Beyond the Gramma

"This is an outstanding book on a timely topic—the place of language in the English classroom. It is ideal for graduate classes in English education, offering new perspectives on the ongoing debates about language teaching from an impressive international lineup of contributors."

Louann Reid, Colorado State University

"An important contribution to contemporary discussions about grammar and grammatics, pedagogy and metalinguistic understanding."

Wendy Morgan, Queensland University of Technology, Australia

"Well-conceived and timely. The field is certainly ready for a reconsideration of the role of 'knowledge about language' in the language arts curriculum."

Steve Vanderstaay, Western Washington University

Questions about the effectiveness of grammar teaching on literacy development have been so fraught in recent years that they are referred to metaphorically as the "Grammar Wars." Are there evidence-based answers to the broad question "What explicit knowledge about language in teachers and/or students appears to enhance literacy development in some way?"

Distinguished by its global perspective, its currency and its comprehensiveness, *Beyond the Grammar Wars* approaches this question systematically, offering both a range of theoretical approaches and "takes" on the issues raised, and examples of how these approaches are being realized in actual classrooms. All of the contributors are acknowledged experts in their field. Activities designed for use in language and literacy education courses actively engage students in reflecting on and applying the content in their own teaching contexts.

Terry Locke is Professor of Education and Chair of the Department of Arts and Language Education in the School of Education, University of Waikato, New Zealand.

Beyond the Grammar Wars

A Resource for Teachers and Students on Developing Language Knowledge in the English/Literacy Classroom

Edited by
Terry Locke

Routledge
Taylor & Francis Group

NEW YORK AND LONDON

First published 2010
by Routledge
270 Madison Avenue, New York, NY 10016

Simultaneously published in the UK
by Routledge
2 Park Square, Milton Park, Abingdon, Oxon OX14 4RN

Routledge is an imprint of the Taylor & Francis Group, an informa business

Typeset in Minion by Wearset Ltd, Boldon, Tyne and Wear
Printed and bound in the United States of America on acid-free
paper by Walsworth Publishing Company, Marceline, MO

Library of Congress Cataloging-in-Publication Data
Beyond the grammar wars : a resource for teachers and students
on developing language knowledge in the English/literacy
classroom / edited by Terry Locke.
p. cm.
1. Second language acquisition. 2. Language and languages–
Grammars. 3. Grammar, Comparative and general. I. Locke,
Terry, 1946–
P118.2.B485 2010
428.0071–dc22   2009041037

ISBN10: 0-415-80264-4 (hbk)
ISBN10: 0-415-80265-2 (pbk)
ISBN10: 0-203-85435-7 (ebk)

ISBN13: 978-0-415-80264-2 (hbk)
ISBN13: 978-0-415-80265-9 (pbk)
ISBN13: 978-0-203-85435-8 (ebk)

Contents

Preface

For over 100 years now, as the title of the book suggests, a battle has raged about grammar and its place in the English/literacy classroom. Participants in this battle have included politicians and policy-makers, professional associations of English or literacy teachers, linguists, teacher educators, educational researchers and theorists of textual practice. Classroom teachers and those preparing to teach have also found themselves caught in the crossfire.

At the simplest level, the battle can be reduced to the question: Does the explicit knowledge of language contribute positively and productively to a learner's developing repertoire of textual practices as readers (viewers) or composers (makers) of texts?

If the answer to this question is yes – and this book indeed *does* answer this question in the affirmative – then the two pivotal questions which follow are:

1. *What* explicit linguistic or grammatical knowledge are we talking about? and
2. *What* pedagogical form might this positive contribution take?

Writing out of a range of educational settings, the contributors to this book offer a variety of responses to this question, all drawing on a range of empirical and conceptual research studies. Moving *beyond* the grammar wars, the contributions in this book collectively point to a reorientation of the grammar/literacy debate, which focuses on the rhetorical demands of those social occasions wherein textual acts of textual production and textual interpretation and response are situated. As social players in these situations, we are all called upon to make choices in respect of how we read situations and how we compose our textual acts. Explicit language (or grammatical) knowledge enhances language-users in these choices, and it is *this* knowledge that we owe the students in our English/literacy classrooms.

We have written this book for two main groups of people: The first comprises teacher educators specifically concerned with the pre-service and in-service education of teachers of English and/or literacy and those pre-service and in-service teachers undergoing either initial teacher education or in-service professional development. The second group comprises postgraduate education students with an interest in language and literacy together with their course lecturers. Needless to say, we would also like this book to be read by educational policy-makers, educational researchers in the field of literacy education and linguists with an interest in the relationship of schooling to linguistics.

As indicated above, this is a research-based textbook. It has four parts:

- Part I, "The 'Grammar Wars' in Context", provides an historical overview of the debates around grammar and English/literacy teaching in four settings: the United States, England, Scotland and Australia.
- Part II, "The Effectiveness of Grammar Teaching: The Research Record", offers an up-to-date account of what the research is telling (and not telling) us about the effectiveness of certain kinds of grammar-based pedagogies in English/literacy classrooms.
- Part III, "Into the Classroom: Integrating Knowledge about Language with Learning", takes us into the English/literacy classroom and offers a range of examples of language/grammar-based pedagogies which have been found to be successful at the classroom level.
- Part IV, "Beyond Print: A Metalanguage for Multimodal Texts", explores the challenge of digital and multimodal textual practices to teachers and educators who are committed to finding a "usable grammar" to contribute to teaching and learning in relation to these practices.

This book has a number of distinctive features:

- *Authority:* The contributors are acknowledged experts in their field, most with international reputations and impressive publication records.
- *Scope:* The book offers a global perspective.
- *Currency:* The book draws on recent research and addresses metalinguistic issues related to changes in textual practice in a digital age.
- *Comprehensiveness:* The book situates issues historically, but is located in the present moment. It offers a range of theoretical approaches and "takes" on the issues raised, but also explores ways in which these approaches are being realized in actual classrooms.

Acknowledgements

This book has had a very long gestation period. It began for me with an invitation from Richard Andrews to join the English Review Group at the University of York, which engaged in a now famous (or infamous, depending on your point of view) review of the impact of formal grammar teaching on the writing of 5- to 16-year-olds. It was given further impetus by encouragement from Hilary Janks who, with Richard, had been a contributor to a double issue on "Knowledge about language in the English/literacy classroom" of the journal *English Teaching: Practice and Critique* (a project undertaken after an encouraging conversation with Dick Hudson at University College, London). For its realization, of course, the book needed an editor. I have been served unstintingly and graciously by Naomi Silverman at Routledge and her assistant Meeta Pendharkar. I have a huge debt of gratitude to the contributors to the book who have trusted me with their work. I feel humbled by this. I also have debt of gratitude to colleagues at my own institution, the University of Waikato, and especially to Michael Collins who helped out with the graphics. Finally, and for me not least, I thank my wife, Linda, who knows the inside story of this project and tolerated my absent-mindedness when I was afflicted with bouts of preoccupation.

Chapter 1

Introduction

"Grammar Wars" and Beyond

Terry Locke

For me as editor, this book has had a multiplicity of prompts. Some of these stem from dilemmas I faced as a classroom teacher and Head of English in a number of New Zealand secondary schools; others stem from conversations subsequent to my involvement as an educational researcher in perhaps the biggest ever review of the impact of two kinds of formal grammar teaching (syntax and sentence-combining) on the quality of student writing (see Andrews et al., 2004a, 2004b). In this introduction, I will be aware of donning a variety of hats at different times: former classroom teacher, teacher educator and educational researcher. This is appropriate, I think, since my co-contributors and I would see ourselves as addressing a broad audience: English/literacy/L1 teachers, pre-service teachers, teacher educators and members of the academic community with an interest in this topic.

The over-riding question driving this book is: What explicit/implicit knowledge about language in teachers and/or students appears to enhance literacy development in some way? It is a question which takes many forms depending on context. It is also the question that has arguably generated more acrimonious debate than any other among English/literacy teachers, linguists and educationalists in the last five decades (see Locke, 2009).

The acrimony is reflected in the kinds of metaphors used to draw attention to the various ways this question has been framed, and the attack and defense mode of much of the argumentation. Urszula Clark (2001) played on this when she entitled her account of language, history and the disciplining of English, *War Words*. In a Bernsteinian analysis of the "Grammar Wars" in England, Clark (2005 and in this book) views the conflict in terms of Conservative government attempts starting in 1984 to reverse a curriculum trend that "had become increasingly decentralized, relocated from the government to the teaching profession, with both content and assessment becoming increasingly deregularized" and

> to pull control over education back towards the centre even more. The curriculum envisaged by this reversal amounted to a restoration of a grammar school curriculum, with the privileged text in English returning to the teaching of Standard English, its grammar and its literature. (2005, p. 37)

In the United States, a major focus of conflict has been the position and positioning of grammar within American classrooms. As Kolln and Hancock argue in their chapter in this book, a range of forces (again, the military metaphor) in the United States signaled the demise of a systematic focus on grammar in US classrooms and a shut-down to dialogue between linguists and educationalists in respect of ways in which grammar could be used in the service of literacy acquisition. For these authors, these forces include NCTE policy, "minimalist" grammar and its anti-knowledge stance, whole-language approaches to language acquisition, the ascendancy of process approaches within composition and the primacy of literature within English curriculums at all levels. Interestingly, Kolln and Hancock view Constance Weaver, who also contributes to this book, as associated with the first two items on this list. In the New Zealand context, as Elizabeth Gordon has described, while there have been pressures to accord traditional grammar knowledge the same kind of status in the educational system as that advocated by conservatives in England, a different kind of "grammar war" was fought in the early 1990s, when it was suggested that the indigenous language, Maaori (an official language), be used as a comparison language for enhancing students' understandings of the workings of English (see Gordon, 2005).

What makes the "grammar wars" in the Australian context interesting, as Frances Christie explains in her chapter, is that it involved the kind of debate that Kolln and Hancock lament the lack of in the United States. In Australia, the debate was between two versions of subject English, both of which offered a social, "progressive" view of English but which viewed the place of explicit grammatical knowledge and what constituted such knowledge (i.e. *whose* knowledge) very differently. The central issue, to use Christie's words, was "What knowledge about language should be taught in the name of subject English?"

Activity: Reflecting on the Teaching of Grammar as Controversial

Is the teaching of grammar a controversial issue in your own educational setting? If so, identify some of the positions that appear to be in conflict in your setting. What sorts of beliefs about the teaching of grammar do advocates of opposing positions have?

Some of my own prompts in initiating this project have their origins close to home – in my experiences as a teacher, teacher educator and researcher in the New Zealand context. It is a context that has had its own share of social upheaval and educational "reform" in the last 20 years (Locke, 2001, 2004). As in other settings, reform drivers were often underpinned by discourses of crisis and a panic about falling standards, especially literacy standards. In the New Zealand setting, the panacea was less a turn back to traditional grammar (as educational conservatives would have it), but rather a turn to a focus on pre-specified learning outcomes (as neo-liberals driving an extrinsic accountability agenda would have it). In the larger context of struggles over administrative, curriculum and assessment policy and practice, questions of "grammar" and "language" were minor blips on the radar screen.

I was, however, one of a generation of teachers that was asked to implement a sociolinguistic approach to language study in the senior secondary English class in the 1980s. My university English degree had not prepared me for this role, though the core degree still required majors to do "language" papers and had yet to suffer the slings and arrows of critical theory. The sociolinguistic resources teachers worked with came with plenty of terminological baggage – you couldn't analyze the language of conversation without talking about *anacoluthons*, could you? This metalanguage was certainly a different breed from the traditional grammar I was subjected to as a student in the 1950s and 1960s as I worked my way through endless, decontextualized parsing exercises. But while it aroused in some students and teachers an interest in the way language worked *in situ*, it didn't appear to be designed to help students write better and seemed marginally related to reading, especially literary reading.

As a secondary teacher in the late 1980s and early 1990s, I had little linguistic training, some knowledge of traditional grammar (augmented by my learning of additional languages) and no clue whatsoever in respect of the place of knowledge about language in the English/literacy classroom. I identify with a recollection of Richard Andrews (2005), who writes: "As a practicing English teacher … I created my own mix of top-down (research-informed) and bottom-up (pragmatic, inventive, intuitive) approaches to the teaching of writing, and employed whichever method seemed right for the learners I was teaching" (p. 69). Nevertheless, in 1992, as a recently appointed HOD English of a large, rather multilingual secondary school, I was struck by the realization that ignorance about language was widespread. Undeterred by my own shortcomings, I wrote and published a small book entitled *Every Student's English Language Manual*. The first part of the book covered "Elements of Language" (morphology, diction, spelling, punctuation, word classes and syntax) and the second "Applications", by relating language use to particular genres (for example, formal letters, reports, essays, display ads and lyric poems). If you had asked me to indicate how "research-informed" the book was, I would have mentioned Halliday and Hasan (1985), Andrews' work on rhetoric and argumentation (1992, 1993) and the work of Australian genre theorists such as Jim Martin that had snuck across the Tasman Sea in the dead of night (Cope & Kalantzis, 1993). But I couldn't have told you whether or not English teachers should teach "grammar" in their classrooms.

Activity: Identifying Sources of Knowledge

Do you identify with the quotation from Richard Andrews above? Identify a course of action you took as a teacher in relation to your language/English teaching that you might describe as intuitive. In addition, identify a "top-down" source that has influenced your teaching or your thinking about teaching. This source might be a textbook, or a model lesson you have observed, or some other kind of document or practice.

The "Exploring Language" project was initiated by the New Zealand Association for the Teaching of English (NZATE)[1] and led to a book of the same title (Ministry of Education, 1996). However, there was never an adequate professional development program, underpinned by coherent theory and sound research, to help teachers know how to use in classrooms that "knowledge about language" the big blue book contained. Meanwhile, as I write, pedagogical practice in respect of language in New Zealand schools is being increasingly shaped by the availability of cheap, write-on, "basic English" texts, diagnostic testing regimes such as AsTTle[2] and ways in which worthwhile knowledge (including knowledge about language) is being shaped by high-stakes, summative assessment regimes such as the National Certificate of Educational Achievement (NCEA).

So much for prompts from my own backyard. In respect of the bigger stage, I was (perhaps) fortunate enough to be involved in an English Review team, based at the University of York and chaired by Richard Andrews, which undertook two systematic reviews in association with the Evidence for Policy and Practice Information and Coordinating Centre (EPPI-Centre) on (1) whether the formal teaching of sentence grammar or (2) whether instruction in sentence-combining was effective in helping 5- to 16-year-olds write better (see Andrews et al., 2004a, 2004b). Andrews' take on this project and the debate that has occurred in its aftermath are a focus of his chapter in this book.

For my own part, involvement in the project raised many questions in my own mind about the virtues of systematic reviews and how they construct "best evidence".[3] In respect of grammar and knowledge about language, I was left with the uneasy sense that our published reviews begged a lot of questions. For instance, the framing of our research questions encouraged a separation of sentence-level grammar considerations from a wider view of what "grammar knowledge" might mean. A definition such as the following from Cope and Kalantzis (1993, p. 20) would have fallen outside this frame:

> "Grammar" is a term that describes the relation of language to metalanguage; of text to generalizations about text; of experience to theory; of the concrete world of human discursive activity to abstractions which generalize about the regularities and irregularities in that world.

In addition, because the focus of the review was on effectiveness, there was a tendency to favor studies reporting trials that were controlled in various ways, but whose measures of writing effectiveness were constrained, narrow and sometimes fatuous. This tendency also led to a selection of studies which focused on

---

1. NZATE is the professional association of New Zealand secondary English teachers and is equivalent to such organizations as AATE, NATE and NCTE.
2. AsTTle is a system of diagnostic testing for a range of competencies, including reading comprehension.
3. I am broadly sympathetic to Maggie MacLure's assault on systemic reviews in MacLure, M. (2005). "Clarity bordering on stupidity": Where's the quality in systematic review? *Journal of Education Policy, 20*(4), 393–416.

the intervention proper, as if such interventions were neutral and separable from the classroom teacher and his/her professional knowledge (including knowledge about language) and value system.

My own list of questions subsequent to the English Review Group's having done its work was included in the rationale for a special issue on "Knowledge about Language in the English/Literacy Classroom" for the journal *English Teaching: Practice and Critique*.[4] They were:

- What is meant by "knowledge about language"?
- Whose knowledges are we talking about when we refer to "knowledge about language"?
- In what ways is "knowledge about grammar" subsumed under the term "knowledge about language"?
- What relationships exist (as productive or non-productive) between the development of linguistics as an academic domain and educational policy and practice in respect of the presence of "knowledge about language" in the English/literacy classroom?
- What (if any) justifications exist for the inclusion of "knowledge about language" in an "intended" curriculum as knowledge worth knowing for itself?
- How is knowledge about language affected by the technologized nature of its object?
- Put another way, how does metalanguage need to change under pressure from the increased digitizing and graphicization of texts and text-based practice?
- Are there any sustainable arguments for a positive relationship between knowledge about language (however understood) and increased effectiveness in some aspect of textual practice (reading/viewing or production)?
- What is the relationship between metalanguage and metacognition?
- What pedagogical frameworks or approaches appear to render "knowledge about language" effective or ineffective as a component of literacy teaching and learning?

The chapters in this book address these questions and others in different ways and out of different contexts. The pivotal question, of course, is: What is meant by knowledge about language? Once a meaning is attributed to the term, then claims can be made for a relationship between either explicit or implicit knowledge and the enhancement of some aspect of literacy acquisition, for example, writing. If a positive relationship is claimed, more particular claims can be made in respect of whether explicit or simply implicit knowledge is needed for students to develop the sorts of literacies deemed to be desirable in terms of an intended curriculum or the requirements of a fulfilling life and citizenship, and the kinds of explicit knowledge deemed to be a desirable aspect of a teacher's content and pedagogical content knowledge (Shulman, 1986).

4. December 2005 (Vol. 4, No. 3) and May 2006 (Vol. 5, No. 1).

As will be clear, such claims can be warranted in a number of ways. One such warrant is grounded in "common sense" and tradition. "Since writing involves the manipulation of language", this argument might go, "then knowledge about language is necessary for its manipulation. Therefore students need grammar. Anyway, a knowledge of grammar didn't do *me* any harm and in fact I benefited from the discipline needed for its mastery." A second kind of warrant constructs a series of theorized propositions which together constitute a kind of a priori argument for the desirability for students having an explicit knowledge about language. Here is one such argument: All texts set out to manipulate readers in certain ways. This manipulation is managed by the deployment of a range of linguistic or textual features. An explicit knowledge of how these features function is required if readers are to develop the critical ability to bring the modus operandi of this manipulation to consciousness. Such a bringing to consciousness is required if readers are to resist the manipulations of texts.

A third kind of warrant is based in research, which can be divided into two broad approaches. The first takes a theorized position and tests it. The systematic review research referred to above (Andrews, 2004a, 2004b) is an example of such research, as are the studies this review analyzed. A second approach attempts to generate theory on the basis of an investigation of what works in respect of the learning and teaching of a particular literate practice, for example, writing. Such an approach might begin with broad questions such as: "What does it mean to write?" and "What are the successful features of a successful teaching program?" Once such features have been identified, *then* a relationship with some mode of knowledge about language might (or might not) be identified and the relationship theorized.

Activity: Reflection on Your Reasons for Engaging with This Book

Which of the above questions (bulleted, p. 5) are you most interested in having an answer or answers to? Why?

The first section of this book puts the "Grammar Wars" in context in a number of settings. Over a distinguished career, Martha Kolln has argued for a rhetorical grammar, to be productively deployed in classrooms for a different purpose

> from the remedial, error-avoidance or error-correction purpose of so many grammar lessons. I use rhetorical as a modifier to identify grammar in the service or rhetoric: grammar knowledge as a tool that enables the writer to make effective choices. (1996, p. 29)

The American scene is traversed historically by Craig Hancock and Kolln in their chapter, "Blowin' in the Wind: English Grammar in United States Schools", where they revisit debates around the inclusion/exclusion of grammar in the classroom. Both Kolln and Hancock are members of ATEG (Assembly for the Teaching of English Grammar), a sub-group of NCTE, and NPG (New Public

Grammar), a group formed to promote and develop a new public grammar through the cooperative effort of linguists and English teachers. Beginning with a consideration of debate precursors, they identify a watershed which produced a demise of the promise of grammar/pedagogy dialogue. They identify a range of factors related to this demise: NCTE policy-making; new approaches to writing (for example, process approaches) and a focus on composition; concerns with elitism; the two-edged contribution of the rise of generative grammar; and changes in the nature of English language arts as a "subject". In their view, this demise produced a crisis, with knowledge about language – in teachers as well as in students – languishing, and a marginalization of debate about possible relationships between knowledge about language and effective literate practice. You could say that the baby had been thrown out with the bath water (that is, sterile routines of teaching formal grammar for the purpose of error correction). In keeping with the title of their chapter, however, they detect a windshift which appears to be a harbinger for renewed interest in the question of the role grammar (depending on how this is defined) might play in English language arts pedagogy.

Chapter 3, by Urszula Clark, is entitled "The Problematics of Prescribing Grammatical Knowledge: The Case in England". Central to Clark's account is the contestation of professional knowledge (content and pedagogical). Who should decide what teachers need to know (and on what basis)? Who should decide what students need to know (and on what basis)? Both questions have a direct bearing on the issue of knowledge about language. Using a Bernsteinian analytical frame, Clark shows how with the election of a Conservative government in the 1970s, England went the route of direct prescriptivity, with powerful forces working, not necessarily in harmony, to rescue the school system from "grammar neglect". Ironically, with the election of a Labour government in 1997, the degree of prescription intensified, not so much via the means of direct policy, but rather through the successive implementation of a series of "strategies", each with its own accountability technology, beginning with the National Literacy Strategy (NLS) in 1998. As Clark points out, one of the most "tenacious shibboleths of governmental educational policy" has been a belief that teaching students grammar will result in improved writing. However, in more recent government reports, Clark suggests, there appears to be a shift in attitude and approach. In her conclusion, Clark calls for a "recontextualization" of pedagogic grammar in English, one that would restore it to a more integrated place in the curriculum.

Frances Christie was Foundation Professor of Language and Literacy Education in the University of Melbourne's Faculty of Education and has had a long-time association with systemic functional linguistics as an approach to language and with what has become known as the "Genre School" in Australia. Her research and teaching interests include English language and literacy education, particularly writing development, the relationship of talk and writing, teaching about language and the development of an educational linguistics. In Chapter 4, on "The Grammar Wars in Australia", she positions herself clearly as "an SFL genre theorist, still interested in the debates after all these years, still following the ongoing evolution of SFL genre theory, and still willing to argue a case for the relevance of the theory for pedagogy" (p. 56). Like Hancock and Kolln in relation to the American setting, she traces the origins of a number of debates over grammar and the question: What knowledge about language should be taught in the English/literacy classroom? Like Kolln, she works within a framework that sees a close relationship between grammar and rhetoric. What makes the Australian setting unique, however, has been the emergence under the influence of M.A.K. Halliday of systemic functional linguistics as a powerful framework for analyzing language in use. A Hallidayan linguistic framework was adopted and adapted by genre theorists such as Martin, Rothery and Christie herself in the 1980s in the development of a pedagogy particularly aimed at identifying and helping students master the genres of schooling. As Christie explains, the special feature of the "grammar debate" in Australia has been the response by teachers and critics (often working out of a "progressive" view of English) to genre pedagogy and its attendant linguistic nomenclature and KAL advocacy.

Graeme Trousdale is a linguist and currently a secretary for the International Society for the Linguistics of English (ISLE), the central aim of which is the promotion of the study of English Language, that is, the study of the structure and history of standard and non-standard varieties of English, in terms of both form and function, at an international level. The significance of Trousdale's chapter ("Knowledge about Language in the English Classroom: A Scottish Perspective") in this collection is that it locates debates about what counts as knowledge about language in the English classroom in a setting characterized by the general use of non-standard varieties of English (Scots) and by the widespread use of an "indigenous" language (Scottish). Questions about what counts as KAL, then, are inextricably related to questions about the status of non-standard dialects and about the status and need for retention strategies for Scots and Scottish as languages. Writing as a linguist with an interest in education, Trousdale discusses ongoing changes in respect of teaching about language in Scottish schools and the importance of links between schools and university departments of English Language, Linguistics and Education. He also looks closely at some specifics of grammar teaching and issues of teacher confidence in their own content and pedagogical knowledge. In addition, he engages with the debate over the nature, function and role of Scots in English teaching in Scottish schools, issues of ethnic and linguistic diversity, and how these impact on the broad question of what constitutes relevant and productive knowledge about language in English/literacy classrooms, particularly at secondary level.

The second section of this book addresses the research record in relation to the effectiveness of grammar teaching, though I should hasten to add that questions of research are addressed in other chapters as well. Richard Andrews, Professor in English in the Faculty of Culture and Pedagogy at the London Institute of Education, has a long interest in argumentation, rhetoric, the teaching of literature and the role of ICTs in literacy education. As Chairperson of the English Review Group that undertook, in 2003–2004, two systematic reviews into the effectiveness of the formal teaching of sentence grammar and instruction in sentence-combining in enhancing student writing (mentioned previously), Andrews is no stranger to controversy. In the United Kingdom and beyond, ripples from these two reviews still occur and form the subject of Andrews' con-tribution to this volume: "Teaching Sentence-Level Grammar for Writing: The Evidence So Far" (Chapter 6). In this chapter, Andrews concludes that there have been no subsequent studies which would moderate the review finding that know-ledge about grammar helps pupils write more fluently and accurately. However, he agrees with another contributor to this book, Debra Myhill, that "the connec-tion between grammar taught in context and the accuracy and quality of writing is under-researched" (p. 94), and supports the position that knowledge about language should more properly be seen as related to teachers' academic and pro-fessional knowledge. Meanwhile, like Clark, he is critical of continuing ways in which national education policy and its instrumentation in the Primary National Strategy mandate frame the teaching of knowledge about language for students. In conclusion, he proposes a model that might provide a starting point for recon-sidering the relationship of grammar (more widely defined) and pedagogies of writing instruction.

Amos van Gelderen, senior researcher at the SCO-Kohnstamm Institute of the University of Amsterdam, has conducted research into language learning and instruction at the primary and secondary levels both for mother-tongue teaching and second- or foreign-language teaching. Chapter 7 on the "Does Explicit Teaching of Grammar Help Students to Become Better Writers?" focuses on the controversial issue of whether learning explicit grammar rules benefits students' mastery of written language. Van Gelderen writes out of a context which con-trasts with most Anglophonic settings in that, as he writes, "the traditional grammar curriculum … is still alive and kicking" in the Netherlands (p. 110). A particular value of this chapter is that van Gelderen provides a systematic mapping of the separate issues which are subsumed (and often confused) under the general heading of "debate about grammar". Drawing on a range of empiri-cal research evidence, he questions the effectiveness of explicit grammar instruc-tion in helping students improve their use of formal language structures and (like Andrews) the overall quality of their writing. However, he does not rule out the productiveness of "approaches to grammar teaching directed at the implicit learning of structures" (p. 110).

Professor Debra Myhill, from the University of Exeter, is currently involved (2008–2010) in a major research project on "Grammar for Writing? A three-year study of the effectiveness of contextualized grammar teaching". In the introduc-tion to Chapter 8, "Ways of Knowing: Grammar as a Tool for Developing Writing", she concedes that "Our understanding of the linguistic, cognitive and social processes involved in learning to write and its rootedness in a secure research base is still developing" and that our "theoretical understanding of the role of grammar in the process of becoming a proficient writer is limited" (p. 129). She positions herself as an educator and researcher who works within a "knowledge about language" frame, rather than a "knowledge about grammar" one, because of the latter's neo-conservative associations. In her chapter, her major focus is writing. In it, she engages in the "risky enterprise" of exploring "a theorized interpretation of how knowledge about grammar might inform both learners' and teachers' understanding of writing" and thereby "position grammar constructively within the frame of reference encompassed by knowledge about language" (pp. 129–130). Her claim, then, is for the value of particular explicit forms of knowledge about grammar, for teachers and students alike, as a productive aspect of the writing classroom. In this respect, while seeing the distinction between explicit and tacit (or implicit) grammar knowledge as an important one, she is more optimistic than either Andrews or van Gelderen in respect of the value of explicit grammatical knowledge instruction, though she is very careful to define precisely the pedagogical contexts consonant with this knowledge being productive.

The third section of the book focuses on the English/literacy classroom itself. The contributors here, while not ignoring the research basis for their claims, discuss ways in which explicit "knowledge about language" can play a productive role in the classroom for students as they engage in textual work, either as viewers/readers or writers/composers.

Professor Hilary Janks is an Associate Professor in Applied English Language Studies (AELS) at Witwatersrand University. With a background in secondary English teaching, she switched her academic interest to Linguistics and Applied Language Studies in the 1980s in order to address the needs of students and teachers in multilingual classes. Her research has consistently been in the area of language, literacy and social justice with a focus on English education in multilingual contexts, critical literacy and language policy. In Chapter 9, on " 'Language as a System of Meaning Potential': The Reading and Design of Verbal Texts", she argues a case for the value of explicit metalinguistic knowledge – based in systemic functional linguistics – for a critical approach to text production and reception. She argues that:

> Explicit knowledge gives one more conscious control for both the reception and production of language. It helps us to see what we are doing when we use language, and to locate the effects in particular linguistic choices. It gives us a metalanguage to talk about these choices. It is important to understand that choice of any linguistic option necessarily implies rejection of other options. (pp. 153–154)

Using an SFL framework, she identifies key linguistic features and shows how each can work as a different lens for developing a critical understanding of how texts work to position readers to respond to them. Using, as examples, seemingly benign texts (a series of UNHCR refugee posters), she models how a study of transitivity helps one to understand agency; a study of modality aids the understanding of such things as certainty/authority or uncertainty/hesitation, lack of authority; and a study of pronoun use can sharpen awareness of practices of inclusion and exclusion.

I wrote Chapter 10, "Discovering a Metalanguage for All Seasons: Bringing Literary Language in from the Cold", out of a number of concerns. One of these is teacher insecurity around their own language knowledge, a concern shared with other contributors to this book. Another is a concern with a certain dichotomizing tendency in the English/literacy classroom that puts the metalanguages related to literary study and broad textual or language study into two separate boxes. I do three things in this chapter. First, drawing (like Clark in her chapter) on a Bernsteinian model (Bernstein, 2000), I investigate ways in which the pedagogic discourses available to teachers have undergone a shift in a number of settings and why this should be. I ask questions about *where* the language a beginning teacher might use to conduct talk about texts might come from. Second, I look specifically at the kind of metalanguage teachers might utilize in their conversations with students around the reading and composition of literary texts. Third, I imagine myself as a teacher beginning my career in English language arts/literacy, and suggest a strategy that might be adopted for developing one's own metalanguage, useful to oneself and to one's students, for making meaning of the texts they read/view and write.

Connie Weaver, Professor Emerita of English at Western Michigan University, has spent a lifetime engaged with aspects of the grammar question. She has authored a number of books related to this book's topic, including *Teaching Grammar in Context* (1996) and, more recently, *The Grammar Plan Book* (2007). As an advocate for what her detractors would label a minimalist approach to explicit grammar teaching and as a leading figure in the development of NCTE's official position on grammar teaching (see Hancock and Kolln in this volume), she is no stranger to controversy (see also, Locke, 2005). In Chapter 11, "Scaffolding Grammar Instruction for Writers and Writing", Weaver positions herself as someone who "almost became a linguist but instead became more and more a teacher of writing" (pp. 202–203). Defining "scaffolding" as teaching that supports the learning process throughout, Weaver describes why and how she abandoned the naming of grammatical parts and the assigning of exercises in grammatical conventions for an approach that scaffolds grammar instruction through various phases of the writing process. A brief foray into what "the research" says about teaching grammar to improve writing is followed by an extended illustration of how grammatical options and skills can be taught throughout the process of writing, from drafting through editing. With a focus on the classroom teacher, she suggests possible and productive steps for introducing a grammatical concept and then scaffolding writers in applying the concept, revising their writing, and editing. For Weaver, the word "minimal" has two senses: the first related to the economy of how teachers spend time; the second related to those key grammatical concepts and terms teachers of writing may find most useful. In her conclusion, Weaver raises the key question in relation to research on the efficacy of teaching grammar: "Works to accomplish *what*?" She offers her own view of those aspects of grammar worthy of deliberate selection for explicit classroom instruction and what the knowledge of certain sociolinguistic concepts might offer the English/literacy classroom.

With Ruth French's chapter, "Primary School Children Learning Grammar: Rethinking the Possibilities", the spotlight moves decisively on to the primary school classroom. French's interest in this topic dates back to 1993 when she was involved as a teacher of a case-study class in an inner Sydney school, in a project initiated and coordinated by Geoff Williams, then at the University of Sydney and now at the University of British Colombia. Since this time, she has conducted her own research, adding to the "comparatively small body of academically documented research explicitly dealing with primary school children using functional grammar" (p. 214). French addresses two broad questions: Can young children learn grammar? and, If so, what's the point of their learning it? She argues that not all grammars are equal for educational purposes and that systemic functional grammar (as a component of systemic functional linguistics) has advantages over other grammars because it conceives of grammar as a meaning-making resource linked to the need of language-users to make conscious choices in situations conceived in rhetorical terms. Drawing on Williams' research and her own, she provides evidence (contrary to received Piagetian wisdom) that children can learn a range of grammatical concepts and even enjoy learning and applying them. In respect of the second of her broad concerns, that is, the *utility* of children learning grammar, she makes the claim that "grammatics was found to be useful to students across a number of dimensions of their school literacy programs" enabling them to develop: (1) conscious control of their writing; (2) critical understandings in their reading; (3) improved expression in reading aloud; and (4) improved punctuation of direct speech (pp. 215–216). The claims are warranted by reference to a particular kind of qualitative research methodological design implemented across a range of classrooms with children of different ages.

The last four chapters of this book address issues raised by the following questions from the list presented earlier:

- How is knowledge about language affected by the technologized nature of its object?
- Put another way, how does metalanguage need to change under pressure from the increased digitizing and graphicization of texts and text-based practice?

These chapters hardly constitute an exhaustive response to such questions. But they *do* provide pointers toward an emerging view of the place of knowledge about language in English/literacy classrooms, where textual study is more and more being asked to recognize increased multimodality and digitization in textual practice. To put the position of these writers in blunt terms, if grammar is a way of describing textual practice, then grammar itself must change in the face of increased multimodality and digitization.

Gunther Kress, currently Professor of Education in the Department of Learning, Curriculum and Communication at the London Institute of Education, has a distinguished reputation for his theoretical work on the relationship between language, culture, human meaning-making (mediated via sign systems) and technology, not just in relationship to print texts, but more recently in relationship to visual and other representational resources. After an early but somewhat ambivalent relationship with the Australian Genre School (discussed by Christie in this volume; see Kress, 1993), Kress moved to England where he teamed up with Theo van Leeuwen to produce *Reading Images: The Grammar of Visual Design* (1996), a ground-breaking attempt to generate a grammar, drawing on Hallidayan linguistic theory, for largely visual texts. Chapter 13, "A Grammar for

Meaning-Making", might be thought of as setting the scene for the chapters which follow. Building on his earlier work, Kress sets about confronting a contemporary world characterized by a kind of "distributed power" that calls into question traditional notions of "grammar" and demands answers to questions such as: "What actually is 'a grammar'?" and "On whose authority could it be founded?" and "What *are* the principles for meaning-making?" (p. 234). Kress guides his readers to consider a number of ways of addressing these questions, beginning with a "communicational framing" of the issue which draws attention to the essentially multimodal character of social discourse and the place of signs and how these are interpreted – a framing that "does not conform to the conception of (a) grammar traditionally held" (p. 239). If contemporary meaning-making is increasingly being made via "multimodal ensembles", the question arises as to the language that might best be used to name the "categories, entities, process and relations" that exist in these ensembles. Kress addresses this issue by drawing attention to the "resources for meaning-making" potentially available in a given social situation, each with its own particular "affordances". He then proceeds to show how these resources can be strategically (or rhetorically) deployed for effect by individuals doing "semiotic work ... in their social lives" (p. 243). In this model, three factors dominate, "the rhetor/designer, resources and principles of design" (p. 249). What Kress offers in this chapter is a radical contestation of the very terms in which earlier chapters in this book are couched and a reorientation of the debate around the sorts of questions raised earlier in this introduction.

Like Kress, Bill Cope and Mary Kalantzis were associated with the Australian Genre School in the early 1990s (see Cope & Kalantzis, 1993) and have made this association a point of departure as they have sought to find a way of theorizing multimodality in texts and the diversity of practice embraced by the word "literacy". This diversity is recognized in the term "multiliteracies", made popular by the New London Group which Kress was also a member of. As outlined in a famous article in the *Harvard Educational Review* (New London Group, 1996), the ten members of the group met for a week in September 1994 in New London, New Hampshire, in the United States, to discuss the state of literacy pedagogy.[5]

> The main areas of common or complementary concern included the pedagogical tension between immersion and explicit models of teaching; the challenge of cultural and linguistic diversity; the newly prominent modes and technologies of communication; and changing text usage in restructured workplaces. (p. 2)

Besides the concept of *multiliteracies* itself, a key concept emerging from the group's deliberations was that of "design". In their construction of a responsive and adequate literacy pedagogy for New Times, the idea of *design* connects with

5. The members were Courtney Cazden (United States), Bill Cope (Australia), Norman Fairclough (United Kingdom), James Gee (United States), Mary Kalantzis (Australia), Gunther Kress (United Kingdom), Allan Luke (Australia), Carmen Luke (Australia), Sarah Michaels (United States) and Martin Nakata (Australia).

ways "in which we are both inheritors of patterns and conventions of meaning and at the same time active designers of meaning. And, as designers of meaning, we are designers of social futures – workplace futures, public futures, and community futures" (p. 5). What will be apparent here is that questions in respect of knowledge about language (and grammar) are being contextualized to wider social agendas and the need to relate theories of learning and literacy to these agendas.

In "Schemas for Meaning-Making and Multimodal Texts", Cope and Kalantzis, now based at the University of Illinois, team up with Anne Cloonan, based at Deakin University in Australia, to write a chapter that outlines three schemas designed to enhance teachers' professional learning as they grapple with ways of helping students engage with texts that are increasingly multimodal, that is, where print-verbal modes of meaning interface with the visual, spatial, auditory and gestural. These schemas are:

- a multimodal schema;
- a dimensions-of-meaning schema;
- a pedagogical knowledge processes schema.

The *multimodal* schema views multimodality as the interplay of linguistic, visual, audio, gestural and spatial literacy meaning-making resources. The concept of *design* is used to describe linguistic, visual, audio, gestural, spatial and multimodal codes and conventions or grammars within a dynamic conception of representation in that it affords meaning-makers to shift *between* modes. The *dimensions-of-meaning* schema is seen as emerging from Hallidayan systemic functional linguistics and critical literacy traditions and is aimed at offering five broad types of textual interrogation as a way of helping students and teachers articulate a multimodal metalanguage. According to the authors, the development of an accessible, pedagogically context-friendly multimodal metalanguage remains an urgent research agenda, to be undertaken in partnership with teachers? As discussed in this chapter, *dimensions-of-meaning* questioning affords teachers a pedagogy to help students make conscious connections between five kinds of textual meaning and mode-related semiotic features:

- Representational meaning: *What do the meanings refer to?*
- Social meaning: *How do the meanings connect the persons they involve?*
- Organizational meaning: *How do the meanings hang together?*
- Contextual meaning: *How do the meanings fit into the larger world of meaning?*
- Ideological meaning: *Whose interests are the meanings skewed to serve?*

The discussion is anchored in the particular instance of particular primary school teacher's deployment of the *pedagogical knowledge processes* schema as the frame for a unit of work with 4- to 6-year-olds on "Body talk: I see what you mean". The underlying argument here is that the *multimodal* and *dimensions-of-meaning* schemas can constitute the basis for an emergent functional grammar, for naming the "what" of the particular representation of a particular meaning. In respect of its utility, the ground is located in its power as a tool which teachers and students can use to assess the reasons why particular design choices are made in particular cultural and situational contexts, that is, the ground lies in the schema's rhetorical utility.

In Chapter 15 on "Resourcing Multimodal Literacy Pedagogy: Toward a Description of the Meaning-Making Resources of Language–Image Interaction", Len Unsworth, Professor in English and Literacies Education and Director of the Centre for Research in English and Multiliteracies Education at the University of New England (Australia), also concedes that "research on an evolving metalanguage of multimodality is in the very early stages and emerging descriptions remain quite tentative" (p. 290). However, like Christie and French in this volume, he makes a case for systemic functional linguistics as offering a robust set of foundational principles for the development of such a metalanguage, especially in respect of its rhetorical concern for language in use (form as following function) and its key metafunctional principle, that is that "all texts, visual and verbal, separately and in combination, always simultaneously entail ideational, interpersonal and textual/compositional meanings" (p. 290). Building on the work of Kress and van Leeuwen (1996), his major emphasis is on the *what* of explicit grammatical (or metalinguistic) knowledge. Specifically, he takes on the challenge of "systematically describing resources for the construction of meaning at the intersection of language and image" (p. 276). What of the question of utility? In the first instance, Unsworth makes the assertion that redefining literacy in the digital age necessitates the development of a "metalanguage that will facilitate metatextual awareness of image–text relations" and that current English syllabi (at least in the Australian context) require the understanding and using of such a metalanguage. The warrant for such an effort, in Unsworth's argument, is the value of such a metalanguage in enhancing "the development of critical social literacies" (p. 289), that is, the focus for the utility argument tends to be related more to the reception than to the production of texts.

A number of seemingly entrenched dichotomies have bedeviled the history of subject English, not the least of which is that between literature and language. Even in this book, there is a tendency for metalinguistic systems to focus on words and sentence-level structures more consonant with the discourse of applied linguistics than that of literary criticism. A number of writers (for example, Andrews, 1992) have posited the concept of rhetoric, suitably refurbished, as pointing to a way of developing a sort of "unified field" theory of subject English. In Chapter 16 on "Rules of Grammar, Rules of Play: Computer Games, Literacy and Literature", Andrew Burn also seeks to find a way of moving beyond "colliding ideologies" of literary appreciation and linguistic analysis, but via the unlikely topic of computer games. Burn teaches in the Department of Learning, Curriculum and Communication at the London Institute of Education, but is also an Associate Director of the Centre for the Study of Children, Youth and Media (CSCYM) at the London Knowledge Lab. Like other writers in this volume, he begins by developing a theory of the *what* of grammar, with reference to computer games, and builds on the work of Kress and van Leeuwen

(1996). He draws on their "three overarching functions of visual media" – the *representational, interactive* and *textual* (which he renames the *compositional*) – to show how they can be applied to computer games and can illuminate the relationship between such games and narratives in other and older media. What Burn does, quite selectively, is to establish a metalanguage that can operate across modes and media and which is both usable and, on the basis of research studies quoted, learnable. Is such knowledge useful? Like French in respect of writing, Burn would seem to argue that explicit grammatical knowledge (as he has modeled it) is useful for young game-composers in their conscious choice-making. Burn's main point about utility, however, as he discusses in the conclusion of his chapter, relates to the capacity of a certain kind of grammatical (or metalinguistic) knowledge to help students appreciate (in a critical sense) the "cultural and social functions of the text" (p. 309).

References

Andrews, R. (Ed.). (1992). *Rebirth of rhetoric: Essays in language, culture and education.* London: Routledge.

Andrews, R. (1993). Argument in schools: The value of a generic approach. *Cambridge Journal of Education, 23*(3), 277–285.

Andrews, R. (2005). Knowledge about the teaching of [sentence] grammar: The state of play. *English Teaching: Practice and Critique, 4*(3), 69–76.

Andrews, R., Torgerson, C., Beverton, S., Locke, T., Low, G., Robinson, A., & Zhu, D. (2004a). *The effect of grammar teaching (syntax) in English on 5 to 16 year olds' accuracy and quality in written composition.* London: EPPI-Centre, Social Science Research Unit, Institute of Education (http://eppi.ioe.ac.uk/reel).

Andrews, R., Torgerson, C., Beverton, S., Locke, T., Low, G., Robinson, A., & Zhu, D. (2004b). *The effect of grammar teaching (sentence-combining) in English on 5 to 16 year olds' accuracy and quality in written composition.* London: EPPI-Centre, Social Science Research Unit, Institute of Education (http://eppi.ioe.ac.uk/reel).

Bernstein, B. (2000). *Pedagogy, symbolic control and identity: Theory, research, critique* (Rev. ed.). Lanham, MA: Rowman & Littlefield Publishers, Inc.

Clark, U. (2001). *War words: Language, history and the disciplining of English.* Oxford: Elsevier Science.

Clark, U. (2005). Bernstein's theory of pedagogic discourse: Linguistics, educational policy and practice in the UK English/literacy classroom. *English Teaching: Practice and Critique, 4*(3), 32–47.

Cope, B., & Kalantzis, M. (1993). Introduction: How a genre approach to literacy can transform the way writing is taught. In B. Cope & M. Kalantzis (Eds.), *The powers of literacy: A genre approach to teaching writing* (pp. 1–21). Pittsburgh: University of Pittsburgh Press.

Gordon, E. (2005). Grammar in New Zealand schools: Two case studies. *English Teaching: Practice and Critique, 5*(1), 48–68.

Halliday, M., & Hasan, R. (1985). *Language, context, and text: Aspects of language in a social-semiotic perspective.* Geelong, Vict.: Deakin University.

Kolln, M. (1996). Rhetorical grammar: A modification lesson. *English Journal, 85*(7), 25–31.

Kress, G. (1993). Genre as social process. In B. Cope & M. Kalantzis (Eds.), *The powers of literacy: A genre approach to teaching writing* (pp. 22–37). Pittsburgh: University of Pittsburgh Press.

Kress, G., & van Leeuwen, T. (1996). *Reading images: The grammar of visual design.* London: Routledge.

Locke, T. (2001). English teaching in New Zealand: In the frame and outside the square. *L1 – Educational Studies in Language and Literature, 1*(2), 135–148.

Locke, T. (2004). Someone else's game: Constructing the English teaching professional in New Zealand. *Teaching and Teacher Education, 20,* 17–29.

Locke, T. (2005). Editorial: Grammar in the face of diversity. *English Teaching: Practice and Critique, 5*(1), 1–15.

Locke, T. (2009). Grammar and writing – The international debate. In R. Beard, D. Myhill, J. Riley & M. Nystrand (Eds.), *The Sage handbook of writing development* (pp. 182–193). London: Sage.

MacLure, M. (2005). "Clarity bordering on stupidity": Where's the quality in systematic review? *Journal of Education Policy, 20*(4), 393–416.

Ministry of Education. (1996). *Exploring language.* Wellington: Learning Media.

New London Group. (1996). A pedagogy of multiliteracies: Designing social futures. *Harvard Educational Review, 66*(1). Retrieved December 20, 2009 from http://banista. wikispaces.com/file/view/Multiliteracies.pdf

Shulman, L. (1986). Those who understand: Knowledge growth in teaching. *Educational Researcher, 15*(2), 4–14.

Weaver, C. (1996). *Teaching grammar in context.* Portsmouth, NH: Heinemann.

Weaver, C. (2007). *The grammar plan book.* Portsmouth, NH: Heinemann.

Part I

The "Grammar Wars" in Context

Chapter 2

Blowin' in the Wind
English Grammar in United States Schools

Craig Hancock and Martha Kolln

In many ways, the situation for grammar instruction in United States schools is unresolved and, perhaps, not solvable without change in the widely differing world-views of the opposing participants. There have long been reasonable criticisms of traditional school grammar, including a criticism that it does not easily transfer to writing. Attempts to reform it have met with resistance from the public and grassroots professionals. The closest we have come to public acceptance of a reform grammar in the schools was with the structural grammar of the 1950s and early 1960s. It's worth a close look to see the "perfect storm" that derailed its possibilities. A number of major forces allied against acceptance of that grammar: the Dartmouth initiative and a movement toward "process" approaches in composition away from the product approach that was often seen as formal correction; the replacement of structural grammar by generative/transformational grammar, an approach that proved even less suited to pedagogy than traditional grammar, as the principal linguistic grammar of the time; and political movements of the 1960s and 1970s, which often characterized Standard English as regressive and reactionary and asserted students' right to their own language.

Even progressive educators, though, have not tried to wish grammar entirely away, acknowledging a need for at least minimalist intervention in the service of fluency and correctness. The movement away from formal grammar and toward a "grammar in context" approach has had the unfortunate consequence of diminishing knowledge about language, not just for the public, but for successive generations of teachers as well. In the wider public and in the teaching professions, there seems little acknowledgment that grammar is an inherent aspect of language, deeply tied to meaning and to rhetorical effect. Most of the debate still seems to assume that grammar is inherently formal and primarily concerned with correctness, though the pendulum in linguistics is swinging toward the functional, cognitive side.

New understandings of language have the potential for healing the grammar/ writing split, though this healing might require significantly more knowledge about language in the teaching profession and significantly more attention paid to language within the English curriculum.

Activity: Reflecting on Your Own "Grammar History"

Reflect back on your own grammar instruction through your school years. Do you feel the instruction was helpful or adequate? What aspects of the instruction were most helpful? What was missing? Were your teachers able to explain the role of grammar within language? Were you made aware of different perspectives on grammar, or was one perspective presented as a given?

Early History

Doubts about the efficacy of teaching grammar and its place in the curriculum are by no means new. According to The Commission on English (1965), "winds of revolutionary doctrine began to blow … shortly before World War I with empirical demonstrations that traditional grammar, as conventionally taught, had relatively little effect on writing and was of negligible value in improving oral usage" (p. 20). The "language" strand of the English curriculum has never been easy to describe or to assess, as Gleason (1965, p. 11) explained:

> The place of grammar in the curriculum varied from school to school, and even from classroom to classroom. It had been practically eliminated from a few schools and drastically cut in some others. It remained strong in most. Indeed, in some it was clearly the dominant element in the English curriculum, receiving more attention than either literature or composition, or even than both together. Even today for many English teachers, the purpose for including grammar lessons is restricted to error correction and error avoidance.

Research to measure the success of grammar in the curriculum began early in the 20th century, when educational research was gaining prominence:

> One of the characteristic movements affecting the schools in this century has been educational research, the statistical study of curriculum, materials, methods, and so on, against certain measurable criteria of usefulness. This has become a standard way of approaching any educational problem. Experiment, evaluation, and statistical interpretation have become familiar devices to every curriculum specialist.
>
> It has usually been assumed that a major purpose of English instruction was to teach "good," "error-free" language. The success of grammar teaching could be measured against this. Grammar might be justified if it could help in preventing "errors" in writing, or if it could contribute in any other way to composing ability. (Gleason, 1965, p. 13)

In addition to questions about effectiveness in reducing error, a study conducted by Hoyt in 1906 and replicated by Rapeer in 1913 questioned the place that formal grammar study occupied in the elementary school curriculum, mainly because of what was known about children's psychological development. Influenced by Thorndike's research into learning, Hoyt considered the mental exercise of classification and parsing and grouping of words ill adapted to immature pupils. Both Hoyt and Rapeer emphasized the need to evaluate the amount of time devoted to formal grammar study in an overcrowded curriculum, when the schools had to provide "the whole range of vocational, hygienic, and socializing training needed by our 'nation of sixth graders'" (Kolln, 1981, p. 143). Both the design and the conclusions of the Hoyt and Rapeer studies, along with five others studies carried out between 1923 and 1961, have been called into question (Kolln, 1981). There is no doubt, though, that they influenced an anti-grammar groundswell.

In 1935, under pressure from educators, the National Council of Teachers of English (NCTE) appointed a committee to look into the role of grammar and to make recommendations for the curriculum. The result was a program called *An Experience Curriculum in English*, which recommended that grammar be taught in connection with writing, rather than as an isolated unit of study. This recommendation was by no means the minimalist approach to grammar in context that is popular today – nor did it emphasize the "teachable moment" for correcting errors. On the contrary, the *Experience Curriculum* set out a systematic program of study, with grammar lessons to be introduced in Grades 2 through 12, objectives having to do with sentence sense, preventing errors and providing sentence variety, along with suggestions to the teacher for introducing these concepts.

The primary resistance to the program came from those defending the older practices. The recommendations were not universally well received – not because the program laid out a systematic plan for grammar, but because it substituted a kind of functional grammar for the formal method that teachers were used to. Two months after the report was published, Wilbur Hatfield, chair of the committee and the editor of *English Journal*, felt a need to answer the critics. Here is an excerpt from his editorial in the January 1936 issue:

> First, it must be pointed out that this recommendation is not so radical as it sounds. Actually *An Experience Curriculum in English* lists 24 items of grammar to be taught, and these include practically all the grammar of function ever taught in the schools. The grammar of classification is, of course, omitted.... All the basic conceptions of the parts of a sentence, of the parts of speech, of concord, and of case appear in the list.
>
> Why, then, the angry denunciations? Because the method of presentation recommended is unconventional. The traditional procedure is to offer, first, an abstract definition; second, illustrations; third, exercises in pointing out the construction in bookish sentences; and only fourth and last, if at all, practical application of the conception in avoiding errors. The procedure now recommended is to show by example how some part of a sentence may be manipulated – moved to a different position, changed from a phrase to an adverb or from an awkward second sentence into an effective gerund with object and modifiers, just for example – and to have the pupils manipulate other sentences in imitation of the teacher or book. When by this activity they have become really familiar with the construction, a name

– adverbial phrase, gerund, participle, subordinate clause, for example, is applied to it. (pp. 65–66)

It is clear that Hatfield's argument was not convincing. And while research studies continued to discredit formal grammar taught as a separate unit, the suggestions for a more integrated grammar laid out by the *Experience Curriculum* were never implemented.

Nothing altered the conditions of this debate until Fries' structural linguistics (in the 1950s) and Chomsky's generative-transformational grammar (in the 1960s) came to public attention. By then, the profession was ripe for new ideas; both the English-teaching establishment and the textbook publishers took an interest. The NCTE convention program of 1963 offers evidence that the "growing ferment of interest in the potential utility of structural grammar" – and interest in generative grammar as well – was strong. The program lists 20 different sessions on language, which was one of four general areas, with 50 individual papers.[1] In 1963, without doubt, grammar occupied a place in NCTE's inner circle; new grammar was being explored and experimented with; hopes were high for the emergence of a new paradigm establishing the utility of grammar in the English program.

The Structural Revolution

In 1952, Charles Carpenter Fries published an acclaimed rethinking of public grammar, *The Structure of English: An Introduction to the Construction of English Sentences*. In the introduction, he likened the current understanding and congruent practices in the schools to the bleeding of patients in medicine, practices lagging far behind "modern scientific study" (p. 1). "Too often those who have opposed the conventional grammar analysis have had nothing to offer as a substitute, and no practical suggestions as to how an understanding of the mechanisms of our language must be gained" (pp. 2–3). Fries' book was an attempt to provide that substitute in a form accessible to what he called "the educated lay reader" (p. 7).

The science of linguistics has moved on in some ways since Fries, but the public situation he described in 1952 looks remarkably similar.

> The usefulness of the materials and the study of "formal grammar" has been challenged and many have insisted that school programs should "eliminate as much as possible" this type of grammar. But the defenders of "formal grammar" seem just as numerous and as articulate as those who would cast it out. (p. 276)

1. The other three areas were literature, composing and curriculum. Titles of the language sessions included Semantics, Structural Linguistics for the Junior High School, Generative Grammar, Some Creative Approaches to Grammar, and the Relationship of Grammar to Composition. Among the speakers were Neil Postman, Roderick Jacobs, John Mellon, Leonard Newmark, James McCrimmon and S.I. Hayakawa. Some of the other sequences also included language-related sessions. In the "composing" sequence, for example, Josephine Miles spoke on "Grammar in Prose Composition".

The point Fries made so emphatically, though, is that the grammar (that is, formal grammar) being argued about is scientifically unsound and the unsoundness of that grammar had been largely ignored in the argument. It is not, according to Fries, that all the details of the formal grammar are false, but that the grammar itself is a bit like a "Ptolemaic astronomy, falsely oriented" and so "cannot be expected to provide any satisfactory insights into the mechanisms of our language or any grasp of the processes by which language functions" (p. 277). The same argument, of course, could be updated today, since any new grammar is by definition "unproven" in its pedagogical utility.

For Fries, there were three kinds of meanings an approach to language needed to account for: lexical meaning, provided by the lexicon; structural meaning, provided by the grammar; and social meaning, provided by social context (1952, pp. 293–296). Fries argued for the utility of learning this structural grammar, pointing out that "knowing" *about* it is different from the "knowing" that constitutes our automatic use of these forms. He argued that it would be of help in learning and teaching new languages, which can benefit greatly from an accurate description of similarities and differences in the structural patterns of the languages. It could aid in understanding the nature and source of structural ambiguities – ambiguities created more from syntax than from lexicon. It could be of great value in mastering punctuation since, from the beginning, conventions "have been based in grammatical structure" (p. 282). It could aid in bringing into conscious use more of "the resources of our language" (p. 291). Ultimately, though, he argued for conscious understanding of these underpinnings of language as "*education* as distinct from *training*" (p. 296). It should be valued for the "insight it can give concerning the way our language works, and, through English, into the nature and functioning of human languages" (p. 296).

In 1954, W. Nelson Francis described structural linguistics as a revolution "as sweeping in its consequences as the Darwinian revolution in biology" (p. 46). In 1958, Harold B. Allen collected his "readings" – 65 recent articles on the topics of grammar and applied linguistics (including the "revolution" article by Francis). In looking back from our vantage point in the 21st century, at a time when grammar remains outside NCTE's inner circle and non-traditional grammar is absent from K–12 textbooks, it's surprising to find the wealth of material, much of it from NCTE publications, that Allen had to choose from in putting together his book of readings, most of them published between 1950 and 1956. When grammar finds its way into NCTE journals today, it is not a topic for elucidation, but an issue to be debated.

We can learn a great deal about our profession's history from the "readings" in Professor Allen's collection. Many of the discipline's pioneers are represented in its pages.[2] The new discipline of applied linguistics was just beginning to make an impact on textbooks and teacher training in the 1950s. Future teachers were learning the utility of structural linguistics with C. C. Fries's *The Structure of English* (1952); they were studying phonology and morphology with *An Outline*

---

2. Among them C. C. Fries, Leonard Bloomfield, Karl Dykema, James Sledd, Albert Markwardt, Raven I. McDavid, Francis Christensen, Paul Roberts, Archibald Hill and Donald Lloyd.

of English Structure by George L. Trager and Henry Lee Smith, Jr. (1951). Secondary students were learning the principles of structural grammar from Paul Roberts's *Patterns of English* (1956), based on the work of Fries. Clearly, the decade of the 1950s held promise as a watershed period, a turning point for the possibility of a reform grammar based on scientific understanding of language. The "long overdue revolution" that Professor Francis predicted in 1954 was on the move. However, within 10 years, it had virtually come to nought.

The century's brightest star in the field of linguistics, whose name is missing from the list of contributors to Allen's collection, is, of course, Noam Chomsky. It was 1957[3] when Chomsky's *Syntactic Structures* exploded onto the linguistic scene. And by 1965, when his expanded *Aspects of the Theory of Syntax* made its appearance, both structural grammar and the traditional "school" variety were beginning to feel the winds of change. Indeed, the whole enterprise of scientific grammar as an integral part of the curriculum was under a cloud.

Generative Grammar and Its Influences

Generative (sometimes called transformational or generative/transformational) grammar has evolved considerably over the years. We will concentrate mostly on its earliest formulations because they have had the most impact on the public understanding of grammar and on pedagogy. One primary influence, certainly, is that generative grammar gained primacy as the dominant linguistic grammar for several decades, supplanting the interest in structural grammar that had begun to influence pedagogical grammar by pushing it toward what its advocates thought of as a more solid, scientific ground.

One primary difference between structural grammar and generative grammar, as articulated by Noam Chomsky, is that structural grammar based itself largely on observations about syntactic patterns of Standard English. For generative grammar, the prime focus is not on patterns in the output of language, though those are not irrelevant, but in the internal rules for the generation of those forms. It is, in Chomsky's words, "mentalistic". In determining whether a given structure is grammatical or not, we can have recourse to the intuitions of a native speaker, quite possibly the linguist herself. Chomsky's view also differs from mainstream views about acquisition, a topic that structural grammar didn't directly address. To Chomsky, attempts to explain language acquisition on the basis of empirical observation or deduction would inevitably fall short. Language, he felt, was far too rich and complex not to be somewhat innate. He posited what he called a "language acquisition device", somewhat separate from other cognitive faculties of the mind.

> It seems reasonable to suppose that a child cannot help constructing a particular sort of transformational grammar to account for the data presented to him, any more than he can control his perception of solid objects or his attention to line and angle. Thus it may well be that the general features of language structure reflect, not so much the course of one's experience, but rather the

3. Allen's *Readings* was probably "in press" at that time.

general character of one's capacity to acquire knowledge – in the traditional sense, one's innate ideas and innate principles. (Chomsky, 1965, p. 59)

There are a few inevitable corollaries to this position. One is that every human being is equally "competent" in grammar by virtue of being human. Though Fries could contrast "vulgar" English with Standard English, no generative grammarian would make the same judgment; whatever the idiosyncrasies of a local grammar, it is essentially a manifestation of the same universal grammar we all inherit genetically. The other corollary is that grammar, though not irrelevant to pragmatics or semantics (communication or cognition), is best thought of as a separate system. "Only imperfect correspondences hold between formal and semantic features in language. The fact that the correspondences are so inexact suggests that meaning will be relatively useless as the basis for grammatical description" (Chomsky, 1957, p. 101). "I think we are forced to conclude that grammar is autonomous and independent of meaning" (1957, p. 17). The prime interest in a generative grammar is the enterprise of discovering the underlying universal grammar, essentially the internal rules for the generation of syntactic forms. The third corollary, directly related to pedagogy, is that grammar is NOT obtained by "conditioning", by "drill and explicit explanation", or even by "elementary 'data processing' procedures" (Chomsky, 1965, p. 51). Chomsky seems to be in agreement with Humboldt that "one cannot really teach language but can only present the conditions under which it will develop spontaneously in the mind in its own way" (1965, p. 51). This last formulation, in particular, echoes the basic position of "whole language" approaches to literacy, which posits that language acquisition will occur while the mind is engaged in literate practices, reading great literature and engaging ideas in composition.

Activity: Reflecting on the Challenge of "Generative" Grammars

Is grammar something that is innate within us, or is it deeply tied to our interactions with the world? Is grammar a neutral conveyor of meaning, or is it deeply connected to the making of meaning? Would answers to these questions influence your position on what kind of grammar and how much grammar to teach?

Grammar as "Elitist"

In Fries' structural approach to grammar, as he describes in his Preface, "I procured the means and the opportunity to record mechanically many conversations of speakers of standard English in this North Central community in the United States" (1952, p. vii). Though he made clear that his purpose was not usage, but structure, choosing the conversations of a group of "Standard English" speakers as the basis for a description of the overall language would seem naive to us these days, not only because we now have access to huge corpus grammars, but because we have lived through the Civil Rights struggles of the 1960s and the concomitant questioning of what "mainstream" language implies.

What might be termed an anti-elitist philosophy helped intensify NCTE's anti-grammar policy. In 1968, NCTE passed a resolution voicing concerns about the neglect of the language needs of non-standard dialect speakers. And while the official statements focused on the preparation of teachers to meet the needs of these students, including the need to teach edited English, teachers were also encouraged to recognize the legitimacy of the home-language dialects in their classrooms. Because traditional school grammar had historically been based on normative rules and the standards of edited English, those traditions, which appeared to promote one "correct" way for every rule and pronunciation, were understood as elitist. Even terms like "Standard English" were seen as an affront to students whose home language deviated from the so-called standard.

This anti-elitist effort came about in part as a response to the "back to the basics" movement of the late 1960s and early 1970s, when public concern was being voiced about student achievement. The NCTE's response can be found in a 1976 document written by Charles Suhor, entitled "Back to the Basics: Grammar and Usage". The document is one of a series of so-called "Starter Sheets" from Support for Learning and Teaching of English (SLATE), NCTE's intellectual freedom network, which are labeled "resources for dealing with current issues affecting the teaching of English". This particular SLATE document quotes the NCTE Commission on Composition, which recognized "the importance of the study of the structure of language as a valuable asset to a liberal education" (para. 4). It went on to say that such study should not be "an instrument for presenting the grammar of a particular dialect as 'right' or 'pure' or 'logical' or better than others". A later paragraph reported that "[m]any English teachers ... feel a responsibility to reject approaches to grammar and usage study that support the linguistic imperialism of prescriptive 'school grammars'" (para. 6).

This Starter Sheet stated the NCTE's position toward the new grammar as well: "The most accurate descriptions of grammatical structure – if, indeed, abstract knowledge of grammar is to be emphasized – are found in generative grammar and generative semantics" (para. 6). While clearly out of date in many respects, including the assumption that generative grammar is the central linguistic grammar of our time, this Starter Sheet is available on the NCTE website and continues to represent the organization's policy on grammar and usage. The lingering concept of "linguistic imperialism" remains an impediment in re-establishing grammar in the curriculum. We don't, in effect, have a way of teaching Standard English that does not clash with our celebration of diversity.[4]

Activity: Reflecting on the Place of Home and Community Languages

Do students need to learn a mainstream "academic" or "standard" language to be successful? Is it also important for students to be able to trust the language they have learned at home and in their communities? How would you balance these goals?

---

4. One exception to this would be the work of Rebecca Wheeler, which advocates the teaching of "code switching" for speakers of non-Standard dialects (see Wheeler & Swords, 2006).

Anti-Formalism and Anti-Elitism in Literature

Similar anti-elitist and anti-formalist movements have come out of literature study as well. If we take the 1960s as point of reference, literature was thought of as the most important component of English studies and was certainly thought of as a deeply humanizing activity. The dominant critical approach of that decade was New Critical and Formalist. A common New Critical perspective was that a text exists independently of its rhetorical context, that it cannot be reduced to its author's intentions, its various interpretations, or even its mirroring of an outside world. But the underlying assumption was always that these canonical texts were among the greatest legacies of civilization, and mining their wisdom was a way of civilizing sensibilities and cultivating humanized adults. There was considerable attention to form and language within this tradition (image patterns, for example, or plot structure, or shades and kinds of irony), though this was an attention that seemed to owe very little to the discipline of linguistics. In the light of disciplinary battles that followed, this was a period of unusual harmony and unity within the field, and it did not, in any serious way, make common ground with linguistics. If grammar was attended to or tolerated, it was a traditional grammar for the most part, and the expectation was that this was to have been taken care of in grammar school, that attention to grammar at the college level would be essentially remedial.

If we looked at an English department 30 years after the 1960s, we would find that the old consensus had been lost. Critical Theory not only challenged the old, disinterested, humanist approaches, but established a somewhat contentious ground for its own importance. We no longer easily accept the fact that there is or should be a monolithic central culture or a received wisdom embodied in the canon. Previously canonized texts can be read as manifestations of a sexist, racist or repressive culture. Rather than simply describe the text in a detached way, we try to place it within a sociocultural framework, as part of the battleground of competing social forces. We can "deconstruct" meanings rather than construct them, particularly when that means helping to bring about important cultural change. Since cultural change is of great importance, we can also look at texts that are not considered literature in the old, high, elitist sense of the word. The focus of English studies can include popular culture. This, of course, often creates a huge disjunct between what a teacher can study in college and what has been the historical norm within a local public school curriculum. But it has been one other way in which the activities of the discipline of English take us further away from the direct study of language (see Locke in this book). The text is often thought of as a stepping-off point for a critical response, which may be thought of as more important than the text.

A Process Revolution in Composition

In addition to these lines of interest, we would need to add composition, which became an emerging field of its own in the last few decades. The roots of this are in the Process movement, which was essentially an attempt to root the study of writing in a study of what writers actually do when they write. The old model of composition, that a student should narrow a topic, select a thesis, write an outline, write a draft following the outline, and then correct the surface errors in the writing, was shown to be faulty, precisely because it is far different from what successful writers report about their writing experience.

For the late Donald Murray (see especially *A Writer Teaches Writing* (1968)), the key insight was always that writing is both discovery and revision, and that revising is not at all a matter of "correcting" writing, but a matter of bringing ideas into form and into clearer focus, for the writer as well as the reader. Error-focused attention to writing emphasized product over process. A great deal of attention was then devoted to ways, other than correctness, that a text could be successful (see especially Elbow (1973, 1981) and Macrorie (1980)) with some sense that this can only happen when an attention to grammar is somewhat held in abeyance.

A great deal of effort was made to establish composition as an important discipline in its own right, and the notion of correcting grammar or correcting texts as central activity had to be dismissed before a more professional ground could be established for the field. Murray collected thousands of comments by writers about the nature of their craft as a sort of informal research. This was followed up more systematically by writing researchers, like Janet Emig (1971), Sondra Perl (1979) and Nancy Sommers (1980, 1982), who focused attention on the contrasting composing processes of successful and inexperienced writers. Inexperienced writers, according to Sommers, "decide to stop revising when they decide that they have not violated any of the rules for revising.... In general, students will subordinate the demands of the specific problems of the text to the demands of the rules" (1980, p. 383). Experienced writers, on the other hand, see changes as "part of the process of *discovering meaning* altogether" (1980, p. 385). In research on teacher comments and their effects, Sommers reported that error-focused comments

> can take students attention away from their own purposes in writing a particular text.... Such comments give the student an impression of the importance of these errors that is all out of proportion ... The comments create the concern that these "accidents" of discourse need to be attended to before the meaning of the text is attended to. (1982, pp. 149–150)

Process approaches to composition, then, which seemed far more grounded in what writers actually do and was establishing itself as a research-based approach, also positioned itself as opposed to the usual overemphasis on error (which was and continues to be a somewhat mainstream association with grammar).

Activity: The Place of Error Correction

Is there still a place for grammar instruction focused on error correction? Argue your case. Design a classroom-based activity that addresses the problem of error correction but is in accordance with the case you have just argued.

The Meta Research Reports

The most influential of the meta research reports was that by Braddock, Lloyd-Jones and Schoer (1963), which contained the oft-quoted statement that: "The teaching of formal grammar has a negligible or, because it usually displaces some instruction and practice in actual composition, even a harmful effect on the improvement of writing" (pp. 37–38). In the introduction to his own meta-report in 1986, George Hillocks Jr. related how important that statement was to him. "My colleagues and I rejoiced" (p. xv). He and his colleagues had developed a junior high school curriculum which "deemphasized formal grammar" and "emphasized developing higher-level skills in reading literature and writing" (p. xv).

The notion of displacement may have been a key to the progressive argument against comprehensive, formal grammar instruction. You cannot learn to write by studying grammar; then studying grammar would take time away from activities that might directly develop the ability to write. As Hillocks Jr. reported, he was "under attack by teachers at the high school our graduates attended. They demanded that we teach nouns, verbs, prepositions, introductory verbal clauses, indirect objects, retained objects, and all the other paraphernalia of traditional school grammar" (p. xv). The report by Braddock and colleagues (1963) was of considerable assistance to those progressive educators who wanted to buy room in the English curriculum for what they thought of as more progressive activities.

Hillocks Jr.'s meta-analysis largely backed up the Braddock report conclusions. He reported on studies that showed "superior performance on STEP writing tests, STEP essay tests, and teacher-assigned themes" for a group that studied a linguistic grammar. He reported on another that showed significant gains in "language knowledge and writing ability" for a class that studied "linguistic grammar" when compared to a group that studied "traditional grammar". Both studies, though, Hillocks Jr. conceded, "had inadequate teacher controls" (p. 134). He reported studies that showed gains on such measures as "syntactic sensitivity", but discounted those that did not directly measure writing quality in pre-test and post-test samples. He reported on a comprehensive study (Elley, Barham, Lamb & Wyllie, 1976) of three groups of students in New Zealand, all of which had instruction in rhetoric and composition, with one group studying transformational grammar, another traditional grammar and the third no grammar at all. He found that the "the grammar groups did outperform the no-grammar classes on a test of usage and mechanics", but on elements that he concluded "appear to be amenable to direct, discrete instruction" (p. 138). Perhaps the most important conclusion of that study was that the transformational grammar curriculum was "not popular" (p. 137).

Hillocks Jr. spent considerable time looking at the research on language acquisition, specifically what has been called "syntactic maturity" in the literature. Much of this dates back to Kellogg Hunt's seminal study (1965) and the establishment of the T-unit as a measure of complexity. The T-unit, in short, includes a main clause and all its subordinate clauses. This differentiates a hierarchical kind of complexity from the complexity formed solely from compounding, which can create sentences that are long without being necessarily complex. Hunt's work can be thought of against the background of generative grammar, which considers acquisition of grammatical forms a more or less biologically ordained process, but nevertheless recognizes that the right sort of environment is necessary for this to happen. It stands to reason that we ought to be able to measure the acquisition of these forms over time as a measure of "syntactic maturity". The problem, as Hillocks Jr. summarized it, is that "several researchers working independently with student writing in a wide variety of modes and at a variety of grade levels have obtained extraordinarily low correlations between mean T-unit length and rated quality" (p. 75).

This correlation problem carries over to the activity of sentence-combining, itself an activity that has grown out of the generative views of language (see especially Mellon, 1969). Students are given "kernel" sentences and asked to combine them in increasingly complex ways. "Mary sat in a room. The room was warm. She looked at a paper. The paper was blank." A typical solution to that problem would be: "Mary sat in a warm room and looked at a blank paper." Students, the theory goes, not only learn transformational patterns, but have concrete practice with their application. In O'Hare's version of it (1973), sentence-combining is taught without any direct attention to grammatical terminology. This, inevitably, has an appeal to writing instructors interested in avoiding the difficulties of teaching a complex grammar. The exercises are somewhat open and the activity somewhat playful, and students seem to enjoy it.

The biggest difficulty seems to be dealing with the reality that syntactic complexity does not directly relate to writing quality. Hillocks Jr. summarized the conjecture this way:

> Perhaps a more useful emphasis would be on *facility*. Facility would appear to involve an expanded repertoire of syntactic structures, the ability to sort through the available structures to select and test those that are feasible, and finally the judgment to select effective structures for a given rhetorical context. (1986, p. 150)

This is a rather extraordinary prescription in a meta-analysis that generally opposed the direct teaching of grammar, as it seems to call for a rhetorically focused attention to grammar. If the Braddock report provided support for a retreat from formal grammar, the literature on sentence-combining had the potential to provide support for the reintroduction of grammar into the curriculum in rhetorically friendly ways.

Hillocks Jr. shared many of the views of the progressive educators of his time, among them the notion that attention to grammar is distant from the "higher-level" concerns of writing.

> If the process of writing is brought to bear on the composing processes at all, it is likely to influence only the most concrete levels, the planning and editing of specific sentences. But such study would have no impact on the higher-level processes of deciding on intentions and generating and organizing ideas.... The study of mechanics and usage (what might be called

"conventional correctness") is likely to have effect only in the last-minute editing done during transcription or in the editing process that follows it. (1986, pp. 226–227)

Clearly, any serious argument for reinstating grammar needs to deal with these concerns. It would need to move us closer toward inclusiveness, closer to higher-level activities, the central purposes and motives for reading and writing. Luckily, more recent linguistic grammars (cognitive and functional) are better suited for this.

Whole Language in Context Approaches

In composition, of course, grammar cannot be completely wished away, and there has been a troubling and troubled relationship to it over the decades. Many people have been attracted to composition precisely because it gives them an opportunity to help people produce important kinds of texts. Teaching WRITING seems fundamentally so much more important than simply policing people's mistakes. On the other hand, students do write texts and texts need to achieve certain "standards", at least in the public mind. There is and has been resistance to a notion of writing that reduces it to correctness. At the same time, there is an uncomfortable recognition that correctness needs to be addressed.

Both 4 C's (The Conference on College Composition and Communication) and NCTE have tended to take the progressive position that every child is entitled to his/her home language and to have that home language respected within school. Another is the resolution, addressed elsewhere in this chapter, that there is no evidence that formal instruction in grammar has any effect on reducing error in student writing. As part of that, also, is the notion that time spent on grammar would be time better spent on actual reading and writing. This is closely tied to "whole-language" approaches to language acquisition, and those are heavily influenced by generative grammar and the theoretical positions of Noam Chomsky.[5] From their perspective, language is acquired rather than learned. Since that happens best in a language-rich environment, language itself does not need to be the focus of instruction. A minimum of attention to the conventions of Standard English is all that is necessary.

One very influential presentation of that progressive view is the work of Constance Weaver, especially *Teaching Grammar in Context* (1996), which made the case for minimalist attention to grammar. If we think of grammar as "the functional command of sentence structures that enable us to comprehend and produce language", then "we do not need to teach grammar at all: the grammar of our native language is what we learn in acquiring that language" (1996, p. 2). Weaver dismisses fairly quickly the notion that conscious understanding of these forms would help, largely by citing the studies that purport to show attempts to teach formal grammar as failures. She does acknowledge the need for a student

5. For a description of the influence of generative grammar on NCTE positions, see MacDonald (2007).

to master the principles of standard written English, but believes this can be done with a minimum of terminology and minimum of intervention. She does present a somewhat comprehensive "scope" for grammar instruction, but emphasizes that there is no one-size-fits-all sequence for the presentation of these, and advocates individualized intervention (for the elimination of error) or occasional "mini-lessons" for larger groups of students or for a whole class. Erica Lindemann's highly influential *A Rhetoric for Writing Teachers* (2001) echoes Weaver in affirming that students can learn to write grammatically without having to know about grammar. Lindemann asserts that English teachers should have considerable knowledge about language but doesn't have direct recommendations about where and how that knowledge should be acquired.

Those of us who have had roles teaching English-teaching majors may echo Susan Peck MacDonald: "They fear learning how to do grammatical analysis, are not prepared for the task, and may have received prior assurances that knowing anything about the grammar of English is either inessential or harmful" (2007, p. 605). English majors preparing to teach may do so with a single class in language, often a survey of the field in linguistics in which just a few weeks are spent on syntax. Typically, a student entering college in the United States may or may not have considerable error in their written work, but will almost certainly not have a metalanguage available to talk about that. Since the emphasis is on behavior (error avoidance) and not on knowledge, it is difficult to intervene and difficult to know who or what to blame for that situation.

Perhaps the main weakness in the whole-language approach is the lack of accountability within the system and in the progressive diminution of knowledge it brings about over time. There is no way of blaming the teacher for not teaching grammar, when it has already been "proven" that teaching grammar is harmful. The fault then lies within the students' failure to somehow soak it up from exposure or from the teacher's non-technical remarks. Or perhaps, because everyone grows at their own pace, that student is simply on a path that will lead them toward maturity somewhere down the road. Unfortunately, some of those students, unschooled in an understanding of grammar, become English teachers in their own right. Even if they have become writers not prone to error, they do not carry into teaching a deep grounding in knowledge of the language. Editing student writing becomes more a matter of what "feels right". They don't have the knowledge base necessary to put the quirks of textual convention into perspective. They don't see a connection between formal choices and rhetorical effect.

Alternative Possibilities

The grammar wars as currently fought may well be unwinnable by either "side". Both seem to assume that grammar is primarily a set of formal restrictions or constraints, the "rules" that govern its use in more formal registers. Therefore, it is either the main goal of writing instruction or a somewhat unfortunate minor concern that has the potential to become a major distraction if given too much attention. You can't write well with a central focus on traditional grammar, and you can't write acceptably without it. (Any attempt to promote more structural freedom is met with charges of a lessening of standards.)

The solution may very well be offered by grammars that show a close, dynamic connection between the forms of grammar and the meanings they convey, including the meanings we most often associate with discourse. These grammars have, in fact, been under development for the past few decades: systemic functional grammar, largely the work of Michael Halliday (see Halliday and Matthiessen, 2004 for the most recent version), and cognitive grammar, largely under the leadership of Ronald Langacker (see Langacker, 2008 for an accessible overview), developed largely in the United States as a counter to generative grammar, which is now losing its hold on linguistics in the States. Since these rhetorically friendly grammars have not been widely understood, they have yet to find their way into pedagogy in any kind of significant way.

According to Myhill (2005 and in this book), "The truth is that teaching grammar and knowledge about language in positive, contextualized ways which make clear links with writing is not yet an established way of teaching and it is, as yet, hugely under-researched" (p. 81). She argues the need to theorize or observe aspects of grammar most readily relevant to writing, ask whether conscious knowledge is helpful and "what teaching strategies are most successful in enabling this to happen" (p. 80).

The generative model of language acquisition, which posits grammar as an innate formal system, has been called into serious question by functional and cognitive linguists, who posit a "usage-based" model as much truer (and empirically grounded). Put quite simply, children learn language the same way they learn other things, on the basis of their experience. Michael Tomasello (2003) posits "intention reading" and "pattern finding" as central cognitive processes. "The process of acquiring language conventions serves to focus children's attention on aspects of experience that they might not otherwise have focused on. The relation between children's language and cognition is a two-way street" (p. 63).

For Mary Schleppegrell (2004), this means, also, that the "language of schooling" is not the language a child brings with her when she enters school. "School-based texts are difficult for many students precisely because they emerge from discourse contexts that require different ways of using language than students experience outside of school" (p. 9). Schleppegrell, who believes much insight can be gained through systemic functional grammar, argues that

> researchers and educators need a more complete understanding of the linguistic challenges of schooling. In the absence of an explicit focus on language, students from certain social class backgrounds continue to be privileged and others to be disadvantaged in learning, assessment, and promotion, perpetuating the obvious inequalities that exist today. (p. 3)

In *Reading in Secondary Content Areas: A Language-Based Pedagogy* (2008), co-authored with Zhihui Fang, she argues for a language-based teaching as a way to give students productive access to reading texts as well. The work of Kolln (*Rhetorical Grammar*, 2006) and Hancock (*Meaning-Centered Grammar*, 2005) have

been attempts to merge rhetorical and functional approaches with more traditional terminology. The future of grammar probably depends on people who can
draw on advances in linguistics and can describe a basis for understanding language that can be both practical and accurate.

Perhaps grammar can be embraced by progressive educators if they can see
that it is not meaning neutral or discourse neutral, but deeply bound up within
the effectiveness of text. Perhaps it will also appeal to traditionalists because
increased understanding of language, a more highly developed metalanguage,
should make formal conventions much easier to understand and master. Knowledge about language can empower us in many ways. It can help us resist standards as well as follow them. It helps make the power and effectiveness of
non-traditional dialects incontrovertible fact, not just a political assertion. It can
help guide us in thoughtfully nuanced expression, in recognizing the inherent
connection between formal choice and rhetorical effect. The questions should be
about which grammar, not about if or when.

References

Allen, H. (1958). *Readings in applied English linguistics.* New York: Appleton-Century-Crofts.
Braddock, R., Lloyd-Jones, R., & Schoer, L. (1963). *Research in written composition.*
    Urbana, IL: National Council of Teachers of English.
Chomsky, N. (1957). *Syntactic structures.* The Hague: Mouton.
Chomsky, N. (1965). *Aspects of the theory of syntax.* Cambridge, MA: MIT Press.
Commission on English. (1965). *Freedom and discipline in English.* New York: College
    Entrance Examination Board.
Elbow, P. (1973). *Writing without teachers.* New York: Oxford University Press.
Elbow, P. (1981). *Writing with power: Techniques for mastering the writing process.* New
    York: Oxford University Press.
Elley, W., Barham, I., Lamb, H., & Wyllie, M. (1976). The role of grammar in a secondary
    school English curriculum. *Research in the Teaching of English, 10*(1), 5–21.
Emig, J. (1971). *The composing processes of twelfth graders.* NCTE Research Report 13.
    Urbana, IL: National Council of Teachers of English.
Fang, Z., & Schleppegrell, M. (2008). *Reading in secondary content areas: A language-
    based pedagogy.* Ann Arbor: University of Michigan Press.
Francis, N. (1954). Revolution in grammar. *Quarterly Journal of Speech, 40,* 299–312.
    (Reprinted in Allen (1958), *Readings in applied English linguistics.*)
Fries, C. (1952). *The structure of English: An introduction to the construction of English
    sentences.* New York: Harcourt, Brace and World.
Gleason, H. (1965). *Linguistics and English grammar.* New York: Holt.
Halliday, M., & Matthiessen, C. (2004). *An introduction to functional grammar* (3rd. ed.)
    London: Arnold.
Hancock, C. (2005). *Meaning-centered grammar: An introductory text.* London: Equinox
    Publishing Company.
Hatfield, W. (1936). Editorial. *English Journal, 25,* 65–66.
Hillocks, G. (1986). *Research on written composition: New directions for teaching.* Urbana,
    IL: ERIC Clearinghouse on Reading and Communication Skill.
Hoyt, F. (1906). Grammar in the elementary curriculum. *Teachers College Record, 7,*
    473–494.

Hunt, K. (1965). *Grammatical structures written at three grade levels.* NCTE Research Report No. 3. Champagne, IL: National Council of Teachers of English.

Kolln, M. (1981). Closing the books on alchemy. *College Composition and Communication, 32*(2), 139–151.

Kolln, M. (2006). *Rhetorical grammar: Grammatical choices, rhetorical effects* (5th ed.). New York: Longman.

Langacker, R. (2008). *Cognitive grammar: A basic introduction.* New York: Oxford University Press.

Lindemann, E. (2001). *A rhetoric for writing teachers.* New York: Oxford University Press.

MacDonald, S. (2007). The erasure of language. *College Composition and Communication, 58*(4), 585–625.

Macrorie, K. (1980). *Telling writing.* Rochelle Park, NJ: Hayden.

Mellon, J. (1969). *Transformational sentence combining: A method for enhancing the development of syntactic fluency in English composition.* Urbana, IL: National Council of Teachers of English.

Murray, D. (1968). *A writer teaches writing.* Boston: Houghton Mifflin.

Myhill, D. (2005). Ways of knowing: Writing with grammar in mind. *English Teaching: Practice and Critique, 4*(3), 77–96.

National Council of Teachers of English. (1935). *An experience curriculum in English.* New York: D. Appleton-Century.

O'Hare, F. (1973). *Sentence combining: Improving student writing without formal grammar instruction.* NCTE Committee on Research Report Series, no. 15. Urbana, IL: National Council of Teachers of English.

Perl, S. (1979). The composing processes of unskilled college writers. *Research in the Teaching of English, 13,* 317–336.

Rapeer, L. (1913). The problem of formal grammar in elementary education. *The Journal of Educational Psychology, 4,* 124–137.

Roberts, P. (1956). *Patterns of English.* New York: Harcourt, Brace and World.

Schleppegrell, M. (2004). *The language of schooling: A functional linguistics perspective.* Mahwah, NJ: Lawrence Erlbaum.

Sommers, N. (1980). Revision strategies of student writers and experienced adult writers. *College Composition and Communication, 31,* 378–388.

Sommers, N. (1982). Responding to student writing. *College Composition and Communication, 33,* 148–156.

Suhor, C. (1976). Back to the basics: Grammar and usage. *Support for learning and teaching of English.* Urbana, IL: National Council of Teachers of English.

Tomasello, M. (2003). *Constructing a language: A usage-based theory of language acquisition.* Cambridge, MA: Harvard University Press.

Trager, G., & Smith, H., Jr. (1951). *An outline of English structure.* Studies in linguistics occasional papers (No. 3). Norman, OK: Battenberg Press.

Weaver, C. (1996). *Teaching grammar in context.* Portsmouth, NH: Boynton/Cook.

Wheeler, R., & Swords, R. (2006). *Code-switching: Teaching Standard English in urban classrooms.* Urbana, IL: National Council of Teachers of English.

Chapter 3

The Problematics of Prescribing Grammatical Knowledge
The Case in England

Urszula Clark

Introduction: A Brief Curriculum History

To understand current debates about the role of grammar and knowledge about language in the UK English school curriculum, one has to understand the ways in which language is inextricably linked with notions of social class. Standard English in England is associated with the middle class, for reasons which are historical and date back to the 18th century and the processes of standardization (see, for example, Leith, 1997; Clark, 2001). Language is also, in the modern world, a key feature of national identity, and thus a key and crucial subject when it comes to reproducing notions of national identity and the maintenance of social order. Indeed, this is why the teaching of English – and notably the teaching of literacy, grammar and literature, as a means of both perpetuating and reproducing notions of Standard English and national identity – occupies curricular centre stage. The very first government report into the teaching of English, the Newbolt Report (1921), for example, argued for the importance of English as a school subject, especially the teaching of Standard English as a written form, including its grammar and literature as a means of ensuring national unity and the continuance of national identity in a society fragmented after the First World War.

In the middle decades of the 20th century, and following the Second World War, emphasis in the teaching of English shifted from the teaching of Standard English and its canonical literature to an emphasis upon creative expression. This shift was supported by research which showed that teaching grammar formally had little or no effect upon the quality of pupils' written expression. This shift was officially endorsed in 1975 with the publication of a second government report into the teaching of English known as the Bullock Report and led to the eventual abandonment of formal grammar teaching. Consequently, from the 1950s and into the 1970s, at a time of increasing social mobility epitomized by the phrase "classless society", it suited government policies of education to support curriculum change within English which abandoned the teaching of Standard English grammar and canonical English literature. In its place came an emphasis upon creative writing, spoken English and contemporary fiction which reflected students' experiences. Little or no reference was made to notions of "accuracy" and "correctness", and with lip-service paid to the demands of the workplace outside the school in the shape of formal letter writing.

Throughout the 20th century, developments in linguistics seemed to support changes in the curriculum for English since, by the early 20th century, linguists realized that the notion of grammar where one size fits all, based on a grammar of Latin, did not apply to all languages, including English. Thus, many of the grammatical "rules" that were being taught in schools no longer had academic credence. No replacement was developed for the Latinate grammars that continued to be written, taught and examined in schools until well into the 1960s, on the grounds that it was better to learn some grammar than none at all.

By the early to mid-1980s, however, civil society in England was characterized by social unrest and racial tension, particularly in the large inner-city areas across England. One of the reasons given by the government for this unrest and tension was the part played by the school curriculum, discussed in more detail below, and especially that of English. More specifically, teachers and the curriculum were blamed for a failure, as the government saw it, to teach Standard English and canonical literature and, through it, social cohesion based upon a common national identity. By the early 21st century, a National Curriculum for English had been legislated for and prescribed, which changed the basis of the curriculum for English once again to one dominated by a functional skills agenda, and emphasis upon accuracy, at the expense of creativity.

This brief overview shows that what constitutes a curriculum subject is as much to do with the external environment of educational policy and the attitudes and approaches taken by policy-makers, as with the internal constructions of the subject and its associated pedagogic practices. As Christie (2004) puts it, "what one does educationally is itself always a part of the period of history in which one is working" (p. 184). One person who attempted to make sense of how this happens was the sociologist Basil Bernstein.

Basil Bernstein and Pedagogic Discourse

Basil Bernstein is perhaps best known for his four-volume series entitled *Class, Codes and Control* (1971 to 1990), in which he investigated the relationship between language and education. He was particularly interested in the ways in which this relationship not only reflects but also structures inequality. He insisted that the relationship between language and social class was fundamental to accessing educational opportunity. In the 1960s, Bernstein argued that the distribution of educational access was very clearly tied to class, particularly through the language used in its distribution, and that educational failure was often, in a very general sense, language failure. In his later work, Bernstein turned his attention to the ways in which discourse functions in society and the part it plays in maintaining social order, especially discourse concerned with education (1990, 1996).

Bernstein identified three principles or rules governing pedagogic discourse in hierarchical relation to one another: those of (1) distribution, (2) relocation or recontextualization and (3) evaluation. In brief, rules of distribution govern the institutional practices and the upper echelons of government; those of recontextualization govern the transformation of school subjects; and those of evaluation govern pedagogic practice (Figure 3.1).

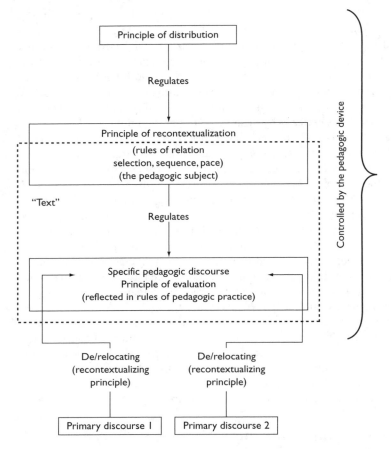

Figure 3.1 Bernstein's View of the Pedagogic Discourse.

To generate these rules or principles, Bernstein distinguishes between the underlying invisible structures through which a pedagogic subject is realized, and what he calls "the text", that is, the actual utterances, written texts and so on, which are privileged through and by these structures – using the term "text" in its widest semiotic sense. In Bernstein's view, for a theory of cultural reproduction to be complete, it has to explain *how* a text came to be constituted as it is and accorded a privileged status (which may change), as well as *what* is transmitted. To achieve this explanation, he proposes a theory of pedagogic discourse within which there is an intrinsic grammar, the "pedagogic device", which controls the three principles of distribution, recontextualization and evaluation. Relevant to our discussion here, a pedagogic discourse such as the school subject English removes or delocates a discourse from the universities and relocates it within the school context, reordering and refocusing it according to the principle of distribution controlled by the pedagogic device.

The relationship between Bernstein's three principles is hierarchical, in that the principle of distribution regulates the principle of recontextualization which in turn regulates that of evaluation. The principle of distribution regulates "the fundamental relationship between power, social groups, forms of consciousness and practice, and their reproductions and productions" (Bernstein, 1990, p. 180). The principle of recontextualization in turn regulates the constitution of a specific pedagogic discourse. The principle of evaluation, in turn, is constituted in pedagogic practice. Bernstein proposes that the pedagogic device makes the transformation of power into differently specialized subjects possible through the distribution and regulation of "knowledges" and the discourses such knowledges presuppose. Change occurs as a consequence of the inner potential of the device and the regulation of knowledge coming into conflict with the social base from which its power is derived. Rather than act as an agent of change, the education system, therefore – including the curriculum taught within it – becomes a site of cultural reproduction that aims to reproduce the society within which it is located.

"English" as a school subject grew out of the 19th-century elementary school curriculum of teaching reading, handwriting and grammar. This curriculum was then influenced in the early 19th century by the new-fangled study of vernacular literature in extension colleges and elsewhere, then became part of the move to professionalize school teaching in the later part of the 19th century. Throughout the 20th century and the expansion of the elementary curriculum into secondary education, the curriculum was further influenced by the publication of several government reports, from the Newbolt Report of 1921, the Bullock Report of 1975, to the Kingman Report of 1988 and then the raft of policy documents that have accompanied the National Curriculum since its introduction in 1991. A range of often contradictory political and theoretical positions are evident within these documents, particularly when issues of "cohesion" and "democracy" hit each other after world wars and financial crises. In short, what becomes the content of a school subject is not something unique or logical. Rather, it is defined by those (including academics and politicians) who regulate and control the curriculum, in ways which they believe to be the most useful and desirable to benefit society. These are social, not logical, facts.

In the case of disciplines such as linguistics and literary studies, for example, their primary location is in universities, whence they are relocated and refocused into the secondary school curriculum through a complex combination or prism of the rules of relation, selection, sequencing and pacing which are not derived from some logic internal to linguistics and literary studies, or from the practices of those who produce these disciplines. Rather, these rules are derived from social and political considerations, where aspects of linguistic endeavor, for example, are selected from their primary location and recontextualized into a pedagogic context, a process which involves selecting aspects believed to be the most useful and desirable to benefit society. Bernstein's theory also proposes that the recontextualizing rules, in addition to selection, sequence, pace and relations with other subjects, regulate the theory of instruction from which the transmission rules are derived. Consequently, the way in which the subject is taught is not one that is intrinsically linked to it, but dictated by those who regulate and control its content.

Bernstein's theory of pedagogic discourse has the merit of providing an empirical description of how cultural reproduction works and the ways in which it positions different sections of society. As has already been argued, the school curriculum plays a central and pivotal role in maintaining and reproducing notions of national identity, centering upon the teaching of Standard English, particularly its written form. An excellent example of Bernstein's theory at work is repeated government attempts in England from the late 1980s to the present day to make the content of the school curriculum a matter of state legislation, including the teaching of Standard English and its grammar, as a means of re-establishing social order and social cohesion.

The Grammar Wars

Recontextualizations of a curriculum subject such as English and redefinitions or recategorizations of a language (for example, Standard English) have to be understood within the wider external educational, political, cultural, social and historical contexts within which they occur as well as within the internal workings of the subject itself. Bernstein calls these two "sites" through which recontextualizations occur, the official and pedagogic fields. The pedagogic field has control over the regulation of its own discourses and practices only insofar as this is sanctioned and allowed by the official one. Although the relationship between these two fields is hierarchical, it is also discursive, interdependent and to some degree circular.

Conflict between the two fields occurs when the official one seeks to curtail the autonomy of the pedagogic one, as has been happening in England since the 1980s. Such conflict was brought to the fore following the return of the Conservative Party to a second term in office in 1983. For example, the Centre for Policy Studies (CPS) published a pamphlet ironically titled *No Turning Back* (1985). This pamphlet set out a political agenda for education, employment, health and housing. In its section on education, changes to the funding and administrative structures of schools were proposed. These structures would effectively make them self-governing and independent of local authority control, regulated by the application of the principles of consumerism to education. As part of its implementation, regulation of the principle of distribution was taken away from regional, autonomous local education authorities (LEAs) and given back to the central state. This changed the role of government from a mediational and supervisory one to one of administration. As a result, it shifted the location of power and distribution of knowledge from LEAs, subject organizations and regional examination boards to central agencies. Pupil numbers would in future determine the level of funding for each school and parents would be free to choose to send their children to any school with places available.

At the same time, curriculum content that had been undermined in traditional terms by non-selective comprehensive schools was to become more prescriptive and centralized. The objective was to prepare children for their place in a formal and class-stratified socioeconomic order which was not the same for all, aided by the introduction of a National Curriculum. A Department of Education and Science memo summed up this objective when it justified the introduction of entry into school by selection on the grounds that: "we are beginning to create aspirations which increasingly society cannot match ... People must be educated once more to know their place" (quoted in Chitty, 1988, p. 88).

The task which faced the Conservative government during the 1980s was how to give pupils knowledge without also giving them the power that goes with it. One way of achieving this was to concentrate attention on literacy standards. Although the centrality of English in the curriculum as the provider of initial literacy had long been established in infant schools, the methods used to teach it had embraced progressive pedagogy. Its other major role as a unifying agent of social cohesion had considerably lessened. Rather than celebrating Englishness, English had come to celebrate cultural and social diversity.

It is clear that the first set of "people" referred to in this statement is not the same as the second. Together with a concern for increasing standards of literacy, therefore, was the need to re-establish a sense of a distinct, homogeneous national cultural identity so that the second set of "people" did not subsume the first. All should be educated to know their place in a very different way from the one which had informed previous, post-war, educational policy. The National Curriculum in English was written with these requirements in mind, where questions of language became key issues in the teaching of literacy, English literature and Standard English. Standards of literacy were said to have declined during the period when English pedagogy had become less concerned with teaching the formal properties of language as a separate component of English.

At the same time, a decline in standards of behavior was also attributed to the lack of such teaching. Reintroducing the requirement that all pupils learn to speak Standard English and read its literature would, it was believed, bring about a corresponding rise in standards of both literacy and behavior. The much-quoted words of Norman Tebbit, a Conservative government minister, from a 1985 interview, illustrate this belief:

> we've allowed so many standards to slip ... teachers weren't bothering to teach kids to spell and punctuate properly ... if you allow standards to slip to the stage where good English is no better than bad English, where people turn up filthy ... at school ... all those things cause people to have no standards at all, and once you lose standards then there's no imperative to stay out of crime. (cited by Carter, 1997, p. 22)

Tebbit's use of the word "standards" alters its meaning every time he uses it. It also illustrates an elision between spoken and written forms of English, as if they were one and the same. First, it is taken to mean a concern with achieving a certain degree of literacy. Second, it is used as a judgment regarding the kind of English that is used, with Standard English presumably being "good" and everything else "bad". Using "bad" English is taken as an indication of a lack of moral standards that leads to its users committing crime. A person's linguistic behavior, therefore, is linked to their moral behavior. Bourne and Cameron point to the social significance of beliefs such as those expressed by Tebbit. They write that: "anxieties about grammar are at some deeper level anxieties about the break-down of order and tradition, not just in language but in society at large" (1988, pp. 149–150).

In summary, a return to traditional grammar would mark a return to the associated social values, with the "national language" being used as a point of unity and social cohesion. Such a position finds linguistic diversity threatening, a force to be contained or even eliminated. Such controversy bears out Bernstein's premise that the rules of recontextualization – in this case, those of the Conservative government and its supporters – regulate not only selection, sequence, pace of a subject and relations with other subjects, but also the theory of instruction from which the transmission rules are derived. A child-centered view of learning, preoccupied with the pupil and their own use of language, which emphasized linguistic diversity, individuality and creativity, was wholly inappropriate to a curriculum centered upon the teaching of Standard English and the literary canon.

A major problem, however, faced the government in its desire to recontextualize English. Teaching formal grammar as part of the curriculum for English had been abandoned during its previous recontextualization in the 1960s and 1970s, because linguistics had shown that a Latinate grammar was wholly inappropriate as a model for living languages such as English. Therefore, it suited a theory of pupil-centered instruction to abandon its teaching altogether. In order to resurrect the teaching of Standard English, the government also sought to resurrect the theory of instruction which went along with it: that is, a model based upon transmission which shifted the center of learning away from the pupil and back onto the teacher. The controversy surrounding the introduction of a National Curriculum in English is well documented (Cox, 1991; Clark, 1994, 2001). What is worthy of further comment here is the *way* in which the government sought to impose the teaching of grammar. The teaching favored by government ministers was that based upon a prescriptive, Latinate grammar of the kind taught in schools until the 1960s.

By the 1980s, that grammar had long been linguistically discredited. However, it was not until 1957, with publications such as Chomsky's *Syntactic Structures*, and the 1980s, with the publication of Halliday's *An Introduction to Functional Grammar* (1985; 2nd ed. 1994) that alternatives became available. The approach in these grammars is radically different from any which existed previously, and did not suit government purposes at all. Halliday's grammar, particularly, stressed the social, cultural and creative aspects of language that influenced and altered its use. The social dimension of language, Halliday (1973) argued, was crucial to discussions of language in education. He pointed out that learning was, above all, a social process. The classroom, the school and the education system form a social institution, each with clearly defined social structures. Consequently, knowledge is transmitted, acquired and learnt in social contexts through relationships that are defined in the value systems and ideology of our culture.

The situation was not helped by the government's inability to harness the support of linguists and educationalists in its desire to reintroduce the teaching of Standard English into schools and to produce either a grammar or support materials for the kind of teaching desired. The materials produced by a multi-million-pound national project headed by Ronald Carter, *Language in the National Curriculum* (LINC) (Carter, 1996), for example, were scrapped, mainly because they did not interpret teaching grammar and knowledge about language in the same way as the government had intended them to do.

One of the many controversies which surrounded the formalizing of a curriculum for English in England was that recontextualizing grammar into a pedagogic context was, first, considered by many as being tantamount to prescribing a grammar; and second, thought to signal a return to teaching by mechanistic drill. This was viewed as contrary to the spirit of much modern linguistic inquiry, which aims at language description, that is, rules of description based upon how language *is* used, and not prescription, which generates rules that language is then forced to fit and *ought* to use. Modern theories of language favor the former, whereas traditional grammar favored the latter.[1] During one of the many rewrites of the National Curriculum for English, one version claimed that what characterized dialects of English other than Standard English is their inaccuracy. Modern linguistics has shown, in fact, that dialects have and do generally abide by their own internal rules of construction in as logical a way as Standard English. In the dialect of the Black Country, for example, a region in the English West Midlands, the verb "be" is regular throughout the first two categories of person singular: "I am, you am". This is not an incorrect form of English. However, it is not a form which would go down well in writing or speech made for formal public consumption.

For politicians who wished to re-emphasize the teaching of grammar based upon traditional models, modern linguists proved to be more of a hindrance than a help. This was compounded by the fact that in England results of appeals to the profession (the pedagogic field of recontextualization) that had resulted in the Kingman Report (1988), the original national English curriculum document in England (1989) and the LINC project which followed it, all stressed the socio-linguistic aspect of a curriculum for language, but stopped short of prescribing what the government wanted (that is, a list of grammatical terms and explanations with which to describe language). The 1980s and early 1990s provide an interesting case of the complexity of the situation which exemplifies Bernstein's principles at work. On the one hand are the nationalizing, modernizing, standardizing imperatives of the high Tories on the distributive level, but on the other there are also many bottom-up, profession-led, enabling interventions that led to the Oracy Project and Writing Project on the evaluative level. Trouble occurred when the two levels clashed spectacularly at the recontextualization one, exemplified most graphically by the government dumping of the LINC project and the total abandonment of any such further bottom-led initiatives.

---

1. An often-quoted Latinate rule of English, for example, is that one should not end a sentence with a preposition, when in English it is patently obvious that you can, and many canonical literary works do just that.

The fact that a pedagogic grammar based upon sound theoretical grammatical principles did not as yet exist, coupled with the perceived refusal of the academic and teaching profession to engage in such an activity, left the way open for politicians to devise their own. In other words, failure by the pedagogic field to prescribe a pedagogic grammar left the way open for the official field to decide these terms for itself in other ways. In England, this has been achieved through the requirements for assessment in primary and secondary schools through key stage tests that purport to test pupils' knowledge of the curriculum, but actually focus on a narrow set of assessment foci, and also through the introduction of various strategy documents. Furthermore, as assessment at the various key stages became ever more divorced from the curriculum it was supposed to assess, the curriculum itself came to be rewritten, not through the legislature but through the introduction of various "strategies" which have resulted in a "renewed framework for English".

Beyond the Grammar Wars

One might have thought, given the change of government in the United Kingdom in 1997, when the Conservatives, after 18 years in power, gave way to the Labour Party, that this might signal a change in government education policy, of the kind which had occurred in 1945. However, such had been the shift to the center within Labour party politics that, within the sphere of education, a change of government made absolutely no difference to education policy. Furthermore, not only did the Labour government continue with previous Conservative education policy, but took it beyond even anything the Conservative government may have dreamed of in terms of prescribing both content and pedagogy associated with the teaching of English. The late 1990s, under New Labour, provide the most startling example of central control with fairly vicious monitoring and penalties for non-compliance.

However, having watched from the sidelines previous Conservative attempts to legislate change and the negative publicity such actions had generated, the Labour government introduced a series of strategies instead, which linked to the National Curriculum. Much of this initial "innovation" was initially linked to the United States' "curriculum 2000", which included setting targets for literacy levels across the whole population. Thus, grass-roots "bottom-up" projects of the kind which had occurred in the late 1980s and early 1990s were replaced by ones which were very much "top-down". The concept of "literacy" at this time also moved beyond the primary curriculum into the secondary.

Unlike the introduction of the National Curriculum under the Conservatives, the introduction of various strategies under Labour occurred beneath any public gaze, and with scant media coverage. Once again, as with the National Curriculum, the strategies had little basis in research or theoretical underpinning, being informed instead by a benign, highly centralized and controlled approach, not only to curriculum reform but also to pedagogic practice (see Andrews, 2008, p. 80). The introduction of the various strategies has been accompanied by an unprecedented increase in bureaucracy and accountability, in addition to that which resulted from the introduction of the National Curriculum. Small wonder then, as Andrews points out, that such initiatives have sent many teachers in search of early retirement or jobs elsewhere. With the introduction of league tables in the late 1980s, primary schools and individual departments in secondary schools became publicly accountable for their assessment results. Each school was given a target which, if not met, triggered a government inspection. Furthermore, if schools or departments failed to meet targets, they became subject to intervention strategies by the LEA, which also involved the withholding of funds to ensure that heads of department and literacy coordinators attend prescribed courses.

The first such strategy to be introduced was the National Literacy Strategy (NLS), introduced into primary schools in 1998. The NLS centers upon a "literacy hour" and a document called the *NLS Framework for Teaching*. The contents of this folder not only detail *what* should be taught – the activities that should take place in that "hour", but also details *how* the activities should be taught. Focusing on a "literacy hour" every day in schools implies at least two things: (1) that teachers have somehow been neglecting the teaching of literacy to such an extent that such an initiative is needed, and (2) supposes that what occurs outside the hour somehow has nothing to do with literacy. Clearly, neither supposition is true. In 2000, the government produced a revised NLS called: *The National Literacy Strategy: Grammar for Writing*. One of the most tenacious shibboleths of government education policy and thinking is that teaching pupils grammar will of itself result in improved writing. From Baranyai in 1949 to Dominic Wyse in 2001 and beyond, research not only continues to contest this premise, but often shows the opposite.

Undeterred, the government commissioned its own research study via a unit based at the London Institute of Education, in yet another attempt to resolve the issue of whether or not teaching pupils explicitly about grammar improved their writing skills. The English Review Group (ERG), an international group of academics which acts as an advisory board based at the Institute of Education in London, reviewed research undertaken since the beginning of the 19th century: in effect, back to the point when universal schooling was introduced, to the present day. Unsurprisingly for academics and practitioners, but disappointing once again for politicians, the report from this group argued that there was not a single bit of evidence that the teaching of traditional grammar, specifically word order and syntax, had any effect whatsoever in assessing writing quality or accuracy among 5- to 16-year-olds (Andrews, in this book). Consequently, the report concluded that the teaching of formal grammar, of the kind taught as part of the NLS which focuses upon parts of speech, is ineffective when it comes to improving the quality of writing. Not unsurprisingly, the ERG recommended that the National Curriculum be revised. As yet, no such revision has been undertaken.

Undeterred, the government continued and continues to revise and introduce new policy in the form of "strategy" documents, not only for pupils of primary age, but also for English at secondary school level. Such a move has been in tandem with the introduction of Learning and Skills Councils across the United Kingdom, tasked with overhauling the 14–19 curriculum with a view to making education align more closely with the needs of employment. In 2007, the NLS became subsumed under the Primary National Strategy (PNS), which, among other things, integrated the teaching of literacy and numeracy. It also set out "end-of-year" objectives, which list the kinds of grammatical knowledge pupils should acquire during the course of each year.

As with all such lists, these flirt with incoherence for the sake of ticking a box. An example given by Andrews (2004) is separating the learning of punctuation from any integration with the form and functions of sentence structure. Research undertaken by Andrews and others cautiously supports the notion of teaching grammar based upon "sentence combining" (Andrews, 2004). That is, pupils learn how clauses are constructed and put together into sentences. From this, one can then go on to talk of textual structure, where sentences combine to make coherent texts. Such an approach would bring together knowledge about written language with the study of texts in ways which are meaningful to the pupils, giving them insight into how language works. Such activity cannot, however, have as its fundamental premise that such knowledge *of itself* improves students' own writing.

Having laid the foundations for strategy documents in primary schools, and despite a growing body of research evidence which questioned the efficacy of such strategies, successive Labour governments continued to introduce strategy after strategy. With the NLS firmly embedded in primary schools, the government in 2001 launched *The Framework for Teaching English: Years 7, 8 and 9* (FTE). The express intention of this strategy was to build upon the NLS in primary schools and take it forward into secondary schools and the 11–16 curriculum. This strategy implied that the NLS had provided in all pupils a foundation for the "learning" of grammar and other aspects of English upon which the secondary curriculum could then be built.

As yet, such a belief remains unproven, and even the government's own research into the effect of the NLS in 2004 failed to endorse underlying assumptions. Nevertheless, notwithstanding the lack of proof, government strategies continue to be produced. Unsurprisingly, the FTE was modeled upon the NLS, with a framework of teaching objectives, a recommended lesson structure, catch-up provision and a parallel infrastructure for support and training, which has also been the case with the NPS. In other words, although not legislated for and ostensibly voluntary, the "strategies" and all their accompanying requirements are anything but. The FTE also recontextualizes the notion of English into one dominated by predominantly functional concepts of "literacy" (see Locke in this book).

A feature of all these various "strategies" has been to provide teachers with "guidance" on how to translate the requirements of the National Curriculum into classroom activities, thereby increasing the *prescribed* content of the subject as a whole (including grammar). Not only do the strategies provide "guidance" on content; they also provide "guidance" on the pedagogic methods used to teach it. Consequently, these various so-called "strategies", although ostensibly designed to form a bridge between the statutory requirements of the National Curriculum on the one hand and the day-to-day activities that occur in the classroom on the other, become, in fact, mandatory. As a result, teachers have become increasingly deprofessionalized.

While previous Conservative governments recontextualized the curriculum for English at the external, policy level, subsequent Labour governments have gone much further. The introduction of the various strategies recontextualizes the curriculum for English at the internal level of evaluation, that is, within the classroom itself, telling teachers not only *what* to teach but, in primary schools and increasingly in secondary schools, *how*. While teachers had to comply with the requirements of the National Curriculum through key stage assessment, so long as they incorporated coverage of assessment requirements in their teaching, the pedagogic methods they employed continued much the same. At the time of writing this chapter, this is no longer the case. In 2008, the government abolished assessment at Key Stage 3 and turned its attention to Key Stage 4. Until then, curriculum and assessment requirements at Key Stage 4 (14–16-year-olds) – as those of AS-, A- and undergraduate, degree-level English – had remained outside those of both the National Curriculum and any accompanying strategy. They had been regulated instead by the syllabi and accompanying assessment at GCSE level. However, in 2008, a "renewed" Framework for Secondary English (FSE) was introduced, building upon that introduced in 2001 and extending its scope from Key Stage 3 to include Key Stage 4.

On the government's *National Strategies* website,[2] in the section called "secondary", the first page dealing with the secondary curriculum is entitled *Addressing the New Secondary Curriculum for English* (DCSF, n.d. [a]). This gives an overview of the new programs of study, which includes a new structure for the subject and separate programs of study for Key Stages 3 and 4. The site also claims that the degree to which content is prescribed has been reduced, further stating: "The common structure presents more opportunities for making links between subjects and so helps to develop more coherent experiences of the curriculum and independent learning" (paragraph 1). As has become common in such documents, the document states as fact – the development of a more coherent experience – something which remains at best an unproven assertion.

The framework divides English into four major strands – speaking and listening, reading, writing and language – subdivided into a total of 10 strands. Whereas the original knowledge about language strand in the National Curriculum was interwoven across the three key areas of speaking and listening, reading and writing, in the FSE aspects of it are separated out into a "Language" strand. At the same time, running throughout the three other strands, are requirements to do with something called "Functional English". A link from the *Addressing the New Secondary Curriculum for English* page takes you to a page called *Functional English*.[3] This page defines "Functional English" thus:

> The term "functional" should be considered in the broad sense of providing learners with the skills and abilities they need to take an active and responsible role in their communities, everyday life, the workplace and educational settings. Functional English requires learners to communicate in ways that

2. See www.nationalstrategies.standards.dcsf.gov.uk/node/16082.
3. See http://nationalstrategies.standards.dcsf.gov.uk/node/16039.

make them effective and involved as citizens, to operate confidently and to convey their ideas and opinions clearly. (DCSF, n.d. [b], paragraph 1)

The concept of "functional English" features large in a further policy document called *Functional Skills Standards* (FSS) introduced by the Qualifications and Curriculum Authority (QCA) in 2007 and specific to Key Stages 3 and 4. This gives a description of the functional skills the DfEE deem pupils should have acquired throughout their schooling, in English, mathematics and ICT. The site states that: "It is essential to think of learners becoming functional in their English rather than thinking there is a vital body of knowledge known as functional English" (DCSF, n.d. [b], paragraph 3). It goes on to say that: "Functional English is not a discrete component of the new programs of study but is embedded within them" (DCSF, n.d. [b], paragraph 4). Precisely what relation "Functional English" has with the remainder of the secondary curriculum in English, however, is unclear, and it is difficult to distinguish the curriculum for functional English from that of "English" itself.

Teaching literature and expressions of creativity, rather than being at the heart of the English curriculum, have instead been marginalized. Furthermore, not since the Revised Codes of the 19th century has such a recontextualization occurred at the hands of politicians and their quangos, rather than by the teaching profession. Most recently, the notion of "functional skills" has been replaced by "key skills", which seems to suggest that English itself has come full circle in being recontextualized into the skills model it once was in the late 19th and early 20th centuries or, as Locke discusses (in this book), a narrowly competence-based version of English.

In short, the kind of English (including the teaching of grammar) currently being taught in English schools has, since 1988, undergone nothing short of a transformation into a skills model of English. Such a transformation is a classic case of Bernstein's example of selection and delocation of what counts as a school subject from its primary location and relocated and refocused in the primary and secondary school curriculum. For Bernstein, the primary location and original site of such a transformation was the university. Debatable though this may be, it has certainly been the case, particularly since 1988, that both the location and site of the subject has shifted from the universities and the teaching profession to government agencies such as the QCA.

New Horizons?

However, at the time of writing, two bright sparks seem to be appearing on the horizon. It appears that the tide of a policy stranglehold by politicians on the primary and secondary curriculum is turning back once again in favor of the teaching profession and educationalists. In January 2008, the government commissioned yet another report, this time on the primary curriculum, which was published on May 2, 2009. This review was led by Sir Jim Rose, who had been a member of Her Majesty's Inspectorate of Education (HMI) and Director of Inspection for the Office for Standards in Education (OFSTED). (Before joining

HMI, Rose held headships of primary schools.) The report sought to answer the question: "What should the curriculum contain and how should the content and the teaching of it change to foster children's different and developing abilities during primary years?" (DCSF, 2009, p. 2).

In the Executive Summary and Recommendations, it is clear that the division of the primary curriculum into the subjects as introduced by the National Curriculum in 1988 has been abandoned with an emphasis upon cross-curricular activities as being central to the primary curriculum. Instead of subjects, the curriculum is grouped into "six areas of learning", of which the first is "understanding English, communication and languages" (DCSF, 2009, p. 17). Crucially, the report states that: "How schools choose to organise their curriculum and timetable will remain a matter for them" (DCSF, 2009, p. 17). And so, the NLS, which has created such controversy and discontent, is abandoned, and a new primary curriculum is to be introduced from September 2011. What "understanding English" will mean in this new curriculum remains to be seen, but maybe, after 20 or so years of neglect, the teaching profession may be coming back in from the cold.

The second bright spark is the publication of the latest OFSTED report into the teaching of English, published in June 2009, called *English at the Crossroads: An Evaluation of English in Primary and Secondary Schools 2005/8*. This report criticizes the teaching of English and, more crucially, the impact recent government initiatives and strategies have had upon its teaching. It states that this has led to a situation where some schools have used initiatives and strategies in a fragmented way, and implemented them unthinkingly, "often because they held no deeply held views about the nature of English as a subject and how it might be taught" (paragraph 19). In relation to the teaching of grammar, the report states that it has led to an "over-emphasis on technical matters such as punctuation or complex sentences, at the expense of helping pupils to develop and structure their ideas" (paragraph 50). Thus, the knowledge about language strand, which threaded its way through the original curriculum and later incarnations of it, appears to have disappeared entirely in the last few years. It remains to be seen whether, as this report seems to suggest, in the next few years, a comparable wholesale review of the secondary curriculum will follow that of the primary one. If so, we might also see the return of grass-roots projects such as the Oracy, Writing and LINC projects. One of the recommendations of the 2009 OFSTED report, for example, is to "establish national programs to increase teachers' own confidence as writers so that they can provide better models for pupils" (p. 6).

Conclusion

In terms of Bernstein's theory of pedagogic discourse, the "text" is the entire curriculum of English, and not just the aspects of pedagogic grammar to be taught. Beginning in 1988 and continuing onward from that point and through two successive, long-running governments, the formalization of that "text" has continued from its enshrinement in the National Curriculum through to the various strategy documents. "The processes of production and reception" are those of the classroom and pedagogic practice within it, for example, those associated with the literacy hour, how teachers interpret its requirements (or not), enact them in the classroom and how they are received and interpreted by pupils. Increasingly, since 1988, not only curriculum content but also its associated pedagogy has become ever more prescriptive, supported by a huge raft of "support" such as dedicated websites which contain suggested lesson plans.

The social conditions of production and interpretation are the political, institutional processes of the education establishment as a whole, which regulate and control the social conditions of production and interpretation and the corresponding processes of production and interpretation. Part of this is also evaluating the institution of education against social processes as a whole. While the NLS, the FTE, PLS and FSS, and any other initiative that may be introduced over the coming years, have all been government's attempts at initiating social democracy and wider equality of access through the teaching of Standard English as the language of power, this practice does not *of itself* result in social equality. It cannot be divorced either from its other policies related to education, health, social welfare and housing or from the social and cultural backgrounds of the pupils themselves. It seems as if, with the publication of two reports, the Rose Report and the 2009 OFSTED Report for English, policy-makers are finally beginning to realize this and the wheel of curriculum change seems once more to be turning from the stranglehold of fragmented government strategies and initiatives reminiscent of a 19th-century skills model of English, which have served to fragment the subject beyond recognition. What such a curriculum will be replaced by, however, remains to be seen.

In terms of the recontextualizations of English, contemporary theories of grammar – most notably those associated with functional grammar, which is firmly rooted in the notion that language, for it to make sense at all, has to be studied in context – seem to be appropriate ones on which to base a pedagogic grammar. Furthermore, such study, which pushes the unit of study beyond the sentence to the text, has much to offer an integrated language and literature curriculum. For example, research undertaken in Australia by Williams (1998, 2000) has shown that pupils are capable of learning formal, linguistic features of language in a literary context from an early age. Furthermore, such knowledge enhances their understanding of the part played by language in structuring the messages the texts being studied convey. Williams' research shows that, if taught as part of the study of a text, rather than as decontextualized exercises, pupils quickly come to acquire the ability not only to reason abstractly, but also to do so enthusiastically. Williams notes: "The teaching of grammar is often associated with authoritarian practices and negative outcomes. The crucial point is that this is not a necessary relation between all grammars and outcomes for children's learning" (2000, p. 128). A functional grammar, and a pedagogy which orients learners to thinking about the effects of grammatical patterning in texts so that their meanings can be uncovered, is not vastly dissimilar from any other kind of literary analysis.

A new recontextualizing of a pedagogic grammar within English, then, might restore it to a more integrated place in the curriculum. Such a restoration would need to take account of modern theories of language which link into the framework of the curriculum for English as a whole. However, such recontextualizations cannot derive totally from a modern grammar, be it transformational generative, systemic functional or any other. Grammar is not a religion, and the key here is the recontextualization of key concepts which underpin functional grammar, and as much terminology as is necessary for a pedagogic context. In short, recontextualizations will need to be selected and drawn upon insofar as they add, extend and reconfigure existing traditions and practices which take account of and build upon teachers' knowledge bases. Such a grammar would go some way toward allowing pupils to understand the ways in which English and language actually structure, convey and position their experiences. How such a selection is effected in practice, of course, brings to the fore issues of power not only within the official field of recontextualization, but also the pedagogic.

References

Andrews, R. (2004). *The impact of ICT on literacy education*. London: Routledge.
Andrews, R. (2008). Ten years of strategies. *Changing English, 15*(1), 77–85.
Baranyai, E. (1949). Learning grammar. *Use of English, 1*(1), 30–47.
Bernstein, B. (1971). *Class, codes and control Vol. I: Theoretical studies towards a sociology of language*. London: Routledge.
Bernstein, B. (1990). *The structuring of pedagogic discourse: Class, codes & control Vol IV*. London: Routledge.
Bernstein, B. (1996). *Pedagogy, symbolic control & identity theory*. London: Taylor & Francis.
Board of Education. (1921). *The teaching of English in England* [Newbolt Report]. London: HMSO.
Bourne, J., & Cameron, L. (1988). Kingman, grammar and the nation. *Language in Education, 2*(3), 147–160.
Carter, R. (1996). Politics and knowledge about Language: The LINC project. In R. Hasan & G. Williams (Eds.), *Literacy in society* (pp. 1–3). London: Longman.
Carter, R. (1997). *Investigating English discourse: Language, literacy and literature*. London: Routledge.
Centre for Policy Studies. (1985). *No turning back*. London: Centre for Policy Studies.
Chomsky, N. (1957). *Syntactic structures*. The Hague: Mouton.
Chitty, C. (1988). *Towards a new education system: The victory of the New Right*. Basingstoke: Falmer Press.
Christie, F. (2004). Revisiting some old themes: The role of grammar in the teaching of English. In J. Foley (Ed.), *Language, education and discourse: Functional approaches* (pp. 158–184). London: Continuum.
Clark, U. (1994). Bringing English to order: A personal account of the NCC English evaluation project. *English and Education, 28*(1), 33–38.
Clark, U. (2001). *War words: Language, history and the disciplining of English*. Oxford: Elsevier Science.
Cox, C. (1991). *Cox on Cox: An English Curriculum for the 1990s*. London: Hodder & Stoughton.
Department for Children, Schools and Families (DCSF). (n.d. [a]). The National Strategies Secondary: Addressing the new curriculum for English. Retrieved May 10, 2009 from www.nationalstrategies.standards.dcsf.gov.uk/node/16082.

Department for Children, Schools and Families (DCSF). (n.d. [b]). *The National Strategies: Functional English*. Retrieved May 10, 2009 from http://nationalstrategies.standards.dcsf.gov.uk/node/16039.

Department for Children, Schools and Families (DCSF). (2009). *Independent review of the primary curriculum: Final report*. Nottingham: DCSF Publications.

DES. (1975). *A language for life: The report of the Committee of Inquiry* [Bullock Report]. London: HMSO.

DES. (1988). *The report of the Committee of Enquiry into the Teaching of the English Language* [Kingman Report]. London: HMSO.

DES. (1989). *National curriculum: English for ages 5 to 16*. London: HMSO.

DfEE. (1998). *The National Literacy Strategy framework for teaching*. London: DfEE Publications.

DfEE. (2000). *The National Literacy Strategy: Grammar for writing*. London: DfEE Publications.

DfEE. (2001). *The Framework for teaching English: Years 7, 8 and 9*. London: DfEE Publications.

Halliday M. (1973). *Explorations in the function of language*. London: Edward Arnold.

Halliday, M. (1994). *An introduction to functional grammar* (2nd ed.). London: Edward Arnold.

Leith, D. (1997). *A social history of English*. London: Routledge.

Ofsted. (2009). *English at the crossroads: An evaluation of English in primary and secondary schools 2005/8*. London: Ofsted.

Qualifications and Curriculum Authority (QCA). (2007). *Functional skills standards*. London: Qualifications and Curriculum Authority.

Williams, G. (1998). Children entering literate worlds: Perspectives from the study of textual practices. In F. Christie & R. Misson (Eds.), *Literacy in schooling* (pp. 40–66). Routledge: London.

Williams, G. (2000). Children's literature, children and uses of language description. In L. Unsworth (Ed.), *Researching language in schools and communities* (pp. 35–52). London and New York: Cassell.

Wyse, D. (2001). Grammar for writing? A critical review of empirical evidence. *British Journal of Educational Studies, 49*(4), 411–427.

Chapter 4

The "Grammar Wars" in Australia

Frances Christie

Introduction

The grammar wars in Australia date from the late 1960s and the 1970s – a period when throughout the English-speaking world there was considerable reassessment and debate, not only about the nature of grammar and its teaching, but more generally about the purposes and preoccupations of subject English. In fact, the issues involved, at least with respect to grammar, had a much longer currency, so that any historical account one offers will depend on which particular period one selects to start from – even of course going back to the period of the Greeks if one chose. Elsewhere (Christie, 1993) I have documented aspects of the history of English grammar from the 17th century to the 20th, arguing the presence of a long tradition of the teaching of rhetoric and grammar: I suggested that where grammar and rhetoric were understood as in close alliance, the one informing the other, the two gave useful direction to much teaching and learning. However, with the advent of mass education in the 19th to early 20th centuries, school grammar was corrupted, reduced to a prescriptive set of rules, while rhetoric largely disappeared for the purposes of schooling, at least in the Anglo-Australian tradition. Though not wishing to traverse all the arguments taken up in my earlier discussion, I shall suggest that many of the issues regarding grammar and its teaching which featured in always heated – and occasionally acrimonious – grammar debates in Australia from the 1970s on did in fact hark back to matters raised in earlier times.

The principal matter at issue in all the debates over grammar concerns the question: what knowledge about language ("KAL", to use Carter's term, 1990) should be taught in the name of subject English? While the notion of knowledge about language covers more than grammar, it nonetheless has always had a significant place in any discussions of English teaching and its knowledge, either because people have wished to defend teaching grammar, or because they wished to decry it, or because they wished to redefine grammar in some way. In the Australian context, arguments about teaching English grammar over the last 25 to 30 years were very much bound up with arguments over genre theory in the tradition of systemic functional linguistic (SFL) theory, using Halliday's functional grammar (for example, Halliday & Matthiessen, 2004)[1] and Martin's model of register and

---

1. It was Halliday's 1985 (Halliday, 1985b) version of his functional grammar (since revised twice) that had a role in the debates mentioned here.

genre (for example, Martin & Rose, 2008). The functional grammar was used to analyze and describe different text-types or genres, which were then proposed for pedagogical purposes (see discussions in Christie & Martin, 1997). Derewianka (1990) produced one of the first widely distributed textbooks on genres for primary schools; a book, incidentally, which is still in print and still selling (though there were others.) The badly named *Write it Right* project of the early 1990s (a name not chosen by its participants, by the way) led to a series of publications on genres in the secondary school, devoted to English, history, geography, science and the media, most of them currently undergoing updating and reissue at the time this chapter was written (for example Korner, McInnes & Rose, 2007; Feez, Iedema & White, 2008; others forthcoming).

A number of critiques of SFL and genre theory have appeared over the years (for example, Reid, 1987; Sawyer & Watson, 1989; Freedman & Medway, 1994a, 1994b; Lee, 1996), some of them helpful in that they caused SFL genre theorists to clarify their work, while others were less helpful because they tended to polarize. I was not myself a disinterested bystander, for I was involved in many of the debates and exchanges. Hence, it needs to be stated that this chapter offers the interpretations of one who is an SFL genre theorist, still interested in the debates after all these years, still following the ongoing evolution of SFL genre theory and still willing to argue a case for the relevance of the theory for pedagogy. Anyone wanting an alternative, and very critical, account of much that occurred in Australia should consult Richardson (1994, 2004).

The Genesis of the Debates

Functional grammar reached Australia in the late 1960s and early 1970s, with the arrival of materials from the Nuffield/Schools Council Program in Linguistics and English Teaching (1964–1971), directed by Halliday. Using the then developing SFL theory, these programs sought to redefine the knowledge base in English language, abandoning traditional school grammar among other things, as well as a great deal of conventional linguistic theory, as taught at the university level (Halliday 1961/2002), and forging new text- or discourse-driven understandings about language (Halliday, McIntosh & Strevens, 1964). Halliday (Halliday & Hasan, 2006) has recently noted how critical to the emergence of his linguistic theory, and his model of language teaching, was his extensive opportunity in the 1960s to work with teachers in Scotland and later in London. Hasan and Martin (1989) and Christie and Unsworth (2005) provide details of the English language programs he refers to, which I shall not pursue here at any length. Suffice to note that probably the best known of the many materials that appeared were *Breakthrough to Literacy* (Mackay & Schaub, 1970) and *Language in Use* (Doughty, Pearce & Thornton, 1973), the former a program for teaching initial literacy, the latter a set of English-language materials intended for the secondary years. Both programs were taken up and used in Australia for some years.

The Nuffield/Schools Council Program materials arrived over the same period as a large number of other publications on English language, mainly from the United Kingdom, including those associated with Britton (1970) Dixon (1967)

Rosen (Rosen & Rosen, 1973) and Barnes (1976; Barnes, Britton & Rosen, 1969), all of whom became influential in Australia, and all of whom, though differing among themselves about many matters, were generally not well disposed to linguistics, arguing that whatever the merits of such a study as a university discipline, it had little to offer teachers of English in schools. In the course of a visit to Australia in the 1970s, for example, Barnes (1977, p. 92) stated that while linguistics had "its own issues", it was not of use to teachers, for teachers, while certainly interested in language, were primarily concerned "through language with meanings". I mention these matters, not primarily because I wish to revisit the discussions with Barnes (whose work on small-group talk was in fact interesting), but because I want to emphasize the point that even at the time of Halliday's arrival in Australia (in 1976), arguments about linguistics generally had already emerged, while the particular claims of SFL theory would be sharpened after his arrival, and those of his colleagues Ruqaiya Hasan and J.R. Martin. One matter was easily lost sight of: namely that SFL theory was then – and remains now – outside the tradition of mainstream linguistics, so that the formalist traditions (to which Barnes had in fact alluded) were not an aspect of SFL theory. Halliday and his colleagues had rejected formalist linguistic theories of the kind that typically prevailed in university departments of linguistics, a response for which, to this day, they are seen as marginal to much linguistic inquiry (Hasan, Matthiessen & Webster, 2005). Their concern has always been with language as a semiotic or meaning-making system.

Soon after Halliday's arrival, one issue emerged with some force in discussions of English language and learning: it concerned whether children need to be taught any knowledge about language, or whether their language should instead be allowed to "grow" in the English classroom, and in the presence of the teacher who was the "trusted adult", facilitating the child's growth in language (Dixon, 1967). The issue of the propriety of teaching knowledge about language had emerged at the Dartmouth Conference on English Teaching, from whose deliberations Dixon wrote his book, while in Australia it came to the fore with the inception of the national Language Development Project (LDP), coordinated by the then Curriculum Development Centre (Maling-Keepes & Keepes, 1979). This was a project intended to generate new language curriculum materials for the primary to secondary school "interface", covering school years 5 to 8. Halliday became consultant to the LDP, which, among other matters, adopted his model of language development (see Hasan & Martin, 1989). This model stated that language development involved:

- *learning language* (the basic resources of language – its sounds, its lexis and its grammar);
- *learning through language* (learning about the world and relationships, shaping a sense of identity); and
- *learning about language* (learning about its grammar, its spelling and writing systems and its registers, and reflecting on these).

The first two, he suggested, are learned simultaneously, while the third builds upon what is learned, requiring conscious reflection on the language and bringing about new understanding (Curriculum Development Centre, 1979, p. 1).

Since I was very closely associated with the LDP for the period 1978–1981, I can state that no issue in the LDP model of language was more controversial than "learning about language", and the materials that emerged more often addressed matters of "learning language" and "learning through" it in the classroom, than "learning about language". It was an issue that many teachers and language consultants avoided, and a review of English language curriculum materials from all Australian states undertaken as part of the LDP work (Christie & Rothery, 1979) revealed some probable causes. All the state English syllabus documents by the mid-1970s showed the influence of international moves since Dartmouth, reflecting an abandonment of what were seen as the prescriptive English statements of the past in favor of English curricula which promoted growth in language, stressing the value of developing learning in "listening, speaking, reading and writing" and promoting self-expression and/or independent learning in a variety of ways. Teaching knowledge about language was neither discouraged, nor was it foregrounded. Children's experience was, as far as possible, to be used as the basis upon which their learning in English was fostered. As a general principle, any teaching of knowledge about language should be provided at the point of need, rather than as part of a structured teaching program. The way was open for what would become "process-driven" theories and practices of English teaching and learning.

The emergence of "growth" or "process" classrooms was not uniquely a development of subject English. It was, in fact, part of a wider trend in curriculum theory, represented, for example, in the deliberations of the Plowden Report (1967) in the United Kingdom, devoted to the primary curriculum, or the then influential curriculum theories of Stenhouse (1975), with his interest in inquiry learning, or constructivist theories of learning, committed to promoting individual, even private, learning (see Larochelle, Bednarz & Garrison, 1998; Christie, 2004). They are relevant to this discussion in that by the 1970s and early 1980s, they helped create a professional climate among teachers, teacher educators and English-language consultants, in which concerns for the nature of what should be taught as knowledge about language were seriously diminished in the name of a model of the English-language learner involved in a personal and/or private journey of self-discovery. Any knowledge acquired by the learner was to be shaped primarily by his/her needs, rather than by a model of knowledge held by the teacher.

Such preoccupations are still evidenced among some contemporary Australian teachers of English (for example, Doecke, Howie & Sawyer, 2006). Howie (2006), for example, writes of the "opportunity for self-exploration" offered students by the secondary English classroom:

> Within the context of the development and articulation of their own moral and ethical framework, students are able to work towards greater self-understanding, as well as increased awareness of their existing social and cultural relations with others and the imagining of how these relations might otherwise be. (Howie, 2006, p. 287)

In the event, debates regarding knowledge about language, especially knowledge of grammar, became very polarized in the early 1980s. Looking back, I identify two strands of argument; while different in origin, the two became entangled. The one concerned the wisdom claimed for policies of fostering or facilitating growth in the English classroom, with its associated reluctance to engage in any formal teaching of knowledge about language. The other concerned the general rejection of traditional school grammar, understood by many as what grammar teaching was necessarily about. Among the SFL theorists at least, to reject traditional school grammar was not in itself to reject the teaching of knowledge about language in other ways. In fact, it was to create what they held were better opportunities to teach such knowledge, where this included a functional grammar, concerned with texts and their meanings. Among those most committed to models of "growth" in learning English, the teaching of any knowledge about language was to be understood as subservient to the primary goal of facilitating personal growth in and through language; and since knowledge about grammar was generally understood as traditional school grammar, which many teachers had found not helpful to children's learning, it was a relatively easy step to argue for its abandonment.

Regardless of the claims or counter-claims of grammar, there were at issue two different theories of the person: the one involved the individual – sometimes rather romantically conceived – engaged in a personal journey of self-development, exploring experience in private and independent ways; in this model the teacher assumed the role of "facilitator" of learning, pursuing what Halliday once referred to as a policy of "benevolent inertia" (1979, p. 279). The other model – associated with SFL and related social theories – saw the individual as functioning in social processes, shaping understandings of his/her world and building relationships in complex, sociocultural contexts, in which language, though not the only semiotic resource involved, is nonetheless a very important one. In this model the teacher assumed a much more directive role, deliberately guiding the nature of teaching and learning of language, where this included teaching and learning about functional grammar, at least with respect to genre.

Activity: Self-Reflection

How do you think of yourself as a teacher? As a facilitator or someone who overtly guides learning? Can these two "models" of the teacher be reconciled? What are some other metaphors for teacher that you can think of?

Some brief explanation of the two terms "traditional" and "functional" grammar, as they are used here, will be in order.

Traditional and Functional Grammar

By the mid 20th century, traditional grammar had degenerated to the rather arid pursuit of traditional "parts of speech" and "rules of syntax". In my own school days, these matters were still taught, and we spent quite a long time correcting "faulty sentences" (which I actually enjoyed, though I found when I started teaching that they were not very useful for the children I taught). The rules of syntax derived from various descriptions of English grammar developed for schools, particularly in the 18th century (for example, Murray, 1795), and these were in turn best understood when linked to the study of rhetoric (Blair, 1783; Campbell, 1776). Where grammar concerned the organization of the written English sentence, rhetoric concerned the overall rhetorical purpose and organization of the text. Even in earlier times, the relationship of grammar and rhetoric was often debated, though when properly balanced, they could be taught and learned effectively. As I noted in my opening remarks, with the passage of time, school grammar became the rules of syntax, while the study of rhetoric largely disappeared, a fact noted in the early 20th century, when the British government held their first inquiry into the teaching of English (the Newbolt Report, 1921). Since matters to do with teaching syntax are still periodically researched, it is notable that Andrews (2005) and Graham and Perin (2007) have both produced recent reports arguing that the teaching of syntax has little or no influence on the writing ability of children or adolescents. There is some evidence, they argue, that exercises in sentence-combining may be helpful.

Systemic functional (SF) grammar uses all the terms found in traditional grammar, most notably the names of the various parts of speech, or "word classes", though it also uses functional labels. Its principal interest, however, is in language *in use*, and this necessarily involves engagement with meaning in *text* and in *context*. It is, in fact, a text- or discourse-driven grammar, so that its focus and preoccupations are not those of traditional grammar, and it has no primary interest in the written sentence, despite its obvious importance in the written text. In the world of linguistics (rather than that of language pedagogy), the traditional preoccupations of formalist grammars – such as those of Chomsky (for example 1980, 2002), as well as many others – are with syntax, where that eschews an interest in meaning. Indeed, where meaning is taken up at all in many recent traditions of linguistics, it is understood as an aspect of pragmatics, though it can be seen as an aspect of formal semantics. SFL grammar addresses the concerns both of "syntax" and "pragmatics", though these two terms are not typically found in the tradition at all. Halliday (2002) specifically rejects the term "pragmatics", while the preferred term for syntax is "lexicogrammar". Use of such a term is an acknowledgment that meaning resides in both the grammar and the lexis.

In addition, functional grammar needs to be understood as part of wider SFL theory, which proposes that language is a primary semiotic system with which we engage in acts of meaning. All such acts involve participation in contexts of use – or *contexts of situation*, to use the term Halliday and Hasan (1985) proposed, following Malinowski (1923). Any text is to be understood in terms of the context that gives rise to it; conversely context is only understood because of the text that brings it into life. When persons engage in various contexts of situation, they take up different language choices with respect to *field* (what is going on), *tenor* (the relationship of the participants) and *mode* (the channel of communication), where all three collectively are said to create particular *registers*. The texts that are generated can in turn by understood as instances of particular "text-types" or genres, though not all SFL theorists use the latter terms in the same way.

Overall, in the SFL tradition, grammar is not to be understood apart from the texts which it shapes and gives life to – hence the emphasis on the various genres that were identified for pedagogical purposes. To study a text-type or genre is to study a social practice, or a socially valued and constituted way of making meaning. In its pedagogical interest in genre and grammar as intimately related, SFL theory is thus in many ways close to the traditional concerns of rhetoric.

The Issue of Genres

To engage in activity in the classroom is to engage with the negotiation and construction of meaning, and for the purposes of school learning – in English as in any other subject – this will involve mastering socially valued ways of making meaning. This brings us to the matter of knowledge about language, for English is unique among subjects in that, while language is certainly the instrument of teaching and learning (as in other subjects), it is itself an object of study. Hence, for the SFL theorist, to promote learning in English is to promote teaching and learning about the very resource with which students shape their ideas, information, experience and values. Neither traditional grammar on the one hand, nor rather open exhortations to "personal growth" in English on the other, will adequately address the needs of the English student.

It was against a background of considerable professional support for the notions of "process" and "inquiry" models of English-language learning that the first discussions of genre-based pedagogy emerged, particularly with respect to writing, and some of these appeared in course books that I either edited and con-tributed to, for the B.Ed. program at Deakin University in the 1980s, or commis-sioned from others in the two Master's subjects we developed (for example, Halliday & Hasan, 1985; Halliday, 1985a; Hasan, 1985; Martin, 1985b; Kress, 1985). The SFL ideas involved were considered controversial by many at that time. The B.Ed. Study Guide, *Children Writing* (1984), included sections that I had written and another by Rothery (1984), while an associated course reading was written by Martin (1984) (though my colleagues involved in the B.Ed. course wrote from very different perspectives). Various genres of the primary school were identified and they emerged as Martin and his colleagues were still pursu-ing register and genre studies, following the work of Halliday and Hasan (for example, 1985) as well as Hasan (1984/1996), who had originally written about genres. While the community of teachers became variously interested in, and sometimes concerned about, genres as we were discussing them for the purposes of writing pedagogy, debates developed both within the SFL community and within the community of language and literacy educators, particularly English teacher educators.

Activity: Reflection

What is your own view of the distinction made between process and product? Why do you think it may have come into use? Does it have any value for the practicing teacher? Design an imagined teaching sequence for some topic of your choice and identify points at which either "process" or "product" is foregrounded. Is it a helpful way to think about teaching?

In the SFL tradition of Halliday and Hasan (1985) already alluded to, the terms "register" and "genre" were conflated, and Martin originally worked with their ideas. However, he and his colleagues went on to propose that register and genre operate on different "planes of experience" (Martin, 1985a), the former shaping the language choices in a text with respect to the immediate "context of situation", the latter with respect to the broader "context of culture" (Malinowski, 1935), first adopted by Halliday and Hasan (1985). A genre was defined as a "staged, goal-oriented social process" and the decision to propose register and genre as having two levels or planes of experience arose from the early work of Martin and his colleagues, including Rothery, investigating young children's writing development, and leading to a series of books for primary schools (Christie et al., 1990–1992), a series that was in fact quite widely used in adult literacy classes as well. Over the ensuing years, the work extended into studies of writing in the secondary school (for example Macken-Horarik, 2002) and elsewhere (Christie & Martin, 1997), writing in history (Coffin, 2006), patterns of talk (Eggins & Slade, 1997; Christie, 2002); language and knowledge construction (Christie & Martin, 2007) and a study of children's writing development from K to 12 (Christie & Derewianka, 2008). Feez and Joyce (1998) offered an account of genre-based curriculum design. Fang and Schleppegrell (2008) have offered a recent account of reading pedagogy in secondary school, using SFL theory. Martin's model of register and genre proved more influential for pedagogical purposes than that of Halliday and Hasan, though they have never accepted it. They have both (Halliday, personal communication; Hasan, 1996, pp. 399–403), with qualifications, conceded its strengths in educational discussions. While Hasan (1995) has written about her reasons for disagreeing with Martin, Halliday has declined to do so.

Criticisms of Genre-Based Pedagogy

A number of criticisms have been offered concerning genre theory and pedagogy, from within the SFL community and the wider profession of language educators, some of which were captured by Cope and Kalantzis (1993) in a volume they edited. These issues include: the claim that in genre pedagogy the "product" (or genre) is more important than the "process" of learning; the apparent determinism implied in the accounts offered of genres, which are explicitly described and, it is implied, understood as "static"; the associated concern that in teaching these to children, we compromise their capacity to act independently, teaching them instead to conform by unthinkingly adopting the genres of power and influence. Threadgold (1988), Threadgold and Kress (1988), Freedman and Medway (1994), Hasan (1995), Lee (1996), Richardson (2004) and Turner (2007) offer representative discussions, though the particular emphases given depend on the writer. In what follows I shall address these criticisms or concerns.

The argument concerning "process" and "product" rests on a very superficial reading of SFL genre theory, and was exacerbated by two factors. One was the influence in the early 1980s of the work of Graves (1981), who made at least one visit to Australia, and whose work studying young children's writing led to proposals for "process writing" classrooms, in which it was argued children must be given opportunity to write in largely self-directed ways, proposals that SFL theorists rejected. The distinction between "process" and "product", while it may have some heuristic value, is really a nonsense: the two are merely two aspects of the same phenomenon, namely the text and its writing. The other factor was that in developing their genre-based pedagogy, SFL theorists described the text-types or genres in reasonably explicit ways, identifying their overall "schematic structures" by using functional grammar. The claims for "explicit" text descriptions and their teaching were challenged on the grounds, earlier noted, that they led to "static" descriptions of texts, which would be "prescribed" or "imposed" on children in repressive ways.

Despite her reservations in other ways, Hasan took issue with those who would criticize genre theorists on such grounds, noting that those who offered such criticism did so from the comfort of the indeterminate or "fuzzy" ways in which literacy pedagogy was "traditionally" discussed. The strength of "genre-based pedagogy", she noted, is that "its intellectual program is made explicit", (and) "it permits discussion about itself in a way that the fuzz around the traditional approaches cannot" (Hasan, 1996, p. 403). This remains one of its strengths to this day in my view, though as Halliday has more than once suggested, the task of bringing language to consciousness is often "unpopular".

As for the specific claim that texts, once described, are "static", this again rests on a serious misreading of the theory. Texts – or genres – come into being as ways of enacting social practices. Like all social practices, they are dynamic, even volatile, shaped in the act of (re)creating them, for genres are ways of making meaning. Having said that, for the purposes of a literacy pedagogy, it needs to be stated that genres require patience and effort in their learning, and students need practice in mastering them, learning the patterned ways they are created, in order, ultimately, to critique or overturn them, should the need arise. Using the schematic structures, with their associated register values to do with language choices in which they are realized, is a productive way to learn. The genres of schooling, like those of the wider community, evolve and change, and learning to play with them as an aspect of school learning, particularly in the English classroom, can be a rewarding thing to do.

Another of the alleged limitations of genre-based pedagogy in the tradition of Martin and others concerns the claims of critical literacy, for it is said that such a pedagogy induces conformity and unthinking adoption of the genres of power – those perhaps of the "status quo". The pedagogy does not, it is said, develop critical students, capable of challenging where challenge is needed. Of all the arguments ever advanced against SFL genre pedagogy, this is in my view the least convincing. It is only ever argued by very competent writers of the genres of academic argument, who presumably believe that they themselves argue independently, and do not merely ape others in some unthinking way. Why, then, suggest that children who are taught to identify and use the various genres of power and privilege will not also go on to manipulate and use them in independent ways? Looking to the work of Gray and Rose (for example, Gray, Rose & Cowey, 1998; Rose, 2008) with Aboriginal students in Australia – surely among our most under-privileged – one must state that any continued denial of the genres of power and influence to such students is a serious injustice.

Finally, there is the issue of "reflection" on the practices of literacy associated with genre-based pedagogy, often also proposed in the name of critical literacy, for, it is said, students should be encouraged to reflect back on their literacy efforts. Here Hasan (1996, p. 405) shows herself in some agreement with the critics, for she suggests that SFL genre pedagogy has "no explicit element" designed to promote reflection back on the genres written or read (Hasan, 1996, p. 405).

Activity: Task Design

The word "reflect" or "reflection" has been used a number of times in the preceding paragraph. In your view, what does it mean in practice to engage students in acts of reflection? Design a task that engages pupils in some way in reflecting on some aspect of literacy practice, particularly in relationship to the study of a particular genre. What value do you attach to this task? Why would you have students engage in it?

If I turn to the first of the publications where I wrote about genre pedagogy using functional grammar (Christie, 1984) in the Deakin B.Ed., course materials, it is true that there was no suggestion that students be encouraged to reflect upon the genres they wrote, though equally there was no suggestion that this should be discouraged. Moreover, none of my three colleagues who designed and taught the program with me, while taking up very different theoretical positions, proposed such critically reflective activity either. The call for critically reflective practices came a little later in the decade and into the 1990s. I would suggest that SFL genre theorists actually contributed to such calls, so that the genre-based pedagogy that soon emerged actually revealed a commitment to critique and reflection (Martin, 1999). Macken-Horarik (1998, 2002) also addressed matters to do with critical literacy, stressing the importance of developing the necessary skills in recognizing and manipulating genres as a necessary step toward acquiring critical capacities, a point also noted by Unsworth (2001, pp. 14–16).

As a general principle, SFL genre theorists today would still argue both that genre pedagogy can be used to promote critical literacy and that, without some essential knowledge about language of the kind that the functional grammar provides, it is difficult to develop appropriately critical skills. This brings me to some reflections on the uses of SFL grammar in educational ways that are not overtly genre-based.

In two editions of *English Teaching: Practice and Critique* (December 2005 and May 2006), a number of very interesting papers offered various "takes" on grammar and its teaching, not all of them using SFL grammar. Both Janks (2005, pp. 97–110) and Macken-Horarik (2006, pp. 102–121) make use of SFL grammar, though in rather different ways, revealing that functional grammar is a very useful tool for many purposes. Janks undertakes what she calls "lexical and grammatical analyses" in order to expose the "design of texts", where her model of text is drawn from Fairclough's discourse analysis. This, she argues (Janks, 2005, p. 109), is a contribution to development of critical literacy skills, reminding us that Halliday has said of analyses of the kind she undertakes:

> A discourse analysis that is not based on grammar, is not an analysis at all, but simply a running commentary on a text: either an appeal has to be made to some set of non-linguistic conventions, or to features that are trivial enough to be accessible without a grammar, like the number of words per sentence ... or else the exercise remains a private one in which one explanation is as good or bad as another. (1985b, p. xvii)

Macken-Horarik (2006, pp. 102–121), who also takes seriously the claims for discourse analysis in this sense, uses the functional grammar to analyze the written texts of students who scored high marks in Year 10 English examinations in New South Wales. This leads her to explore the notion of what she terms "symbolic abstractions", found among successful writers, and what they reveal of the capacities for reasoning about experience that such writers possess. Elsewhere and in other contexts, writers such as Love and Simpson (2005) use the functional grammar to analyze and interpret online discussion of texts by students while Unsworth (2001; Christie & Unsworth, 2005) uses the grammar to develop accounts of multiliterate, multimodal texts.

Grammar and the Emergent National Curriculum in Australia

In the interval of time between my being first invited to write this chapter and its acceptance for publication by the editor, Australia had moved toward the adoption of a National Curriculum, involving the development of shared curriculum statements for all states in English, mathematics, science and history. What I have written thus needs to be understood against a background of rapid change in Australian education policy. As part of the ongoing debate about education "standards" that has emerged over the first years of the new century, the word "grammar" has appeared regularly in the daily press and a number of the issues I have traversed above have reappeared.

The position statement – referred to as a "Framing Paper" for English in the National Curriculum – was released in late 2008, and a process of public discussion and consultation has been initiated by the National Curriculum Board. Three "Elements" of the National English Curriculum were proposed, to be taught and developed incrementally across the years of schooling:

- *Knowledge about the English language*
- *Informed appreciation of literature*
- *Growing repertoires of English usage.* (National Curriculum Board, 2008, p. 9)

The intention to assert the claims for a knowledge base for subject English was strong in the Framing Paper. Among other matters, it noted that the teaching of grammar had been at times "strongly contested", though it went on to observe:

> As part of a strong commitment to equity and quality, the teaching of grammar, progressively building knowledge and fluency over the full course of the school years, will be a significant feature of the national English curriculum. This commitment includes traditional word- and sentence-level grammar, text-level grammar that teaches text types and patterns, and the functional relations between these levels. (National Curriculum Board, 2008, p. 9)

Grammar is back on the agenda in Australia, and as Snyder (2008, p. 40) has noted, it has emerged in various ways across Australian schools, some incorporating more functional grammar elements than others. There is much that is commendable about the Framing Paper for English though, as many observers acknowledged, even at the time it was released, the important work of moving on from a reasonably coherent set of first principles (which is what the paper represents) to fleshing out the substance of the English curriculum remains to be done. At the time of writing this chapter, working groups, whose members included some who worked with SFL theory, had begun to develop accounts of the knowledge about language to be taught, including accounts of grammar, though it was not clear how the claims of sentence grammar and text grammar were to be reconciled. History shows it is possible to reconcile the two, and much will depend on the skill and scholarship of those involved. We live in interesting times.

Activity: Developing Your Own Position

Where do you stand in relation to the claim made in the draft Framing Paper for an Australian National English Curriculum (see above) that the teaching of grammar is a matter of "a strong commitment to equity and quality" in educational practice? Summarize your position in a number of bullet points.

To Conclude

At the time of writing this chapter, Halliday's *Introduction to Functional Grammar* had been published in its third edition (Halliday & Matthiessen, 2004), and many other versions of the grammar and related publications had appeared for applied linguistic and/or educational audiences (see Coffin, Hewings & O'Halloran, 2004; Martin & Rose, 2003; Schleppegrell, 2004; Droga & Humphrey, 2002, 2003; Christie, 2005). The theory has attracted very broad interest in many parts of the world, and in a period in which discourse studies generally have emerged as more significant than some 20 years ago, SF grammar is a respected tool for discourse analysis. As for genre theory, this also has achieved greater prominence over the years, and several schools of genre theory are now recognized (Hyon, 1996; Johns, 2002; Christie, 2008), though it does not follow that they all agree. However, what is apparent is that the notion of genres is established in the wider studies of texts and social practices, and among the several approaches, SFL genre theory continues to evolve.

The SFL genre theory is still used and taught in many parts of Australia, and though its influence waxes and wanes, I doubt it will disappear any time soon. In the English-speaking tradition, we have a very long history of arguing about and debating the rival claims of grammar generally, as I noted earlier, and our present period shows no waning of that. The issues do not go away, and that is not only because of the periodic calls to correct "declining standards" promoted in the press that provoke often defensive responses from the teaching profession. It is because the issues to do with knowledge about language remain very significant for teaching and learning. In my view, SFL theory continues to have a lot to offer, not least in its capacity to contribute to the metalanguage necessary for mounting programs devoted to teaching critical literacy.

Activity: Reflection

The history of English teaching over many years reveals periodic debates over the teaching of grammar. In fact of all aspects of English teaching it is probably the most regularly discussed and debated in the profession and in the wider community. Why do you think this is so? Is it a good thing or a distraction in the way of developing pedagogically useful approaches to subject English?

References

Andrews, R. (2005). Knowledge about the teaching of [sentence] grammar: The state of play. *English Teaching and Critique, 4*(3), 69–76.

Barnes, D. (1976). *From communication to curriculum*. London: Penguin.

Barnes, D. (1977). The study of classroom communication in teacher education. In M. Gill & W. Crocker (Eds.), *English in teacher education* (pp. 85–94). Papers of the National Conference: English in Teacher Education, at the University of New England, 1977. Armidale, NSW: University of New England.

Barnes, D., Britton, J., & Rosen, H. (1969). *Language, the learner and the school* (Rev. ed.). Harmondsworth and Ringwood, Australia: Penguin Books.

Blair, H. (1783). *Lectures on rhetoric and belles lettres* (Vols. 1 and 2). London: W. Strahan and T. Cadell.

Britton, J. (1970). *Language and learning*. London: Penguin.

Campbell, G. (1776). *The philosophy of rhetoric*. London: T. Tegg and Son.

Carter, R. (Ed.). (1990). *Knowledge about language and the curriculum*. London: Hodder and Stoughton.

Chomsky, N. (1980). *Rules and representations*. New York: Columbia University Press.

Chomsky, N. (2002). *On nature and language* (Eds. A. Belletti & L. Rizzi). Cambridge: Cambridge: University Press.

Christie, F. (1984). *Varieties of written discourse (Section 1, Children Writing: B.Ed. Study Guide)* (pp. 11–51). Geelong, Vict.: Deakin University Press.

Christie, F. (1993). The "Received Tradition" of English teaching: The decline of rhetoric and the corruption of grammar. In B. Green (Ed.), *The insistence of the letter. Literacy studies and curriculum theorizing* (pp. 75–106). London: Falmer Press.

Christie, F. (2002). *Classroom discourse analysis. A functional perspective*. London and New York: Continuum.

Christie, F. (2004). Authority and its role in the pedagogic relationship of schooling. In L. Young & C. Harrison (Eds.), *Systemic functional linguistics and critical discourse analysis. Studies in social change* (pp. 173–201). London and New York: Continuum.

Christie, F. (2005). *Language education in the primary years*. Sydney: University of New South Wales Press.

Christie, F. (2008). Genres and institutions: Functional perspectives on educational discourse. In M. Martin-Jones, A. de Mejia, & N. Hornberger (Eds.), *Encyclopedia of language education* (2nd ed.), *Vol. 3: Discourse and education* (pp. 29–40). New York: Springer.

Christie, F., & Derewianka, B. (2008). *School discourse: Learning to write across the years of schooling*. London and New York: Continuum.

Christie, F., & Martin, J. (Eds.). (1997). *Genre and institutions: Social processes in the workplace and school*. London and New York: Continuum.

Christie, F., & Martin, J. (Eds.). (2007). *Language, knowledge and pedagogy: Functional linguistic and sociological perspectives*. London and New York: Continuum.

Christie, F., & Rothery, J. (1979). English in Australia. An interpretation of role in the curriculum. In J. Maling-Keepes & B. Keepes (Eds.), *Language in education. The Language Development Project, Phase 1* (pp. 193–242). Canberra: Curriculum Development Centre.

Christie, F. & Unsworth, L. (2005). Developing dimensions of an educational linguistics. In R. Hasan, C. Matthiessen, & J. Webster (Eds.), *Continuing discourse on discourse: A functional perspective* (Vol. 1, pp. 217–250). London and Oakville: Equinox.

Christie, F., Gray, P., Gray, B., Macken, M., Martin, J., & Rothery, J. (1990, 1990, 1992). *Language: A resource for meaning: Procedures, Books 1–4 and teachers' manual; Reports, Books 1–4 and teachers' manual; Explanations, Books 1–4 and teachers' manual*. Sydney: Harcourt Brace Jovanovich.

Coffin, C. (2006). *Historical discourse*. London: Continuum.

Coffin, C., Hewings, A., & O'Halloran, K. (Eds.). (2004). *Applied English grammar: Functional and corpus approaches*. London: Hodder Arnold.

Cope, B., & Kalantzis, M. (1993). *The powers of literacy: A genre approach to teaching writing*. Pittsburgh: University of Pittsburgh Press.

Curriculum Development Centre. (1979). *The language development project discussion paper no. 1*. Canberra: Curriculum Development Centre.

Derewianka, B. (1990). *Exploring how texts work*. Rozelle, NSW: Primary English Teaching Association.

Dixon, J. (1967). *Growth through English*. London: National Association for the Teaching of English and Oxford University Press.

Doecke, B., Howie, M., & Sawyer, W. (2006). *"Only connect": English teaching, schooling and community*. Kent Town, SA: Australian Association for the Teaching of English.

Doughty, P., Pearce, J., & Thornton, G. (1973). *Language in use: Schools Council program in linguistics and English teaching*. London: Edward Arnold.

Droga, L., & Humphrey, S. (2002). *Getting started with functional grammar*. Berry, NSW: Target Texts.

Droga, L., & Humphrey, S. (2003). *Grammar and meaning: An introduction for primary teachers*. Berry, NSW: Target Texts.

Eggins, S., & Slade, D. (1997). *Analyzing casual conversation*. London and Washington, DC: Cassell.

Fang, Z., & Schleppegrell, M. (2008) *Reading in the secondary content areas: A language-based pedagogy*. Ann Arbor: University of Michigan Press.

Feez, S., with Joyce, H. (1998). *Text-based syllabus design*. Sydney: National Centre for English Language Teaching and Research, Macquarie University.

Feez, S., Iedema, R., & White, P. (2008). *Media literacy* (Ed. H. de Silva Joyce). Sydney: NSW Adult Migrant English Service.

Freedman, A., & Medway, P. (Eds.). (1994). *Genre and the new rhetoric*. London: Taylor & Francis.

Graham, S., & Perin, D. (2007). *Writing next: Effective strategies to improve writing of adolescents in middle and high schools. A report to the Carnegie Corporation of New York*. Washington, DC: Alliance for Excellent Education.

Graves, D. (1981). *Robert Graves in Australia: Children want to write* (Ed. R. Walshe). Roseberry, NSW: Primary English Teaching Association.

Gray, B., Rose, D., & Cowey, W. (1998). *Scaffolding reading and writing for indigenous children in school*. Canberra: Department of Education, Science and Training: Indigenous Education Branch and the University of Canberra.

Halliday, M. (1961). Categories of the theory of grammar. *Word, 17*(3), 241–292. (Republished in J. Webster (Ed.). (2002). *On grammar. The collected works of M.A.K. Halliday* (Vol. 1, pp. 37–94). London & New York: Continuum.)

Halliday, M. (1979). Linguistics in teacher education. In J. Maling-Keepes & B. Keepes (eds.), *Language in education. The Language Development Project, phase 1* (pp. 279–286). Canberra: Curriculum Development Centre.

Halliday, M. (1985a). *Spoken and written language*. Geelong, Vict.: Deakin University Press.

Halliday, M. (1985b). *An introduction to functional grammar*. London and Melbourne: Arnold.

Halliday, M. (2002). Introduction: A personal perspective. In J. Webster (Ed.). (2002). *On grammar. The collected works of M.A.K. Halliday* (Vol. 1, pp. 1–16). London and New York: Continuum.

Halliday, M., & Hasan, R. (1985). *Language, context & text: A social semiotic perspective*. Geelong, Vict.: Deakin University Press.

Halliday, M., & Hasan, R. (2006). Retrospective on SFL & literacy. In R. Whittaker, M. O'Donnell, & A. McCabe (Eds.), *Language and literacy. Functional perspectives* (pp. 15–44). London and New York: Continuum.

Halliday, M., & Matthiessen, C. (2004). *An introduction to functional grammar* (3rd ed.). London: Arnold.

Halliday, M., McIntosh, A., & Strevens, P. (1964). *The linguistic sciences and language teaching*. London: Longmans, Green & Co.

Hasan, R. (1984). The nursery rhyme as a genre. *Nottingham Linguistic Circular, 13*, 71–102. (Produced in a revised form in C. Cloran, D. Butt & G. Williams (Eds.). (1996). *Ways of saying: Ways of meaning* (pp. 51–72). London and New York: Cassell.)

Hasan, R. (1985). *Linguistics, language and verbal art*. Geelong, Vict.: Deakin University Press.

Hasan, R. (1995). The conception of context in text. In P. Fries & M. Gregory (Eds.), *Discourse in society: Systemic functional perspectives* (pp. 183–283). Norwood, NJ: Ablex.

Hasan, R. (1996). Literacy, everyday talk and society. In R. Hasan & G. Williams (Eds.), *Literacy in society* (pp. 377–424). London and New York: Longman.

Hasan, R., & Martin, J. (Eds.). (1989). *Language development: Learning language, Learning culture. Meaning and choice in language. Studies for Michael Halliday*. Norwood, NJ: Ablex.

Hasan, R., Matthiessen, C., & Webster, J. (Eds.). *Continuing discourse on language: A functional perspective* (Vol. 1). London and Oakville: Equinox.

Her Majesty's Stationery Office. (1967). *Children and their primary schools* [Plowden Report]. London: Her Majesty's Stationery Office.

His Majesty's Stationery Office. (1921). *The teaching of English in England and Wales* [Newbolt Report]. London: His Majesty's Stationery Office.

Howie, M. (2006). The importance of being politically correct. In B. Doecke, M. Howie & W. Sawyer (Eds.), *Only connect. English Teaching, schooling and community* (pp. 283–293). Kent Town, SA: Wakefield Press & the Australian Association for the Teaching of English.

Hyon, S. (1996). Genres in three traditions: Implications for ESL. *TESOL Quarterly, 30*, 693–722.

Janks, H. (2005). Language and the design of texts. *English Teaching: Practice and Critique, 4*(3), 97–110.

Johns, J. (Ed.). (2002). *Genre in the classroom: Multiple perspectives*. Mahwah, NJ: Lawrence Erlbaum.

Korner, H., McInnes, D., & Rose, D. (2007). *Science literacy* (Ed. H. de Silva). Sydney: NSW Adult Migrant English Service.

Kress, G. (1985). *Linguistic processes in sociocultural practice*. Geelong, Vict.: Deakin University Press.

Larochelle, M., Bednarz, N., & Garrison, J. (Eds.). (1998). *Constructivism and education*. Cambridge: Cambridge University Press.

Lee, A. (1996). *Gender, literacy and curriculum*. London: Taylor & Francis.

Love, K., & Simpson, A. (2005). Online discussion in schools: Towards a pedagogic framework. *International Journal of Educational Research, 42*, 446–463.

Mackay, D., & Schaub, P. (1970). *Breakthrough to literacy*. London: Longmans.

Macken-Horarik, M. (1998). Exploring the requirements of critical school literacy: A view from two classrooms. In F. Christie & R. Misson (Eds.), *Literacy and schooling* (pp. 74–103). London and New York: Routledge.

Macken-Horarik, M. (2002). "Something to shoot for": A systemic functional approach to teaching genre in secondary school science. In A. Johns (Ed.), *Genre in the classroom: Multiple perspectives* (pp. 17–42). Mahwah, NJ: Lawrence Erlbaum.

Macken-Horarik, M. (2006). Knowledge through "know how": Systemic functional grammatics and the symbolic reading. *English Teaching: Practice and Critique, 5*(1), 102–121.

Maling-Keepes, J., & Keepes, B. (1979). (Eds.). *Language in education. The Language Development Project, phase 1*. Canberra: Curriculum Development Centre.

Malinowski, B. (1923). The problem of meaning in primitive languages, supplement 1. In C. Ogden & I. Richards (Eds.), *The meaning of meaning* (pp. 296–336). London: Kegan Paul.

Malinowski, B. (1935). *Coral gardens and their magic* (Vol. 2). London: Allen & Unwin.

Martin, J. (1984). Language, register and genre. In *B.Ed. Children writing course reader* (pp. 21–30). Geelong, Vict.: Deakin University Press.

Martin, J. (1985a). Process and text: Two aspects of human semiosis. In J. Benson & W. Greaves (Eds.), *Systemic perspectives on discourse* (Vol. 1, pp. 248–274). Norwood, NJ: Ablex.

Martin, J. (1985b). *Factual writing: Exploring and challenging social reality*. Geelong, Vict.: Deakin University Press.

Martin, J. (1999). Mentoring semogenesis: "Genre-based" literacy pedagogy. In F. Christie (Ed.), *Pedagogy and the shaping of consciousness* (pp. 123–155). London and New York: Continuum.

Martin, J., & Rose, D. (2003.) *Working with discourse: Meaning beyond the clause*. London: Equinox.

Martin, J., & Rose, D. (2008). *Genre relations: Mapping culture*. Equinox: London & Oakville.

Murray, L. (1795/1968). *English grammar*. Facsimile reprint no. 106. Menston: Scholar Press.

National Curriculum Board. (2008). *National curriculum English framing paper*. Carlton South, Vict.: National Curriculum Board. Retrieved February 5, 2009, from www.ncb. org.au/communications/publications.html.

Reid, I. (1987). *The place of genre in learning: Current debates*. Geelong, Vict.: Typereader Publications.

Richardson, P. (1994). Language as personal resource and as social construct: Competing views of literacy pedagogy in Australia. In A. Freedman & P. Medway (Eds.), *Genre in education* (pp. 117–142). Portsmouth, NH: Boynton/Cook Heinemann.

Richardson, P. (2004). Literacy, genre studies and pedagogy. In W. Sawyer & E. Gold (Eds.), *Reviewing English in the 21st century* (pp. 119–128). Melbourne: Phoenix Education.

Rose, D. (2008). *Reading to learn: Accelerating learning & closing the gap*. Professional Development Course. Sydney: Rose Publications.

Rosen, H., & Rosen, C. (1973). *The language of primary school children*. London: Penguin Education and the Schools Council.

Rothery, J. (1984). *The development of genres – primary to junior secondary school. Section 23, Children writing, B.Ed. study guide* (pp. 67–114). Geelong, Vict.: Deakin University Press.

Sawyer, W., & Watson, K. (1989) Further questions of genre. *English in Australia, 90*, 27–42.

Schleppegrell, M. (2004). *The language of schooling. A functional linguistics perspective*. Mahwah, NJ: Lawrence Erlbaum.

Stenhouse, L. (1975). *An introduction to curriculum research and development*. London: Heinemann Educational Books.

Snyder, I. (2008). *The literacy wars. Why teaching children to read and write is a battleground in Australia*. Crows Nest, NSW: Allen & Unwin.

Threadgold, T. (1988). The genre debate. *Southern Review, 21*(3), 315–330.

Threadgold, T., & Kress, G. (1988). Towards a social theory of genre. *Southern Review, 21*(3), 215–243.

Turner, G. (2007). Cultural literacies, critical literacies, and the English school curriculum in Australia. *International Journal of Cultural Studies, 10*, 105–114.

Unsworth, L. (2001). *Teaching multiliteracies across the curriculum. Changing contexts of text and image in classroom practice.* Buckingham and Philadelphia: Open University Press.

Chapter 5

Knowledge about Language in the English Classroom

A Scottish Perspective

Graeme Trousdale

I Context

This chapter is about the place of knowledge about language in the secondary English classroom in Scotland, and particularly about the ways in which curricular reform, the changing attitudes of teachers and increased collaboration between schools and universities might allow for a greater and clearer emphasis on knowledge about language in both English and foreign-language teaching. In this chapter, you will be encouraged to think about ways in which collaboration between schools and universities in your own area might be enhanced. The discussion is organized around the following topics. Section 2 is concerned with ongoing changes in the teaching of knowledge about language in Scotland. It explores the various links that are emerging between schools and departments of English Language, Linguistics and Education in the country, and tries to explain why these links are emerging at the present time. This section also discusses existing provision for the teaching of knowledge about language generally and grammar in particular. There is also some discussion in this section of existing curricular arrangements[1] and of the guidance from both the education department at the Scottish government (which, prior to the election of the Scottish National Party to form a minority government in Scotland in 2007, was known as the Scottish Executive[2]) and the Scottish Qualification Authority (SQA).

In section 3, I consider some of the specifics of grammar teaching: for example, how, when and why specific grammatical topics are addressed, and teachers' confidence in exploring such topics. You will be encouraged to reflect on your own practice regarding grammar teaching, with some suggestions for possible work on teaching grammar using non-standard dialect data. In the fourth section, issues of multilingualism in the English classroom are explored. These issues are of relevance not only to the long-standing debate about the nature, function and role of Scots in English teaching in Scotland, but also to our understanding of the effect of more recent migration patterns from natives of

---

1. The issues noted in this brief section are discussed in more detail in Trousdale (2006).
2. Henceforth I use the term "Scottish government" to refer to both the Scottish Executive prior to 2007 and the current organization.

other countries within the European Union to Scotland. This is reflected in a recent government consultation document, *A Strategy for Scotland's Languages*. The issue of language variety is an important topic relating to knowledge about language in the English classroom in Scotland, not least because of the increasing ethnic diversity of students in Scotland's schools. Again, you will be encouraged to consider the issue of linguistic diversity in your own classroom, and to reflect on ways in which this diversity may be seen as a resource for work on knowledge about language. In section 5, I briefly discuss some of the ways in which the debate concerning knowledge about language might be moved forward, and consider how university academics might support teachers who are working on knowledge about language, should such support be required. Section 6 is the conclusion.

In Trousdale (2006), I discussed some of the particular effects of education policy on the teaching of knowledge about language in Scotland, and of the place of knowledge about language in formal examinations in English. This was in part prompted by recent and ongoing curricular reform across the entire Scottish school system, a project known as *A Curriculum for Excellence*,[3] henceforth *ACfE*. This project has conceived of the curriculum as a series of groupings of related subjects (for example, Sciences, Technologies, Expressive Arts). The "traditional" subject of school English falls largely[4] in the "Languages" group, which provides a wealth of opportunities for work on knowledge about language cross-linguistically. What is particularly encouraging about *ACfE*, at least as far as one can gather from the information that is publicly available, is the emphasis on the linguistic diversity of Scotland as a whole. A webpage on languages in *ACfE* states:

> Scotland has a rich diversity of language, including the different languages of Scotland and the growing number of community languages such as Urdu, Punjabi and Polish. This diversity offers rich opportunities for learning. Learning other languages enables children and young people to make connections with different people and their cultures and to play a fuller part as global citizens. (Learning and Teaching Scotland, 2009, paragraph 2)

Activity: Reflecting on Linguistic Diversity as a Learning Resource

Based on your own experience of the languages spoken in your classroom, reflect on some of the ways in which such a diversity "offers rich opportunities for learning". How could you use the multilingual classroom to develop schemes of work about particular aspects of knowledge about language?

This emphasis on multilingual Scotland – where that multilingualism covers not just Gaelic, Urdu and Polish, but Scots and English too – foregrounds the need

---

3. Accessible at www.ltscotland.org.uk/curriculumforexcellence.
4. Drama appears within Expressive Arts.

for putting knowledge about language at the centre of the languages strategy.[5] This has been emphasized by those working on the Languages component of *ACfE*, since they stress the importance of students developing a good understanding of how language works. They have also been keen to recognize the value of local indigenous cultures, by highlighting the pleasure and benefits of studying Scottish literature. In other words, some aspects of this important curricular review are encouraging: part of the Languages curriculum is local, but it is not parochial – it recognizes that the diversity of language in the local communities of Scotland is a resource in itself, which can help children become proficient in a range of competencies. There are therefore a number of initiatives linked to government policy (whether specifically concerned with education or not) that foreground the importance of language awareness and language learning that are likely to impact on English teaching in the Scottish secondary system.

The material presented here is based on a range of sources, including documentation from the Scottish government and the SQA. I have also included, where relevant, some matters arising from work, discussions and interviews with (and reports from) some teachers of English from state secondary schools in central and southern Scotland. These discussions and interviews were sometimes carried out as part of larger collaborative projects, but some specific questions were asked in order to clarify what seemed to be the critical issues in the teaching of knowledge about language among a very small sample of teachers. Therefore, the views expressed should not be seen as in any way representative of the views of the English teaching profession in Scotland as a whole, nor is there as yet sufficient material to provide detailed quantitative analysis. But the comments do at least provide some insight into some of the problems that particular teachers have faced when working on knowledge about language with their students, and ways in which some of the these problems have been overcome. As noted above, the chapter also provides some discussion of ways in which academics and teachers can collaborate with the aim of promoting a fuller understanding of knowledge about language in the classroom; recent work on this in Scotland has brought about a network of teachers who are keen to do further work on knowledge about language, both at Higher and Advanced Higher (the Scottish national school exams typically taken towards the end of one's school career), and more generally elsewhere in the curriculum.

2 Knowledge about Language in the Curriculum in Scotland: Status, Support and Practice

Knowledge about language has always been important in the English classroom in Scotland, but there is some evidence that it is becoming increasingly central. In the research I have begun on the teaching of language in schools, I have been

---

5. In fact, *ACfE* suggests that competence in literacy is a responsibility of all teachers, not just those who teach English and Modern Languages.

particularly keen to find out why this change seems to be happening at the present time, and initial responses from teachers have tended to cluster around the following views: that the time was simply right; that for some teachers there had been an evolution in what the subject of "English" is; and that there had a been a shift in understanding of what the students required. In the words of one of the teachers I talked to, "we are just moving on".[6]

It may be that some of this feeling is based on a comparison with some of the developments in England, such as the Literacy Strategy (DfEE 1998, 2000), since some of the teachers contacted as part of the research for this chapter had some experience of teaching in both England and Scotland, and noted significant differences regarding the place of knowledge about language in the English classroom in both countries. To a certain degree – but only to a certain degree – this was felt to be related to the existence of a separate A-level in English Language in England. In Scotland, there is currently no separate qualification available to students who are keen to explore purely linguistic topics. There is a separate section on "Language Study" at Advanced Higher, which encourages the study of a number of linguistic topics, such as regional and social varieties of English and Scots, the historical development of those languages, multilingualism in contemporary Scotland, the language of informal communication, and the language of political communication. However, very few centres prepare students for this optional topic: the majority of candidates for Advanced Higher English either answer a question on textual analysis or submit a creative writing portfolio, in addition to answering a question from the compulsory section on literary topics. Furthermore, the teachers suggested that issues regarding the place of knowledge about language in the English classroom were of importance across the entire secondary school-age range, and not simply (or even primarily) pertinent to advanced work in the subject. The issue, then, becomes one of embedding work on knowledge about language earlier in the curriculum; but questions remain as to how to do this, what resources are needed, and what kind of support is required. This is partly where collaborative work between schools and universities can be relevant.

One recent initiative in this regard has been the establishment of the Committee for Language Awareness in Scottish Schools (CLASS). CLASS is concerned with knowledge about language generally, not just in the English classroom, though the majority of the teachers on the committee are English teachers. The committee is organized by academics at the University of Edinburgh (which funds the work of the committee), but the aim of the group is to support teachers working in Scottish classrooms, and it is hoped that the

6. It should be noted that teachers were not of the opinion that a developing interest in the teaching of knowledge about language was tied to the worsening of standards in literacy in Scotland – indeed, there was no sense that literacy standards had been falling. A recent report on levels of literacy among children, in different countries across the globe, who had received about five years of formal schooling (detailed in Twist, Schagen & Hodgson, 2007) suggested that, although the relative ranking of Scotland had fallen between 2001 and 2006, the actual mean scores of reading achievement had not changed substantially over the five-year period.

agenda, where possible, will be set by teachers, with academics simply providing support where necessary. Discussions with teachers have suggested that academic support in the form of the creation of functional and cheap resources would be particularly valued. To that end, the committee has decided to develop a website to enable users to share resources for working on knowledge about language topics. This website, since it would be hosted by the University of Edinburgh, would be moderated by an academic. But the aim is to have resources posted by teachers and academics, some of whom would occasionally be working together[7] to produce such material. The committee has been particularly concerned to focus on language issues that are relevant to the lives of Scotland's students, and to embed knowledge about language within a wider educational framework; it is for that reason that the teachers (not the academics) are the most central members of the committee (see section 6 below).

The amount of time dedicated to knowledge about language is variable both across schools and within individual departments, though there does seem to be an increase in interest in explicit work on language (especially varieties of English and Scots, both synchronic and diachronic). An important factor here is the extent to which "language" ought to be seen as a separate topic within the discipline of "English", or whether issues in knowledge about language ought to be addressed only when they emerge from the study of a particular written text. Discussions with some teachers have shown that opinions can vary quite substantially on this matter. Some teachers have voiced approval for what they perceived as the "Scottish" system (in contrast with what they considered to be the pattern in England), whereby knowledge about language is taught through the medium of the written text; at the other extreme, some teachers (particularly those with substantial training in linguistics) have wanted to switch the focus almost entirely to spoken language, exploring how meaning is created cooperatively in conversation, and examining the lexical, grammatical and phonetic ways in which accents of English and Scots vary. One teacher went so far as to say that work on knowledge about language was central to his teaching, not simply because he was an English teacher, but because work on knowledge about language teaches children "how to think" more generally.

Knowledge about language operates across the curriculum (an issue highlighted in *ACfE*, as noted above), but improving attainment in knowledge about language seems to be seen (particularly by teachers of subjects other than English) as the responsibility of the English teacher. Most teachers fall somewhere between the two extremes noted above, and to a certain extent feel hamstrung by time constraints – there is only so much time available for English in the curriculum, and not everything that in an ideal world should be covered, can be covered. This then becomes a matter of prioritization, as a result of which many issues in knowledge about language become more marginalized.

7. For an example of a recent collaborative project between a teacher and an academic working on a particular topic, see section 4 below.

Activity: Reflecting on the Place of Knowledge about Language

To what extent do you think knowledge about language should be treated separately from other aspects of English teaching? List some of the advantages and disadvantages of teaching knowledge about language as a separate discipline. How does your own teaching practice relate to the practices of the teachers mentioned in the paragraph above?

There has been some attention paid to particular issues regarding knowledge about language in recent (that is, post-2000) documentation from the Scottish government. Attitudes towards the provision of guidance on knowledge about language provided by government officers and examination boards varied quite considerably among teachers. In one school, there was some criticism of the 5–14 National Guidelines on English Language (SOED, 1991). The knowledge about language strand here was considered to be unhelpful and even "obstructive", with the result that teachers tended to rely on local arrangements agreed within the school. My own reading of the guidelines confirms this: there is little significant discussion of grammatical terminology in the guidelines, and what is there is focused almost exclusively on writing, and is also not particularly transparent. Of course the 5–14 National Guidelines are simply guidelines, and not a "national curriculum", but as Ellis and Friel (2003, p. 380) have noted, the document typically serves as a focal point for work on knowledge about language in both the primary and lower secondary schools. The guidelines have (at least in part) a clear focus on the importance of knowledge about language (see, for example, SOED, 1991, pp. 4, 7) in a multilingual society like contemporary Scotland (see McGonigal, 2003; Donovan & Niven, 2003).

Yet a problem remains in defining what precisely constitutes knowledge about language, and particularly the relationship between knowledge about language and grammar. It is clear that knowledge about how grammar works is part of knowledge about language; there is also some evidence that knowledge about how to form standard written English sentences may benefit from explicit grammar teaching (though the extent – and even the existence – of such a benefit has been a subject of some debate recently).[8] But it is less clear that terms like "play" or "scene" warrant inclusion in the knowledge about language strand given the existence of a parallel strand on genre and text-type in the guidelines (see Trousdale (2006) for a fuller discussion of the 5–14 National Guidelines on knowledge about language). These are not merely minor quibbles; in a situation where confidence in knowledge about language among English teachers themselves may be low (see below, and also Hudson & Walmsley, 2005), clarity in the official documentation from government departments is crucial.

---

8. For a detailed discussion of extant research, see Hudson (2001); see also Andrews et al. (2004) for a discussion of research on how decontextualized teaching of traditional "parts of speech" grammar or Chomskyan transformational grammar has little effect on writing skills.

3 Knowledge about Language and the Teaching of Grammar

Philp (2001) identifies three main strands of grammar teaching which have been adopted in various places at various times across the United Kingdom. These three strands are: the "Traditional Grammar Approach"; the "Creative Writing Approach"; and the "Language-Study-Based Approach". The first of these typically involves explicit teaching of what is perceived as the "correct" forms of English (for example, the avoidance of multiple negation markers in a clause, or of split infinitives). Such an approach privileges the written language above the spoken language, though usually this approach to grammar makes little if any reference to any context. The second approach typically makes little explicit reference to the formal teaching of grammar for its own sake, relying instead on the belief that knowledge about language will emerge simply through repeated practice in using language in different styles and for different purposes. The third approach has been divided into two subcategories. In "implicit" language study, attention is still paid to certain aspects of language structure, but specific linguistic metalanguage is avoided; by contrast, with "explicit" language study, teachers will make use of specific terminology drawn from the field of linguistics, but (in contrast to the "Traditional Grammar" approach) may make use of differences between the structure of spoken and written English, or may explore differences between local and standard varieties, or between different varieties of English across the globe. This is often done in order to allow the students to describe language structure and variation more clearly and consistently.

From discussions with teachers, it seems that all three approaches may still be used in contemporary Scottish classrooms, but the first is used far less frequently than the others, and the third used most frequently of all. The first approach, since it is typically a decontextualized and prescriptive exercise in promoting correct forms of English, is rare, but used sometimes in order to clarify a particular grammatical point (on which see further below). The third approach, which as noted may be implicit or explicit, is the approach that is typically promoted in Scottish education policy and has been commended in earlier inspection reports on the teaching of English in Scotland[9] (SOED, 1992). The textual basis of grammar teaching was remarked upon by a number of the teachers who were contacted as part of this research. Issues relating to grammar in poetry, of "alternative ways of saying the same thing", were sometimes addressed; and if students were repeatedly using similar, non-standard forms, then the teachers would take time to explain a particular grammatical point. But non-standard language per se was rarely considered, unless the study of a particular text raised particular issues of non-standard grammar. The focus is primarily therefore on the grammar of standard written English; but teachers agreed that this can only be understood by contrasting it with non-standard and spoken forms of the language, and it was in these areas that they were keenest to explore possible schemes of work.

9. The report also warned against the decontextualized teaching of grammatical terminology (cf. Andrews et al., 2004, referred to in note 8 above.)

Activity: Incorporating Non-Standard Dialects into Grammar Teaching

Which of the strands of grammar teaching identified by Philp (2001) do you adopt in your own teaching of grammar? How might you incorporate data from non-standard dialects into your model of grammar teaching? What might be the advantages and disadvantages of doing so?

One significant area where work on grammar may feature more substantially concerns the study of texts in Scots. Teachers reported that Scots texts were not only read, but also created, by their pupils and, in such cases, teachers typically worked on both lexical choices and grammatical structures. In addition to developing students' knowledge of more formal matters of language structure, creative writing in Scots can also lead to a discussion of sociolinguistic and applied linguistic matters, such as the status of Scots as a language in comparison to English. In some cases, teachers have used this as a way into discussing more general issues of multilingualism in the classroom (see section 4 below).

Particular issues relating to knowledge about language and public examinations in Scotland, such as Standard Grade and Higher, are not explored in detail here for two reasons. First, the Standard Grade qualification has been replaced by new qualifications at the "pre-Higher" stage of secondary education; and second (and more importantly), the SQA, in November 2007, revealed plans for a wholesale revision of the content of and assessment relating to the Higher English qualification, and this may involve a change as to whether knowledge about language will be formally assessed in the Higher examination. However, in light of this proposed revision, it is interesting to note one point that was made to me quite forcibly by a group of teachers whom I interviewed, and who saw a link between the marginalization of grammar in assessment and its impact on teaching in the classroom. The problem relates to the fact that in many of the formal examinations (that is, not just Higher, but Standard Grade and Intermediate 1 and 2), students are expected to show a command of standard written English (in terms of spelling, grammar and punctuation) but explicit knowledge about language is not separately assessed (except, of course, in the Language Study section of the Advanced Higher English qualification). Teachers felt that because grammar was not necessarily seen as central in assessment, there was a tendency to sideline explicit work on grammar in the Higher English classroom, and they found this frustrating. They also felt that explicit teaching of grammar – as part of a more widespread and substantial articulation of knowledge about language in the English classroom – was essential in improving their students' literacy skills.

4 Varieties and Multilingualism in Contemporary Scotland: Another Aspect of Knowledge about Language

The rich linguistic and literary tradition in Scotland provides students with many opportunities to explore non-standard varieties, and also the historical evolution of standard and non-standard forms. The issue of multilingual and multicultural diversity in the classroom, and the ways in which this can enhance students' understanding of a range of topics, have been well documented recently (for example, Rickford, Sweetland & Rickford, 2004; Gordon, 2005; Wheeler, 2006). The discussion has illustrated some of the advantages of a focus on linguistic variation (particularly through the application of Contrastive Analysis). One such advantage is that students gain confidence in talking and writing about linguistic concepts by using examples from the (standard and non-standard) varieties they know and use (cf. also Rickford, 1996). As Barton and Hudson (2004) point out, the exact proportion of children in the United Kingdom who have to learn standard English as a "second dialect" is not clear, but is somewhere in the region of 90%. Such a high proportion provides a great opportunity for exploring the nature and function of linguistic diversity. The increase in multilingualism in Scotland's classrooms will highlight this issue even further.

Activity: Exploring Non-Standard Grammar

Encourage your students to list some of the features of non-standard grammar that characterize the dialect of the local area in which the school is situated. Think about some of the ways you could use that list to do the following:

1. Explore children's knowledge of the relationship between language choices and the social context in which language was used (for example, why non-standard dialect is not typically appropriate in a job interview).
2. Explore the relationship between language and identity (for example, how particular features are local to the area, and how other features might be more widespread).
3. Explore attitudes to language variation (for example, what is meant by "incorrect" grammar and "bad" language).

A significant issue in the Scottish context is likely to be the effects of the enlargement of the European Union and migration patterns across the continent. For example, on 9 November 2005, the *Scotsman* newspaper reported that in the 18 months since Poland had joined the European Union, the Polish population in Scotland had risen by about 50% to around 30,000 people, the majority of whom had settled near Edinburgh. This influx has given rise to an increase in the visibility of the Polish language in the capital, from labels on Polish foodstuffs in the supermarket to signs in Polish about opening a current account in a high-street bank. From interviews with teachers that I have conducted, it would seem that the education of children who, for example, have Polish as a first language, presents both a challenge and an opportunity for work on knowledge about language in the English classroom. The teachers recognized the need for developing particular activities for some of these students, who were having difficulty mastering particular grammatical phenomena associated with the standard language. They were concerned about the availability of training and resources to help these students. However, the teachers also recognized that the linguistic diversity which such students brought to the classroom was in itself an excellent resource for other work on knowledge about language. Specifically, the teachers saw an increase in multilingualism and multicultural diversity in Scotland as a "resource that is growing": the more varieties that are used in the classroom, the more diverse the linguistic issues that can be discussed.

A second advantage is that, since knowledge of variation relates to knowledge of culture, students become more aware of diversity and have the opportunity to explore the ways in which such diversity is socially beneficial. Work on varieties (including local varieties of Scots, and those of speakers who have English as a second or other language) allows students to understand cultural diversity and the various ways in which societies change. Work on such variation need not be restricted to work on spoken languages; investigating, in a serious and purposeful way, the ways in which different technologies use different forms of written English, can be both stimulating and challenging for students. Understanding why the kind of writing used in mobile/cellphone messages (that is, in texting) is perfect for that medium, but inappropriate for use in formal letters, raises awareness of how language use is related to context, and can be used to illustrate particular points associated with the standard spelling system and of the diversity in orthographic practices cross-linguistically (see Sebba, 2007).

In a number of ways, then, working on linguistic diversity within Scotland goes some way to meeting the four capacities at the heart of *ACfE*, namely: developing successful learners; developing confident individuals; developing responsible citizens; and developing effective contributors. It is therefore not surprising that work on linguistic varieties has been increasingly popular in the English classroom. In addition to my own discussions with teachers, other studies (SOED, 1992; Donovan & Niven, 2003) have reported on opportunities for a range of activities in which teachers and pupils have worked on Scots, from reading Scottish texts to creative writing projects in Scots.

It was also clear that students were keen on and able to handle work which involved analysis of historical data. A particularly fine example of this concerns a project on lexical change in the history of English given to the top stream of an S3 cohort (that is, with students aged around 14 or 15) in one school. Having been introduced to some external history associated with the Old and Middle English periods, the students were given an extract from Chaucer's *Franklin's Tale*, and asked to identify which words they thought came from Germanic, and which had been borrowed from Norman French. The teacher reported that the students identified words in the extract that were associated with government, aristocracy and high culture as those they would expect to be derived from Norman French, given their understanding of the external history of medieval England. The teacher then went on to talk more generally about poetic verse traditions in different cultures, linking this to poetic concepts with which they were already familiar (such as metre and alliteration). Further work might also include the relationship between Scots and Standard English in writing from contemporary Scotland, exploring the distribution of lexical items in different genres of varying degrees of formality, and showing how a situation that obtained in a historical period may have resonances in the modern day.

A different project for the same age-group at a different school in Scotland concentrated on the linguistics of names. This project involved collaboration between a high school teacher and a university linguist, which included a school lesson taught by the linguist. This lesson involved many key areas of knowledge about language, all based around onomastics. For instance, basic principles of sociolinguistics were introduced by showing how names function as linguistic variants that can indicate the social relationship between speaker and addressee, the formality of the discourse and the social context of the speech act. This was illustrated through an examination of names used in a particular scene in the movie *Spiderman*, and in an extract from a Harry Potter novel. Basic grammar was introduced by showing how combinations of given and family names varied cross-linguistically, and how names behaved differently from common nouns. Issues of cross-linguistic variation and multilingualism were addressed by exploring differences between naming practices in Germanic and Arabic languages. Other issues addressed included the relationship between linguistic variation and identity, which was tied in to work the students had been engaged in prior to the lesson (including work on names in *Romeo and Juliet*) and work to be undertaken in the following lessons (including a discussion of passages from a contemporary novel on names), and on recent UK newspaper articles on identity and changing one's name (either by deed poll or at marriage), and on the relationship between names and success in one's professional life.

This work, then, represents a number of intersections of work on knowledge about language. In particular, work on different kinds of media texts (a film, two novels, a play, some newspaper features) combined with work on "old-school" linguistics (grammatical categories, linguistic variables, cross-linguistic variation) produced an interesting perspective on the teaching of knowledge about language. Furthermore, the students were introduced to ways of thinking about knowledge about language based on a range of textual evidence, and were invited to consider what counts as a text. The lesson was introduced through an examination of a birth certificate, both as an official identification document (which opened up a discussion of identity more generally) and as a piece of linguistic evidence for the study of names. The teacher and the academic linguist involved felt that this overall approach was a successful synthesis of the traditional text-based work on knowledge about language with more formal issues in language structure and linguistic variation.

Recent political developments are also of relevance for the place of the study of multilingualism in the curriculum. As mentioned in section 1, in early 2007, the then Scottish Executive proposed a consultation exercise entitled *A Strategy for Scotland's Languages*. The strategy was intended to serve as reference point for policy-makers, and to highlight the principal goals of the Executive. The strategy documentation focused attention on the various issues of relevance to multilingual Scotland: the importance of English as a global medium of communication; the local cultural heritage associated with both "indigenous" languages like Scots and Gaelic, and those languages which arrived in Scotland as a consequence of more recent migrations, such as Urdu and Punjabi; the linguistic consequences of the arrival of even more recent immigrant groups (such as the large contingency of Polish migrants, as highlighted above); and the importance of other community languages, such as British Sign Language, in the social and economic life of Scotland.

Part of the strategy was concerned with the opportunities for language learning, of "European languages, other major world languages and Scotland's indigenous languages" (Scottish Government, 2007, "Enriching Education"), and this is reflected in the holistic approach to language elsewhere in the document. The strategy recognized the importance of locating literacy in English within a wider framework of language learning, of recognizing the cultural and personal enrichment that can be achieved by devoting time to the study of Scots (in its spoken and written forms), and of understanding the needs of those for whom English is a second or additional language. Indeed, the special place of Scots in the whole curriculum (cf. Corbett, 2002; Niven, 2002; Donovan & Niven, 2003) is highlighted in the strategy. One of the guiding principles focuses on Scots, and states that the "use of Scots should be promoted in the school curriculum" (Scottish Government, 2007, "Principles", paragraph 4). It is disappointing to report that, following the 2007 election, this excellent initiative was not taken forward by the new Scottish government. In the next section, I suggest some ways in which those keen to work more extensively on knowledge about language might be supported, should such support be required.

5 Some Ways Forward

As noted in Trousdale (forthcoming), the provision and easy means of distribution of free and functional resources on knowledge about language seem to be an important issue for teachers, and one which might usefully be addressed in collaboration with university academics. A striking feature of some of the discussions with teachers was the desire to develop work that was purely on "language for language's sake", particularly through work on language puzzles, and through work on language variety. To this end, a group of teachers who form part of CLASS is currently working with a university linguist to produce resources which will be freely downloadable from the CLASS website. Such collaboration means that teachers have the opportunity to consult with an academic about new research in the field, and to have any particular questions or issues clarified, while the university community becomes more aware of what work is being carried out in schools, which may facilitate the planning of a freshman curriculum.

Specifically, the teachers are able to organize the material as they see fit, tailoring particular resources either by topic, or by (expected) level of attainment at different stages in the school curriculum. Furthermore, such collaborative work allows teachers who are particularly interested in knowledge about language to form a virtual community to supplement the face-to-face meetings, which for practical reasons occur less frequently. Initial discussions with teachers suggested that a number of resources had already been prepared, and teachers were looking for an outlet through which to share such work with interested colleagues. Thus, an important objective for CLASS (and perhaps for similar organizations, elsewhere) is the creation of a network of teachers who share common interests in the study of language at school.

Curricular reform is also central to raising the profile of knowledge about language in Scotland's schools. As noted above, the revisions as part of *ACfE* and the promise of a review of the Higher English exam are two examples of such reform that will impact on how knowledge about language is viewed by English teachers. But it is critical that the teachers themselves are appropriately supported, and have adequate resources, to enable them to take forward work on knowledge about language in the way they wish to.[10] Seeking to increase the level of support along such lines can only be beneficial.

6 Conclusion

In discussions I have had with teachers of my own age and younger (that is, under 40), one theme that has arisen on a number of occasions concerns the extent to which they themselves were taught about language, as school students and as undergraduates, with many current teachers feeling that they lack sufficient knowledge about language; anxiety associated with aspects of knowledge about language is sometimes experienced by teachers and pupils alike. Such an anxiety needs to be acknowledged; but we also need to move on, having recognized this as a problem, to establishing a set of workable solutions. It is important further to recognize that the situation in Scotland is by no means unique to that country; it is a more general problem, certainly in the United Kingdom as a whole. As Hudson and Walmsley (2005) observe, documentation from the Qualifications and Curriculum Authority (QCA) in England and Wales in 1998 reported that many younger teachers lacked explicit training in grammar as part of their own education.

Simply lamenting the current situation is not acceptable. It seems to me that this is where the establishment of links between schools and English Language or Linguistics departments becomes paramount (as discussed elsewhere in this chapter, and in Trousdale, forthcoming), but this will require a frank and open discussion of what exactly knowledge about language means, and in particular, what the teaching of grammar might mean. Various stakeholders have an interest in and/or responsibility for establishing what knowledge about English as a language a graduating high school student should have: employers, teachers, university academics, parents and students themselves. But what constitutes that knowledge is clearly a matter of debate. For some, what students should know about language is how to spell according to the conventions of the standard language, and how to form sentences which accord with the grammatical conventions of the standard written language; for others, this forms only part of knowledge about language,

---

10. In Scotland, many materials are available from a range of different sources, for example the Learning and Teaching Scotland website (www.ltscotland.org.uk) and the Language into Languages Teaching project (www.arts.gla.ac.uk/SESLL/EngLang/LILT/frameset.htm).

and an exploration of wider linguistic issues (including a questioning of the ideology associated with standard languages) is also relevant.

References

Andrews, R., Beverton, S., Locke, T., Low, G., Robinson, A., Torgerson, C., & Zhu, D. (2004). *The effect of grammar teaching (syntax) in English on 5 to 16 year olds' accuracy and quality in written composition.* London: Evidence for Policy and Practice Information.

Barton, G., & Hudson, R. (2004, 20 February). Standard English. *Times Educational Supplement, 5.*

Corbett, J. (2002). The language components of the "Higher Still" examinations in English: Confessions of an item-writer for a token exam. In J. Kirk & D. Ó Baoill (Eds.), *Language planning and education: Linguistic issues in Northern Ireland, the Republic of Ireland, and Scotland* (pp. 203–211). Belfast: Cló Ollscoll na Banríona.

Department for Education and Employment. (1998). *The National Literacy Strategy: The framework.* London: Department for Education and Employment.

Department for Education and Employment. (2000). *The National Literacy Strategy: Grammar for writing.* London: Department for Education and Employment.

Donovan, A., & Niven, L. (2003). The Scots language in education. In T. Bryce & W. Humes (Eds.), *Scottish education* (2nd ed., pp. 262–271). Edinburgh: Edinburgh University Press.

Ellis, S., & Friel, G. (2003). English language. In T. Bryce & W. Humes (Eds.), *Scottish education* (2nd ed., pp. 380–384). Edinburgh: Edinburgh University Press.

Gordon, E. (2005). Grammar in New Zealand schools: Two case studies. *English Teaching: Practice and Critique, 4*(3), 48–68.

Hudson, R. (2001). Grammar teaching and writing skills: The research evidence. *Syntax in the Schools, 17,* 1–6.

Hudson, R., & Walmsley, J. (2005). The English patient: English grammar and teaching in the twentieth century. *Journal of Linguistics, 41*(3), 593–622.

Learning and Teaching Scotland. (2009). Languages: Introduction. In *A curriculum for excellence. Building the curriculum 1. Languages.* Retrieved 23 June 2009, from www.ltscotland.org.uk/curriculumforexcellence/buildingthecurriculum/guidance/btc1/lan/intro.asp.

McGonigal, J. (2003). English language education. In In T. Bryce & W. Humes (Eds.), *Scottish education* (2nd ed., pp. 518–523). Edinburgh: Edinburgh University Press.

Niven, L. (2002). Nae chiels: Scots language in Scotland. In In J. Kirk & D. Ó Baoill (Eds.), *Language planning and education: Linguistic issues in Northern Ireland, the Republic of Ireland, and Scotland* (pp. 198–202). Belfast: Cló Ollscoll na Banríona.

Philp, A. (2001). English grammar in British schools. In R. Mesthrie (Ed.), *The concise encyclopedia of sociolinguistics* (pp. 723–735). Oxford: Elsevier.

Rickford, J. (1996, 26 December). The Oaklands Ebonics decision: Commendable attack on the problem. *San Jose Mercury News.* Retrieved 12 June 2009, from www.stanford.edu/~rickford/ebonics/SJMN-OpEd.html.

Rickford, J., Sweetland, J., & Rickford, A. (2004). African American English and other vernaculars in education: A topic-coded bibliography. *Journal of English Linguistics, 32*(3), 230–320.

Scottish Government. (2007). *A strategy for Scotland's languages: Draft version for Consultation.* Retrieved 11 January 2008, from www.scotland.gov.uk/Publications/2007/01/24130746/8.

Scottish Office Education Department. (1991). *English language national guidelines 5–14.* Edinburgh: Scottish Office Education Department.

Scottish Office Education Department. (1992). *Effective learning and teaching in Scottish secondary schools: English.* A report by HM Inspectors of Schools. Edinburgh: SOED.

Sebba, M. (2007). *Spelling culture: Political, social and cultural aspects of orthography around the world.* Cambridge: Cambridge University Press.

Trousdale, G. (2006). Knowledge about language in the English classroom in Scotland. *English Teaching: Practice and Critique, 5*(1), 34–43.

Trousdale, G. (Forthcoming). Supporting the teaching of knowledge about language in Scottish schools. In K. Denham & A. Lobeck (Eds.), *Linguistics at school: Language awareness in primary and secondary education.* Cambridge: Cambridge University Press.

Twist, L., Schagen, I., & Hodgson, C. (2007). *Readers and reading: National report for England 2006.* Slough: National Foundation for Educational Research.

Wheeler, R. (2006). "What do we do about student grammar – all those missing -*ed*'s and -*s*'s?" Using comparison and contrast to teach Standard English in dialectally diverse classrooms. *English Teaching: Practice and Critique, 5*(1), 16–33.

Part II

The Effectiveness of Grammar Teaching

The Research Record

Chapter 6

Teaching Sentence-Level Grammar for Writing
The Evidence So Far

Richard Andrews

Introduction

This chapter focuses on the teaching of sentence-level grammar and confines itself to first-language learning in English and to the construction of meaning in words. It takes a particularly close and critical look at the ways in which education policy in England continues to frame and reframe the way in which the teaching of grammar can assist (or not) writing development.

In two previous articles, I have addressed with colleagues the question of whether teaching formal grammar to young learners is an effective or sensible way of proceeding, if the aim is to improve their writing development. The first of these (Andrews et al., 2006) reported a systematic review of research on the effect of grammar teaching on writing development. It was the result of a team-based approach in which 4,691 papers on the topic were identified that had been written between 1900 and 2004, of which 64 were relevant to the particular criteria for that review. Essentially, the results were that formal grammar teaching was not effective in teaching writing development; but that sentence-combining (a more practical, compositional approach that included embedding within as well as combining sentences) looked as though it might be more effective. The review did not look at other kinds of approach to the improvement of writing and the command of sentence structure, but limited itself to these two methods.

The second article was a summary evaluation of knowledge about the teaching of sentence grammar (Andrews, 2005), and was more limited in scope. Although published earlier than the first article, it was written later and built on the systematic review (which had been conducted in 2004). It concluded that there was no evidence for the assumption made by policy-makers and some researchers in the United Kingdom that knowledge about sentence grammar helps pupils write more fluently and accurately.

Neither of the two articles claimed to be comprehensive in its coverage of the efficacy of grammar teaching, nor on the usefulness of knowledge about grammar – though the systematic review on which the first article was based was the most comprehensive undertaken to date on the efficacy of teaching formal grammar in order to improve writing. Both articles were narrow in their focus in that they were concerned with the grammars of and the development of sentence structure in English, not with large units of language like text and its relation to context, nor with other languages. These limitations are important to state at the start of the present chapter, which continues to limit its aperture to sentence structure and the development of writing,[1] and which aims to provide an update, in 2009, on the state of play in the field at that point.[2] It seeks to explore further, rather than return to, the territory already charted in the previous two articles.

Despite an extensive search for recently published research on the topic, there is little new evidence to support the teaching of sentence-level grammar to first-language learners of English as a way of enhancing writing ability. By formal "grammar", I mean specifically descriptions and pedagogic prescriptions about how sentences are constructed. Formal grammar teaching would depend on a metalanguage to account for the ways sentences are constructed; would identify and generate rules to be observed; and would generate a taxonomy. Its key identifying feature would be *abstraction* from actual sentences. Such abstraction would be reified (often distilled, dumbed down) into rules and/or guidance for the construction of sentences in pedagogic grammars, as they appear in textbooks, guides for teachers and/or students, etc.

It appears that the research base for the teaching of formal grammar[3] to first-language learners is diminishing. There has been little recent research on the topic, and when such research has appeared, it concludes that sentence-level teaching is ineffective. Most of the recent research in the field, since 2004, has been in *second*-language learning.[4] The stimulus to look again at grammar

1. The present chapter uses the term "grammar" to describe descriptions of language structure, and limits its focus (while acknowledging the connections with text and context) to sentence grammar or syntax. It does not use the term grammar metaphorically, as in Rex, West Brown, Haniford and Schiller's (2005) "expanded notion of grammar" which "more broadly recognizes language as an instrument in the negotiation between the self and social worlds" (p. 115). In particular, the notion of "a 'grammar' of pre-service teaching" seems too broad to be useful in the present debate; as does the notion of people creating "their own 'grammars' to operate successfully in the world" (p. 114).
2. In the present review, covering literature from 2005 to May 2009, the following sources have been used: the onlinebooks.library.upenn.edu resource at the University of Pennsylvania; the Australian Education Index; the British Education Index; the British Humanities Index for both the humanities and social sciences; ERIC; Linguistics Abstracts Online; Linguistics and Language Behavior Abstracts; the MLA Bibliography; PsycInfo; SSCI on the Web of Knowledge; and Sociological Abstracts. In addition, the following e-journals have been checked: *English Language: Practice and Critique, Language, Language Acquisition, Language and Cognitive Processes, Language and Education, Language and Literacy News, Language and Literature, Language and Communication, Language Culture and Curriculum, Language in Society, Language Learning, Language Learning and Technology, Language and Literacy.*
3. By "formal grammar", I mean versions of teaching grammars which focus on form rather than function. These range from descriptions of parts of speech and how they link in a sentence at one end of the spectrum, to teaching of formal systems of sentence generation, like generative transformational grammars, at the other.
4. A good example is Macaro and Masterman (2006). This paper, as its abstract sets out,

    investigates the effect of explicit grammar instruction on grammatical knowledge and writing proficiency in first-year students of French at a UK university. Previous research suggests that explicit grammar instruction results in gains in explicit knowledge and its application in specific grammar-related tasks, but there is less evidence that it results in gains in production tasks. A cohort of 12 students received a course in French grammar immediately prior to

teaching in modern foreign-language learning has come also from England's Key Stage (KS) 3 framework for teaching modern foreign languages.[5] There is gradual convergence of interests between English as "mother-tongue" teaching, ESL/EAL/ESOL and modern foreign-language teaching, not only around grammar and how it should be taught (if at all), but also in other aspects of language learning. Such convergence, if it happens, may lead to a reappraisal of the usefulness and applicability of knowledge about grammar in the teaching of writing.

The exception to the general picture is two intensely focused editions of *English Teaching: Practice and Critique*, edited by Locke (2005, 2006a). In completing the present brief survey and update on research on the topic of grammar teaching, I will focus on those articles in the two issues of the journal which address the relationship between grammar teaching (whether conceived as systemic, systemic functional, generative, "part of speech"-based, context-based or any combination of these; or in any other way) and the improvement of writing skills. In doing so, I accept that my own aperture is a narrow one, in its focus on sentence-level grammar's use in writing development.

Clark (2005) usefully sets the debate about grammar teaching within a context in which politics shapes educational policy more than any notion of a coherent, academic approach. She uses Bernstein's theory of pedagogic discourse (1990) to shed light on the successive curriculum and assessment framings of English and, more specifically, grammar teaching. Myhill (2005a) notes a relative dearth of research on knowledge about grammar for writing – in relation to a wealth of research on reading.

In a critique of the EPPI report[6] on the teaching of syntax to improve writing (Andrews et al. 2004a), Myhill does not take account of the limitations that were

---

their university studies in order to determine whether a short but intensive burst of explicit instruction, a pedagogical approach hitherto unexamined in the literature, was sufficiently powerful to bring about an improvement in their grammatical knowledge and performance in production tasks. Participants were tested at three points over five months, and the results were compared with a group which did not receive the intervention. Our results support previous findings that explicit instruction leads to gains in some aspects of grammar tests but not gains in accuracy in either translation or free composition. (sourced at http://ltr.sagepub.com/cgi/content/abstract/10/3/297)

5. See, for example, Rendall (2006). Rendall, like many modern foreign-language practitioners, suggests that awareness of the structures and patterns of the first language have to be developed before they can be applied to second-language learning. This move from implicit understanding to explicit understanding is part of that development of awareness. She records the fact that many modern foreign-language teachers bewail the fact that they have to do two jobs: teach children first about their own language structures; then teach them the modern foreign language. Despite the fact that Rendall feels that the literacy strategies have provided a common basis for learning more about one's first language, the interesting scenario that could develop – and that perhaps has already been the case for some years – is that knowledge about the structures and procedures of the first language might *only* be gained in the process of learning a second or third language.

6. One of the two technical reports that served as the basis for the 2006 *British Educational Research Journal* article. The other was Andrews et al. (2004b), on sentence-combining.

explicitly acknowledged in the systematic review: that the connection between teaching formal grammar and the development of writing was not theorized; that the report explored instead the assumptions informing practice in policy circles; that pedagogic confidence of the teacher was not addressed because the research that we examined did not address it; and that our attention was on experimental trials because our research question was about effectiveness. What the EPPI reports (there were two, including one on sentence-combining that is not mentioned in the critique) wanted to achieve and did achieve, I would argue, was a ground-clearing exercise in the field. The ground that has been cleared is principally an assumption that the teaching of formal grammar is efficacious in the teaching of writing.

I would entirely agree with Myhill that the connection between grammar taught in context and the accuracy and quality of writing is under-researched; as is the significance of teacher knowledge about grammar and its application (tacitly or explicitly) in the classroom. Myhill's three principles of research into the connection between knowledge about grammar and writing development – that writing should be seen as a communicative act; that linguistic resources are to be seen as meaning-making resources; and that of connectivity – are all good ones. So too are the possibilities for future research, building on Hayes and Flower's (1980) content, formal and audience schemata and on the need to know more about what teachers know and need to know in order to be excellent teachers of writing.

My feeling is that there is still not an understanding at policy level in the United Kingdom that knowledge about grammar at sentence level might best be positioned as a requirement for teachers' academic and professional knowledge, not as something to *teach* to young people. In other words, teachers need to know about grammar in order to deploy their knowledge *as they see fit* in the service of the teaching and learning of more accurate and better-quality writing. This is a different position from that enshrined in *Grammar for Writing* (DfEE 2000), which assumed that *pupils* needed to know about language in order to write well.[7]

There was one further article that I could find, published in the period since the EPPI review and beyond those papers published in *English Teaching: Practice and Critique*. Wyse (2006) looks at how pupils' word choices within sentence construction are influenced and finds five features that seem to influence word choice: topic knowledge, interaction with others (teachers, family and peers), tone, text features and audience awareness. He concludes that these text-level influences are stronger than sentence-level approaches, and that more individualized support for young writers is needed to provide contextualized learning. This is an interesting conclusion, because it suggests that text- and word-level

7. I also agree with Myhill's criticism that the systematic review of sentence combining (Andrews et al., 2004b) drew largely – though not exclusively – on research and practice in the 1960s and 1970s. That does not disqualify it – indeed, there has been a revival of interest in sentence-combining in the United States in the last 10 years. Again, the aim of sentence-combining was/is limited and technical: it is a practical way of embedding clauses within sentences and of combining sentences. But nowhere has the English Review Group claimed that it is the panacea, nor the only way, to develop young learners' command of sentence structure in English.

choices are closely connected, but that syntax considerations are not such a strong part of the influence on word-choice when composing. However, Wyse also admits his empirical study is based on a small sample (eight children) and that further research is necessary to begin to build a new foundation for work in this field.

Activity: Exploring the Teaching of Sentence Grammar

Draw up a two-column table. In the left-hand column, list what you know about sentence grammar. The list need not be systematic in its first draft, but you may wish to reorder the various elements when you see what your first draft reveals.

In the right-hand column, list which of these elements you think you would teach to your students, and under what circumstances. How would you go about this teaching? In whole-class or small-group teaching, or via 1:1 tutoring?

Once you have completed the two columns, extend the exercise by listing what you do not know about sentence grammar and what you would like to know.

Repeat the exercise in the right-hand column regarding what you would do about your students.

The Politics of Grammar Teaching in England

In Andrews (2005), I critiqued the papers that had come from the thinking about grammar teaching at the level of policy development in the late 1990s: from England's Qualifications and Curriculum Authority (QCA, 1998, 1999) and its Department for Education and Employment (DfEE, 2000). The critique was aimed at an eclectic approach that was suggesting that knowledge about language, and specifically knowledge about grammar, would help young writers to gain command of the written language. The approach may have contributed to an increase in performance in *reading* in the first years of the 21st century, but the impact on *writing* development seems less assured in the light of research studies alluded to in this chapter.

The standard of pupils' writing has, however, been rising in the last few years in some respects. The performance of pupils moving from KS1 (ages 5–7) to KS2 (ages 7–11) between 2001/2 and 2005/6 improved during that period, across the transition. Furthermore, the trend has been consistently upward in writing performance at KS2 since 1997, from 53% of pupils achieving level 4+ (the government's median target) in 1997 to 67% in 2006 (an advance of 4% on 2005 results). Since 2003, writing performance at level 5 has improved significantly (those attaining a level 5 in writing rising from 65% to 75% between 2003 and 2006) whereas reading scores remain between 65% and 70%, without significant improvement. Writing performance continues to improve from KS2 to KS3 (ages 11–14), and from KS3 to the General Certificate of Secondary Education (GCSE) (ages 14–16), with a significantly better conversion from KS2 to KS4 than from KS3 to KS4. While there has been improvement, it is probably more to do with an overall strategy and with upward trends in performance (for example, teachers teaching to the test), rather than with a specific focus on knowledge about language (see Andrews, 2008); and it has to be admitted that the improvement is not sufficiently fast, especially in relation to reading development.[8] Although the figures offered above look positive, on the whole, one has to remember that the seemingly upward performance is based on the government setting its own targets and then claiming that those targets have been met. There is no *independent* verification of such an improvement.

The difference between reading performance and writing performance is marked, however, particularly at KS2. Between 1997 and 2007, writing performance lagged an average 20 percentage points behind reading for 10–11-year-olds in England. At KS2, the gap was 14 points in 1997, reached its widest at 28 points in 2000, narrowed to 16 points in 2006 and widened again to 20 points in 2008. Only two-thirds of KS2 pupils attained level 4+ in writing in 2006, whereas since 2000, 80% or more pupils per annum have attained level 4+ in reading. The gap in performance is wider for boys than for girls. Not enough pupils gain level 4+ in writing at KS2, or advance sufficiently at KS3 (despite considerable improvements at this stage) to push beyond 60% the number of pupils gaining a C (the standard expected for those entering the post-compulsory school world) or above at GCSE. As the Office for Standards in Education (Ofsted) puts it "many schools are finding difficulty in raising standards in writing" (2006, p. 55). On the basis of 2007 and 2008 results, this statement applies particularly to primary/elementary schools.

The Primary National Strategy (DCSF, 2007) is a major curriculum programme within England, building on the National Literacy Strategy that was initiated by the Blair government in 1998 and which gave rise to the results discussed above. This new strategy is an attempt to take forward gains made within the National Literacy Strategy and to raise standards yet further.

Within the Primary National Strategy is a new framework for literacy[9] in which communication, language and literacy are integrated and used as the basis for the specific identification of 12 strands. These strands are intended to make clear the elements of literacy, and to enable the charting of progression within each strand. The strands attempt to cover the literacy objectives in the primary curriculum. Strand 11 is devoted to sentence structure and punctuation. The weakness in the conception is that although there is sharper definition of the characteristics and developmental direction of each strand, the relationships between the strands (for example, between creating and shaping texts; text structure and organization; sentence structure; and punctuation) are not fully articulated.

The progression identified for movement between the years of primary school – for which I will focus on the age group 7–11 for the purposes of this chapter – is spelt out for each year. Although these are not "end-of-year" objectives, the expectation at age 7/8 is that writers will:

---

8. We cannot be sure that the quality of data is high or reliable across the 5–16 age range. However, what we can say is that it is better than it was 10 years ago, when the previous decade of data was not based on a single set of comparable annual test scores.

9. See www.standards.dfes.gov.uk/primaryframeworks/foundation/cll.

- show relationships of time, reason and cause through subordination and connectives;
- compose sentences using adjectives, verbs and nouns for precision, clarity and impact; and
- clarify meaning through the use of exclamation marks and speech marks.

In Year 4 (ages 8/9) writers will:

- clarify meaning and point of view by using varied sentence structure (phrases, clauses and adverbials);
- use commas to mark clauses, and use the apostrophe for possession.

In Year 5 (ages 9/10), they will:

- adapt sentence construction to different text-types, purposes and readers;
- punctuate sentences accurately, including using speech marks and apostrophes;

and in Year 6, the last year of primary schooling in England (ages 10/11), writers will:

- express subtle distinctions of meaning, including hypothesis, speculation and supposition, by constructing sentences in varied ways;
- use punctuation to clarify meaning in complex sentences.

Interestingly, for the first time, there is provision and guidance for the transition from primary to secondary schooling. Across this transition, pupils will be expected to:

- extend their use and control of complex sentences by deploying subordinate clauses effectively;
- use punctuation to convey and clarify meaning and to integrate directly quoted speech into longer sentences; and
- use Standard English confidently and consistently in formal writing, with awareness of the differences between spoken and written language structures.

Such progression is interestingly structured. First we have the grammatical requirements for the construction of sentences, couched in terms of function, technical awareness of the parts of speech, and syntactic terminology (this may be for the teacher's awareness only, to be deployed as he/she sees fit). Second, in each cluster of objectives, we have punctuation marks as a requirement. These are not assumed to derive from an understanding and use of accurate and elegant sentence structure, but appear to stand by themselves as markers to be used. The emphasis on punctuation as a separate requirement appears to be reinforcing the surface markers of language without full integration into the functions and forms of sentence structure.

At around the same time, the QCA (2007) in England consulted on the future of the secondary (that is, for age group 11–16) curriculum.

As part of the program of study for *reading* at Key Stage 3 and Key Stage 4, students should be able to "understand how meaning is constructed within sentences and across texts as a whole". The gloss on this requirement was quite technical and specific:

> This could include recognising the effect of different connectives, identifying how phrases and clauses build relevant detail and information, understanding how modal or qualifying words or phrases build shades of meaning, and how the use of adverbials, prepositional phrases and non-finite clauses give clarity and emphasis to meaning.

Furthermore (and still with reading), under a requirement to understand and comment on how texts are crafted, pupils would learn that sentences can be varied in length and focus to affect meaning; that impersonal constructions might be used; and that dialogue, action and description might be interwoven for effect. And as part of a requirement to understand and comment on how writers' use of language and rhetorical, grammatical and literary features influences the reader, there would need to be coverage of the active and passive voice, and the use of abstract and concrete nouns. At Key Stage 4, in addition, the craft of texts would include "shifts in pace or tense, choice of personal pronoun, use of modal verbs (for example, *can, could, must, would, shall, may*), use of rhetorical and literary techniques".

As far as *writing* is concerned at the key stages in secondary/high school, the elements of language that pertain to syntax included, at Key Stage 3, the variation of sentence structure,

> using a range of sentence features to clarify or emphasize meaning (for example, adverbials such as *Reluctantly, he* or *Five days later, it*, or complex noun or prepositional phrases), varying word order and using a range of connectives to clarify the relationship between ideas, *although, on the other hand*.

At Key Stage 4, further features included the use of repetition, antithesis, comparison, figures of speech, deliberate use of cliché, balanced structures and the "full use of punctuation marks" which includes "full stops, commas, apostrophes, exclamation and question marks, brackets for parentheses, colons, semicolons, inverted commas, commas to mark clauses and clarify meaning, and the full punctuation of speech".

Although the detail was considerable, and was replicated at different levels[10] of language description and production, there was no connection between the various levels; no recognition that, for example, decisions on structure and

---

10. By "level" here I mean levels of language description, for example, phoneme, morpheme, word, phrase, clause, sentence, paragraph, text. Whenever the meaning "*assessment level*" is intended, I make the distinction clear.

meaning at textual level, in relation to a particular audience, might affect the choice of sentence structure and vocabulary. Furthermore, there was no connection made between learning to write and learning to read, thus missing the opportunity to draw on the reciprocal nature of writing and reading – and perhaps missing a major chance to help teachers and learners build on that connection. In other words, this was a highly prescribed and proscribed set of programmes of study (curriculum) at its various levels, but there was little connection between them, nor between writing and reading.

There is clearly no let up in practices (curricula, textbooks, websites, teachers' approaches) that apply grammatical parts of speech and rules of sentence structure to teach writing, despite the fact there is no research evidence to support such practices; and there is a continued belief in the naming of parts, or knowledge about grammar, as part of this process. It appears that curriculum designers and textbook writers are hooked into the notion that formal grammar teaching is valuable and effective in the improvement of writing, even though there is no evidence to support their claims.

Activity: Researching Approaches to Teaching Sentence Grammar

Collect together the books, worksheets, online and other material on sentence grammar that you can find. Make them available to colleagues, then meet to decide:

1. what are the underlying language principles that inform the way the material is presented?
2. what are the underlying or explicit pedagogic principles that inform how the material might be used?
3. what lessons can you learn about such material?

Then work out your own philosophy of sentence grammar teaching, and devise some practical ways of implementing that philosophy in the classroom.

In the next section, I take a critical look at the continuing attraction of such "naming of parts".

Review of a Particular Approach

In the wake of key earlier books on the place of grammar in teaching, like Perera (1984) and Hudson (1992), Cameron's (2007) *The Teacher's Guide to Grammar* has recently appeared. It is described by the publishers as:

> unique in focusing directly on the aspects of grammar that teachers need to know. Assuming little or no formal linguistic education, this concise and accessible book provides the necessary background knowledge required in the classroom context. There are detailed chapters on the nuts and bolts of language: words, morphology, sentences, phrases, verbs, and clauses. Other

important educational issues concerned in the teaching of English are discussed: the grammatical variation that differentiates standard and non-standard English; how grammar varies in relation to the purpose and audience of a text; and the different grammatical characteristics of different languages. Throughout, illustrations are given using examples from the real spoken and written language produced by learners. Here are the essentials every English and literacy teacher needs to know about grammar in one practical and relevant guide.

The focus on what teachers need to know is welcome. Few would dispute that a teacher of first-language English needs to know about the various aspects of language listed above. An intuitive teacher of writing and reading may be a wonderful teacher, but he/she will be better still with a knowledge (preferably a working knowledge) of the language he/she is teaching. In the craft of being an expert teacher of writing, knowing the possibilities that are afforded by a comprehensive knowledge of how language works and the terms used to denote it must be an advantage. In other words, I am not arguing in this chapter that teachers should not *know about* language as well as teach the craft of writing – and preferably practise the craft themselves.

But the subtle shift to features of language needing to be *taught* is evident in the publisher's (not necessarily the author's) clause above: "other important educational issues concerned in *the teaching of English* are discussed" [my italics]. Van Gelderen's (2005 and this volume) distinction between explicit and implicit knowledge about language/grammar is useful here, and I share his position that the drive towards explicitness is not supported by research. In the light of the research reviews and subsequent published research, it is my contention that these language features do not need to be *taught* as part of a systematic program; rather, the teacher needs to know them so that he/she can deploy that knowledge as and when appropriate in the teaching of writing. Such deployment may not be overt (as in a naming of parts). It might be grounded in the actual examples and practice of writing that is going on in- and outside the classroom. The guidance from the teacher may be direct, abstract and overt, or indirect and conveyed via analogy or example. In practice, what the learner needs to develop is command of the *craft* of writing, not the machinery of its constituent parts.

Cameron herself (2007, pp. 10ff.) reviews the debate about whether grammar should be taught to pupils, citing Perera (1984) and Andrews and colleagues (2004a) as examples of research that finds that formal grammar teaching is not effective in helping pupils to write more accurately or with better quality. She also mentions work that has come to the opposite conclusion: "that grammatical instruction *can* enhance writing skills" (p. 10), citing three sources for such a claim. Let us look at each of these in turn.

The first two are cited as coming from the newsletter of the National Association for the Teaching of English, though only Hudson (2005) appears there in an article called "Grammar for Writing". In the article, he expresses "belief" that grammar teaching can improve writing skills, and explains why. First, there is a suggestion that the systematic review (it is not clear which one) "misses the point of grammar teaching in the government's 'English strategy'" (it is not clear what the point is), but there is also an acceptance that "the grammar teaching in the research didn't work" (it is not clear what research). Second, Hudson cites a study in which a term's study of word morphology gave a class of 11-year-olds "significantly better spelling than a control group" – but the topic in question is sentence grammar, not spelling. Third, the article claims that the systematic review mis-classified sentence-combining as not grammar teaching – which is not the case. We distinguished between formal grammar teaching and sentence-combining as just two types of grammar teaching. In a defence of "Grammar for Writing", Hudson suggests that every point of grammar is "linked as soon as it is taught to a writing activity which is designed to exploit it"; that grammar is taught systematically rather than "as needed"; and that grammar teaching has the positive aim of "language expansion rather than the negative one of eliminating 'errors'" (2005, p. 2). None of these "key innovative features" has a research-based warrant to underpin its claims.

The second source is more substantial. Myhill (2005b) is a paper for a QCA conference/seminar. It finds the EPPI reviews on grammar teaching disappointing because they do not engage with exactly *how* the grammar was taught or with the pedagogical confidence of the teacher. Our reason for these omissions is that none of the papers we studied in the reviews described these particular aspects. The objection, I think, is a useful one, and identifies a perceived gap in the research literature which *does* need to be filled. I agree that it would be interesting and valuable to explore what aspects of grammar and knowledge about language are most relevant to writing development; that contextualized grammar teaching might be one aspect of the way forward; and that the distinction between explicit and implicit grammatical knowledge might prove to be a useful one, if we can also distinguish between what teachers and learners need to know.

The third source is referenced, also incorrectly, as Wyse (2004); it should be Wyse (2001). In fact, Wyse does *not* support the claim that grammatical instruction can enhance writing skills; on the contrary, his abstract reads:

> Governmental concerns about primary children's performance in writing in the Standard Assessment Tasks (SATs) have resulted in the "Grammar for writing" Initiative. This resource and the associated in-service training is intended to raise standards in the teaching of writing. The article reviews SATs reports, inspection reports and research evidence in order to address the question: to what extent can this development be justified by empirical evidence on the teaching of grammar? *It is concluded that the initiative is not supported by research evidence* and that changes will need to be made to English curriculum policy and pedagogy if children's writing is to further improve. (p. 411; my italics)

It would seem, then, that Cameron's broad counter-claim – that grammatical instruction *can* enhance writing skills – is based, respectively, on research that provides evidence that does not withstand scrutiny; on the perception of a gap in knowledge; and on a mis-citation and mis-reading.

The next point made by Cameron is that

> the EPPI-Centre [report, i.e. Andrews et al., 2004a] did not consider whether
> the teachers in the studies they reviewed related grammar to writing. If they
> did not, that in itself might explain why pupils did not make the connection.
> (2007, p. 11)

It is not true that the English Review Group did not take into account whether
teachers in the studies related grammar to writing. In all of the studies we looked
at in depth, the very nature of the teaching was to improve writing through
formal grammar teaching. We can only assume that pupils did not make the
connection between formal grammar on the one hand, and writing accuracy and
quality on the other, because the gap between the two is too wide – not because
teachers did not try to provide such a bridge for the pupils.[11]

Finally, Cameron simplifies the debate in order to make a rhetorical point.
She suggests that

> The whole debate which the EPPI-Centre review is part of focuses on a
> single question: whether grammar teaching makes children better writers.
> Improving writing is by implication the only purpose teaching grammar in
> the classroom could possibly serve: if the evidence suggests that it does not
> serve that purpose, it is axiomatically a waste of time. (2007, p. 11)

Interestingly, media coverage of the publication of the EPPI-Centre report
(Andrews et al., 2004a) used the same phrase – "a waste of time" – to refer to the
teaching of formal grammar in the curriculum. This was not a phrase or notion
used in the report itself, its summaries nor indeed in the press release. It is worth
repeating the actual summary position from the full technical report:

> The evidence base to justify the teaching of syntax in order to improve the
> quality and accuracy of writing, whether traditional or transformational/
> generative, is very small. This is not to say that the teaching of such gram-
> mar may not be of value in itself; or that it might lead to enhanced know-
> ledge and awareness of how language works, and of systems of language use.
> But the clear implication, based on the small number of studies providing
> high quality research evidence, is that the teaching of syntax in English to
> 5–16 year olds in order to improve writing should cease to be part of the
> curriculum ... (p. 49).

The report does not imply that the teaching of grammar is a waste of time, nor
that the improvement of writing is the only learning outcome that such teaching
may, or may not, serve. On the contrary, the discipline of the systematic review

11. It may be the case that different kinds of grammar require different pedagogical "bridges" to
make them accessible, and useful, to emergent writers; and that such bridges *could* be built
between formal grammars and effective pedagogical approaches to the improvement of writing.

requires caution in the conclusions and implications. The writers of the report would agree with Cameron that there may be other uses for the teaching of formal grammar in the curriculum.

Indeed, Cameron is right to warn us that the national curriculum "is not a seamless and monolithic document" (2007, p. 13) – I would go further and say that neither it, nor the strategies documents, are based on a systematic look at the research evidence, nor on an intellectually coherent theory of writing development (see Beard, Myhill, Nystrand & Riley, 2009; Smith & Andrews, 2009) – and that such latitude "leaves scope for teachers to develop their own agendas, and to translate those into imaginative teaching" (p. 13). Here, in the space we would wish teachers to have to make their own judgements about what and when to teach, is where we agree. Cameron's book is a well-written and useful guide for teachers, taking a descriptive and imaginative approach to aspects of grammar; its emphasis is on teachers using their knowledge of language and their professional judgement to intervene in the development of young people's writing in a helpful and timely way.

There is, however, more work for the government in fashioning a coherent approach to the writing curriculum: one which does not assume the justification of the teaching of sentence grammar in isolation as leading magically to enhanced writing ability, but which links such teaching more closely to other levels of language description and production, and to the teaching of the craft of writing.

The Way Forward

I accepted earlier that the focus of the current chapter was relatively narrow: on the teaching of sentence-level grammar's use in the development of writing skills. Before looking forward to further research, policy and practice in the field, I want to widen the aperture to take in approaches to grammar that go beyond sentence structure. There is no sense of a claim here that the grammar of sentence structure is the true and only focus, and that other grammars are somehow only metaphorically related to such an *ur*-grammar. Far from it. But how do the various grammars sit in relation to each other? And, once that relationship is established (and various didactic and pedagogical selections and transformations have taken place in relation to the model), how can teachers best help emerging writers to develop the range, accuracy and quality of their writing?

The creation of such a model, and explication of its didactic, pedagogic and teacher-education implications, is the challenge facing us. The beginnings of such a model, with consideration of the teaching material that would be associated with each level of language description, appeared in Andrews (2001, p. 10; see also Locke, 2006b). That provisional model moved (from the top down) from context to text to sub-units of text (like paragraphs, stanzas) to the sentence, to sub-units of the sentence (phrases, clauses), to the word level, and thence down through morphology to the phonological and grapho-phonemic levels. It is not a new model; and yet, at the same time, it does not align itself with either a systemic functional grammar approach nor with syntactics-based grammar or transformational grammar. Essentially, it could be termed the beginnings of a *pedagogic* grammar for use in the teaching of written English as a first and/or second language. A similar model underpinned the thinking of the literacy hour and the early versions of the National Literacy Strategy. However, what has been lost sight of in the last few years has been:

- a sense that the top-down and bottom-up models of language learning are reciprocal, and that learners need to move in both directions as they make sense of the integration of the various levels of language;
- the fact that teaching rules and systems of sentence description in isolation from the other levels of language description is counter-productive;
- the need to make the learning of sentence structure part of the functional aspect of writing; in other words, to make meaning and communication the drivers of motivation for getting sentence structure right;
- productive connection between the two different grammars of speech and writing;
- acknowledgement of, and more focused use of the reciprocal connection between reading and writing in the teaching of both;
- a clearer sense of what teachers need to know about sentence structure and levels of language description in order to help their students become better writers;
- a sense that meta-languages and taxonomies of sentence structure are of limited use for learners;
- any sense of the pedagogy of when and how best to intervene with learners, as a teacher, in the process of learning to write.

The development of teachers themselves as writers – not just of "essays" they might have written at university, but of a much wider range of texts – will be central to the next phase of development in this field, so that the rhetorical choices they make in the act of writing/composing can be understood from the inside. With such a core knowledge of the craft of writing, they will be that much better prepared to select what aspects of the meta-knowledge of writing process and description might be useful for their students, and at what point.

As a practical guide to how best to position oneself as a prospective teacher, teacher or teacher educator in relation to the question of sentence-level grammar learning by students, I would suggest the following as starting points:

- read widely, not only in the field of grammars of the language, but also in reflecting on literature in English and other languages: what can you learn that will help you in advising and guiding students in their own writing?
- transform your knowledge so that it can be accessible to young writers at the moment they need it, in a form that they can understand and apply;
- check your developing knowledge against government requirements and guides on teaching grammar, and ask yourself what angle *you* should take as a teacher;

- write yourself, in a range of genres, to get at the process of selection and structuring from the inside;
- share the problems of writing, and how you have overcome them, with your students.

Acknowledgements

I am grateful to Deborah Cameron, Terry Locke and Debra Myhill for comments on an earlier draft of this chapter, and for their generosity in allowing this critique. Its shortcomings, however, are entirely my own.

References

Works Cited

Andrews, R. (2001). *Teaching and learning English: A guide to recent research and its implications.* London: Continuum.

Andrews, R. (2005). Knowledge about the teaching of [sentence] grammar: The state of play. *English Teaching: Practice and Critique, 4*(3), 69–76.

Andrews, R. (2008). Ten years of strategies. *Changing English, 15*(1), 77–85.

Andrews, R., Torgerson, C., Beverton, S., Freeman, A., Locke, T., Low, G., et al. (2006). The effect of grammar teaching on writing development. *British Educational Research Journal, 32*(1), 39–55.

Andrews, R., Torgerson, C., Beverton, S., Locke, T., Low, G., Robinson, A., & Zhu, D. (2004a). *The effect of grammar teaching (syntax) in English on 5 to 16 year olds' accuracy and quality in written composition.* London: EPPI-Centre, Social Science Research Unit, Institute of Education. Retrieved from http://eppi.ioe.ac.uk/reel.

Andrews, R., Torgerson, C., Beverton, S., Locke, T., Low, G., Robinson, A., & Zhu, D. (2004b). *The effect of grammar teaching (sentence-combining) in English on 5 to 16 year olds' accuracy and quality in written composition.* London: EPPI-Centre, Social Science Research Unit, Institute of Education. Retrieved from http://eppi.ioe.ac.uk/reel.

Beard, R., Myhill, D., Nystrand, M., & Riley, J. (Eds.). (2009). *The handbook of writing development.* London: Sage.

Bernstein, B. (1990). *The structuring of pedagogic discourse: Class, codes and control* (Vol. 4). London: Routledge.

Cameron, D. (2007). *The teacher's guide to grammar.* Oxford: Oxford University Press.

Clark, U. (2005). Bernstein's theory of pedagogic discourse: Linguistics, educational policy and practice in the UK English/literacy classroom. *English Teaching: Practice and Critique, 4*(3), 32–47.

DCSF (Department for Children, Schools and Families) (2007). *Primary framework for literacy and mathematics.* London: Department for Children, Schools and Families. Retrieved 26 April 2007, from www.standards.dfes.gov.uk/primaryframeworks.

DfEE (Department for Education and Employment). (2000). *The National Literacy Strategy: Grammar for writing.* London: Department for Education and Employment.

Hayes, J., & Flower, L. (1980). Identifying the organization of writing processes. In L. Gregg & E. Steinberg (Eds.), *Cognitive processes in writing* (pp. 3–30). Hillsdale, NJ: Lawrence Erlbaum.

Hudson, R. (1992). *Teaching grammar: A guide for the National Curriculum.* Oxford: Basil Blackwell.

Hudson, R. (2005). Grammar for writing. *NATE News, 34*, 2.

Locke, T. (Ed.). (2005). *English Teaching: Practice and Critique, 4*(3) (December 2005).

Locke, T. (Ed.). (2006a). *English Teaching: Practice and Critique, 5*(1) (May 2006).

Locke, T. (Ed.). (2006b). Editorial: Grammar in the face of diversity. *English Teaching: Practice and Critique, 5*(1), 1–15.

Macaro, E., & Masterman, L. (2006). Does intensive explicit grammar instruction make all the difference? *Language Teaching Research, 10*(3), 297–327.

Myhill, D. (2005a). Ways of knowing: Writing with grammar in mind. *English Teaching: Practice and Critique, 4*(3), 77–96.

Myhill, D. (2005b). *Writing and grammar.* Paper presented at the "Grammar and knowledge about language: its place in teaching English" conference, QCA ENGLISH 21, Nottingham, 13 June 2005.

Ofsted. (2006). *The annual report of Her Majesty's Chief Inspector of Schools.* London: The Stationery Office.

Perera, K. (1984). *Children's writing and reading: Analyzing classroom language.* Oxford: Basil Blackwell.

QCA (Qualifications and Curriculum Authority). (1998). *The grammar papers: Perspectives on the teaching of grammar in the National Curriculum.* London: Qualifications and Curriculum Authority.

QCA. (1999). *Not whether but how: Teaching grammar in English at key stages 3 and 4.* London: Qualifications and Curriculum Authority.

QCA. (2007). *The secondary curriculum review.* Retrieved 19 May 2008, from www.qca.org.uk/secondarycurriculumreview/subject/index.htm.

Rendall, H. (2006). *Patterns and procedures.* London: Centre for Information on Language Teaching and Research.

Rex, L., West Brown, D., Haniford, L., & Schiller, L. (2005). Understanding and exercising one's own grammar. *English Teaching: Practice and Critique, 4*(3), 111–140.

Smith, A., & Andrews, R. (2009). *Toward a comprehensive, contemporary model: Writing development.* Paper given at American Educational Research Association convention, San Diego, 13–17 April 2009.

Van Gelderen, A. (2005). What we know without knowing it: Sense and nonsense in respect of linguistic reflection for students in elementary and secondary education. *English Teaching: Practice and Critique, 5*(1), 44–54.

Wyse, D. (2001). Grammar for writing? A critical review of empirical evidence. *British Journal of Educational Studies, 49*(4), 411–427.

Wyse, D. (2006). Pupils' word choices and the teaching of grammar. *Cambridge Journal of Education, 36*(1), 31–47.

Selection of Works from the EPPI Grammar Review

Asker, W. (1923). Does knowledge of formal grammar function? *School and Society* (27 January), 109–111.

Bateman, D., & Zidonis, F. (1966). *The effect of a study of transformational grammar on the writing of ninth and tenth graders.* Urbana, IL: National Council of Teachers of English.

Bazerman, C. (2005). An essay on pedagogy by Mikhail Bakhtin. *Written Communication, 22*(3), 333–338.

Benfer, M. (1935). *Sentence sense in relation to subject and predicate.* Unpublished Master's thesis, University of Iowa.

Benjamin, A., & Jago, C. (2006). Teacher to teacher: What is your most compelling reason for teaching grammar? *English Journal, 95*(5), 18–21.

Boraas, J. (1917). *Formal grammar and the practical mastery of English*. Unpublished doctoral thesis. University of Minnesota.

Britton, J. (1983). Shaping at the point of utterance. In A. Freedman, I. Pringle, & J. Yalden (Eds.), *Learning to write: First language/second language* (pp. 13–19). London: Longman.

Catherwood, C. (1932). *A study of the relationship between a knowledge of rules and ability to correct grammatical errors and between identification of sentences and knowledge of subject and predicate*. Unpublished Master's thesis, University of Minnesota.

Combs, W. (1976). Further effects of sentence-combining practice on writing ability. *Research in the Teaching of English, 10*, 137–149.

Combs, W. (1977). Sentence-combining practice: Do gains in judgments of writing "quality" persist? *Journal of Educational Research, 70*(6), 318–321.

Cope, B., & Kalantzis, M. (1993). Introduction: How a genre approach to literacy can transform the way writing is taught. In B. Cope & M. Kalantzis (Eds.), *The powers of literacy: A genre approach to teaching writing* (pp. 1–21). Pittsburgh, PA: Falmer Press.

DES (Department of Education and Science). (1975). *A language for life* [The Bullock Report]. London: Her Majesty's Stationery Office.

DES. (1988). *Report of the committee of inquiry into the teaching of English language* [The Kingman Report]. London: Her Majesty's Stationery Office.

Elley, W., Barham, I., Lamb, H., & Wyllie, M. (1975). The role of grammar in a secondary school curriculum. *New Zealand Council for Educational Studies, 10*, 26–41.

Elley, W., Barham, I., Lamb, H., & Wyllie, M. (1979). *The role of grammar in the secondary school curriculum*. Wellington: New Zealand Council for Educational Research.

EPPI-Centre. (2002a). *Core keywording strategy: Data collection for a register of educational research. Version 0.9.7*. London: EPPI-Centre, Social Science Research Unit, Institute of Education.

EPPI-Centre. (2002b). *EPPI-reviewer. Version 2.5.2*. London: EPPI-Centre, Social Science Research Unit, Institute of Education.

EPPI-Centre. (2002c). *Guidelines for extracting data and quality assessing primary studies in educational research. Version 0.9.7*. London: EPPI-Centre, Social Science Research Unit, Institute of Education.

Fellowes, J. (2006). Grammar knowledge and students' writing. *Practically Primary, 11*(3), 40–43.

Feng, S., & Powers, K. (2005). The short- and long-term effect of explicit grammar instruction on fifth graders' writing. *Reading Improvement, 42*(2), 67.

Fogel, H., & Ehri, L. (2000). Teaching elementary students who speak black English vernacular to write in standard English: Effects of dialect transformation practice. *Contemporary Educational Psychology, 25*(2), 212–235.

Hawkins, E. (1987). *Awareness of language: An introduction*. Cambridge: Cambridge University Press.

Hilfman, T. (1970). Can second grade children write more complex sentences? *Elementary English, 47*, 209–214.

Hudson, R., & Walmsley, J. (2005). The English patient: English grammar and teaching in the twentieth century. *Journal of Linguistics, 41*(3), 593–622.

Hunt, K. (1965). *Grammatical structures written at three grade levels*. NCTE Research Report No. 3. Urbana, IL: National Council of Teachers of English.

Hunt, K., & O'Donnell, R. (1970). *An elementary school curriculum to develop better writing skills*. Washington, DC: Office of Education, Bureau of Research.

Kitzhaber, A. (Ed.). (1968). *The Oregon curriculum: A sequential program in English*. New York: Holt, Rinehart and Winston.

Locke, T., & Wilkins, M. (2001). *Grammar for starters*. Auckland: Pearson Education.

Macaulay, W. (1947). The difficulty of grammar. *British Journal of Educational Psychology, 17*, 153–162.

McNeill, J. (1994). Instruction for deaf students in syntactic cohesion. *Acehi Journal/ Revue Aceda, 20*(3), 88–95.

Mellon, J. (1969). *Transformational sentence combining. Research Report No. 10*. Urbana, IL: National Council of Teachers of English.

O'Hare, F. (1973). *Sentence combining: Improving student writing without formal grammar instruction. Research Report No. 15*. Urbana, IL: National Council of Teachers of English.

Purpura, J. (2004). *Assessing grammar*. Cambridge: Cambridge University Press.

Reynolds, R. (2004). *Simply grammar: English grammar for beginners*. Auckland: New House Publishers Ltd.

Rice, J. (1903). Educational research: The results of a test in language and English. *Forum, XXXV*, 209–293, 440–457.

Roberts, C., & Boggase, B. (1992). *Non-intrusive grammar in writing*. Paper presented at the Annual Conference on Computers and Writing, Indianapolis, USA, 1–3 May.

Robinson, N. (1960). The relationship between knowledge of English grammar and ability in English composition. *British Journal of Educational Psychology, 30*, 184–186.

Rousseau, M., & Poulson, C. (1985). *Using sentence-combining to teach the use of adjectives in writing to severely behaviorally disordered students*. Unpublished research report. New York: City University of New York. (ERIC document number ED342153.)

Saddler, B., & Graham, S. (2005). The effects of peer-assisted sentence combining instruction on the writing performance of more and less skilled young writers. *Journal of Educational Psychology, 97*(1), 43–53.

Satterfield, J., & Powers, A. (1996). Write on! Journals open to success. *Perspectives in Education and Deafness, 15*(2), 2–5.

Segal, D., & Barr, N. (1926). Relation and achievement in formal grammar to achievement in applied grammar. *Educational Research, 14*, 401–402.

Sipe, R. (2006). Grammar matters. *English Journal, 95*(5), 15–17.

Stock, R. (1980). *The effect of teaching sentence patterns on the written sentence structures of grade two children*. Unpublished research report, Manitoba, Canada (ERIC document number ED208414).

Stone, A., & Serwatka, T. (1982). Reducing syntactic errors in written responses of a retarded adolescent through oral patterning. *Education and Training in Mental Retardation and Developmental Disabilities, 17*(1), 71–74.

Symonds, P. (1931). Practice vs. grammar in the learning of correct usage. *Journal of Educational Psychology, 22*, 81–96.

Thomas, G., & Pring, R. (Eds.). (2004). *Evidence-based practice in education*. Maidenhead: Open University Press.

Thompson, C., & Middleton, M. (1973). Transformational grammar and inductive teaching as determinants of structurally complex writing. *California Journal of Educational Research, 24*, 28–41.

Thornbury, S. (2005). *Uncovering grammar*. Oxford: Macmillan Education.

Weaver, C., Bush, J., Anderson, J., & Bills, P. (2006). Grammar intertwined throughout the writing process: An "inch wide and a mile deep". *English Teaching: Practice and Critique, 5*(1), 77–101.

Wilkinson, A. (1971). *The foundations of language*. London: Oxford University Press.

Chapter 7

Does Explicit Teaching of Grammar Help Students to Become Better Writers?

Insights from Empirical Research

Amos van Gelderen

Introduction

The teaching of grammar in primary and secondary schools is a controversial issue in countries all over the world. It is not easy to explain why this issue is so controversial, because the debate is rather fuzzy. The main reason for this fuzziness is that the concept of "grammar teaching" is not well defined. Many people refer to grammar as the traditional practice in which students label word classes and parts of speech. This certainly is the most popular meaning of "grammar teaching". From here on, I will refer to this practice as "traditional grammar teaching". On the other hand, there are other meanings of grammar teaching in which the purpose is to stimulate students' linguistic reflection about language, not necessarily based upon a given set of classifications but upon students' own observations of regularities. Still another form of grammar teaching is at stake when students are simply taught about correct language forms in their first or second language. In this case students do not have to learn much explicit meta-language about those forms; they only learn how to pronounce or write the forms correctly. This teaching may therefore aim primarily at the *implicit* learning of grammar, which means that the students are unaware of underlying rules and accompanying linguistic terminology. In addition, there are different sorts of arguments being put forward in support of grammar teaching. Some arguments stress the instrumental function of grammar knowledge. Students should learn grammar in order to master their mother-tongue language[1] or to learn a second or foreign language. Other arguments, however, maintain that grammar teaching is valuable in its own right, for example because grammatical terminology has cultural value or because it helps develop abstract thinking.

This chapter will give a brief overview of the main grammar issues in order to clarify the outlines of the big grammar debate in education. However, it will mainly focus on one of the most controversial issues at stake: the question whether the learning of explicit rules for grammar is beneficial for students' mastery of (written) language. This issue lies at the heart of grammar curricula of schools

---

1. Here and in the rest of this chapter I will refer to mother-tongue language as the dominant language that is taught in schools (L1) and at the same time is the dominant language of instruction. For immigrant students and some minorities, however, this language is not necessarily their native language.

(both traditional and non-traditional) and reveals the assumptions on which they are based. It seems that many teachers and teacher educators have been carried away in ideological discussions, clouding their sight on the most important aspects of grammar teaching: when is grammar teaching beneficial for students and when not? Many are for or against "grammar", leaving little room for a more balanced view in which the teaching of grammar rules and metalinguistic terminology is weighed against less abstract or more implicit forms of grammatical acquisition in the process of producing (or grasping) meaning in texts (see, for example, Long, 1991). If teaching explicit linguistic rules and terminology is not as efficient as we would like, this does not exclude approaches to grammar teaching directed at the implicit learning of structures. Such implicit grammar learning may, for example, be triggered by linguistic reflection in the classroom specifically tuned to the needs and insights of students in their acquisition of forms of (written) language.

It is appropriate to point out that in the context from which I speak, the Netherlands, the status of the grammar debate is not completely comparable to the situation in Anglophone countries such as England (see Hudson & Wamsley, 2005; Clark, 2005) and the United States (see Kolln & Hancock, 2005). From these commentaries, an image arises of a general neglect of grammar practice in primary and secondary schools over the last three decades. This neglect seems to be legitimized by a negative attitude towards "grammar", not only in teaching and teacher-education circles, but also among policy-makers and the general public. An important factor is the utilitarian ideology that supports this attitude: there are more important things to do than learn abstract linguistic rules with an, at best, uncertain contribution to the mastery of (written) language.

In the Netherlands, however, such a general negative attitude towards "grammar" has never gained the upper hand. Though there exists a critical attitude among teacher educators and theoreticians of mother-tongue pedagogy (supported by official policy) towards traditional grammar, in *practice* the traditional grammar curriculum in the Netherlands is still alive and kicking. Many teachers, publishers of textbooks *and* parents are still supporting it. Official core objectives for Dutch in elementary education define a very limited set of traditional concepts to be taught, but regular textbooks still devote much attention to the learning of traditional grammatical terminology. Labelling word classes and parts of speech, morphological knowledge, idiom, sentence structure and conjugation were the most prominent grammatical objectives in these textbooks in an analysis of Jacobs and Van Gelderen (1997).

The same contradictory situation is observed in secondary education. According to Van Gelderen, Couzijn and Hendrix (2000), the teaching of traditional grammar in the first years of secondary education (Grades 7–9) is much more extensive than required by the official core objectives. Many concepts regarding sentence analysis and the labelling of word classes are being taught here, even though they are not included in the core objectives (Hoogeveen & Bonset, 1998). Many schools use special textbooks for traditional grammar or develop their own syllabus. According to the Dutch Inspectorate (Inspection, 1999) the time spent on grammar in secondary schools is much more than expected on the basis of the official curriculum.

Recently, however, policy has taken a new turn in the Dutch mother-tongue curriculum. In reaction to public criticism concerning poor writing skills of students in secondary and higher education, a review committee had to make proposals for the Ministry of Education for a "continuous" curriculum from elementary till the end of secondary education with a strong focus on grammar and spelling (Expertgroep Doorlopende Leerlijnen, 2008). Although the committee did its best to also include other parts of mother-tongue learning (such as reading, writing and oral skills) in the proposal, the typical policy-maker's reflex of "back to basics" is well demonstrated: when poor writing is the symptom, devote more attention to grammar and spelling. This indicates that the real problems underlying poor writing are not well understood, but it also provides an opportunity to rethink the pros and cons of linguistic reflection in the classroom and why and when the teaching of explicit grammatical concepts makes sense. This is important in the Dutch situation as in other countries. At least, it is much more important than one would suspect on the basis of the few studies on the basis for grammar teaching in the mother-tongue (L1) curriculum that have been carried out in the last 30 years.

Issues in the Grammar Debate

As mentioned, the debate about grammar teaching is a fuzzy one, because the concept of grammar teaching itself is ill-defined. In an international comparison of different forms of grammar teaching in elementary and secondary education (Grades 4–9) (Van Gelderen, 1988), the following main issues regarding grammar teaching appeared, discriminating the approaches found. First, there is the issue of the validity of the approach. Some approaches see grammar teaching as *inherently* valid from an educational perspective. According to this view, there is no question whether students should learn linguistic knowledge and/or reflect on that knowledge in the classroom. This sort of teaching serves a goal in its own right, for example, because it makes students conscious of important elements of language or because the knowledge acquired has a certain cultural value. In contrast, other approaches see grammar teaching merely from an *instrumental* point of a view: as a means to an end, such as learning to read or write better, fostering critical language use or learning foreign languages.

Second, there is the issue of explicitness of the teaching. In *explicit* grammar teaching, it is assumed that students need explicit metalanguage and explicit rules explaining how the concepts learned should be applied. In contrast, *implicit* approaches aim at developing grammatical intuitions by confronting students with exemplars of the target structures without explicit metalanguage or rules.

Third, there is the issue of product versus process-oriented approaches of grammar teaching. In a *product*-oriented approach, grammatical knowledge is used for error-correction or for the improvement of (written) texts. In a *process*-oriented approach, students are encouraged to use grammatical knowledge for reflection on language use.

The fourth issue concerns the pedagogical function of grammar teaching. We can distinguish between *prescriptive/deductive* ways of grammar teaching, using grammatical rules as strict guidelines to determine whether language is used correctly or not. In contrast, there are approaches towards grammar teaching that are characterized by a *descriptive/inductive* focus: the observation of language phenomena comes first followed by a description of regularities or irregularities.

The fifth issue concerns the place of grammar teaching in the mother-tongue curriculum. In many cases, grammar teaching takes the form of a *systematic* course not related to other aspects of the language curriculum. This contrasts with approaches in which grammar teaching is primarily *incidental* and takes place in close relation to meaningful language use.

Finally, the sixth issue concerns the topics that are regarded as important for grammar teaching. Because there is a large diversity of topics that belong under the umbrella term grammar, there is also a large diversity of propositions in the literature of topics for grammar teaching, varying from the macro (such as dialects, sociolinguistics, comparative language study) to the micro (such as morphology, phonology, phonetics). A rather general distinction can be made between three so-called perspectives of grammar teaching: the formal, the semantic and the pragmatic perspective (Van Gelderen, 1988). The formal perspective is specifically directed to the structure of words and sentences (including syntax); the semantic perspective has as its target the meaning of words and sentences (both in and out of context) and the pragmatic perspective is directed to functions of language use in specific communicative contexts.

Activity: Describing Your Own L1 Grammar Education

Describe the L1 grammar teaching you had in primary and secondary education in terms of the issues mentioned above. Was it mainly inspired by the instrumental or the inherent validity view? Did it mainly aim at explicit or implicit learning? Was it more product- or process-oriented? Was the focus more prescriptive or more descriptive? Was it a more systematic or more incidental approach? Explain your answers, using examples of the dominant grammatical topics that were taught. Don't hesitate to state your opinion: did you find the grammar education you received useful?

These three perspectives (formal, semantic and pragmatic) are used by Van Gelderen (1988) to define what is meant by *declarative* knowledge about language, as opposed to *procedural* knowledge. The distinction between declarative and procedural knowledge is derived from Anderson's (1982) ACT theory about skill acquisition. Whereas declarative knowledge refers to "knowing that", procedural knowledge refers to "knowing how". According to Anderson (1982), the acquisition of skills starts with a declarative phase in which students have conscious knowledge about specific rules (in the form of IF–THEN statements) followed by a phase of fine tuning, which finally results in a procedural phase in which students have no conscious control over the application of rules, because this application is automatized. Explicit and systematic grammar teaching can thus be based on the assumption that students first need declarative formal, semantic and/or pragmatic knowledge before they use this knowledge (procedurally) in a correct and efficient way in their speaking, listening, reading and writing. It is clear that Anderson's theory of skill acquisition can be used as a *basis* for teaching students explicit (declarative) knowledge about grammar. In this line of thinking, for example, procedural mastery of formal structures in language must be preceded by the learning of explicit rules explaining these structures. Later on, when these rules have gone through extensive fine tuning (correction of errors by confrontation with many exemplars) they become proceduralized, which means that application proceeds more and more fluently and automatically.

In contrast, however, there are theories of skill acquisition that deny the need for declarative knowledge as a first stage (De Keyser, 2001; N. Ellis, 1998; Hulstijn, 2002). Such theories assume that frequency of and associations between stimuli determine learning, resulting in the efficient application of (procedural) knowledge. It follows that for the acquisition of correct linguistic forms, frequent exposure to these forms (in different combinations) is sufficient. The more frequent this exposure, the more likely is the acquisition of the correct form and the more fluent is the recognition and production of the form. Also, if a form is frequently combined with a certain meaning, the more likely is the acquisition of the form–meaning association, thus explaining vocabulary acquisition and the development of pragmatic competence (often associated with non-verbal cues such as intonation, facial expression and gestures). When certain forms are frequently presented in a fixed combination (such as collocations, or recurring grammatical structures, especially in oral language), such combinations will also be learned without any conscious declarative knowledge of rules that can be used to describe such combinations. This learning mechanism is thus characterized by *implicit* rule learning. Instead of producing correct forms of language by applying declarative knowledge, this production is exemplar-based and generalizes only by the acquisition of more and more exemplars, until all exemplars are produced correctly even without any knowledge of underlying linguistic rules.

Activity: Examples of Explicit and Implicit Rule Learning

Think of a skill that you have learned (for example, walking, driving a car, swimming, playing a musical instrument) and explain which roles explicit and implicit learning have played in the acquisition of this skill. Which parts of learning this skill where probably predominantly based on implicit learning and which parts on explicit learning? Explain your answers.

These two contrasting accounts of skill acquisition bring to the fore a crucial issue. For which aspects of language learning is the explicit learning of declarative knowledge the better model and for which aspects is exemplar-based implicit learning the better model? An obvious criterion, of course, is frequency of exposure. If exposure to structure (in "naturally occurring" oral and written language[2]) is supposed to be sufficiently frequent for acquisition, there is no need for explicit teaching of rules. But in cases of doubt, rules might help to speed up acquisition, for example, by helping students to identify structure or by explaining the structure. Focusing on the function of explicit grammar teaching therefore reveals a dominant theme in the grammar debate that underlies many of the issues mentioned above.

From the instrumental point of view that grammar teaching is not an end in itself, but a means towards better mastery of language, the question of when (and why) the explicit teaching of rules and metalanguage is beneficial is crucial. However, whether we discuss grammar teaching from an instrumental viewpoint or from the viewpoint that knowledge about language is an end in itself (so-called inherent validity) does not matter in this respect. In either case, it has to be demonstrated that students are able to *understand* the meaning of the knowledge about language taught and are able to use it in a *sensible* way. For that reason, evidence from empirical studies showing that students benefit from one or other grammar approach is essential from both viewpoints.

Below, I will first review evidence concerning explicit grammar teaching for three different goals: mastery of formal structures in the mother tongue, writing in the mother tongue and learning a foreign or second language. I will conclude with a section describing grammar-teaching practices that deviate from the previous (mostly form-oriented) approaches and aim at improving writing via the implicit teaching of grammar or from developing student awareness of semantic and pragmatic topics.

Explicit Grammar Teaching in Relation to Formal Structures in Mother Tongue

In this section I will focus on the empirical evidence relating to the effects of explicit grammar teaching on structural aspects of language use, from an instrumental point of view. The main issue here is whether students improve their use of formal structures by learning explicit rules and metalanguage.

My first example comes from Dutch morphology. Dutch diminutives are formed in five different ways, depending on the syllable preceding the diminutive part (*-je*, *-kje*, *-tje*, *-pje* and *-etje*).[3] It may come as a surprise to speakers of other languages, but this rather complex set of rules is not part of the Dutch grammar curriculum. In grammar textbooks for primary and secondary education, these rules will not be found, nor do I know of suggestions for teachers to acquaint students with these rules by training or awareness-raising exercises.

2. With "naturally occurring" language, I do not wish to exclude language that is purposefully included in textbooks for students or in classroom interactions, in order to provide a sufficiently rich experience of language for implicit learning to take place.
3. For a complete explanation of Dutch diminutives, see Lagelands Grammar: www.ucl.ac.uk/dutch/grammatica/diminutives.htm#INTRODUCTION.

Nevertheless, mastery of these rules is accomplished by virtually *all* native speakers of Dutch. Most students by the end of primary education make no errors in their use of diminutives. For example, a grammar test administered by Van Gelderen and colleagues (2004) contained three items in which Grade 8 students (from high *and* low tracks of secondary education, including also students from immigrant backgrounds) had to fill in the correct diminutive (trui-*tje*, man-*netje*, beest-*je*). The mean percentage correct (of the 355 students that answered these questions) was 91. So on average, in the whole student population, very few errors were made.

A contrasting example is the spelling of the conjugation of verbs (with a stem ending on the letter *d*) in the second- and third-person present tense and perfect participle (ending on *t* or *d*). Learning how to spell these forms takes up a lot of time in the Dutch grammar curriculum. This learning consists of elaborate explicit rules in which students use phonological (Do you hear a "d"?), morphological (What is the stem?) and syntactical knowledge (Is it a verb? Is it in its finite form or is it a perfect particle?). However, correct spelling of this type is not mastered in a satisfactory way by a large majority of the student population, not even in adulthood. This fact gives rise to yearly public outcries that grammar education is being neglected, and recently it was one of the main political issues regarding the mother-tongue curriculum (as mentioned in the introduction). For many, including politicians, the spelling of conjugated verbs as indicated above has become the symbol – if not the main issue – of the poor outcomes of language education.

So, what can we say about the usefulness of explicit linguistic rules for students based on these two extreme examples? The first example concerns oral language to which students are being exposed frequently, even before they enter school. In addition, the different forms manifest themselves as audible sounds that make the phenomena rather salient. The second example concerns written language use, to which students are exposed for the first time at school, with limited occasions for practice (although these forms are frequent in writing). Unlike diminutives that are often used in spoken language and for which correct forms are signalled by feedback from adults and peers, the spelling of conjugated verbs is not part of children's normal language use and is made relevant to them only in specially designed exercises. In addition, the spelling (or misspelling) of these conjugations has no audible consequence in the Dutch language.

More importantly, the first type of rule (diminutives) is learned without any awareness of the underlying linguistic structure. Only specialized linguists can explain these rules. Native speakers do not know the rules consciously (that is, they do not have declarative knowledge about the rules) and do not reflect upon them, because it would seriously disrupt their language production. In contrast, the second type of rule (spelling conjugated verbs) is *not* learned, despite the fact that the explicit rules are discussed and exercised over many years of Dutch grammar education. Most students are confronted with these rules from Grade 3 up to Grade 10, and even later, because errors are still frequently made. Even experienced and highly educated writers keep on making this type of error, despite the fact that they know the rules well.[4] So, even when these explicit rules are correctly understood, the correct form does not come automatically. We can conclude that for linguistic structures of Type 1 (frequent exposure/oral language/audible consequence), the learning mechanism seems to be implicit, with no need whatsoever for explicit instruction of the underlying rules of the structure,[5] and that for structures of Type 2 (infrequent exposure/written language/inaudible consequence) explicit instruction of rules has no convincing effect on mastery of the structure.

Activity: Describe a Structure in Your L1

Give an example of a morphological or syntactical structure from your L1 or mother-tongue language that probably is learned implicitly. Describe the structure precisely (in such a way that non-natives also understand what you are talking about) and explain why you think it is implicitly learned. Which factors determine that implicit learning is the most probable route?

The case for teaching explicit grammatical rules is thus not very strong on the basis of these two examples. The fact that forms that are frequently practised are perfectly learned without an awareness of underlying linguistic rules illustrates that children do not *need* explicit instruction and conscious reflection on rules. The fact that forms that are *infrequently* practised are *not* learned by a majority of the population *despite* elaborate courses teaching explicit linguistic rules illustrates that explicit rule teaching is not very effective. The latter seems a rather devastating argument against the teaching of explicit declarative knowledge, because explicit rule knowledge should be helpful, *especially* for learning to use structures for which normal student language use does not supply sufficient practice, making implicit learning less likely.[6]

---

4. It must be added that at least part of the explanation why students in the Netherlands do not learn to apply the rules for verb conjugation properly is that many do not *understand* these rules properly. According to Sijtstra, van der Schoot and Hemker (2002), even the best students at the end of elementary education make many errors in basic sentence grammar needed for applying the rules for verb conjugation (such as determining the function of verbs in the sentence and identifying perfect particles), despite the fact that they have already "enjoyed" 3–4 years of traditional grammar teaching.
5. This does not mean that there is no explicit knowledge involved in this implicit learning. Ellis (2005), for example, contends that one does not exclude the other and that there are connections between the two (a so-called interface). However, in the present chapter, I am focusing on explicit *instruction*, which, of course, is distinct from explicit *knowledge* that students acquire in the learning process.
6. For example, Hudson and Walmsley (2005) plead for explicit grammar teaching to expand the grammatical competence of children in grammatical patterns that are needed in adult life but not found in children's casual conversation. But the argument for explicit grammar teaching is also valid in the context of learning foreign languages, because normally there are not enough occasions for using a foreign language for implicit grammar learning to occur.

These two examples suggest that, in relation to effectiveness, explicit grammar teaching directed to forms cannot compete with the implicit learning that occurs when students are confronted frequently with salient (in this case audible) exemplars. This advantage of exemplar-based implicit grammar learning is probably not restricted to language forms that can be audibly discriminated (making them salient), but also applies to forms that cannot, as long as the written forms are frequently met (and produced). A demonstration is provided by some items of a spelling test administered in Grade 8 by Schoonen and colleagues (2003). These items asked students to choose from one of the alternatives "i", "y" or "ie" in some words (juli, viking, pyjama, bizar, ledikant, intimiteit and individu). The alternative spellings in Dutch language all sound the same (IPA notation: i), but the spellings "i" and "ie" can be regarded as the regular spellings in Dutch, whereas "y" is highly irregular. So, if an awareness of grammatical rules dictated the difficulty of these spellings, then one would expect that "pyjama" would be the most difficult of them. However, the opposite was found. "Pyjama" was spelled correctly by 92% of the 362 students that answered these items, making it the easiest of the items. The most difficult one, "ledikant" (that is, a specific type of bed) was spelled correctly by only 41% of the students. It appears that not grammatical regularity, but the frequency with which students have been exposed to the unique exemplars explains the spelling difficulty. "Pyjama" is a word that students quite often encounter, presumably not only in oral but also in written contexts, whereas "ledikant" is rather infrequent.

There are as yet many unresolved issues relating to the effects of the explicit teaching of formal aspects of mother-tongue language. One of these issues in the Netherlands is whether other (more implicit and less abstract) approaches towards spelling of conjugated verbs are more effective. Surprisingly, given the enormous amounts of time that are being spent on the traditional approach and its deplorable results, there has not been systematic empirical investigation into this question. Other issues relate to the systemic and empirical characteristics of language forms that determine whether explicit teaching can be beneficial or whether we can better rely on implicit learning. We know that frequency of exposure is an important determinant (N. Ellis, 2002; Biber & Reppen, 2002), but it is hard to define this exposure generalized over all students of a certain age and over all sorts of forms to be taught. Exposure may be intense for some students from literate environments and with positive reading attitudes, but limited for others with family backgrounds that are less literate or even illiterate. Another issue is rule complexity, which determines the chance of success (Ellis, 2005; Williams, 2005). In the case of the spelling of Dutch conjugated verbs, this complexity might well be an important cause for the failure of explicit rule teaching, because many students do not understand the abstract concepts underlying the declarative knowledge (see note 3). Salience of structure is also recognized as an important factor, because salient structures are easily noticed by students (Schmidt, 1992), which makes implicit learning more likely. Furthermore, there are issues concerning individual differences among learners, such as aptitude, intelligence, motivation and learning style (Robinson, 2001). For example, intelligent students may benefit more from explicit grammar teaching than less intelligent students and motivation can be a crucial factor in students spending extra effort on learning and applying explicit rules.

Although normally not considered grammar teaching, there is an example of teaching explicit rules related to language forms in the Dutch mother-tongue curriculum that *is* successful for the large majority of the students. This is the teaching of sound–letter associations for beginning readers in Grade 1. If we use this as a model for the explicit teaching of structure with a reasonable chance of success, we can derive the following features: newness (beginning readers barely have any experience with the coding and decoding of words), interest (beginning readers are normally eager to unravel the secrets of the written code), simplicity (rules usually have the form of simple IF–THEN statements) and quick results (learning takes place stepwise, while each step leads to a satisfying result, such as the correct pronunciation of a letter symbol, a syllable or a whole word). It seems a good idea to use this model for checking other forms of explicit teaching of structure as a rough estimation of its effects on students' mastery of the intended structures. It is but an observation, but it appears that traditional grammar teaching directed at labelling word classes and analyzing sentence structure has almost none of the above features.

Activity: Compare Instruction in Sound–Letter Associations to Traditional Grammar

Compare the explicit instruction in sound–letter combinations in your L1 or mother-tongue language to the explicit labelling of word classes in traditional grammar education. How do the two activities compare on the aspects of newness, interest, simplicity and quick results in your view, and what does this comparison reveal about the usefulness of the two sorts of explicit instruction?

Explicit Grammar Teaching in Relation to Mother-Tongue Writing

The previous section dealt with the effects of explicit grammar teaching on students' mastery of language forms, which is important for writing, but is certainly not the only element that determines the quality of writing. It has often been claimed that the explicit teaching of grammar is not only helpful for the mastery of formal aspects such as correct spelling or word order, but also for writing in a more general sense (for example, Hudson & Walmsley, 2005). Although this claim is seldom specified, it suggests that there are not only beneficial effects in terms of avoiding errors, but also in more general terms, such as the efficacy of texts and their overall quality. Therefore, it is appropriate to review the empirical evidence that has been gathered over the years regarding the effect of explicit grammar teaching on writing as a complex activity.

Tordoir and Wesdorp (1979), for example, reviewed 53 experimental studies (from 1931 to 1975) that probed the effect of different approaches to grammar education on language abilities (for the greatest part writing composition). Their conclusion was that the effect on writing composition – measured by intensive evaluation of writing products – of the "direct" approach (no grammar, but practice in writing and reading) was superior to grammar approaches. Hillocks (1984), in his meta-analysis of 39 studies related to the focus of instruction in teaching composition, concluded: "The study of traditional school grammar (i.e. the definition of parts of speech, the parsing of sentences etc.) has no effect on raising the quality of student writing. Every other focus of instruction examined in this review is stronger" (p. 160).

Recently, a meta-analysis was published of studies into the effectiveness of writing instruction for students in Grades 4–12 (Graham & Perin, 2007). This analysis was based on 123 documents, including also the studies analyzed in five, prior meta-analytic studies (Hillocks' 1984 study was also included). Nevertheless, almost two-thirds of the effect-sizes obtained were from new studies. The authors distinguished 11 different types of interventions: strategy instruction, summarization, peer assistance, setting product goals, word processing, sentence combining, inquiry, prewriting activities, process-writing approaches, the study of models and finally grammar instruction. The largest effect-sizes, indicating a large positive effect on writing quality, were found for strategy instruction, summarization and peer assistance. The lowest effect-sizes were found for the study of models and grammar instruction. More specifically, grammar instruction was the only type of intervention that yielded a negative effect-size (−0.32), indicating a general negative effect of this type of intervention in comparison with other interventions. Although this result must be interpreted with caution because grammar teaching was the control condition for all but one of the effect-sizes involved, the authors note that "grammar instruction was not an efficient treatment in any of these comparisons" (p. 462).

Results of meta-analytic reviews can be criticized because of the heterogeneity of the studies reviewed, the narrowness of the measures taken (especially for composition skill, because this is a very complex construct) and other methodological shortcomings. However, there are still further reasons to doubt that explicit grammar teaching has a positive effect on writing composition. The empirical studies mentioned above probed the so-called transfer of explicit grammar knowledge to writing composition. From theories of the writing process, however, we know that writing consists of numerous sub-processes, such as idea generation, text organization, selection of content, translation of ideas into language, evaluating, reviewing, rewriting and editing (Hayes & Flower, 1980; Bereiter & Scardamalia, 1987). Many of these sub-processes are on the conceptual level of the text and have little to do with linguistic structure. Only the translating process is predominantly oriented towards the linguistic proficiency of the writer. It is therefore hard to understand how a treatment (traditional grammar instruction) can affect the whole writing process if only one of many sub-processes is targeted. In addition, it is questionable how *free* composition can benefit from *specific* explicit knowledge about language structure. It is hard to explain the underlying mechanism of transfer when students are free to use any structure that suits their ideas, regardless of whether these structures are part of the traditional grammar teaching they have received.

A study into the effects of explicit versus implicit training in linguistic structures on writing probed the effects on writing more directly to avoid this transfer
problem (Van Gelderen & Oostdam, 2002, 2005). Some 240 students from
Grades 5 and 6 were trained in using target structures that students of that age
normally do not use in writing (although these structures were familiar to them).
The purpose of the training was to improve students' writing fluency in order to
facilitate their paying attention to meaning in the process of writing. Four types
of linguistic operations were taught: adding commentaries to sentences (such as
adverbs and adjectives), adding subordinate clauses to main clauses, combining
sentences and using anaphora. Training occurred in textual and meaningful contexts, instead of with isolated sentences. The implicit condition consisted of
many exemplars of the structures that students had to recognize or to produce.
The explicit condition contained the same exercises, but here students were also
taught explicit rules and metalanguage for carrying out the operations (for
example, "add commentary to the kernels"). Outcome measures were designed
to evoke the target structures. They consisted in the improvement of a given text
and the writing of a text on the basis of phrasal elements. The students in the
experimental conditions (implicit or explicit instruction of target structures) out-
performed students in a control group (no instruction), showing that both
implicit and explicit training had resulted in a better application of the linguistic
operations in writing. However, no differences were found between the students
in the implicit and explicit conditions. This result shows that even with limited
room for repetition (four lessons of 45 minutes), the implicit learning of
grammar can be effective and explicit rule knowledge does not seem to have an
additive effect.

Explicit Grammar Teaching in Relation to L2 Learning

Within the logic and limitations of experimental training programs, strictly
focused output measures are needed to detect beneficial effects of explicit
grammar teaching. However, as mentioned above, the studies relating to mother-
tongue (or L1) writing normally do not have this focus. They are only interested
in effects on the global level of writing, which is determined not so much by
grammatical processes on the sentence level, but predominantly by conceptual
processes for planning, evaluating and revising text. In addition, in L1 writing
studies there is normally no clear link between the (traditional) grammatical
knowledge taught and the structures used in the outcome measures. To expect
an effect of explicit grammar teaching on such complex and free writing seems
unrealistic. Therefore, the negative results of the reviews discussed above are not
surprising. But, on the other hand, they fail to give us an answer to the more fundamental question of whether the explicit teaching of grammar can help students
to become better writers.

In the context of foreign-/second-language (L2) learning, however, many
empirical studies have been carried out directed at the question of whether the
explicit teaching of specific target structures leads to improved production of

those structures in speaking or writing (for example, Doughty & Williams, 1998; Norris & Ortega, 2000; Robinson, 1997; VanPatten, 2002). Typically, studies compare a condition in which explicit knowledge is taught about a few structures in the second language with a control condition (no instruction) and/or with a condition in which implicit instruction is given (repetitive presentation and/or production of the structures). The outcome measures are sometimes oral responses to stimuli that are designed to evoke the learned structures, but quite often they consist of written responses of a more or less restricted nature.

In contrast to the cited L1 reviews, the evocation of target structures in the outcome measures is essential in these studies, allowing a direct appraisal of the treatment effects. If explicit grammar teaching is beneficial from an instrumental viewpoint it should at least be demonstrated in such studies, where the primary goal of students is simple: learn to produce unfamiliar structures in a language correctly. Norris and Ortega (2000) published a review of 49 studies directed towards explicit and implicit L2 teaching, of which the main conclusion was that, indeed as expected, explicit instruction was more effective than implicit instruction. However, the authors themselves question the applicability of these results, because the studies are often of questionable quality and lack experimental rigor. In addition, there is a general bias in these studies towards outcome measures that favor explicit, declarative knowledge, such as metalinguistic tests, while skill-oriented measures such as oral or written use of target structures are under-represented.

Therefore, a review by R. Ellis (2002) is of more interest to our main question. Using six out of the 49 studies analysed in Norris and Ortega (2000) and adding five more recent studies, this review seems to support the conclusion that teaching explicit rules directed at linguistic forms (so-called explicit, form-focused instruction) is effective. This conclusion is based upon outcome measures with language-production tasks (spoken or written) evoking the target structures (thus bias towards tests for declarative knowledge is certainly not the case). Examples of such language-production tasks are oral interviews, information-gap tasks, science reports and short written essays based on pictures. Target structures were, for example, passive verb forms, past tenses, question forms and sociolinguistic expressions of politeness. It is hard to precisely evaluate the results reported by R. Ellis (2002), because it is not clear whether there were control groups involved in these studies and, if present, whether the control groups received any treatment at all. We can conclude, however, that it is rather disappointing that in five out of 11 studies, no positive results were found for the explicit grammar conditions. Apparently, even in such experiments directed at specific L2 target structures, expectations of the effectiveness of explicit, form-focused teaching were often over-optimistic.

Moreover, results of other L2 studies do not unequivocally support the instrumental view of the explicit teaching of linguistic rules – even in the limited sense of enabling students to produce the learned structures correctly – and show mixed results (Ellis & Laporte, 1997; Robinson, 1997; Segalowitz, 2003). For example, in a recent study, Andringa (2005) taught Dutch degrees of comparison and subordinate clauses to 101 recently immigrated students aged 12–18.

Although he found a difference in favour of the explicit condition in the case of a grammaticality judgement test (students evaluate whether given sentences are syntactically correct), no difference was found in terms of correct *use* of the target structures between groups that were trained explicitly and implicitly.

Implicit and Explicit Teaching of Forms and Other Topics of Linguistic Reflection

The studies discussed hitherto probing the beneficial effects of explicit grammar teaching are directed at the teaching of formal structure. They concern grammar in the narrow sense of knowledge about word and sentence structures. The review has shown that instruction in explicit rules and relevant metalinguistic terminology in this formal domain has a limited effect on students' skills. In many cases implicit grammar teaching – understood as not using explicit rules and terminology but studying and using many exemplars of the target forms – is just as effective, even in some short, experimental interventions with relatively few occasions for repetitive practice.

The popular view on which the teaching of traditional grammar is based holds that explicit (declarative) rule knowledge about language structure is a means to the end of improved (written) language ability. This view is not generally corroborated by the research evidence and is at odds with prevailing theories of writing process and language learning. For the grammar curriculum directed at mastery of formal structures, it would be advisable if a more rational choice were made between explicit rule teaching and implicit alternatives. At this time, however, such a rational choice is hard to make, because research into the effectiveness of implicit grammar teaching in the mother-tongue curriculum is very rare. While the L2 research literature is rich in comparisons between implicit and explicit grammar teaching, the L1 research agenda has almost completely ignored the subject. Maybe this is a side-effect of the strong beliefs about "grammar" on which mother-tongue curricula are based (positively or negatively). Teachers choose for or against a grammar approach, and to them this is synonymous with the explicit teaching of formal structure. Examples of systematic implicit approaches in mother-tongue education are very rare indeed. The first implicit curriculum for the spelling of Dutch conjugated verbs, for example, has still to be developed.

An example of implicit grammar teaching that seems worth experimenting with concerns the teaching of unfamiliar or complex sentence structures by the reading of texts containing these structures, and undertaking follow-up writing assignments intended to evoke the same structures. This type of instruction supposes that the implicit learning of grammatical structures can be successful when students use the structures in ways that are meaningful to them. In the absence of such meaningful applications of grammar (and the implicit learning accompanying these applications), explicit rule knowledge and metalinguistic terminology may offer no realistic alternative. This view of grammar learning, however, poses a new challenge for textbook writers for mother-tongue education. In the studies mentioned above, exemplary experimental materials have been developed, but it is not an easy task to combine meaningful reading and writing with implicit grammatical training focused on certain structures. Research into the feasibility and success of such approaches in the mother-tongue curriculum is certainly worth the effort.

For teaching focused on language structures to be beneficial for students' writing there need to be stronger connections with the teaching of writing than is the case in the traditional grammar approach. Instead of using linguistic theory as backbone, *actual* usage of structures in relevant kinds of texts should guide teaching.[7] Consequences of this latter grammar approach (which can use both implicit and explicit pathways or a mixture of both) are different for mother-tongue (L1) and L2 writing contexts. For L1 writing, it is important to be fluent in using certain types of operations (such as adding and deleting information, for example, by using adjectives, subordinate clauses, adverbs) to produce interesting expository texts. In such texts, writers must use several operations in order to convey information in a clear but also interesting way. It is better for the training in these operations to take place in the context of writing texts of this specific genre, rather than in isolated sentences in which concerns of connectivity and text coherence are absent, inhibiting transfer to textual contexts. Appendix A contains an example of a text that has been used for such instruction in the study of Van Gelderen & Oostdam (2002, 2005).

For L2 writing contexts, however, fluency in using linguistic operations is not the first objective. L2 grammar education must focus on the correct use of structures first. Given the divergent results in the research in this field, it is difficult to advise on the role of explicit grammar teaching. At best, it has a complementary role in addition to sufficient practice and implicit learning. But it probably depends on other factors, such as complexity of structure, degree of L2 experience, motivation and possibly other learner characteristics, whether explicit rules and terminology can help accelerate the learning process.

As mentioned previously, grammar teaching can be directed to issues other than formal structure, which may or may not have a beneficial effect on students' language use. At this time, we can only speculate on the areas for grammar teaching that are defensible from an instrumentalist point of view as parts of the elementary or secondary curriculum, because there is hardly any research evidence to cling to. For example, on face value, it seems plausible that teaching about pragmatic aspects of language – such as speech acts, manipulative language use and pragmatic aspects of word meaning – has an awareness-raising effect. It can make students aware of the fact that taken-for-granted modes of expression that they (or others in their environment) often use are not always the best form of expression or can be an undesirable means of manipulation. The basis for reflection may be found in interactions that occur in the classroom (for example, irony, rhetorical questions, hidden commands), in daily, out-of-school situations (for example, advertising, propaganda, selective news, rumours) or in

---

7. An illustration of the conflict that exists between grammatical theory and usage is the definition of the sentence in relation to punctuation. Whereas students often learn that sentences consist at least of a verb in a finite form and a subject, in the real world of texts there are many utterances that look like sentences (starting with a capital letter and ending with a full-stop) but do not fit the definition.

children's literature. Also in the field of semantics, there are many topics for teaching and reflection that could make students more aware of what they can "do" with words (or what words can "do" with them). Being aware, for example, that synonyms have different meanings ("man–gentleman") or that some words define very general concepts while others refer to more specific sub-categories ("animal–dog") may help students to become more critical in their choice of words and therefore may also contribute to their writing.

These types of linguistic reflection normally take on an explicit form, because it is hard to trigger them simply by presenting a lot of exemplars in texts. At the very least, the teacher (or a peer) needs to make the students notice the phenomena at hand; normally, also, a framework for discussing it is necessary. On the other hand, students do not *need* explicit rules and formal metalanguage for describing the phenomena at hand, but can make use of their own observations and phrase their findings in their own language. This is what was referred to as inductive pedagogy in the section about issues in the grammar debate.

Activity: Invent a Useful Lesson Focused on Semantic Awareness Raising Using Inductive Pedagogy

Think of a semantic phenomenon that students of a certain level of primary or secondary education can apply in their writing. For inductive pedagogy you will need to demonstrate the phenomenon with several examples in (oral and/or written) text and talk about them with your students. Describe the phenomenon you wish to make your students more aware of, how they can use this in their writing and design the lesson. Give concrete examples of materials that you are going to use to illustrate the phenomenon and a summary of the instructional activities.

Another example is individualized reflection on students' writing. In contrast to the approach outlined above, in which reading and writing activities are structured in the context of implicit grammar teaching, individualized linguistic reflection is based on writing assignments in which students pursue a circumscribed communicative goal. By discussing the links between rhetorical and linguistic levels of a student's text (text structure, word choice and sentence construction) with the teacher (or with peers), the student becomes aware of new linguistic means for increasing text effectiveness. In this way, a gap in writing pedagogy can be closed, namely the gap between idea generation and formulation. This is a part of the writing process that is normally considered a black box and the private (and impenetrable) domain of the student. However, this is also probably the domain in which support from teachers or peers can produce important learning gains. Because the discussion is based on the students' own texts, the learning process can be adapted to their conceptual *and* linguistic level of expertise, a good condition for meaningful learning experience. Hence, this kind of individualized reflection can be seen as an example of the "incidental curriculum", as opposed to the systematic curriculum for grammar (as mentioned in the section on "issues in the grammar debate"). It is remarkable that such an approach is present in descriptions of pedagogy for beginning writers (Grades 1–2), but is almost invisible in relation to later grades. It seems that as soon as students are able to write sentences independently, the need of support for formulation processes is no longer acknowledged in teaching.

Conclusion

This chapter has drawn attention to the reasons why teachers might decide that learning grammar (whether directed to form only, to relations between form and meaning or to language use in concrete situations) is of interest for students in elementary and secondary education. In hindsight, we might argue that the discussion about the effectiveness of traditional grammar started at the wrong end of the problem. Instead of theorizing what declarative knowledge about language would be of interest to students, the attempt was made to justify a traditionally given set of rules and terminology by claiming its beneficial effects on language use. There was, however, no theory guiding this quest for effectiveness. With the knowledge we now have about writing processes, the idea that the explicit teaching of traditional grammar improves students' mother-tongue writing is far-fetched. This is not only because empirical studies fail to show any effect, but also because the underlying mechanism is mysterious. Looking at types of grammar teaching other than the teaching of traditional grammar (both in L1 and L2) has taught us more about the likelihood of beneficial effects on specific forms of writing. Whether explicit grammar teaching is useful or not appears to depend on several factors, such as the frequency of exposure to the forms to be learned, the salience of those forms, the complexity of the rules to be learned and several learner characteristics (such as motivation and intelligence). If we find topics or methods for (implicit or explicit) grammar teaching for which we can formulate plausible theories explaining why awareness is beneficial, whether it should include explicit declarative knowledge and for what kind of language use exactly, this has the advantage that we can refine teaching in ways directed by our theory.

Explanation

These two texts are presented to students (Grades 5–6) to make them aware of linguistic operations for writing expository text. The A text does not contain any commentaries such as adjectives, adverbs or subordinate clauses that can make the text more interesting, while the B text does. Students are invited to compare the two texts by questions about the additions. Questions are asked about each addition. For example: Is the addition "very exciting" extra information about snowboarding, does it help to understand the text better or is it just fun to read? Also general questions are asked, such as: Which of the two texts do you find more interesting, and why? In further exercises students are invited to include "similar" additions in their own texts. No metalinguistic knowledge or terminology has to be applied at all for this grammar learning.

Appendix A: Focusing Students on Specific Linguistic Operations in Expository Text

A

Did you know that snowboarding is a sport? It is the sport of Bianca de Wit. This girl intends to become a champion. Sliding on a board from a slope, is what she likes. Et cetera...

B

Did you know that snowboarding is a *very exciting* sport? It is the *favourite* sport of Bianca de Wit, *a 13-year-old girl with blond tresses and hefty calves from Rotterdam.* This girl, *now already the top-best of her age,* intends to become a *real* champion. Sliding on a *narrow* board *as fast as she can* from a *steep* slope, is what she likes *best on her winter holiday.* Et cetera...

References

Anderson, J. (1982). Acquisition of cognitive skill. *Psychological Review, 89*(4), 369–406.

Andringa, S. (2005). *Form-focused instruction and the development of second language proficiency.* Groningen: Groningen Dissertations in Linguistics.

Bereiter, C., & Scardamalia, M. (1987). *The psychology of written composition.* Hillsdale, NJ: Lawrence Erlbaum Associates.

Biber, D., & Reppen, R. (2002). What does frequency have to do with grammar teaching. *Studies in Second Language Acquisition, 24,* 199–208.

Clark, U. (2005). Bernstein's theory of pedagogic discourse: Linguistics educational policy and practice in the UK English/literacy classroom. *English Teaching: Practice and Critique, 4*(3), 32–47.

DeKeyser, R. (2001). Automaticity and automatization. In P. Robinson (Ed.), *Cognition and second language instruction* (pp. 125–151). Cambridge: Cambridge University Press.

Doughty, C., & Williams, J. (1998). *Focus on form in classroom second language acquisition.* Cambridge: Cambridge University Press.

Ellis, N. (1998). Emergentism, connectionism, and language learning. *Language Learning, 48,* 631–664.

Ellis, N. (2002). Frequency effects in language processing: A review with implications for theories of implicit and explicit language acquisition. *Studies in Second Language Acquisition, 24,* 143–188.

Ellis, N. (2005). At the interface: Dynamic interactions of explicit and implicit language knowledge. *Studies in Second Language Acquisition, 27,* 305–352.

Ellis, N., & Laporte, N. (1997). Contexts of acquisition: Effects of formal instruction and naturalistic exposure on second language acquisition. In A. De Groot & J. Kroll (Eds.), *Tutorials in bilingualism, Psycholinguistic perspectives* (pp. 53–83). Mahwah, NJ: Lawrence Erlbaum Associates.

Ellis, R. (2002). Does form-focused instruction affect the acquisition of implicit knowledge? A review of the research. *Studies in Second Language Acquisition, 24,* 223–236.

Expertgroep Doorlopende Leerlijnen. (2008). *Over de drempels met taal en rekenen* [Crossing the thresholds with language and arithmetic]. SLO: Enschede.

Graham, S., & Perin, D. (2007). A meta-analysis of writing instruction for adolescent students. *Journal of Educational Psychology, 99,* 445–476.

Hayes, J., & Flower, L. (1980). Identifying the organization of writing processes. In L.

Gregg & E. Steinberg (Eds.), *Cognitive processes in writing* (pp. 3–30). Hillsdale, NJ: Lawrence Erlbaum Associates.

Hillocks, G. (1984). What works in teaching composition: A meta-analysis of experimental treatment studies. *American Journal of Education, 93,* 133–170.

Hoogeveen, M., & Bonset, H. (1998). *Het schoolvak Nederlands onderzocht* [Research of the teaching of Dutch language]. Leuven/Apeldoorn: Garant.

Hudson, R., & Walmsley, J. (2005). The English patient: English grammar and teaching in the twentieth century. *Journal of Linguistics, 41*(3), 593–622.

Hulstijn, J. (2002). Towards a unified account of the representation, processing and acquisition of second language knowledge. *Second Language Research, 18,* 193–223.

Inspection (1999). *Inspectierapport Nederlands in de Basisvorming* [Inspection report Dutch language and literature in the first phase of secondary education]. Utrecht: Inspectie van het Onderwijs.

Jacobs, M., & Gelderen, A. van (1997). Taalbeschouwing in moderne taalmethoden: Een gedetailleerde classificatie van leerstof [Language awareness in modern textbooks: A detailed classification of subject matter]. *Spiegel, 15*(2), 9–40.

Kolln, M., & Hancock, C. (2005). The story of English grammar in the United States schools. *English Teaching: Practice and Critique, 4*(3), 11–31.

Long, M. (1991). Focus on form: A design feature in language teaching methodology. In K. de Bot, R. Ginsberg, & C. Kramsch (Eds.), *Foreign language research in cross-cultural perspective* (pp. 196–221). Cambridge: Cambridge University Press.

Norris, J., & Ortega, L. (2000). Effectiveness of L2 instruction: A research synthesis and quantitative meta-analysis. *Language Learning, 50*(3), 417–528.

Robinson, P. (1997). Individual differences and the fundamental similarity of implicit and explicit adult second language learning. *Language Learning, 47*(1), 45–99.

Robinson, P. (2001). Task complexity, cognitive resources, and syllabus design: A triadic framework for examining task influences on SLA. In P. Robinson (Ed.), *Cognition and second language instruction* (pp. 287–318). Cambridge: Cambridge University Press.

Schmidt, R. (1992). Psychological mechanisms underlying second language fluency. *Studies in Second Language Acquisition, 14,* 357–385.

Schoonen, R., Gelderen, A. van, Glopper, K. de, Hulstijn, J., Simis, A., Stevenson, M., & Snellings, P. (2003). First language and second language writing: The role of linguistic knowledge, speed of processing and metacognitive knowledge. *Language Learning, 53*(1), 165–202.

Segalowitz, N. (2003). Automaticity and second language acquisition. In C. Doughty & M. Long (Eds.), *The handbook of second language acquisition* (pp. 382–408). Oxford: Blackwell Publishers.

Sijtstra, J., van der Schoot, F., & Hemker, B. (2002). *Balans van het taalonderwijs aan het einde van de basisschool 3; Uitkomsten van de derde peiling in 1998.* [Balance of language education at the end of elementary school 3; Results of the third sounding in 1998]. Arnhem: Cito.

Tordoir, A., & Wesdorp, H. (1979). *Het grammatica-onderwijs in Nederland: Een researchoverzicht betreffende de effecten van grammatica-onderwijs en een verslag van een onderzoek naar de praktijk van dit onderwijs in Nederland* [Grammar education in the Netherlands: An overview of research into the effects of grammar education and a report of a study into the practice of this education in the Netherlands]. Den Haag: SVO, Staatsuitgeverij.

Van Gelderen, A. (1988). *Taalbeschouwing wat is dat? Deel 1: Een internationale inventarisatie en systematische beschrijving van alternatieven voor het traditionele grammatica-onderwijs* [Reflection on language what is that? Part 1: an international inventory and systematic description of alternatives for traditional grammar education] (SCO-rapport 173). Amsterdam: SCO.

Van Gelderen, A., & Oostdam, R. (2002). Improving linguistic fluency for writing: Effects of explicitness and focus of instruction. *L1: Educational Studies of Language and Literature, 2*(3), 239–270.

Van Gelderen, A., & Oostdam, R. (2005). Effects of fluency training on the application of linguistic operations in writing. *L1: Educational Studies of Language and Literature, 5*(2), 215–240.

Van Gelderen, A., Couzijn, M., & Hendrix, T. (2000). Language awareness in the Dutch mother-tongue curriculum. In L. White, B. Maylath, A. Adams, & M. Couzijn (Eds.), *Language awareness: A history and implementations* (pp. 57–88). Amsterdam: AUP.

Van Gelderen, A., Schoonen, R., Glopper, K. de, Hulstijn, J., Simis, A. Snellings, P. & Stevenson, M. (2004). Linguistic knowledge, processing speed and metacognitive knowledge in first and second language reading comprehension; a componential analysis. *Journal of Educational Psychology, 96*(1), 19–30.

VanPatten, B. (2002). Processing instruction: An update. *Language Learning, 52*(4), 755–803.

Williams, J. (2005). Learning without awareness. *Studies in Second Language Acquisition, 27*, 269–304.

Chapter 8

Ways of Knowing

Grammar as a Tool for Developing Writing

Debra Myhill

Introduction

Learning to write and learning to be a writer are relatively new areas of empirical enquiry. Our understanding of the linguistic, cognitive and social processes involved in learning to write and its rootedness in a secure research base is still developing; unlike learning to read, which is well supported by a considerable body of well-respected research. Psychological models of the writing process, for example, only began to be developed in the 1980s (Hayes & Flower, 1980; Bereiter & Scardamalia, 1987; Kellogg, 1994). Theoretical understanding of the role of grammar in the process of becoming a proficient writer is limited, though there is no shortage of professional and academic viewpoints on the topic. Extending our ways of knowing about how best to teach writing, and how best to address linguistic aspects of writing thus remains an important aspect of pedagogy and practice.

Ways of Knowing

But ways of knowing reflect our subjectivities as teachers or as researchers. I position myself differently as an English specialist if I talk about knowledge about *language*, rather than knowledge of *grammar*: this is not simply because grammatical knowledge is a subset of a broader set of understandings about language but rather that the choice, "knowledge about language", implies a more liberal, learner-centred perspective than the traditional, neo-conservative associations of the word "grammar". The term "knowledge about language" tends to carry positive associations, perhaps implying insider-knowledge, a professional view of what is valuable and important to children learning to be literate; in contrast, the word "grammar" has negative connotations, often implying an outsider view of English teaching, and carrying associations of control and blame. The choice we make signals our identity and the community of practice with which we want to be identified. But, in this chapter, I would like to explore specifically a theorized interpretation of how knowledge about grammar might inform both learners' and teachers' understanding of writing, rather than looking more broadly and generally at knowledge about language. In doing so, I hope to position grammar constructively within the frame of reference encompassed by knowledge about language and to avoid being trapped by "the particular values and standards the idea of grammar has been made to symbolise" (Cameron, 1995, p. 82). This might be a risky enterprise!

Activity: Reflection

Before you read further, where do you stand in your thinking about grammar? What connotations does the concept "grammar" have for you? Were you taught grammar at school? What do you believe about the place of grammar in a forward-thinking language/literacy curriculum?

A difficulty in considering how grammatical knowledge might support an effective pedagogy for the teaching of writing is that one persistent conceptualization of how grammar relates to writing centres upon error: the deficit model of grammar teaching. This was a position identified and criticized in England by the Bullock Report (DES, 1975). Bullock reported that "the traditional view of language teaching was, and indeed in many schools still is, prescriptive. It identified a set of correct forms and prescribed that these should be taught" (p. 169). Indeed, one strong impetus behind the UK Conservative government's introduction of the National Curriculum in 1988 was "to eliminate 'bad grammar' – the only interpretation of grammar that they recognised" (Hudson & Walmsley, 2005, p. 613), an ideological stance not far removed from Newbolt's desire to rid children of the "evil habits of speech contracted in home and street" (Board of Education, 1921, p. 59). As a consequence, grammar suffers "the misfortune of being associated with the negative, the corrective, the inevitable remedial half of English teaching" (Keith, 1990, p. 69).

This is not an exclusively British phenomenon. Micciche (2004) observes that in US composition classrooms "teaching grammar and teaching writing are separate enterprises" and grammar is viewed as "not empowering but disempowering, not rhetorical but decontextualized, not progressive but remedial" (p. 717) and Kolln and Hancock (2005, p. 13) note the tendency to link grammar with error avoidance and error correction. Thus, the dominant orientation towards grammar is concerned with error and correction rather than as a tool for "articulating and expressing relationships among ideas" (Miccicche, 2004, p. 720). It's all about "bad grammar"! Grammar is coupled with notions of error, accuracy, correctness and judgements about individuals and their intelligence. And this association is inimical to professional understanding of language education, as indicated in a National Council for Teachers of English (NCTE) press release: "English teachers do not see themselves as grammar police, on the lookout for mistakes" (NCTE, 2006).

Hudson and Walmsley (2005) rightly observe that in England there has been a significant discourse shift at policy level and in curriculum documentation: references to grammar emphasize making comparisons between standard and non-standard forms, and supporting children in becoming bidialectal in speech and writing, able to make informed choices about the forms which are most appropriate. There is little significant reference to accuracy. The ultimate goal for any teacher of writing is not accuracy, but effectiveness. As a US report on the teaching of writing insists, "basic writing is not the issue" because most students can write, "what most students cannot do is write well" (NCW, 2003, p. 16).

The following extract from a 16-year-old's General Certificate of Secondary Education (GCSE) English examination script was part of a large sample of GCSE examination scripts analysed in a study of children's writing (QCA, 1999; Myhill, 1999), and it exemplifies well how weak writing cannot be crudely correlated with inaccuracy. If you read it, you will notice that, apart from the absence of some initial capitalization, the extract is grammatically accurate. However, correcting these "errors" makes little significant difference to the effectiveness of the piece. There is a story here waiting to get out, and from a pedagogical perspective there might be many things one could recommend to breathe life into it, but improving the accuracy would not be one of them.

> we started to throw bricks in the canal where he had gone in and he still never came back. so I and 2 other chaps went for help and left where he fell in. We went to the factory just up the canal and they helped us. 2 workmen jumped in the canal looking for him. they got him but he wasn't breathing so we called an ambulance. they took him to the hospital and they couldn't get him to breathe. the doctor asked how long he had been under the water for and I said only for a few minutes...

So it is encouraging that the educational thrust of attention to grammar in England in the statutory National Curriculum for English (DfEE, 2000), the National Literacy Strategy (NLS) (DfEE, 1998) and the Key Stage 3 Framework for English (DfES, 2001) is on improving and developing writing, not upon error. And yet, precisely *how* grammar can improve children's writing is neither clearly conceptualized nor clearly articulated.

Activity: Further Reading

If you are interested in exploring the long-running debate about grammar in the curriculum, you might like to dip into the following:

Kamler, B. (1995). The grammar wars or what do teachers need to know about grammar? *English in Australia, 114*, 3–15.
Locke, T. (2009). Grammar and writing: The international debate. In R. Beard, D. Myhill, J. Riley & M. Nystrand (Eds.). *International handbook of writing development* (pp. 182–193). London: Sage.
Wyse, D. (2004). Grammar. For writing? A critical review of the evidence. *British Journal of Educational Studies, 49*(4), 411–427.

A Theoretical Framework for Teaching Grammar to Support Writing

Perhaps the absence of a cogent rationale for advocating teaching grammar to improve children's writing is because, as yet, there is no theoretical framework within which to locate the discussion. The rejection of grammar teaching by the English profession was largely because there was no conviction that it served any useful purpose "because explicit grammatical knowledge was no longer considered a necessary precondition for pupils' ability to communicate" (QCA, 1998, p. 12). Instead, the past 40 years or so have been characterized by rather polarized, ideologically driven debates about whether teaching grammar improves writing, debates which have tended to reveal more about the proponent's stance than about the issue itself. Tracing the story indicates patterns of claim, counter-claim and criticism of current practice. The Bullock report (DES, 1975, p. 16) condemned grammar teaching which was "prescriptive" and which, in terms of writing, "identified a set of correct forms" and no more. The research of Harris (1962) and Robinson (1959), which had partly provided the impetus for whole-scale rejection of grammar teaching in the 1970s, was subsequently rebutted by Tomlinson (1994, p. 20) on the grounds that both studies were methodologically flawed and do not stand up to "critical examination". More recently, two reviews of the empirical evidence (Hudson, 2001; Wyse, 2004), focusing specifically on the impact of grammar teaching on writing, arrive at opposite conclusions.

In the light of this continuing uncertainty, the commissioning of an Evidence for Policy and Practice Information and Coordinating Centre (EPPI-Centre) study into the impact of grammar teaching upon children's writing was a promising endeavour. The final EPPI report (2004) concluded that there was no evidence to counter the belief that teaching syntax "has virtually no influence on the writing quality or accuracy of 5–16 year olds" (p. 4). But the EPPI research, though apparently thorough and extensive, draws its conclusions on the basis of just three studies deemed of high or medium-high significance, none of which were conducted in the United Kingdom, and two of which are 30 and 40 years old respectively (Elley, Barham, Lamb & Wylie, 1979; Bateman & Zidonis, 1966; Fogel & Ehri, 2000). The Elley study, like Harris and Robinson before it, compared classes given reading and creative writing lessons with those given grammar lessons. The Bateman and Zidonis study looked at the effect of teaching generative grammar, focusing on sentence construction, on children's writing and did find, in fact, limited evidence of a positive impact. The third study, by Fogel and Ehri, published in 2000, looked at the impact of practising transforming sentences from Black Vernacular dialect to Standard English – and the children in this study also showed some improvement.

The EPPI review is not without its limitations. In its conduct of the systematic literature review, it does not consider how grammar was taught, particularly whether the grammar teaching made connections between grammar and writing. As a reader, you might consider how, if at all, in your own classroom you establish links between a grammatical construction and how it might enhance communication in writing. Equally, the review does not engage with the pedagogical confidence of the teacher, not just in command of metalinguistic knowledge, but also in applied linguistic understanding relevant to the development of writing ability. Its conclusion, that there was no evidence of any impact of grammar teaching upon written composition, was reported in the media as evidence of the redundancy of grammar teaching to the development of writing: a sign perhaps that, as Tomlinson (1994) argued in the 1990s, this was "what many in the educational establishment wanted to hear" (p. 26). It does, however, make the poverty of the evidence base crystal clear.

Methodologically rigorous and valid evidence concerning the impact of grammar teaching on writing is indeed extremely limited, but sensitive readings of available research do point to pedagogical issues which warrant both systematic research enquiry and professional critique and debate. The Fogel and Ehri study (2000), considered in the EPPI report, was one where the teaching of grammar was directly related to learners' needs and this seems to have borne fruit. Green, Johnson, O'Donovan and Sutton (2003) found, for example, that children's sentence structure in writing had improved between 1995 and 2002, covering the period since the introduction of the NLS which explicitly teaches about sentence structure. More recently, Fearn and Farnan (2007), using an experimental design, found that teaching writers about sentence structures in writing lessons had a statistically significant positive impact on writing quality. The evidence that teaching about sentence structures may be beneficial echoes repeated claims about the value of sentence-combining. Hillocks and Mavrognes (1986) suggested that instruction in sentence-combining has a positive impact on composition; the EPPI review (2004) maintained there was good evidence for the value of sentence-combining; and Graham and Perin (2007) identified sentence-combining as one of 11 pedagogical strategies for writing with a positive effect-size. The latter claimed that, "teaching adolescents to write complex sentences in this way enhances the quality of their writing" (p. 18).

Yet careful scrutiny of the evidence for the positive impact of sentence-combining on the quality of children's writing reveals a considerably more ambivalent picture. Confirmatory evidence of the benefits of O'Hare's (1973) original study on sentence-combining has been argued assertively by Daiker, Kerek and Morenberg (1978), Hake and Williams (1979), Keen (2004) and Saddler and Graham (2005). But critics point out that, in some instances, the evidence simply shows that teaching children to write more complex sentences helps them to write more complex sentences, without necessarily improving the quality of writing. In the Hake and Williams' study, for example, gains in use of complex structures were accompanied by an increase in errors for some students. In other words, they were writing longer, syntactically more complex sentences but were unable to manage them effectively. Crowhurst (1980) challenged the link between syntactical complexity and writing quality, arguing from her own experimental data that while there was a correlation between syntactical complexity and assessments of writing quality, the same did not hold for narrative writing. Furthermore, she argued that sentence-combining "raised to conscious control" certain linguistic resources, but that "the student must still be taught when and how to use these resources to rhetorical advantage" (p. 64). Other critics of sentence-combining (Witte, 1980; Kinneavy, 1979; Faigley, 1980) suggest that the underlying cause of improvement is not the sentence-combining itself but the discussion and rhetorical understanding which accompanies it. Indeed, Faigley argues that, "sentence-combining succeeds not because it mysteriously enriches some cognitive process but because teachers using sentence-combining have conveyed to students certain traditional rhetorical principles characteristic of good writing" (p. 298).

Activity: Research

Take a sample of writing from three or four children that you teach and look closely at how they have used sentences. Is there evidence from these young writers that they need to know how to connect sentences and use subordination? Or do they need to learn how to use short sentences occasionally for effect? Or perhaps do they construct over-long and over-complex sentences in which their communicative expression is disrupted?

In general, sentence-combining teaches grammatical or syntactical principles without the use of a metalanguage. Elsewhere, the consequence of direct instruction of linguistic forms needed in written composition is seen to have less beneficial impacts, including misuse of connectives (Perera, 1987), misunderstanding of the effect of the passive (Myhill, 2003), and the formulaic repetition of taught forms (Kress, 1994). Arguably, direct instruction in grammatical structures used in writing can lead not to effective writing but to "the reproduction of dominant knowledge" (Doecke, Kostogriz & Charles, 2004, p. 30). The truth is that teaching grammar and knowledge about language in positive, contextualized ways which make clear links with writing is not yet an established way of teaching and it is, as yet, hugely under-researched. What is needed is more research which is genuinely open-minded and critical and policy initiatives which encourage professional engagement with the pedagogic issues. Our ways of knowing about how grammar might support writing development need to move beyond simplistic or ideological parameters of agreement or disagreement.

I would argue, therefore, that our understandings about grammar and writing would benefit from stronger theorization and conceptualization which move both theory and practice beyond the confines of proof and rebuttal. In particular, I would like to consider what is understood by the concept of "grammar taught in context"; the relationship between learning theory and a theorization of how grammar might benefit writing instruction; and finally, the significance of teacher linguistic and pedagogical subject knowledge.

Activity: Further Reading

If you are interested in good arguments about how teaching grammar might help writing development, you might like to read the following:

Hancock, T. (2009). How linguistics can inform the teaching of writing. In R. Beard, D. Myhill, J. Riley & M. Nystrand (Eds.), *International handbook of writing development* (pp. 194–208). London: Sage.

Kolln, M. (2002). *Rhetorical grammar: Grammatical choices, rhetorical effects.* New York: Longman.

Myhill, D. (2009). Changing classroom pedagogies. In A. Denham & K. Lobeck (Eds.), *Linguistics at school: Language awareness in primary and secondary education.* Cambridge: Cambridge University Press.

Teaching Grammar in Context: The Acceptable Mantra

For many teachers of English, including myself, the principle of teaching grammar in context has been tantamount to a mantra, uttered whenever the issue of grammar teaching is raised. Teaching grammar in context avoids all the worst excesses of prescriptive grammar teaching, which operates within the deficit model of grammar teaching, focusing on error, or as the Bullock Report (DES, 1975) puts it, teaching where the emphasis is "less on knowing what to say than on knowing what to avoid" (p. 170). Indeed, the three major reports in England into English teaching in the last 50 years, Bullock (DES, 1975), Kingman (DES, 1988) and Cox (DES, 1989) all rejected prescriptive grammar teaching in favour of contextualized grammar, based on a systemic-functionalist view of grammar as "*a dynamic description of language in use*" (DES, 1988, p. 3). The wholehearted espousal of the principle of grammar in context represents a particular way of knowing about grammar teaching, and is one which is very much part of the mainstream professional identity of English teachers (see, for example, NATE, 1997; Barton, 1999; Bain & Bain, 1996).

However, the danger of a mantra is repetition without reflection. The rejection of decontextualized, and with it by implication, prescriptive, grammar teaching was rooted in insightful critique of what was happening in English classrooms. In contrast, the "grammar in context" principle is both less sharply critiqued and considerably less clearly conceptualized. Fearn and Farnan (2007), based on the outcomes of their study, argue that "grammar instruction influences writing performance when grammar and writing share one instructional context" (p. 16), and Weaver and Bush (2006) adopt a similar stance, arguing for the importance of contextualized study which teaches the potentiality of the "grammatical resources that are available for adding detail, creating flow, foregrounding some sentence elements and backgrounding others" (2006, p. 100). In the United States, in particular, there are numerous professional articles (for example, Prain, 1995; Gribbin, 1996; Sams, 2003; Blasingame & Nilsen, 2005; Jayman et al., 2006) demonstrating the benefits of contextualized teaching of grammar in which connections are made between linguistic constructions and rhetorical effect. While these have classroom authenticity, they lack empirical rigour even though they constitute useful descriptions of best practice which might usefully inform more robust future research.

Moreover, there has been little genuine discussion or consideration of what "in context" means. Frequently, observations of classroom practice indicate that the notion of "in context" means little more than grammar teaching which is slotted into English lessons where the focus is not grammar but some other feature of English learning. In other words, "in context" may simply mean "not decontextualized".

Activity: Research

Look at four or five of your lesson plans for a writing lesson, or even better, work in a group and pool a larger set of lesson plans. Investigate whether these lessons address grammar at all and, if so, how the grammar point is addressed. Is it a "mini-lesson" on grammar within the lesson as a whole and does it make explicit connections between grammar and writing?

You could take this further and consider how one or two of these lessons might either introduce a relevant grammar point or improve how a grammar point was introduced to strengthen young writers' understanding of that grammar point as a tool for developing their writing.

From the learners' perspective, there are several dangers in such a definition. First, the context can be so interesting that the grammar learning is lost – what George Keith describes, in the National Association for Teachers of English (NATE) position paper on *Grammar*, as the learner losing sight of the wood "as each tree becomes more and more interesting" (1997, p. 3). There is also a danger of pseudo-contextualization, where separate, discrete grammar lessons are replaced by "mini" grammar lessons in the midst of something else. The latter may be of particular significance in England where, for all children aged 5–14, there are yearly teaching objectives laid out in the Primary National Strategy and the Key Stage 3 Framework for English, some of which have an explicit grammar focus. One undoubted benefit of outlining teaching objectives, but not specifying content, is that it gives teachers considerable freedom about the contexts and content within which they want to choose to teach these objectives. But there is also the tendency for the objective to become more important than applied understanding, and for mini-grammar lessons to occur within writing lessons. This is an issue also raised by Weaver and Bush (2006, p. 78), who argue that in the United States such mini-lessons treat grammar as an "isolated event" rather than being genuinely contextualized. Such pseudo-contextualization can result in children unwittingly acquiring misconceptions such as the notion that complex sentences are good sentences or that liberally sprinkling writing with adjectives improves the quality of the writing. Wray's study of effective teachers of literacy (Wray, Medwell, Fox & Poulson, 2000) looked at primary school teachers using the NLS objectives and found that the most effective teachers were able to make meaningful connections between linguistic points at word and sentence level, and engagement with whole texts. Although these teachers did teach explicitly linguistic objectives, such as sentence structure, they were less likely to highlight it "as the overall aim of a lesson". In contrast, less effective teachers "tended to teach language features directly, without providing children with a clear context in which these features served a function" (p. 81).

Learning Theory and Theorizing Learning Grammar for Writing

So what might a more theorized understanding of grammar in context mean? I am interested in exploring how the teaching of grammar in the context of writing might be located within a clearly articulated framework of how children learn. In this way, I would like to move the debate away from the binary oppositions of "should we/shouldn't we" teach grammar, to a more pedagogically helpful and theoretically robust conceptualization of how writing might be improved by the teaching of grammar.

A recognition that writing is a social practice, determined and influenced by social, cultural and historical contexts (Lankshear, 1997; Street, 1995; Prior 2006) is now well understood. When children are learning to write, "they learn more than the **system** of writing. They learn about the **social practices** of language" (Czerniewska, 1992, p. 2). In this way, writing is not a set of decontextualized skills to be mastered and deployed, but a meaning-making activity, rooted in social contexts, and reflecting power relations between different groups. In her work with high school students, Janks (2000) explicitly explored some of these relationships between language and power, and quotes the post-apartheid Truth and Reconciliation Commission's assertion that "Language, discourse and rhetoric does things: it constructs social categories, it gives orders, it persuades us, it justifies, explains, gives reasons, excuses. It constructs reality. It moves people against other people" (1998, para. 24).

In our own study (Jones & Myhill, 2007; Myhill & Jones, 2007; Myhill, 2008), there was evidence that teenage writers understood that in some genres, their choice of formal language reflected a particular power relationship between writer and reader:

JIM: If this was meant to be like a letter or something, you know, to a higher authority or whatever, where it would be complicated, then I would write it and redraft it much more, you know, to change the words so that they were better words.

JAKE: Well, when you're like speaking to someone more important than trying to, like, make it sound more sophisticated.

JOE: 'Cause it's quite formal and we're writing to someone who's obviously higher up and that.

In terms of formality, these writers and others in the sample were able to articulate explicitly how formality could be achieved through choosing word items appropriately, a form of metalinguistic awareness that demonstrated their ability to make connections between a lexical item and its effect on an implied reader:

- Because "store" to me sounds more formal because a "shop" is something that you might say to your schoolmate.
- I have, you know, used some words like "purchased" instead of "bought".
- Instead of using "happened", I used "occurred".
- Here it was just to use a more formal word. I used "aid" instead of "help".

Developing metalinguistic awareness about linguistic choices made in the design of a piece of writing, at lexical, syntactic and textual levels, has a potential role within a sociocultural view of writing as social practice. At the heart of such a theoretical perspective is the importance of making connections between grammar and meaning. In the 1960s, Gurrey (1962) was arguing that one cause of scepticism about grammar teaching was in "the divorce of grammar and meaning" (p. 8) and Perera (1984), considering the primary school context, noted that, "a body of research has accumulated that indicates that grammatical instruction, unrelated to pupils' other language work, does not lead into improvement in the quality of their own writing" (p. 40). Curiously, this is frequently cited as evidence against teaching grammar, yet her argument is that teaching which is "unrelated to pupils' other language" work is ineffective (p. 40). This principle of making connections between grammar and meaning in writing is more than language awareness: it is perfectly reasonable to argue for the study of grammar to allow children to explore "the rich complexity of language", as the NATE position paper (NATE, 1997, p. 1) does, but this is an argument for the intrinsic value of studying language and grammar. I would argue for a more direct connection to be made between grammar, writing and children's experiences of language as readers and speakers – more clearly focused "guidance about how meanings can be shaped through language", to give writers "freedom and power over language" (Czerniewska, 1992, p. 146). Indeed, Nystrand, Gamoran and Carbonaro (1998) found a positive impact on writing achievement was evident where instruction integrated reading, writing and discussion in meaningful ways.

Connecting Grammar and the Rhetoric of Writing

Making such meaningful connections between communicative purposes and linguistic choices is at the heart of theoretical arguments for a pedagogy of grammar centred upon rhetorical understanding. As a theoretical perspective, this has much to offer the teaching of writing since at its heart is the discussion and analysis of how meaning is crafted and created through shaping language to achieve the writer's intentions. Miccicche (2004) argues that, as writers, the grammatical choices we make "represent relations between writers and the world they live in. Word choice and sentence structure are an expression of the way we attend to the words of others, the way we position ourselves in relation to others" (p. 719). This has resonances with Bakhtin's (2004) insistence that consideration of grammatical forms cannot be undertaken without parallel consideration of their "stylistic significance" (p. 12) and that teaching should help writers make choices about grammatical constructions in the light of stylistic purposes and implications. Several US authors have written convincingly about the impact of adopting such approaches in the classroom (Ehrenworth, 2003; Nunan, 2005; Paraskevas, 2006), though these are not, as yet, rigorously evidenced. Underpinning them all, however, is the principle that grammar knowledge is a "rhetorical tool that all writers should understand and control" (Kolln, 2002, p. xi), a tool which enables the writer to make effective choices.

Although the term "rhetorical grammar" is not familiar in England, there are voices which express similar ideas. Burgess (1998) maintains that grammar teaching should be "an enquiry … a way of talking about language" (p. 106) which reflects on and interrogates how words work and which is embedded in a discursive classroom context. More specific rhetorical connections between grammatical constructions and writing effects are made by Gregory (2003), who calls for more pedagogical attention to "subordination in sentences being explored as dealing with the management of complexity, the holding of related ideas in tension in the development of argument or examination of the role of phrase structures in achieving expressive economy" (p. 17). Approaching rhetorical grammar from a more text-oriented perspective, Kamler (1995), responding to curriculum changes in Australia which required more grammar teaching, argued that "we did not have adequate tools available to us to help our students learn about language" (p. 3) and that better language knowledge would enable us, as teachers, to illustrate how "texts participate in the exercise of social power that result in gender, racial and class inequality" (p. 4).

Explicit and Tacit Knowledge

The principle of rhetorical grammar appropriately raises the issue of tacit and explicit knowledge. Kellogg (1994) notes that it is only through language that our tacit knowledge "becomes explicit or conscious knowledge" (p. 49). Given that at an early age, all children "have mentally internalised an immensely complex system of grammatical rules" (Leith, 1983, p. 88), writers, whether in the early-years classroom or in secondary school, have considerable tacit grammar knowledge to draw upon. Furthermore, children's reading encounters with texts and previous experience as writers furnishes them with tacit knowledge which is specifically concerned with writing. If tacit knowledge acts as an influence upon the composition of successful writing, what can we gain from making that tacit knowledge explicit? One boy in our study (Myhill & Jones, 2007) was able to articulate clearly how exercising grammatical or linguistic decision-making processes during writing is an automatic process for him, drawing on tacit knowledge about effectiveness, rather than making explicit, conscious choices:

OLIVER: My brain sort of … automatically frames how the sentence is going to work and, you know, where to put dashes and colons and everything.
INTERVIEWER: Is that in terms of punctuation?

OLIVER: Yeah, but also how I use the words, which way round the sentence goes.
INTERVIEWER: So having your clauses, I mean, do you actually consciously think about them?
OLIVER: No, not really, that's the point, I don't really consciously think about ... this should go here or this should go here, 'cause I just subconsciously know that if you put the verb here then it makes it seem more angry or more colloquial or whatever than if you put it in the normal place.

But it is important to be aware of the various nuances of tacit and explicit knowledge and to avoid simply counterpointing them as opposites. There are many gradations between tacit and explicit knowledge: as well as explicit knowledge which can be both articulated orally and enacted in their writing, writers may have explicit knowledge which they have temporarily forgotten; or explicit knowledge which they can articulate orally but do not transfer into their writing; or tacit knowledge which is not articulated but can be deployed in their writing. Linked to this is the distinction in cognitive psychology between "declarative knowledge" (knowing that) and "procedural knowledge" (knowing how): knowledge about grammar is not the same as knowing how to make effective and appropriate grammatical choices. Moreover, the assumption that the continuum moves from tacit knowledge to explicit knowledge is not always true, particularly with learners of English as an additional language or weaker writers. For these writers, instruction about linguistic features may generate explicit knowledge where there is no corresponding tacit knowledge. This may be particularly salient when considering stylistic choices in writing, where through meaningful teaching you can draw attention to patterns or characteristics which had not previously been noticed.

As one would anticipate, our analysis of children's writing highlighted greater effectiveness and variety in linguistic features in high-ability writers than in weaker writers, and this was matched by greater ability to articulate explicit choices in interview in relation to specific pieces of writing. All of the comments below, except the final one, come from high-ability writers. If you are not a reader familiar with the English National Curriculum, you might not realize, however, that all the features they choose to mention – rhetorical questions, sentence variety, sentence length – are frequently explicitly taught as part of the Key Stage 3 Framework for English. One important question is the extent to which these articulations are "learned" responses rather than sophisticated metalinguistic understanding.

JANE: Other ones [crossing-out decisions] were connecting ones. Once I had put them quite a few times, I thought it might sound a bit like "and, and, and" sort of thing, so I tried to change those.
SARAH: I made it into a short sentence so it had some effect.
CHARLOTTE: I wanted some one-word sentences, some long sentences and I can't actually think of any one-word sentences at the moment, but I suppose when you see the monster, it could be the monster and it could be, like, scared and the character's scared.

RUTH: I quite, a lot of the time, use a question at the end, a rhetorical question, but I don't know if this is really a rhetorical question.

LUKE: Here as well where it says, "*He crunched the pebbles together on his beautiful polished leather shoes,*" and I was trying to also link polished leather shoes with the inspector 'cause they always like to look right … they kind of want to look posh and make a good appearance.

WILL: Sometimes, you know, the sentences, they all seem to follow the same pattern so I need to change it around to make it more interesting.

Explicit teaching of grammatical features in writing is a key part of the English National Curriculum policy guidance, and the ability to understand and deploy that knowledge in writing is conceived of as part of the writer's toolkit, a repertoire of choices available to the writer as he or she writes. This does not, however, engage with the place of tacit knowledge. Hudson (2004) observes that writers without explicit linguistic knowledge "may even be able to internalise the features of the text to the extent that they can imitate its style" and he argues that these writers "must be analyzing these features implicitly; but they cannot make the analysis explicit" (p. 113). There is a strong argument that if internalization occurs successfully and writing is effective, then there is no need to make the analysis explicit. However, explicit knowledge is, by definition, more cognitively accessible for reflection and decision-making, and may therefore be a powerful enabling tool for writers tackling the cognitively complex task of writing. Carter (1990) expresses this forcefully in critiquing the demise of grammar teaching, arguing that it "disempowered them [children] from exercising the kind of conscious control and conscious choice over language which enables both to **see through** language in a systematic way and to use language more discriminatingly" (p. 119). Of the three studies rated of high or medium-high significance in the EPPI review of grammar teaching, it may be particularly significant that the two which recorded positive effects after the teaching intervention (Bateman & Zidonis, 1966; Fogel & Ehri, 2000), both involved explicit teaching of a particular linguistic feature (sentence structure and standard dialect).

The Significance of Teacher Linguistic and Pedagogic Subject Knowledge

The teaching of writing, as I have attempted to describe above, makes particular demands of English teachers in terms of substantive subject knowledge and pedagogic knowledge. It is axiomatic that meaningful, focused and relevant attention to grammar in the context of teaching writing requires teachers who are confident both about what they are teaching and how to teach it. Yet for many teachers of English in England their career pathway into teaching has not prepared them for this. In a recent research interview with a young teacher about the teaching of writing, she made it very clear that she saw no role for teaching grammar because it stifled creativity and led to a formulaic approach to writing. But in the same interview, she talked enthusiastically about teaching poetry composition and showing writers how caesura and enjambment could contribute to shaping meaning in poetry. I asked about this apparent contradiction – that grammatical metalanguage was limiting but literary metalanguage was enabling – and she told me: "But I am confident about caesura and enjambment and I know how to teach them; I'm not confident about grammar."

Activity: Reflection

How confident are you in your own grammatical knowledge? What grammatical terms would you feel unable to teach without checking definitions and explanations first? If you do lack confidence, how does this influence your professional attitude to grammar?

Cajkler and Hislam (2002) record the difficulties trainee teachers of English experience in trying to demonstrate sufficient linguistic subject knowledge to meet the standards required to qualify as a teacher of English (DfES, 2000). Faced with an English curriculum, especially in primary schools, with a strong emphasis on grammar at word, sentence and text level, these novice teachers struggle to simultaneously understand the linguistic terminology themselves and to teach it effectively. But this is not a problem reserved for new teachers to the profession. For most of the past 100 years, graduates of English have been predominantly graduates from university departments of English Literature, and applicants for teacher training in English have also drawn principally from English Literature degree routes. As a result, as Hudson (2004) notes, not only do we have "far too few teachers of English with an adequate grounding in the linguistics of English" (p. 106) but also limited engagement of linguistics research with pedagogic issues. Perhaps equally relevant is the fact that teachers who come to English teaching through a degree in literature route may have very little interest in linguistics, and their own identity as an English teacher may be heavily shaped by their values and beliefs about what literature can offer learners. It is not surprising that many English teachers eschew grammar or reject its value in English teaching if their intellectual and pedagogical confidence with literature is counterpointed by frustration in attempting to understand clause structures.

Lack of confidence in subject knowledge is nearly always paralleled by a similar lack of confidence in how to teach that element effectively. Research from an earlier study (Myhill, 2003) illuminated how weak subject knowledge of the passive led one teacher to generate misconceptions in her class both about the structure of the passive itself and its effect in texts. Teachers often become dependent upon commercial teaching materials or support materials provided by curriculum authorities, which are often suspect themselves, as Cajkler (2004) has demonstrated. But this kind of dependence means it is difficult for teachers to respond to children's misunderstandings or questions or "to react sensitively to any grammatical issue that may arise unexpectedly" (Hudson & Walmsley, 2005, p. 616). Moreover, grammar teaching which focuses on terminology or fulfilling a particular curriculum objective can establish strange ways of thinking about writing. In

England, the emphasis on grammatical constructions without the corresponding understanding of effect and meaning-making is leading many children to believe that some grammatical features have intrinsic merit. We are nurturing a generation of children who believe that complex sentences are good, that connectives are ace, and that adjectival pile-up before a noun is the path to good description! In our own research study (Jones & Myhill, 2007; Myhill, 2009b), several children referred to personal targets to use more complex sentences, or when evaluating their writing recalled the teacher's emphasis on complex sentences, but without purposeful insight, as the following exchange demonstrates.

INTERVIEWER: Why might that make it better?

SEAN: It's 'cause that's, like, one of my targets this year ... to use complex sentences...

INTERVIEWER: Do you understand why complex sentences might be better?

SEAN: I know, like, that you get a better grade, but I don't actually know, like, why they're better.

However, there has been considerable professional development for teachers in this field in the past five years and, in secondary schools, the existence of teachers who teach A-level English Language and are both enthusiastic and comfortable with pragmatic linguistics has meant that some teachers are indeed helping children to make meaningful connections between grammar and writing. The following set of comments about sentence structure show these children beginning to develop understandings which interrelate form and meaning, even if they are, as yet, struggling to articulate this clearly:

VICKY: I think if it's short, not drags on and it's making a small point that it will make you think about it a bit more because it's like ... I could have just said "the drawer was left open" something like that, and it makes you focus on that because it was quite short.

INTERVIEWER: What is it about complex sentences...

MATT: I wouldn't say they're necessarily good, it depends what you find good in the content, but complex sentences often make it more adult. You can get through stuff a lot quicker, I find as well, otherwise, full stop, new sentence, stop and you're thinking how ... how far have I got? OK, next sentence. A couple of sentences you get it all going...

LUKE: Sometimes I, sort of, got into a sentence that was a bit too long and had too many, like, dashes and brackets and things in so I had to find what I was actually trying to write.

TOM: I probably would introduce more short sentences actually.

INTERVIEWER: Why would you do that?

TOM: Um, it kind of makes it more exciting and long sentences can get quite boring if you have lots of them.

Finally, in terms of pedagogic subject knowledge, we need to consider the "difference between what teachers need to know about language and what they need to teach" (Perera, 1987, p. 3). Understanding the difficulties children face in learning how to create and shape meaning in written form is supportive knowledge for informing decision-making about teaching strategies and content. Equally, being able to recognize the way different linguistic characteristics in writing contribute to their success, as did the QCA *Improving Writing* study (QCA, 1999), can inform formative assessment in precise and purposeful ways, which can move beyond impressionistic judgements to explicit articulation of writers' development needs. Collins and Gentner (1980) have argued for "a linguistic theory of good structures for sentences, paragraphs, and texts" which would have "direct implications for the teaching of writing" (p. 53). But this does not necessarily mean that knowing that good writers use more short sentences than weaker writers should be paralleled by lessons on the virtues of the short sentence. It may mean, however, making the most of opportunities to notice the way short sentences are used and the effects they have in texts being shared in class; or it may mean talking to an individual writer with a tendency to write in sentences of similar length about possibilities in a given piece of writing to shorten sentences to emphasize a particular point. It also means that we need to consider whether the grammatical terminology is important, or whether the teaching point can be addressed through alternative strategies.

Conclusion

It is wholly unsurprising that there is no substantial empirical evidence base demonstrating the beneficial impact of grammar on writing, as there has never been any theoretical or operationalized framework for teaching writing with grammar in mind. It is hard to imagine, though clearly historically there were those who did, that teaching children about nouns or subordinate clauses would be matched by a corresponding improvement in their writing. In England, however, as Hudson and Walmsley (2005) observed, there has been a discourse shift in how grammar is discussed at policy level, and this has been matched at the pedagogical level by clear attempts to teach grammar in a more meaningful way. The evidence of constructivist approaches to teaching, making use of careful scaffolding of children's learning, and the teaching strategies of demonstration and modelling have been positive moves, and were consonant with the findings of the characteristics of effectiveness in literacy teaching in the research of Wray and colleagues (2000), which was conducted prior to the introduction of these national initiatives.

There are, nonetheless, weaknesses in these national initiatives: the variable quality and accuracy of teaching materials (though some are excellent); the insufficient attention to teachers' subject and pedagogic knowledge at the outset; the way teaching objectives relating to grammar and writing have sometimes been addressed as decontextualized teaching within the teaching of writing; and the reluctance to open up debate about the efficacy of teaching approaches. I would argue that these weaknesses stem, in part, from the lack of a theoretical conceptualization of how grammar might support the teaching of writing, and this chapter is an attempt to articulate such a theory.

At the heart of this theory are three principles. First, that *writing as a communicative act* should be the principal pedagogic focus, and any attention to grammar should inform this, rather than using writing as useful context to deliver grammatical learning objectives. Second, writers should be encouraged to see the various linguistic choices available to them as *meaning-making resources*, ways of creating relationships with their reader, and shaping and flexing language for particular effects. And finally, the principle of *connectivity*: children should be supported in making connections between their various language experiences as readers, writers and speakers, and in making connections between what they write and how they write it.

This chapter raises as many questions as it answers. With the curriculum developments that have taken place in England in the past 10 years, now is a ripe time for robust, balanced and critical research which investigates the complex web of interrelationships which surrounds the teaching of writing with a purposeful focus on grammar, where appropriate. This research must include the active involvement of teachers who are prepared to approach the topic in a spirit of open-minded exploration, willing to identify positive learning experiences as well as problematic ones. Only then will we be in a position to supply salient and purposeful answers to the questions raised here.

References

Bain, E., & Bain, R. (1996). *The grammar book*. Sheffield: NATE.

Bakhtin, M. (2004). Dialogic origin and dialogic pedagogy of grammar: Stylistics as part of Russian language instruction in secondary school (L. Gogotishvili, Trans.). *Journal of Russian and East European Psychology, 42*(6), 12–49.

Barton, G. (1999). *Grammar in context*. Oxford: Oxford University Press.

Bateman, D., & Zidonis, F. (1966). *The effect of a study of transformational grammar on the writing of ninth and tenth graders*. Champagne, IL: National Council of Teachers of English.

Bereiter, C., & Scardamalia, M. (1987). *The psychology of written composition*. Hillsdale, NJ: Lawrence Erlbaum Associates.

Blasingame, J., & Nilsen, A. (2005). The mouse that roared: Teaching vocabulary with source-based lessons. *English Journal, 94*(4), 59–64.

Board of Education. (1921). *The teaching of English in England* [The Newbolt Report]. London: HMSO.

Burgess, T. (1998). Mouse and grammar: Connecting use and structure in English teaching. *Changing English: Studies in Culture & Education, 5*(2), 103–113.

Cajkler, W. (2004). How a dead butler was killed: The way English national strategies maim grammatical parts. *Language and Education, 18*(1), 1–16.

Cajkler, W., & Hislam, J. (2002). Trainee teachers' grammatical knowledge: The tension between public expectation and individual competence. *Language Awareness, 11*(3), 161–177.

Cameron, D. (1995). *Verbal hygiene*. London: Routledge.

Carter, R. (Ed.). (1990). *Knowledge about language*. London: Hodder & Stoughton.

Collins, A., & Gentner, D. (1980). A framework for a cognitive theory of writing. In L. Gregg & E. Steinberg (Eds.), *Cognitive processes in writing* (pp. 51–72). Hillsdale, NJ: Lawrence Erlbaum Associates.

Crowhurst, M. (1980). Syntactic complexity and teachers' quality ratings of narrations and arguments. *Research in the Teaching of English, 14*, 223–231.

Czerniewska, P. (1992). *Learning about writing.* Oxford: Blackwell.

Daiker, D., Kerek, A., & Morenberg, M. (1978). Sentence-combining and syntactic maturity in freshman English. *College Composition and Communication, 29*(1), 36–41.

DES. (1988). *Report of the Committee of Inquiry into the Teaching of English Language* [The Kingman Report]. London: HMSO.

DES. (1975). *A language for life* [The Bullock Report]. London: HMSO.

DES. (1989). *English for ages 5–16* [The Cox Report]. London: HMSO.

DfEE. 1998). *The National Literacy Strategy. A framework for teaching.* London: DfEE.

DfEE. (2000). *English: The national curriculum for England.* London: DfEE.

DfES. (2000). *Qualifying to teach: Standards for the awards of Qualified Teacher Status.* London: DfES.

DfES. (2001). *Framework for teaching English: Years 7, 8 and 9.* London: DfES.

Doecke, B., Kostogriz, A., & Charles, C. (2004). Heteroglossia: A space for developing critical language awareness? *English Teaching: Practice and Critique, 3*(3), 29–42.

Ehrenworth, M. (2003). Grammar–comma–a new beginning. *English Journal, 92*(3), 90–96.

Elley, W., Barham, I., Lamb, H., & Wylie, M. (1979). *The role of grammar in a secondary school curriculum: Educational Research Series No 60.* Wellington: New Zealand Council for Educational Research.

EPPI Review Group for English. (2004). *The effect of grammar teaching (syntax) in English on 5 to 16 year olds' accuracy and quality in written composition.* London: EPPI-Centre.

Faigley, L. (1980). Names in search of a concept: Maturity, fluency, complexity, and growth in written syntax. *College Composition and Communication, 31*(3), 291–300.

Fearn, L., & Farnan, N. (2007). When is a verb using functional grammar to teach writing? *Journal of Basic Writing, 26*(1), 1–26.

Fogel, H., & Ehri, L. (2000). Teaching elementary students who speak black English vernacular to write in Standard English: Effects of dialect transformation practice. *Contemporary Educational Psychology, 25*, 212–235.

Graham, S., & Perin, D. (2007). A meta-analysis of writing instruction for adolescent students. *Journal of Educational Psychology, 99*(3), 445–476.

Green, S., Johnson, M., O'Donovan, N., & Sutton, P. (2003). *Changes in key stage two writing from 1995 to 2002.* A paper presented at the United Kingdom Reading Association Conference, University of Cambridge, 11–13 July 2003. Retrieved August 2009, from www.cambridgeassessment.org.uk/ca/digitalAssets/113781_Changes_in_Key_Stage_Two_Writing_from_1995-2002.pdf.

Gregory, G. (2003). They shall not parse! Or shall they? *Changing English: Studies in Culture & Education, 10*(1), 13–33.

Gribbin, B. (1996). The role of generalization in studying grammar and usage. *English Journal, 85*(7), 55–58.

Gurrey, P. (1962). *Teaching English grammar.* London: Longman.

Hake, R., & Williams, J. (1979). Sentence expanding: Not can, or how, but when. In D. Daiker, A. Morenberg, & M. Kerek (Eds.), *Sentence-combining and the teaching of writing* (pp. 134–146). Conway, AR: L&S Books.

Hancock, T. (2009). How linguistics can inform the teaching of writing. In R. Beard, D. Myhill, J. Riley, & M. Nystrand (Eds.), *International handbook of writing development* (pp. 194–208). London: SAGE.

Harris, R. (1962). *An experimental enquiry into the functions of and value of formal grammar in the teaching of English.* Unpublished PhD thesis, London University.

Hayes, J., & Flower, L. (1980). Identifying the organization of writing processes. In L. Gregg & E. Steinberg (Eds.), *Cognitive processes in writing* (pp. 3–30). Hillsdale, NJ: Lawrence Erlbaum Associates.

Hillocks, G., & Mavrognes, N. (1986). Sentence combining. In G. Hillocks (Ed.), *Research on written composition: New directions for teaching* (pp. 142–146). Urbana, IL: NCTE.

Hudson, R. (2001). Grammar teaching and writing skills: The research evidence. *Syntax in the Schools, 17*, 1–6.

Hudson, R. (2004). Why education needs linguistics. *Journal of Linguistics, 40*(1), 105–130.

Hudson, R., & Walmsley, J. (2005). The English patient: English grammar and teaching in the twentieth century. *Journal of Linguistics, 41*(3), 593–622.

Janks, H. (2000). Domination, access, diversity and design: A synthesis for critical literacy education. *Educational Review, 52*(2), 175–186.

Jayman, J., Doolan, L., Hoover, M., Maas, S., McHugh, T., Mooney, K., & Zepp, A. (2006). Sentence patterns: Making meaning with a countywide grammar initiative. *English Journal, 95*(5), 41–47.

Jones, S., & Myhill, D. (2007). Discourses of difference? Examining gender difference in linguistic characteristics of writing. *Canadian Journal of Education, 30*(2), 456–482.

Kamler, B. (1995). The grammar wars or what do teachers need to know about grammar? *English in Australia, 114*, 3–15.

Keen, J. (2004). Sentence-combining and redrafting processes in the writing of secondary school students in the UK. *Linguistics and Education: An International Research Journal, 15*(1–2), 17–97.

Keith, G. (1990). Language study at KS3. In R. Carter (Ed.), *Knowledge about language* (pp. 69–103). London: Hodder & Stoughton.

Kellogg, R. (1994). *The psychology of writing.* Oxford: Oxford University Press.

Kinneavy, J. (1979). Sentence combining in a comprehensive language framework. In D. Daiker, A. Morenberg, & M. Kerek (Eds.), *Sentence combining and the teaching of writing* (pp. 60–76). Conway, AR: L&S Books.

Kolln, M. (2002). *Rhetorical grammar: Grammatical choices, rhetorical effects.* New York: Longman.

Kolln, M., & Hancock, C. (2005). The story of English grammar in US schools. *English Teaching: Practice and Critique, 4*(3), 11–31.

Kress, G. (1994). *Learning to write.* London: Routledge.

Lankshear, C. (1997). *Changing literacies.* Buckingham: Open University Press.

Leith, D. (1983). *A social history of English.* London: Routledge.

Locke, T. (2009). Grammar and writing: The international debate. In R. Beard, D. Myhill, J. Riley, & M. Nystrand (Eds.), *International handbook of writing development* (pp. 182–193). London: Sage.

Micciche, L. (2004). Making a case for rhetorical grammar. *College Composition and Communication, 55*(4), 716–737.

Myhill, D. (1999). Writing matters. *English in Education, 33*(3), 70–81.

Myhill, D. (2003). Principled understanding? Teaching the active and passive voice. *Language and Education, 17*(5), 355–370.

Myhill, D. (2008). Towards a linguistic model of sentence development in writing. *Language and Education, 22*(5), 271–288.

Myhill, D. (2009a). Changing classroom pedagogies. In A. Denham & K. Lobeck (Eds.), *Linguistics at school: Language awareness in primary and secondary education.* Cambridge: Cambridge University Press.

Myhill, D. (2009b). From talking to writing: Linguistic development in writing. In *Teaching and learning writing: Psychological aspects of education – current trends. British Journal of Educational Psychology Monograph Series II (6).* Leicester: British Psychological Society.

Myhill, D., & Jones, S. (2007). More than just error correction: Children's reflections on their revision processes. *Written Communication, 24*(4), 323–343.

NATE. (1997). *Position Paper No 1: Grammar.* Sheffield: NATE.

National Commission on Writing in America's Schools and Colleges. (2003). *The neglected "R": The need for a writing revolution.* New York: College Board.

NCTE. (2006). Beyond grammar drills: How language works in learning to write. *The Council Chronicle Online.* Retrieved August 2009, from www.ncte.org/magazine/archives/125935.

Nunan, S. (2005). Forgiving ourselves and forging ahead: Teaching grammar in a new millennium. *English Journal, 94*(4), 70–75.

Nystrand, M., Gamoran, A., & Carbonaro, W. (1998). *Towards an ecology of learning: The case of classroom discourse and its effects on writing in high school English and Social Studies. Report Series 2.34.* Albany, NY: National Research Center on English Learning and Achievement.

O'Hare, F. (1973). *Sentence combining: Improving student writing without formal grammar instruction. NCTE Research Report No. 15.* Urbana, IL: NCTE.

Paraskevas, C. (2006). Grammar apprenticeship. *English Journal, 95*(5), 65–69.

Perera, K. (1984). *Children's writing and reading: Analyzing classroom language.* Oxford: Blackwell.

Perera, K. (1987). *Understanding language.* London: National Association of Advisers in English.

Prain, V. (1995). Vaporize the verbs: Teaching grammar after Nintendo. *Australian Journal of Language and Literacy, 18*(1), 43–59.

Prior, P. (2006.) A sociocultural theory of writing. In C. MacArthur, S. Graham, & J. Fitzgerald (Eds.), *Handbook of writing research* (pp. 54–66). New York: Guilford.

QCA. (1998). *The grammar papers.* London: QCA.

QCA. (1999). *Improving writing.* London: QCA.

Robinson, N. (1959). *The relation between knowledge of English grammar and ability in English compositions.* Unpublished M.Ed. thesis, University of Manchester.

Saddler, B., & Graham, S. (2005). The effects of peer-assisted sentence-combining instruction on the writing performance of more and less skilled young writers. *Journal of Educational Psychology, 97*(1), 43–54.

Sams, L. (2003). How to teach grammar, analytical thinking, and writing: A method that works. *English Journal, 92*(3), 57–65.

Street, B. (1995). *Social literacies: Critical approaches to literacy in development, ethnography and education.* New York: Longman.

Tomlinson, D. (1994). Errors in the research into the effectiveness of grammar teaching. *English in Education, 28*(1), 20–26.

Truth and Reconciliation Commission. (1998). *Truth and Reconciliation Commission of South Africa report.* Cape Town: The Commission.

Weaver, C., & Bush, J. (2006). Grammar intertwined throughout the writing process: An "inch wide and a mile deep". *English Teaching: Practice and Critique, 5*(1), 77–101.

Witte, S. (1980). Sentence-combining and the teaching of writing. *College Composition and Communication, 31*(4), 433–437.

Wray, D., Medwell, J., Fox, R., & Poulson, L. (2000). The teaching practices of effective teachers of literacy. *Educational Review, 52*(1), 75–84.

Wyse, D. (2004). Grammar for writing? A critical review of empirical evidence. *British Journal of Educational Studies, 49*(4), 411–427.

Part III

Into the Classroom

Integrating Knowledge about
Language with Learning

Chapter 9

"Language as a System of Meaning Potential"

The Reading and Design of Verbal Texts

Hilary Janks

Bertrand Russell once described the word *obstinate* as an "irregular verb". During a BBC radio programme, he offered the conjugation, "I am firm, you are obstinate, he is pig-headed" (Pearson, 2009). I could do the same with the word *fat*: "I am plump, you are fat, he is obese."

The Microsoft Word thesaurus offers the following synonyms for the word fat: *overweight, plump, chubby, stout, portly, obese, heavy, large, big, corpulent, hefty, huge, enormous.* Relative to the other options, *chubby* has an affectionate ring to it and *plump* is not as fat as *obese* or *enormous* or *huge*. *Portly* and *stout* are somewhat old-fashioned and are associated with upright elderly gentlemen in three-piece suits or stiff, matronly women. *Corpulent* suggests men with wide girths. *Big* and *large* could refer to size and height, not just weight, so they are less blunt than *fat* or *overweight*. Given these options, *plump* seems to be among the lesser of the evils, which is why I chose it for the first person form of my "irregular verb".

Activity: Conjugation

"Conjugate" the following "irregular verbs" using Bertrand Russell's method.

I am untidy.
I am fussy.
I am inquisitive.
I am generous.

Although it is possible to view language as a closed abstract system, where each sign, each meaning-bearing unit, is arbitrary and derives its meaning from its place in the system relative to other signs (de Saussure, 1972), this tells us nothing about what happens when language *is* used. When people use language, they have to select from options available in the system – they have to make lexical, grammatical and sequencing choices in order to say what they want to say. This is what Halliday means by the meaning potential of language.

> A language is interpreted as a system of meanings, accompanied by forms through which the meanings can be realized.... Systemic theory is a theory

of meaning as choice, by which a language, or any other semiotic system, is interpreted as networks of interlocking options: either this, or that, or the other. (Halliday, 1985, p. xiv)

For Halliday, the forms are the different elements of the lexico-grammar. Choice from this grammar determines how the meaning potential of language is realised. In 1978, he defined it as follows:

What a speaker can say, i.e., the lexicogrammatical system as a whole, operates as the realization of the semantic system, which is what the speaker can *mean* – what I refer to as the "meaning potential". I see language essentially as a system of meaning potential. (Halliday, 1978, p. 39)

Let us then consider some grammatical options in addition to the lexical options already discussed. We affect the certainty of a statement by opting for tense [1] or modality [2].

[1]   He *is* overweight. (The choice of tense makes the statement categorical.)
[2]   He *might be* overweight. (The choice of modality creates doubt and the statement is hedged.)

The meaning changes entirely depending on our choice of polarity. Compare [1] and [3]. Where [1] is positive and [3] is negative.

[3]   He *is not* overweight.

Transitivity is the technical name Halliday (1985) gives to the range of verbal processes from which to choose. Consider the differences in meaning created by what is selected from this part of the system.

[4]   He *is* overweight. (Relational process.)
[5]   He *feels* overweight. (Mental process.)
[6]   He *says* he is overweight. (Verbal process.)
[7]   He *made* himself overweight. (Material process.)

There is a difference between actually being overweight and feeling or saying one is overweight. Feeling is a perception that may not bear any relation to reality, as in anorexia. The same is true of saying one is overweight. Making oneself overweight is an action for which one has to take responsibility. Being overweight is a statement of what is rather than of action. In [8] responsibility shifts away from the person who is overweight to a different participant.

[8]   McDonald's made him overweight.

Halliday's theory of language as meaning potential (Halliday, 1985) argues that what is selected from the options in the lexico-grammar determines how we realise meaning when we compose and design texts. Understanding the choices that others have made enables us to recognise the linguistic resources that have been harnessed to produce a particular representation of events.

These selections are not neutral. In the examples that I have given, I could have chosen to use "she" instead of "he". I deliberately chose not to because fat has been constructed as a feminist issue (Orbach, 1986) and I did not wish to convey the idea that body image is an issue that predominantly affects women.

Activity: Gender-Switching

Find a text that describes either a man or a woman and switch genders. Change the names and the pronouns. Do the descriptions still ring true?

Lexical and grammatical selections are motivated: they are designed to convey particular meanings in particular ways and to have particular effects. Moreover, they are designed to be believed. Texts work to position their readers; and the ideal reader, from the point of view of the writer (or speaker), is the reader who buys into the text and its meanings. Another way of saying this is to say that all texts are positioned and positioning. They are positioned by the writer's points of view, and the linguistic (and other semiotic) choices made by the writer are designed to produce effects that position the reader. We can play with the word "design" by saying that texts have designs on us as readers, listeners or viewers. They entice us into their way of seeing and understanding the world – into their version of reality. Every text is just one set of perspectives on the world, a representation of it; language, together with other signs, works to construct reality.

Freebody and Luke's (1990) four resources model for reading argues that readers have to be competent in four different roles. They have to be text decoders, text participants, text users and text analysts. Their focus is on the roles involved in text reception. Parallel roles are needed for text production. These roles are summarised in Table 9.1. Each of these roles is underpinned by linguistic knowledge.

Activity: Using the Four Resources Model for Self-Reflection

Draw the four quadrants of the four resources model for reading and writing (Table 9.1). In each of these quadrants fill in as many of your own practices as a text decoder, text participant, text user and text analyst as you can.

This is summarised in Table 9.2. Teachers need to exercise professional judgement to decide what activities are needed to develop their students' implicit knowledge of lexis and grammar. They also have to decide what explicit knowledge is necessary and how to teach it in such a way that it becomes a usable resource in the literacy practices required by each of the roles.

Much of this linguistic knowledge is implicit and is acquired as one learns one's primary language (see van Gelderen in this book). Explicit knowledge gives one more conscious control for both the reception and production of language.

Table 9.1 The Four Roles of the Reader/Writer

Text Decoder/Encoder

The decoder has to understand the relation between letters and sounds and the ways they combine to form words. Practice is needed to link visual and auditory processing with meaning. Automaticity in decoding allows time for both comprehension and interaction. Writers also need to develop the motor skills needed for handwriting, remember spelling patterns and grasp the rules of combination, i.e. syntax.

Text Participant

Text participants do more than comprehend texts. They are active readers who use their own experience and meanings to think about and interact with the writer's meanings when they make sense of a text. As writers they actively engage in making and communicating meaning. They have a purpose for writing and a sense of their audience.

Text User

Users read and write for a range of purposes. They are familiar with different kinds of texts (newspaper articles, personal letters, poems, recipes, science reports, literature essays, text books, advertisements, notes, SMS messages, etc.). They understand that different genres are structured differently and use language in different ways. Implicit understanding of these forms comes from ongoing use. They employ a range of literacy practices.

Text Analyst

Analysts examine the effects of linguistic choices in order to understand how the text is working. They are not only interested in what the text means but who benefits and who is disadvantaged by the position taken by the writer. They are interested in how the text works to maintain or challenge existing relations of power in the society. Writers who are analysts are able to choose language deliberately so that their voices can be heard and the positions they support believed.

It helps us to see what we are doing when we use language, and to locate the effects in particular linguistic choices. It gives us a metalanguage to talk about these choices. It is important to understand that choice of any linguistic option necessarily implies rejection of other options. Because any selection directs our attention to what is present in a text and away from the possibilities that have been elided (Kress & Hodge, 1979), it is useful to consider the range of options from which a choice has been made. Using Saussure's concept of paradigmatic relations, it becomes possible to consider the lexical and grammatical choices in the light of what was not selected but what could have been. Because our choices are constrained by what the language system allows us to choose from, we have to know something about this system. For example, at times we have to choose between two options, for example, the definite and the indefinite article[1] or the

---

1. Even the choice of a word as seemingly innocuous as "the" is not neutral. The definite article is used only when the referent is specific for both addresser and addressee or, in simpler terms, when both the writer and the reader know what is being referred to. The use of the definite article presupposes shared knowledge. It is therefore used to refer to established information, whereas the indefinite article is used to refer to new information. So, for example, referring to "weapons of mass destruction" as "the weapons of mass destruction" presupposes both that we all know what weapons we are talking about and that they exist.

Table 9.2 Linguistic Resources Underpinning the Four Roles of the Reader/ Writer

Text Decoder/Encoder

Print literacy – familiarity with books, pages and print.

Alphabetic literacy – names and shapes of letters.

Phonic awareness – sound–letter correspondences.

Phonemic awareness – sound system of English in relation to the sounds of the languages they speak.

Morphological awareness – word formation (book, book*ing*, book*ings*, book*s*, book*ed*).

Vocabulary – words and their (multiple) meanings; word associations, webs of meaning, connotations, collocations, synonyms and antonyms. Word attack skills. *Spelling patterns.*

Syntax – word order and the rules of combination; grammatical clues.

Contextual clues (in the text and in the context).

Text User

Engage in literacy events – read, write and design texts for a range of social purposes.

Understand the social practices that underpin different literacy events.

Understand genres as text-types tied to different social purposes; work with fiction and non-fiction, functional and aesthetic texts.

Appropriateness – the ability to choose the variety and form suited to the social purposes of texts.

Modes – recognise and use the affordances of verbal and visual modes in the construction of print texts.

Media – use a range of technologies for the reception and production of print texts.

Text Participant – Engaged Reader or Writer

Lexical competence – extensive knowledge of words: formation and meaning.

Grammatical competence – complex syntax and nominalizations.

Pragmatic competence – how context affects meaning: implicature, ambiguity, inferencing.

Sociolinguistic competence – language varieties and their social uses (register); text-types and their social purposes (genres).

Semantic competence – the ability to make and infer meaning; metaphorical uses of language.

Textual competence (above the level of the sentence) – cohesive ties, logical connectors, discourse markers, structure and organisation of texts.

Text Analyst – Resistant Reader or Critical Writer

Critical competence – ask questions to understand whose interests are served by the way the text has been, or is being, constructed and its possible social effects; imagining how the text might be transformed.

- How is language working to position the reader?
- Who benefits? Who is disadvantaged?
- What are the values that underpin the text?
- Who is included? Who is excluded? Who speaks?
- What is foregrounded? What is backgrounded? Why?
- What is assumed or taken-for-granted? Who decides what is appropriate?
- How is language used to maintain or challenge existing relations of power? Whose perspectives are privileged? Whose voices are heard/ silenced?

passive and the active voice. At other times we have to choose from many options: the vast array of synonyms in the lexis of English, the range of tenses and modality, the different logical connectors are all cases in point.

Key Linguistic Features for Designing and Analysing Texts

In focusing on the linguistic features that are key for producing and analysing texts, it is important to recognise that text analysis is just one aspect of discourse analysis. For Fairclough (1989, 1995), there are three dimensions of discourse:

1.   the object of analysis (verbal, visual or verbal and visual texts);
2.   the processes by means of which the object is produced (written, spoken, designed) and received (read, listened to, viewed) by human subjects;
3.   the sociohistorical conditions which govern these processes.

According to Fairclough each of these dimensions requires a different kind of analysis:

1.   text analysis (description);
2.   processing analysis (interpretation);
3.   social analysis (explanation).

Fairclough captures the simultaneity of his method of critical discourse analysis (CDA) with a model that embeds the three different kinds of analysis, one inside the other (see Figure 9.1 (Fairclough, 1989, 1995)).

What is useful about this approach is that it enables text participants, text users and text analysts to focus on the signifiers that make up the text, the specific linguistic and visual selections, their juxtapositioning, their sequencing, their layout and so on. However, it requires them to recognise the historical determination of these selections and to understand that these choices are tied to

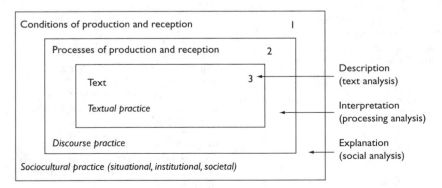

Figure 9.1 Fairclough's Dimensions of Discourse and Discourse Analysis.

the conditions of possibility of that text. This is another way of saying that texts are instantiations of socially regulated discourses and that the processes of production and reception are socially constrained.

Text analysis that focuses only on the semiotic choices that form the text is therefore limited because it says nothing about the text in relation to the social context or the conditions of its production and reception. However, for the purposes of this chapter, which focuses on "language as a system of meaning potential", the focus is on linguistic options in the system and how choice realises meaning. This is not to suggest that text analysis should be done in isolation or that other forms of semeiosis are not as important as language. The template of key linguistic features for text design and analysis (Table 9.3), which is based on Halliday's Systemic Functional Grammar (Halliday, 1985), explains the meaning potential of different linguistic choices. While it provides a useful starting point, it is not intended to be comprehensive. It has three columns. The first names the linguistic feature, the second explains it briefly and the third column is left open for comments about, or examples of, the use of the feature in specific texts.

In order to use this table, writers have to become analysts of what they have written. Analysis enables them to understand how their text is positioned and positioning and it enables them to redesign their texts in relation to their purposes. What matters in text analysis is that it is systematic. If the analyst (either a reader or a writer) decides, for example, to examine the use of pronouns, then every pronoun in the text needs to be considered in order to establish the patterns of use. The same is true of any other linguistic feature. Moreover, a principled reason needs to be given for which linguistic features are examined, should the analyst choose to select only a few.

The text used here as an example is "Spot the Refugee", one of four Lego posters which have appeared on the United Nations High Commission for Refugees website since they were first uploaded on 31 December 1997. I downloaded them again at the following web addresses on 27 July 2009:

> Spot the refugee: www.unhcr.org/4a5484999.html
> What's the difference? www.unhcr.org/4a5466e92.html
> What's wrong here? www.unhcr.org/4a5485ba9.html
> How does it feel? www.unhcr.org/4a5483b39.html

They are not difficult to find if one googles "UNHCR Lego posters" and they make an excellent resource for classrooms.

My analyses of these posters appear in Janks (2005a, 2009). In summary, I argue that in these posters, which set out to construct refugees as "just like you and me", refugees are nevertheless *othered*. They are portrayed as having nothing, which suggests that, without material possessions, they are deemed to be worthless. The assessment of their worth is not based on their skills, their knowledge, their labour or their cultural resources. They are constructed as dependent on us. The historical causes that produce ever-increasing numbers of refugees are absent from the text and the readers (and their respective governments) are exonerated from blame. In order to make the readers more accepting of refugees,

Table 9.3 Template of Key Linguistic Features for Text Analysis (Janks, 2005, 2009)

Linguistic Feature	Meaning Potential	Realisations
Lexicalisation	The selection/choice of wordings. Different words construct the same idea differently	
Overlexicalisation	Many words for the same phenomenon	
Relexicalisation	Renaming	
Lexical cohesion	Created by synonymy, antonymy, repetition, collocation	
Metaphor	Used for yoking ideas together and for the discursive construction of new ideas.	
Euphemism	Hides negative actions or implications	
Transitivity	Processes in verbs. Are they verbs of: • *doing*: material process • *being or having*: relational processes • *thinking/feeling/perceiving*: mental • *saying*: verbal processes • *physiological*: behavioral processes • *existential*	
Voice	Active and passive voice constructs participants as *doers* or as *done-to's* Passive voice allows for the deletion of the agent	
Nominalisation	A process is turned into a thing or an event without participants or tense or modality. This is the central mechanism for reification	
Quoted speech Direct speech Indirect speech Free indirect speech	• Who is quoted in DS/IS/FIS? • Who is quoted first/last/most? • Who is not quoted? • Has someone been misquoted or quoted out of context?	

continued

Scare quotes	• What reporting verb was chosen? • What is the effect of scare quotes?
Turn-taking	• Who gets the floor? How many turns do different participants get? • Who is silent/silenced? • Who interrupts? • Who gets heard? Whose points are followed through? • Whose cultural rules for turn taking are used? Cultures? • Who controls the topic?
Mood	Is the clause a statement, question, offer or command?
Polarity	Positive (yes it is); negative (no it is not)
Tense	Tense sets up the definiteness of events occurring in time. The present tense is used for timeless truths and absolute certainty. The past tense is used for events in the past
Modality	Degrees of uncertainty; logical possibility/probability; social authority Modality created by modals (may, might, could, will), adverbs (possibly, certainly), intonation, tag questions (He'll come, won't he?)
Pronouns	Inclusive we/exclusive we/you Us and them: othering pronouns Sexist/non-sexist pronouns: generic "he" The choice of first/second/third person
Definite article (the) Indefinite article (a)	*The* is used for shared information – to refer to something mentioned before or that the addressee can be assumed to know about. Reveals textual presuppositions
Thematisation	The first bit of the clause is called the Theme. (If the bit before the clause has two bits, the Theme is the first bit) The Theme is the launch pad for the clause Look for patterns of what is foregrounded in the clause by being in Theme position

Table 9.3 continued

Linguistic Feature	Meaning Potential	Realisations
Rheme	The last bit of the clause: the part after the verb. In written English the new information is usually at the end of the clause In spoken English new information is indicated by tone.	
Sequence	Sequencing of information in the clause and of clauses affects meaning Sequence sets up cause and effect, chronology . . .	
Logical connectors	Conjunctions set up the logic of the argument. Conjunctions are • *Additive:* and, in addition • *Causal:* because, so, therefore • *Adversative:* although, yet • *Temporal:* when, while, after, before	
Cohesion	Sets up connections between participants, processes and circumstances in a text Cohesion serves to tie long stretches of clauses together to form a text Effected by conjunction, substitution, repetition, reference and lexical cohesion	

the UNHCR produces a discourse of sameness, which hides differences and does not value diversity as a resource for innovation and growth.

In order to arrive at this interpretation, the transitivity, voice, mood, tense/ modality, theme and lexical choices of every clause in the text were analysed. This first level of description enables one to find patterns by counting occurrences. Table 9.4 shows the rough working that enables the analyst to understand the linguistic and grammatical selections that constitute the data for text analysis.

It is this careful and systematic behind-the-scenes work that enables the analyst to complete the realisations column of Table 9.5.

While there can be no doubt that the intentions of the UNHCR are to improve the ways in which refugees are perceived by making an argument for the recognition of our common humanity, what this analysis shows is that it does this by constructing a discourse of sameness that is problematic. It fails to value our differences and it is a discourse that presupposes a melting-pot ideology as opposed to one which embraces difference.

I began this chapter by playing with lexical and grammatical options for constructing fatness. I will end by stressing the importance of grammatical knowledge for both writers and readers of texts. An understanding of how lexical and grammatical choices realise the meaning potential of language in texts enables writers to design texts purposefully and it gives readers the power to see how texts have been designed – *how* they mean, not just *what* they mean. In the old days of teaching grammar, students were asked to rewrite texts transforming active voice to passive voice or direct speech to indirect speech or present tense to past tense in order to demonstrate their technical facility with these different linguistic forms. Grammar was taught as form not meaning. Such decontextualised grammatical exercise can be redesigned to focus on meaning. If one takes a sentence in a text and makes different linguistic choices, one can ask students to explain what the change does to the meaning. To illustrate this idea, I have suggested some changes in relation to "Spot the Refugee" (see Table 9.6).

These changes serve to draw attention to the choices that were made by the writer and invite students to compare the meaning of the original and the changed version, sensitising them to the effects of particular selections. In rubbing original texts up against transformed texts, we help to see the effects of the original choices and to recognise them as choices, rather than as natural and inevitable ways of encoding meaning. This provides both a purpose for learning and understanding grammar and the motivation for doing so. Where grammar for grammar's sake may be boring, meaning is not. Most importantly, this method of teaching language can be used with any text, at any level.

When we add to this the other dimensions of Fairclough's model and ask students to think about the effects of these meaning choices in particular sociohistorical contexts, then the study of language is immeasurably enriched. In relation to this text, for example, we could ask questions such as:

- Are people the same? Why is it so important to think of people as the same rather than as different?

Table 9.4 Detailed Linguistic Analysis of UNHCR Poster

(Processes in **bold**, pronouns in *italics*)	Transitivity	Voice	Mood	Modality	Theme	Lexis: T=cohesion
Spot the refugee	material	active	command	categorical present tense		the = shared knowledge
There *he* **is**.	relational – being	active	statement	categorical present tense		*he*
Fourth row, second from the left.	no verbs (relational – being?) abbreviated syntax – staccato information. All therefore theme		statement	categorical	fourth row…	pointing out
The one with the moustache.			statement	categorical high modality	the one	the one = with factual info e.g. moustache
Obvious really.			statement		modal: certain	
Maybe not			statement		modal: doubt	
The unsavory looking character **is** more likely to be your average neighborhood slob with a grubby vest and a weekend's stubble on his chin	relational – being	active	statement	more likely – makes "is" less categorical	the unsavory looking character	• Unsavory • average neighborhood slob • grubby vest • weekend stubble
You're **looking at**	behavioral	active	statement		you	
You **see**	mental	active	statement		you	
refugees **are** just like *you and me*.	relational – being	active	statement	categorical	refugees	the real refugee inclusive: you/me/refugee
Except for one thing.			statement?		[except] for one thing	one thing
Everything **has been left behind**	material	passive	statement	categorical	everything	everything
they once **had**	relational – having	active	statement	categorical	they	exclusive
Home, family, possessions [are] all **gone**.	relational – being	active	statement	categorical	home family possessions	Overlexis rheme: all gone

Clause	Process type	Voice	Mood	Modality/Polarity	Participant	
They **have** nothing.	Relational – having	active	statement	categorical	they	nothing T
And nothing **is** all	relational – being	active	statement	categorical	[and] nothing	nothing is all T
They'll ever **have**	relational – having	active	statement	categorical	they	ever T
Unless we all **extend** a helping hand.	material	active	statement	categorical	[unless] we all	helping hand
We **know**	mental	active	statement	categorical	we	
you **can't give** them **back** the things	material	active	statement	can't give back	you	things
that *others* **have taken away**.	material	active	statement	categorical	others	
We're **not** even **asking** for money	material	active	statement	categorical (even)	we (UNHCR)	exclusive we money
(though every penny certainly **helps**).	material	active	statement	certainly helps	every penny	
But we **are asking**	material	active	statement	categorical	[but] we	
And a smile of welcome.	(nominalization)	active			[And] a smile of welcome	smile of welcome
It **may not seem** like much.	relational	active	statement	may not seem	it (a smile of welcome)	[not] much
But to a refugee it **can mean** everything.	?relational/mental	active	statement	can mean	[but] to a refugee	you: it [not much] refugee: it everything
UNHCR **is** a strictly humanitarian organization	relational – being	active	statement	categorical present tense	UNHCR	strictly humanitarian
[that **is] funded** only by voluntary contributions.	material	passive [is] funded	statement	categorical	[UNHCR]	only by voluntary contributions (nom)
Currently it **is** responsible for more than 19 million refugees around the world.	relational – being	active	statement	categorical present tense	currently [UNHCR]	more than 19 million around the world

Table 9.5 Linguistic Analysis of a UNHCR Poster Using the Key Linguistic Features Template

Linguistic Feature	Meaning Potential	Realisations of Meanings
Lexicalisation	The selection/choice of wordings. Different words construct the same idea differently	If you look for the refugee in the *Fourth row, second from the left. The one with the moustache,* you will have been reeled in by the text, only to discover that you have been cheated, because – *The unsavory looking character you're looking at is more likely to be your average neighborhood slob with a grubby vest and a weekend's stubble on his chin. And the real refugee could just as easily be the clean-cut fellow on his left.* In addition, you will have been constructed as someone who assumes that refugees look like "unsavory", unshaved "slobs". And because you are now someone who sees refugees as both different from and inferior to you, you need to learn that *"clean-cut" refugees are just like you and me*
Metaphor	Used for yoking ideas together and for the discursive construction of new ideas	Lego dolls are a visual metaphor – human beings are constructed as look-alike, manipulateable, toy dolls
Euphemism	Hides negative actions or implications	Everything they once had has been left behind
Transitivity	Processes in verbs • *doing:* material process • *being or having:* relational processes • *thinking/ feeling/perceiving:* • *mental* • *saying:* verbal processes	The use of transitivity shows that the refugee is constructed predominantly with relational processes of "being" and "having", whereas the reader and the UNHCR are constructed with very few relational processes. They are given both mental and material processes, and the UNHCR in addition, is given verbal processes. They are shown acting. The UNHCR is the only participant that speaks

Voice	Active and passive voice constructs participants as doers or as "done-to-s". Passive voice allows for the deletion of the agent	All active voice except for "everything has been left behind" which is a passive construction, removing agency. Un-named "others" are blamed
Nominalisation	A process is turned into a thing	
Quoted speech	The use of direct, indirect or free indirect speech	"a smile of welcome"
Turn-taking	• Who gets the floor? How many turns do different participants get? • Who is silent/silenced? • Who interrupts? • Who gets heard? Whose points are followed through? • Who controls the topic?	Only the UNHCR speaks and it speaks for refugees. It alone knows what refugees want and need. No refugee's voice is heard
Mood	Is the clause a statement, question, offer or command?	The opening instruction, SPOT THE REFUGEE, prominent because it is printed in capital letters in a large bold font is the only command in a text that is otherwise made up of statements. Statements providing information are used throughout, suggesting that the reader needs to be informed by the UNHCR
Polarity and tense	Tense is used for categorical statements	Almost all clauses are in the present tense and are categorical.
Modality: degrees of uncertainty	Logical possibility/probability Social authority	Modality is used to create uncertainty only about our ability to recognise or understand the needs of refugees

continued

Table 9.5 continued

Linguistic Feature	Meaning Potential	Realisations of Meanings
Pronouns Generic "he" used to include "she"	The pronouns chosen are also doing interesting work. First the refugee is referred to as "he". The use of pronouns is also interesting because of the way in which it presents the refugee as male, this despite the fact that 80% of refugees are women and children. The gender stereotyping is reinforced in the visual images, where women tend to be shown without the occupation markers of the male figures and with jewellery	
Us and them	The refugee is constructed as just like "you and me" (the reader and the writer, who represents the UNHCR). Having denied any diversity, reinforced by the supposed sameness of the Lego dolls, the text immediately sets up a difference, introduced by the word "except" and encoded in us/them pronouns	*Except for one thing. Everything **they** once had has been left behind. Home, family, possessions all gone. **They** have nothing. And nothing is all **they'**ll ever have unless **we** all extend a helping hand.* [My emphasis]
Inclusive we/exclusive we	"We" is used here to include the reader and the writer, and to exclude refugees. In the very next sentence, "we" is used exclusively. Here, "we" refers to the UNHCR only. The UNHCR is constructed as knowing what can mean everything to a refugee. The reader is in need of instruction on how to behave, and refugees are given no agency and no voice. This sets up the very social divide that the early part of the text is at pains to refute	*We know you can't give **them** back the things that others have taken away.* *We're not even asking for money (though every penny certainly helps).* *But **we** are asking that **you** keep an open mind. And a smile of welcome.* *It may not seem like much. But to a refugee it can mean everything.*
Definite article (the) Indefinite article (a)	The is used for shared information – to refer to something mentioned before or that the addressee can be assumed to know about	Spot the refugee – "the" suggests that there is a refugee in the group of Lego figures and that this is shared information

Thematisation	Look for patterns of what is foregrounded in the clause by being in theme position	An analysis of theme, shows movement in the text from the refugee, to you (the reader), to possessions thematised four times and expressed as everything and as nothing, back to the reader (and his or her attitude) — "a smile of welcome" is thematised twice, once with the pronoun "it". The text concludes with the UNHCR in theme position
Rheme — syntax: the last bit of the clause is called the rheme	In written English the new information is usually at the end of the clause	The bottom right-hand corner of the text, the prime position for new information, is reserved for the UNHCR
Sequencing of information Logical connectors — conjunctions set up the logic of the argument	Sequence sets up cause and effect. Conjunctions are: • *additive*: and, in addition • *causal*: because, so, therefore • *adversative*: although, yet • *temporal*: when, while, after, before	The logic of the text is maintained by the way in which information is sequenced. Additive conjunctions predominate with two noticeable variations — the use of "except" to signify the shift to the one thing that differentiates refugees, and the use of "but" to underscore how important people's attitudes are to a refugee

Table 9.6 Possible Changes to "Spot the Refugee"

Original Version	Changed Version
Spot the refugee	Can one spot a refugee?
They have *nothing*	They have no *material possessions*
We know *you* can't give them back the things that others have taken away	We know *we* can't give them back their stolen possessions
Your average neighborhood slob	Your average neighbor
Picture of Lego people arranged *in rows*	Picture of *real* people *not in rows*

- Why are people who have no possessions viewed as having nothing? What other kinds of "things" might people have?
- Who is said to be responsible for taking the refugees' things? In what ways might our government or other governments be responsible?
- What percentage of refugees in the world are men?[2]
- How are refugees treated in your country?

Such questions teach students to become text participants, who bring meanings to texts, and text analysts who think about the interests at play and the political and social effects that textual representations can have.

Activity: Analysing an Advertisement

Find an advertisement that you find interesting. Analyse the linguistic choices by completing the key linguistic features table introduced in Table 9.3.

If discourse analysis is not possible without an understanding of lexico-grammar, and critical reading is not possible without discourse analysis, then we do our students an educational disservice if we do not teach them grammar. If writers have no means of interrogating the texts they produce, then they have limited resources for redrafting and repositioning their work. In this chapter I have provided the motivation for teaching grammar along with a method and a model for thinking about the use of lexico-grammar for making meaning in texts and contexts. I trust that I have used the meaning potential of language to construct a convincing argument.

References

De Saussure, F. (1972). *Course in general linguistics.* (R. Harris, Trans.) London: Duckworth.
Fairclough, N. (1989). *Language and power.* London: Longman.

2. These questions are addressed in Janks (2005a).

Fairclough, N. (1995). *Critical discourse analysis.* London: Longman.

Freebody, P., & Luke, A. (1990). Literacies programs: Debates and demands in cultural context. *Prospect: Australian Journal of TESOL, 5*(7), 7–16.

Halliday, M. (1978). *Language as social semiotic.* London: Arnold.

Halliday, M. (1985). *An introduction to functional grammar.* London: Arnold.

Janks, H. (2005a). Deconstruction and reconstruction: Diversity as a productive resource. *Discourse, 26*(1), 31–43.

Janks, H. (2005b). Language and the design of texts. *English Teaching: Practice and Critique, 4*(3), 97–110.

Janks, H. (2009). *Literacy and power.* New York and London: Routlege.

Kress, G., & Hodge, R. (1979). *Language and ideology.* London: Routledge.

Orbach, S. (1986). *Fat is a feminist issue.* New York: Berkley Books.

Pearson, P. (2009, 22 May). obstinate/ˈɒbstɪnət/. *The word guy: Blog at wordpress.com.* Retrieved 27 July 2009, from http://thewordguy.wordpress.com.

Chapter 10

Discovering a Metalanguage for All Seasons

Bringing Literary Language in from the Cold

Terry Locke

Recently, I was teaching a class to pre-service English teachers on the topic of metalanguage in the English classroom. As this book has made clear, a "metalanguage" is a language that is used to talk reflectively and to some extent systematically *about* language use. Groups were reading literary texts in order to identify what they considered to be the salient language features present. Sitting in on one group, I discovered that they had identified *personification* as such a feature. In the course of conversation, one of the students (I'll call her Emma) asserted that personification was not a metalinguistic feature. "Personification is a figure of speech", she said, "whereas grammar just is". The comment is indicative of a number of concerns that underpin this chapter: teacher insecurities around their own language knowledge; a persisting dichotomy in English/literacy between "language" and "literature" and their attendant metalanguages; how the discourses teachers use to frame or construct conversations around texts are constituted.

Activity: Map Your Own Metalinguistic Profile

We can think about the metalanguage we use to talk about texts as existing on a number of levels: (1) the relationship of text to context; (2) whole text; (3) sentence-level; (4) word-level; (5) prosodic and kinesic (body language) features; (6) visual/pictorial features. List the metalinguistic terms you would use in talking about each of these levels and categories.

For example, a level 1 term might be "genre", a level 2 text "rhyme scheme" (for a poem), a level 3 term "complex sentence", a level 4 term "noun" or "metaphor", a level 5 term "intonation" and a level 6 term "close-up".

There are three parts to this chapter. In the first part, I draw on a Bernsteinian model (see Bernstein, 2000) to investigate ways in which the pedagogic discourses available to teachers have undergone a shift in a number of settings and why this should be. Putting it another way, I will be asking questions about *where* the language Emma uses to conduct talk about texts comes from. In the second part of this chapter, I look specifically at the kind of metalanguage teachers might utilize in their conversations with students around the reading and composition of literary texts. In the third part of the chapter, I put myself in Emma's shoes, as a teacher beginning her career in English language arts/literacy, and suggest a strategy teachers might adopt in constructing for themselves a metalanguage, useful to themselves and to their students, for making meaning of the texts they read and write.

Talking around Texts

As a teacher educator, I often find myself telling pre-service teachers that their principle task is to conduct productive and interesting conversations around texts, whether the situation is a text being responded to, or a text in the process of being composed. I'm using the term conversation in a rather broad sense here, and include the extension of oral conversation into the kind of dialogue that takes place via the medium of written tasks.

A related assumption is that the meaning that students make of a text (even one they are writing themselves) is a function of the kind of conversation that is taking place. Different ways of interrogating texts elicit different kinds of meaning (Locke, 2003). For example, if you dip into *Understanding Poetry* by Cleanth Brooks and Robert Penn Warren (1976), you will see that a typical segment contains the text of a poem and a set of question prompts. The kind of conversation generated by adherence to the questions in this book assumes an authorized meaning *in* the poem and assigns negligible importance to the contribution individual readers bring to the meaning-making process. They are discoverers rather than co-constructors of meaning. The conversation also demands a common understanding of certain technical terms (a literary metalanguage): stanza, tone, concrete image, run-on lines, caesura, scan and so on.

The metalanguage that teachers like Emma develop becomes part of their professional content knowledge (Shulman, 1986). As I have discussed elsewhere (Locke, 2004b), the various sources that can be viewed as having a constitutive role in the development of the professional knowledge of English/literacy teachers are threefold:

1. textual practice as it operates in society and across cultures;
2. textual practice as it is constructed in the context of undergraduate and graduate degree programs in such "disciplines" as English, Media Studies, Drama, Applied Linguistics, Professional Writing and so on;
3. textual practice as constructed via curriculum designs, qualifications systems, high-stakes assessment practices and resource production.

The virtue in keeping these sources distinct is that it allows for scrutiny of the relationship between each of them. For example, one can ask questions such as: To what extent does the construction of textual practice in a system's intended curriculum reflect textual practice in the wider social context?

Bernstein's contribution to this discussion is his view that the constitution of professional knowledge in discourse as a dimension of pedagogic practice, while apparently haphazard, is in fact the product of a set of "regulatory principles" controlled by what he terms the "pedagogic device [which] acts as a symbolic regulator of consciousness" (2000, p. 37). (For an application of Bernstein's theory to the situation of grammar teaching in Britain, see Urszula Clark's chapter in this volume.) Putting it bluntly, there is nothing neutral about pedagogic discourse, and the hegemonic or dominant position of a *particular* pedagogic discourse is the result of a particular set of power relations (see Figure 10.1). In Bernstein's scheme, the top-level "distributive rules mark and distribute who may transmit what to whom and under what conditions, and they attempt to set the outer limits of legitimate discourse" (2000, p. 31). In the current milieu, Bernstein argues, these rules are increasingly controlled by the state apparatus.

Norman Fairclough defines a discourse as "a practice not just of representing the world, but of signifying the world, constituting and constructing the world in meaning" (1992, p. 64). In the case of a school subject like English, the prevailing discursive mix (in Bernstein's terms, the "specific pedagogic discourse") determines *what* can be said about a particular topic and *how* it can be said – hence

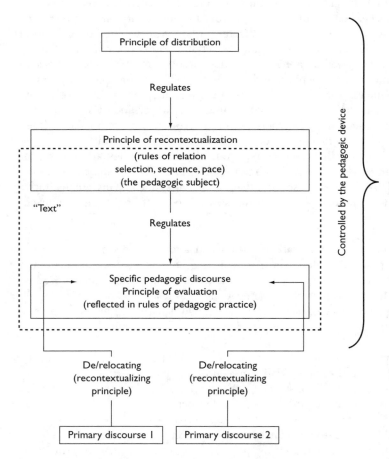

Figure 10.1 Bernstein's View of the Pedagogic Discourse.

the relationship to metalanguage.[1] As Bernstein further points out, a specific pedagogic discourse can be thought of as a principle "by which other discourses are appropriated and brought into a special relationship with each other, for the purpose of their selective transmission and acquisition" (2000, p. 32) via a process he calls "recontextualization" from a range of "primary" discourses that have their origins beyond the confines of the school. We are back here with the question of where Emma's metalanguage comes from and what led to her having her metalanguage constituted in a particular way.

Activity: Reflecting on the Sources of Your Professional Content Knowledge

List the sources of your metalinguistic knowledge, that is, where did this knowledge come from? Rank these sources from more to less important.
This book is an example of a source of textual knowledge about metalanguage. Another kind of source relates to pre-service teacher-education courses. Another source might be a policy document that stipulates the kind of metalanguage students need to know at different stages of schooling.

The example Bernstein uses is the school subject, physics, and its relationship with physics as a primary discourse, produced through the work of physicists in the field. What of English as a pedagogic discourse? If we explore the question of the primary discourses that become recontextualized in the production of English as a school subject, we find a clue as to why Emma and other beginning teachers (see Wild, 2003) struggle to settle on an appropriate metalanguage for themselves. In Bernstein's terms, English as a school subject has always been weakly classified, that is, its boundaries have tended to be permeable to a range of primary discourses. At the beginning of the 20th century, you might describe English as constructed out of discourses such as philology, rhetoric and an emergent discourse called literary studies or literary criticism. For most of the 20th century, it tended to be dichotomized between language (grammar, linguistics) and literary (literary criticism) emphases, with one or the other holding sway at any one time (see, for example, Shayer, 1972; Muller, 1967). In the present time, there is potential for English to be subject to discursive input from applied linguistics, cultural studies, screen and media studies, theatre studies, literary criticism, rhetoric and semiotics, each with its own specialist language.

In the last 20 years, the term "literacy" (or "literacies") has assumed a central role in constructions of English as pedagogic discourse. For teachers of English or English language arts in a number of educational contexts, powerful state-sanctioned messages are positioning them as teachers of literacy rather than teachers of English (Bousted, 2003). Depending on the content of the message,

---

1. Bernstein uses the term "unthinkable" to encapsulate those things which a hegemonic discourse disallows one from saying about a particular topic.

teachers are being positioned as either contributors to this or that literacy crisis or part of its remedy.

This shift in discourse and identity formation has been played out in different ways in different parts of the world, with somewhat different impacts on the professional content knowledge of teachers (including metalinguistic take-up). There is broad agreement that in the Australasian setting, discourses of English were dominated prior to 1990 by cultural heritage and personal growth models of the subject (Locke, 2007; Snyder, 2008), which in different ways made literary response and its attendant metalanguage central to the subject. In the early 1990s, the Australian genre school emerged which advocated powerfully for a particular version of a rhetorical or textual competence model of English (Cope & Kalantzis, 1993; Christie, this volume). This model focused on language-in-use and was concerned to empower students with the competences to read and produce significant genres (or text-types) in a range of social contexts. Genre theorists connected their pragmatic competence agenda with a focus on academic literacy and the adoption of Hallidayan or systemic functional grammar. In this instance of the "linguistic" turn, subject English underwent a huge shift in its primary discursive base, away from literary criticism towards applied linguistics.

Chronologically, the critical practice (or critical literacy) model of English succeeded the rhetorical practice model. Both models tended to decentre the literary. In 1996, the Australian Association for the Teaching of English (AATE) published a resource on critical literacy, which included an address by Wendy Morgan (Morgan, Gilbert, Lankshear, Werner & Williams, 1996). It is a useful resource, which I still use with my pre-service secondary English teachers. At what I now take to be a key moment in her address, Morgan tells her audience that: "These days, we hear less about literary criticism and more about critical literacy" (p. 35). Elsewhere in the address, Morgan acknowledges the widespread use of systemic functional grammar in Australian schools and notes that while it can be seen as supporting the concerns of critical literacy, it should not be seen as synonymous with it. What is evident here is a further discursive shift from literary criticism as a primary discourse in the construction of English towards the discourse of a particular (Hallidayan) school in applied linguistics.[2]

The mantra that "literacy is a social practice", associated with both rhetorical practice and critical literacy models of English, has further consolidated the centrality of "literacy" or "literacies" as the core of the English progamme. While this mantra highlights a particular aspect of literacy, it rather tends to suppress other aspects. Literacy is also an individual practice, and it is individuals who take pleasure in texts. The focus on concepts such as discourse also shifts the focus from literary text-makers and receivers giving and receiving pleasure to the cultural. Critical literacy, almost by definition, is about reading culture *through* texts, with a consequent erasure of pleasure *in* the text and the idea of individual

---

2. Recognition of this shift and perhaps a way of compensating for it is implicit in the book, Misson, R., & Morgan, W. (2006). *Critical literacy and the aesthetic: Transforming the English classroom.* Urbana, IL: NCTE.

artistic genius. Moreover, because of the close link between critical literacy and both critical language awareness and critical discourse analysis, it has been affected by the linguistic turn – by the widespread "take-up" of systemic functional grammar at the expense of forms of literary criticism.

In discussing the function of the "recontextualizing field", Bernstein (2000) distinguishes between "an *official recontextualizing field* (ORF) created and dominated by the state and its selected agents and ministries, and a *pedagogic recontextualizing field* (PBF)" consisting of "pedagogues in schools and colleges, and departments of education, specialized journals, private research foundations" (p. 33). The distinction is a useful one for considering the balance of power relations in relation to who determines the pedagogic discourse at any particular time and in whose interests. Clark's chapter in this book, for example, shows how prescribed grammatical knowledge in the British setting became dominated by the ORF and how individuals associated with the PBF, such as Ron Carter and the LINC (Language in the National Curriculum) project, became marginalized (see Carter, 1996).

A specific illustration of how recontextualization can contribute to the erasure of a literary-related metalanguage is a discussion hosted in 1999 on the International Reading Association's *Reading Online* site, featuring Allan Luke and Peter Freebody, and entitled "Further Notes on the Four Resources Model".

> The model posits four necessary but not sufficient "roles" for the reader in a postmodern, text-based culture:
>
> - Code breaker (coding competence)
> - Meaning maker (semantic competence)
> - Text user (pragmatic competence)
> - Text critic (critical competence). (Luke & Freebody, 1999, paragraph 1)

Having referred to an axiom of the New Criticism that the recovery of "authorial intent is a waste of time" (paragraph 2), Luke and Freebody ironically make it very clear what their intention was:

> It was our position that determining how to teach literacy could not be simply "scientific," but rather had to involve a moral, political, and cultural decision about the kind of literate practices needed to enhance both peoples' agency over their life trajectories and communities' intellectual, cultural, and semiotic resources in multimediated economies. (paragraph 8)

The piece is a powerful reminder of the role human agents can have in the production of discourses, in this case of literacy and education. The four-resources model had wide uptake in the New Zealand context following an address by Luke to the New Zealand Reading Association in 1992. It is ironic that a piece that rejects "magic bullets" was in a way treated as such. In the transcript of the discussion forum, we find Luke outlining changes in the teacher-education curriculum at his then institution, the University of Queensland.

We require that all teacher-trainees (in maths, sciences, economics, all areas): learn functional grammar, critical discourse analysis, how to analyze and teach genres of a range of popular and academic texts, and related teaching/learning theory. This includes theories of discourse and ideology. In other words, all our students learn to "do" grammar – but in relation to issues of how discourse constructs and shapes identity, difference and educational relations of power. p.s. the students really enjoy it, because it's extremely hands on. (transcript of the discussion forum, Reply 1a)

If the "it" that students enjoy includes the literary, it is certainly not mentioned. Luke has arguably been the most influential literacy theorist of his generation, and has been involved in both official and pedagogic recontextualizing fields. It is hardly surprising then, that stances such as the above should have played their part in affecting at the micro level the metalanguage available for Emma to utilize in her English teaching, at least in Australasia.

Activity: Identifying Powerful Sources of Professional Content Knowledge

In relation to your own educational setting, identify the source of metalinguistic knowledge that you would rate as most powerful for English/literacy teachers. Has it always been like this? How did this situation come about? We realize that this is a rather "subjective" question, but it provides an opportunity for you to think about the forces that "shape" your thinking as a literacy/English language arts teacher.

A Language for Talking about Literary Texts

In this section of the chapter, I focus on literary texts as a significant category (however defined) in a typical English/literacy programme. I will be addressing two questions:

- Is there a specialized language for talking about responses to literary texts that teachers should know?
- Is there evidence that it is useful for student readers of literary texts to have a specialized language (or metalanguage) for making meaning?

At the outset, let me reiterate a point I make at the end of my introduction to this book, that there is more evidence for the usefulness of a metalanguage in responding to texts than in the production of them. However, as producers of texts we are also potentially responders to and reflectors on the texts that we produce. In the latter metacognitive role, I believe, knowledge of a metalanguage is useful.

As a way of approaching the first of these questions, let me quote a recent comment by Eagleton (2007) that "quite a few teachers of literature nowadays do not practice literary criticism, since they, in turn, were never taught to do so" (p. 1). *How to Read a Poem* was published 24 years after Eagleton wrote his highly influential book *Literary Theory: An Introduction* (1983), where he argued famously "not only that literature does not exist in the sense that insects do, and that the value-judgements by which it is constituted are historically variable, but that these value-judgements themselves have a close relation to social ideologies" (p. 16). You could say that his 2007 book is ironic testimony to the fact that books of poetry and silverfish really do coexist materially in bookshops, but that a shift has occurred in the pedagogic discourse of English teaching that his book seeks to remedy.

Eagleton makes no bones about the *value* of poetry (and by extension, other literary texts).

> Poetry ... puts on show what is true about language anyway, but which goes generally unnoticed. In everyday language, too, "content" is the product of "form".... Meanings are a matter of how we use words, rather than words being a matter of conveying meanings which are formed independently of them. (2007, p. 68)

Putting this another way, poetry is the literary form par excellence, that highlights the role all language plays in human sense-making. For Eagleton, a consequence of the disappearance of literary critical practices has been a classroom focus on content rather than form, with a correspondingly reduced grasp of textual meanings that are form-dependent. Form, in respect of poetry, Eagleton tells us,

> concerns such aspects of the poem as tone, pitch, rhythm, diction, volume, metre, pace, mood, voice, address, texture, structure, quality, syntax, register, point of view, punctuation and the like, whereas content is a matter of meaning, character, idea, storyline, moral vision, argument and so on. (p. 66)

The medicine his book dispenses includes two key chapters, one entitled "In Pursuit of Form", and the other "How to Read a Poem", both of which model ways in which form contributes to meaning in a range of texts.

There are three points to be made here that may be of use to Emma in her search for a metalanguage. First, there is a specialized language for talking about responses to literary texts and that a case can be made for its necessity in understanding the way in which *form-dependent* meanings are constructed in literary (and other) texts. Second, literary criticism as primary discourse has a role to play in the construction of pedagogic discourse of English/literacy that is different from the role of, say, Hallidayan linguistics. You would not find anything remotely resembling Eagleton's list of terms in a book such as Knapp and Watkins' *Genre, Text, Grammar* (2005), which draws on the primary discourse of systemic functional linguistics as recontextualized in the educational setting by Jim Martin (for example, 1993). What you *will* find is a section on "literary descriptions" in a chapter on "The Genre of Describing", and a chapter entitled

"The Grammar of Narrating" which focuses on sequencing and structure. Emma's term "personification" is missing from the index. In fact, a focus on the metalanguage of texture is markedly absent from this text. Third, within the primary discourse of literary criticism, there is no settled, agreed-upon metalanguage. This is unsurprising, given the varied schools that make up the patchwork of literary criticism as an intellectual discipline (or, some would say, indiscipline). The literary metalanguage you will find in a book such as Beach, Appleman, Hynds and Wilhelm (2006) will not be identical to that found in Eagleton (2007), but there will be areas of overlap.

Is there evidence that it is useful for student readers of literary texts to have a specialized language (or metalanguage) for making meaning? A study that attempted to address this question in relation to the reading of poetry·was conducted by Joan Peskin (1998) at the University of Toronto. Among other things, the study asked "whether, in a subjective and idiosyncratic area such as poetry reading, experts differed from novices in terms of their deep structure of knowledge in a manner similar to the study of expertise in other domains" (p. 237) and "whether, if novices are having greater difficulty constructing meaning in poetry, this will diminish their appreciation of the poem" (p. 239).

Of relevance to this discussion, Peskin viewed literary expertise as the possession of knowledge content and organization. Besides their ability to identify allusions to other works and categorize poems by genre, experts were able to focus on aspects of form in ways which enriched the meaning-making process for them, that is, they "mine[d] their knowledge resources to provide a deeper, richer exploration of the poetic significance and of how the poet has effected meaning, where the form echoes the content, and whether the conventions were adhered to or subverted" (p. 243). Eagleton would have used a word like "construct" rather than "echo". However, like Eagleton, Peskin suggests that literary meaning-making cannot be separated from a focus on form. Her experts, when confronted with interpretive challenges, resorted to attending to their knowledge of the formal qualities of the writing. Their metalinguistic (formal) knowledge cued them to attend to such things as structure, wordplay and word choice, rhyme and rhythm and patterns of various kinds. Compared to the novices, expert readers showed a greater appreciation of the texts read and of "specific effects and imagery" (p. 252). It would seem, then, that a major source of pleasure from a literary or aesthetic text derives from one's delight in its formal qualities and an awareness of the relationship and appropriateness of those qualities to the meanings that are being made in and around the text.

An Eclectic Strategy for Constructing a Metalanguage for English/Literacy Classrooms

My starting point and "frame" for this section of this chapter is the old concept of rhetoric, defined by Eagleton (1983) as the oldest form of "literary criticism" in the world, which analysed "the way discourses are constructed in order to achieve certain effects" (p. 205), and which I tell my own students is the art of making language work for you. In relation to this definition, *function* is the work that language performs at a particular instance in a text. A rhetorical approach to textual study can be summed up in the following points.

- People construct texts to achieve a desired result with a particular audience.
- Textual form follows function.
- Texts are generated by contexts.
- Texts assume a social complicity between maker and reader.
- The expectations of participants in such acts of complicity become formalized in the conventions of genre.
- These conventions relate to such language features as layout, structure, punctuation, syntax and diction.
- In a rhetorical approach, literature is not devalued but revalued.

At the heart of the rhetorical approach is a concern for a relationship between a text producer and an audience of some kind, either explicitly or implicitly present. Peskin (1998) makes precisely this point using the metaphor of a contract when quoting Jonathan Culler (1976, p. 95) in the report on her research discussed previously.

> Culler wrote of a "contract between reader and writer" whereby "expectations about the forms of literary organization, implicit models of literary structures, practice in forming and testing hypotheses about literary works ... guide[s] one in the perception and construction of relevant patterns". (p. 254)

The term "genre" – regardless of how it is defined – reflects a view that the context of an utterance has a determining effect on its formal qualities. Bakhtin (1986) uses the word in two senses, both for the complex of factors that make up the utterance as he defines it and for the "form of construction" of the utterance as textual product. Kress, in his early work, defines genres as "typical forms of text which link kinds of producer, consumer, topic, medium, manner and occasion" (Hodge & Kress, 1988, p. 7). Writers in the new rhetorical tradition incline to definitions of genre, focusing on similarities in the context of situation (to use Halliday's term) rather than in the text as artefact. Freedman and Medway (1994), for instance, define genres as "typical ways of engaging rhetorically with recurring situations" (p. 2).

Viewed through this lens, Emma's task as an English/literacy teacher is to make her students aware that context-specific, textual engagement is an inevitable facet of their social lives as human beings and that different contexts have different rules of textual engagement. As Bakhtin would have it, we are socialized into differing repertoires of genres. It is in students' interests that they understand these rules, however provisional and subject to change they might be. It is also in their interests that they expand their genre repertoire and understand that certain genres are more powerful in certain societies than others. (For instance, the submission, editorial, policy document and press release are powerful genres in most Western societies.)

The following headings can be useful for describing a genre (see Locke, 2004a).

1. Context of culture
2. Context of situation
3. Function/purpose
4. Typical content
5. Features:
   - layout
   - diction
   - punctuation
   - syntax
   - structure.

The first two of these draw on Halliday and Hasan's work in the 1980s, when they were laying the foundations of systemic functional grammar (see Christie in this volume). The *context of situation* was the immediate social context of a text which allowed for meaning to be exchanged, whereas the *context of culture* was the broader institutional and cultural environment within which the context of situation is embedded (see Halliday & Hasan, 1985, p. 12).

By framing Emma's search for a metalanguage rhetorically, I'm doing two things. I'm recommending that she adopt a top-down approach to grammar, that is, begin with the social context and view the particulars of any text as rendered meaningful *only* in relation to the function they serve in that context (conveying a particular stance on particular content to a particular audience). Second, I'm foregrounding certain metalinguistic terms that reflect the text–context orientation, terms such as *genre, context of situation, words* and *function*. The use of such terms orient Emma (and by extension her students) to text–context considerations, regardless of the text-type being studied.

I must acknowledge at this point that using a rhetorical frame is a value-laden decision. It is encouraging a particular slant on, say, a literary genre such as the short story, a slant that would not be reflected in New Critics such as Brooks and Warren (1976). However, in my defence, I am suggesting that a rhetorical framing offers a useful way of grasping ways in which literary texts operate socially in ways that are similar to those not normally categorized as literary, a point suggested by Eagleton (2007), when he notes that "A poem ... is a rhetorical performance, but (unlike most rhetorical exercises) not typically an instrumental one. It does things to us, though not usually so that we can get something done" (p. 89). It is also, I argue, an accommodating frame, that is, it permits a range of approaches to literary texts to be adopted by classroom teachers such as Emma (for examples of such approaches, see Soter, 1999; Beach, Appleman, Hynds & Wilhelm, 2006). At its heart, a rhetorical orientation is pragmatic, that is, it judges a text by its effects, whether these effects be moving mountains, moving barriers or moving hearts.

The adoption of a rhetorical frame, then, is not meant to commit Emma to a particular approach to the teaching of literary and non-literary texts. Rather it presents her with the above list of genre headings and says to her: *You* identify the language features that *you* think are most useful for metacognitive reflection in relation to the reception and composition of texts that you have chosen to put before your students. *You* consider the ways in which the headings for features needs to change, when the text under consideration is multimodal. (See, for example, Unsworth in this volume).

Activity: Describing a Genre You Use with Your Students

Using the headings listed above, describe a genre that your students engage with (as readers or producers) in the context of your own classroom or in a classroom you are familiar with. (If your text is multimodal, you may want to modify the feature categories under 5, drawing on the work of Cloonan, Kalantzis and Cope, or Unsworth in this book.

In a recent research project on teaching literature in the multicultural classroom (Locke et al., 2008), participating teacher-researchers were asked to identify the terms they expect themselves and their students to use in their classroom discourse. Table 10.1 shows the terms identified by one teacher (I'll call her Bronwen) in relation to different textual levels suggested by the genre headings above. Asked how confident she felt about her own "technical" vocabulary, she wrote in her reflective profile: "I don't worry when I don't know. I explain to students that we're in a changing world with changing language. So sometimes I discover new words only when they do." Bronwen had been teaching for around 24 years, and had Emma asked her about her approach to teaching English, the more experienced colleague would have indicated that she drew on a range of paradigms of the subject and varied the emphasis in her teaching from lesson to lesson and in response to the kind of class she had in front of her.

The approach I have taken in this chapter views English teaching in practice as drawing on a number of paradigms of the subject, each with its own attendant metalanguage. While recontextualization processes in different educational settings are likely to propel a particular version of the subject into a hegemonic position, English/literacy teachers need to be cannily aware of ways in which the pedagogic discourse of their subject is shaped by various power relations. For teachers as professionals, a way of strategizing a response to the political situation is to spread the net widely in terms of the way one garners a metalinguistic vocabulary for use with students and constructs one's identity as a teacher. (A currently under-utilized source of such a vocabulary, I have been suggesting, is literary criticism in its various forms.) Elsewhere, I have termed this critical eclecticism (Locke, 2003). For a young teacher like Emma, it provides a strategy for exercising some power in her situation. If language creates reality, Emma can become an agent in the process, exercising and modelling choice-making and thereby affecting/effecting the realities and meanings for the students in her care.

Table 10.1 Textual Levels and Metalinguistic Terms

Textual Level	Metalinguistic Term
Text in relation to social context	Cultural context, context of situation, discourse, story, genre, position (as noun and verb), version of reality, representation, partial, rhetoric, function, purpose, audience, intention, novel, stage play, lyric poem, ballad, short story, biography, autobiography, review, hyperfiction, literary, literature, literary non-fiction, tragedy, comedy, absurd, existential, fate, theme, hero, anti-hero, concrete poetry
Text structure	Script, structure, plot, form, exposition (or orientation), rising action, suspense, initial incident, problem, complication, predicament, dilemma, choice, conflict, resolution, turning point, climax, catastrophe, denouement, foreshadowing, motif, point of view, first person, second person, third person, restricted access, omniscient, composition, architecture, meter, stanza, paragraph, coherence, cohesion, setting, character, characterization, mood, atmosphere, hypertext, hotlink, animation
Sentence-level	Syntax, sentence (various types), phrase (various types), clause (various types), rhythm, meter, iambic, non-metrical, non-syntactical pause, lineation, indent, dialogue, indirect speech, reported speech, punctuation, run-on sentence, semi-colon, full stop, capital letter, tone, exclamation, question-mark
Word-level (diction)	Figures of speech, metaphor, simile, symbol personification, oxymoron, hyperbole, metonymy, figures of sound, assonance, alliteration, assonance, onomatopoeia, synaesthesia, sound colouring, formal, informal, literal, figurative, concrete, abstract, image, visual, aural, tactile, olifactory, gustatory, rhyme, redundant, tautology, synonym, antonym, word class, noun, verb, adjective, pronoun, determiner, conjunction, pronoun, preposition
Prosodic and kinesic (body language) features	Prosodic features, transcription, pitch, pause, pace, volume, intonation, emphasis, tempo, paralinguistic features, kinesic signals, body language, body movement, gesture, facial expression, stance
Visual/pictorial features	Symbol, icon, index, composition, layout, border, font, size, bold, italic, plain, point, gutter, text block, autoflow, highlight, perspective, disposition, point of view, close-up, medium shot, long shot, establishing shot, distance, angle, objective, subjective, element, relationship, mock up, mise-en-scène, costume, make-up, lighting, pagination, justification, alignment, tabulation, bullets

References

Bakhtin, M. (1986). The problem with speech genres. In C. Emerson & M. Holquist (Eds.), *Speech genres and other late essays: M.M. Bakhtin* (V. McGee, Trans.) (pp. 60–102). Austin: University of Texas Press.

Beach, R., Appleman, D., Hynds, S., & Wilhelm, J. (2006). *Teaching literature to adolescents*. Mahwah, NJ: Lawrence Erlbaum Associates.

Bernstein, B. (2000). *Pedagogy, symbolic control and identity: Theory, research, critique* (Rev. ed.). Lanham, MA: Rowman & Littlefield Publishers, Inc.

Bousted, M. (2003). English or literacy? That is the question. *English Teaching: Practice and Critique, 2*(3), 72–82.

Brooks, C., & Warren, R.P. (1976). *Understanding poetry* (4th ed.). New York: Holt, Rinehart and Winston.

Carter, R. (1996). Politics and knowledge about language: The LINC project. In R. Hasan & G. Williams (Eds.), *Literacy in society* (pp. 1–3). London: Longman.

Cope, B., & Kalantzis, M. (1993). *The powers of literacy: A genre approach to teaching writing*. Pittsburgh: University of Pittsburgh Press.

Culler, J. (1976). *Structuralist poetics: Structuralism, linguistics and the study of literature*. Ithaca, NY: Cornell University Press.

Eagleton, T. (1983). *Literary theory: An introduction*. Oxford: Basil Blackwell.

Eagleton, T. (2007). *How to read a poem*. Malden, MA: Blackwell Publishing.

Fairclough, N. (1992). *Discourse and social change*. Cambridge: Polity Press.

Freedman, A., & Medway, P. (Eds.). (1994). *Teaching and learning genre*. Portsmouth, NH: Boynton/Cook.

Halliday, M., & Hasan, R. (1985). *Language, context, and text: Aspects of language in a social-semiotic perspective*. Geelong, Vict.: Deakin University.

Hodge, R. & Kress, G. (1988). *Social semiotics*. Cambridge: Polity Press.

Knapp, P., & Watkins, M. (2005). *Genre, text, grammar: Technologies for teaching and assessing writing*. Sydney: University of New South Wales Press.

Locke, T. (2003). 13 ways of looking at a poem: How discourses of reading shape pedagogical practice in English. *Waikato Journal of Education, 9*, 51–64.

Locke, T. (2004a). *Critical discourse analysis*. London: Continuum.

Locke, T. (2004b). Reshaping classical professionalism in the aftermath of neo-liberal reform. *Literacy Learning: The Middle Years, 12*(1)/*English in Australia, 139*, 113–121.

Locke, T. (2007). Constructing English in New Zealand: A report on a decade of reform. *L1 – Educational Studies in Language and Literature, 7*(2), 5–33.

Locke, T., Cawkwell, G., Sila'ila'i, E., Cleary, A., de Beer, W., Harris, S., et al. (2008). *Teaching literature in the multicultural classroom*. Report commissioned by New Zealand Council for Educational Research. Hamilton: Wilf Malcolm Institute of Educational Research (WMIER), School of Education, University of Waikato.

Luke, A., & Freebody, P. (1999). Further notes on the four resources model. *Reading online*. Discussion posed August 1999. Retrieved September 26, 2008, from www.readingonline.org/research/lukefreebody.html.

Martin, J. (1993). A contextual theory of language. In B. Cope & M. Kalantzis (Eds.), *The powers of literacy: A genre approach to teaching writing* (pp. 116–136). Pittsburgh: University of Pittsburgh Press.

Misson, R., & Morgan, W. (2006). *Critical literacy and the aesthetic: Transforming the English classroom*. Urbana, IL: NCTE.

Morgan, W., Gilbert, P., Lankshear, C., Werner, S., & Williams, L. (1996). *Critical literacy: Readings and resources*. Norwood, SA: AATE.

Muller, H. (1967). *The uses of English: Guidelines for the teaching of English from the Anglo-American conference at Dartmouth College.* NewYork: Holt, Rinehart and Winston.

Peskin, J. (1998). Constructing meaning when reading poetry: An expert–novice study. *Cognition and Instruction, 16*(3), 235–263.

Shayer, D. (1972). *The teaching of English in schools: 1900–1970.* London: Routledge & Kegan Paul.

Shulman, L.S. (1986). Those who understand: Knowledge growth in teaching. *Educational Researcher, 15*(2), 4–14.

Snyder, I. (2008). *The literacy wars: Why teaching children to read and write is a battle-ground in Australia.* Crows Nest, NSW: Allen & Unwin.

Soter, A. (1999). *Young adult literature & the new literary theories: Developing critical readers in middle school.* New York: Teachers College Press.

Wild, A. (2003). What am I doing and where am I going? Conversations with beginning English teachers. *English Teaching: Practice and Critique, 2*(1), 68–79.

Chapter 11

Scaffolding Grammar Instruction for Writers and Writing

Constance Weaver

In education, "scaffolding" means helping learners do what they can't yet do by themselves, an important step toward independence (Jerome Bruner, in Ninio & Bruner, 1978; Bruner, 1986). It's like training wheels on a bicycle or water wings for swimming, a temporary support. For me, scaffolding means genuinely teaching, not merely assigning and grading: guiding apprentice learners in developing knowledge and skills. In writing instruction, scaffolding includes guiding writers from the process of discovering ideas through editing and sharing work with a broader audience – until eventually they can do this with only the feedback and editing that we published writers enjoy. Where and how does grammar instruction serve as scaffolding for writers and writing? Over decades, I have developed and refined my own answers, an evolving process that continues yet today.

> ### Activity: Reflecting on the Meaning of "Scaffolding"
>
> Before reading on, it may be valuable to think about this concept of "scaffolding" in learning. Can you think of instances when someone scaffolded your learning of something – that is, they provided support not unlike training wheels or water wings? Or when they worked with you to accomplish something that you could not yet accomplish alone, like guiding you step-by-step through a writing project or creating a science project together. Can you think of examples where you scaffolded learning for others? Think and discuss what it might mean to "scaffold" grammar instruction for writers and writing.

At the beginning of my career, I was teaching grammar to future English teachers. It was the late 1960s, our soldiers slogging through Vietnam, razing villages, killing civilians who could not always be distinguished from soldiers, dying from sniper's bullets, mortar shells, or air raids. Here in Kalamazoo, some of our university students were enlisting, or fleeing to Canada, or protesting the war outside the administration building. In our English Language classes, students preparing to be secondary teachers engaged in the naming of parts. I remembered Henry Reed's poem by that name – actually a section of his poem called "Lessons of the War" (1942) – and thought of the irony. In Reed's poem, the instructor drones "To-day we have naming of parts", the parts of a rifle, while the soldier-narrator – and surely many of his fellow recruits – juxtaposed the instructor's voice with his own vision: "Japonica/Glistens like coral in all of the neighboring gardens,/And to-day we have naming of parts."

The parallel irony seeped into my consciousness. While war blossomed with deadly Agent Orange, destroying everything like japonica, we, too, had naming of parts. Though eschewing traditional schoolroom grammar and its famous/infamous diagramming of sentences, we teachers indulged in our own kind of dissection: immediate constituent analysis, a procedure developed by structural linguists like W. Nelson Francis (1958) to divide a sentence into increasingly smaller parts, surrounding each part with a box, until no unit larger than a word (or morpheme) remained in any box. The result was a set of nesting boxes. We teachers then demonstrated how this boxing procedure was inadequate to demonstrate some of the structural differences that we and our students intuitively perceived. Enter transformational grammar, courtesy of the intellectual giant Noam Chomsky (*Syntactic Structures*, 1957), then Owen Thomas's popularization of transformational grammar (1965), and eventually our own book (Malmstrom & Weaver, 1973). Thomas was my teacher and Chomsky my idol – he once hung his hat in my office – so no wonder I, like my senior colleagues, was enamored of transformational grammar.

We were now growing transformational trees instead of merely naming the parts. We were showing how the basic structure underlying a sentence such as, "A new surgeon performed the operation" could surface either as that sentence or, with a passive transformation, could surface as "The operation was performed by a new surgeon." We demonstrated how "Visiting relatives can be a nuisance" can derive from two different underlying structures, with us doing the visiting in one version but relatives visiting us in the other. Our cadre of six English Language teachers was fascinated by the ways in which transformational/generative linguistics "accounted for" native speakers' understanding of the language, but not so most of our students. They must have viewed both immediate constituent analysis and transformational sentence generating with as little interest as the soldier in Reed's poem viewed the naming of rifle parts. Whatever flowers and trees and shrubs caught our students' attention beyond the windows, whatever their own "japonica" here in Michigan, their hearts were not with us in the naming or generating of parts. And when the heart is not engaged, the mind seldom remembers.

And these students were going to be our next generation of English teachers!

Across campus, the old and the new bisected by a couple of busy streets and the state psychiatric hospital, I was also teaching freshman writing. Or trying to. Often I found the students' writing almost devoid of content and their sentences dull and boring, lumbering across the page, one medium-length sentence after another, typically with a subject–verb–object structure that led me to suspect – often quite accurately – that these students were scarcely readers. They could read, but they didn't. They could write, but only minimally. Fortunately, I soon discovered sentence-combining (Mellon, 1969), found that no grammatical terminology was needed for teaching sentence-combining

(O'Hare, 1973), and then fell in love with Francis Christensen's work on sentence-generating (1967). His idea was not to combine sentences already generated by the teacher or the textbook, but to create a bare-bones sentence of one's own, and then add to it. Christensen used examples from published writers with his students, showing them how the writers embedded modifying elements within modifying elements. He emphasized the use of appositives, participial phrases, and absolutes, all of which he found common in the writing of professionals (some more than others), but not in the writing of 12th-grade students. Here's an example (Christensen, 1967, p. 20) cited from science writer Loren Eisley:

> It is with the coming of man that a vast hole seems to open in nature,
>   a vast black whirlpool spinning faster and faster,
>   consuming flesh, stones, soil, minerals,
>   sucking down the lightning,
>   wrenching power from the atom,
>   until the ancient sounds of nature are drowned out in
> the cacophony
>   of something which is no longer nature,
>   something instead which is loose and knocking at
>   the world's heart,
>   something demonic and no longer planned –
>   escaped, it may be –
>   spewed out of nature,
>   contending in a final giant's game against its
>   master.

Each time a line is indented more deeply than the previous, the more deeply indented line modifies something that came before. Parallel lines, such as those beginning with "consuming", "sucking", and "wrenching", all modify the same thing, in this case "whirlpool" – or, in my opinion, the whole action of the whirlpool spinning. With examples like this, Christensen illustrated the point quoted from John Erskine (1946, p. 254): "When you write, you make a point, not by subtracting as though you sharpened a pencil, but by adding. When you put one word after another, your statement should be more precise the more you add." I was beginning to understand one way that grammar – or at least my own grammatical knowledge – could be used to help writers. I could scaffold for them how to develop bare-bones sentences into sentences with more detail, perhaps even voice; they, too, could command structures professional writers use to engage readers.

Of course, not all professional writers or writings use such constructions equally, but why not help students add to their repertoire? Recently (Weaver with Bush, 2008), I began sharing more examples from expository writing, demonstrating that writing about a process, any kind of process, may call forth the kinds of constructions emphasized by Christensen – and the "adjectives out of order" now emphasized by Harry Noden (1999, 2007):

Looking closely at the skeletons, paleontologists could see that none of the bones of any of the dinosaurs or the other animals seemed to be cracked from drying a long time in the sun. (Gillette, *Dinosaur Ghosts*, 1997, p. 15) [present participial phrase]

Drenched but unhurt, Manly was rescued, while the Aerodrome was fished out of the Potomac. (Freedman, *The Wright Brothers: How They Invented the Airplane*, 1991, p. 22) [past participial phrase]

David Richard Steinman (1886–1960) grew up in a poor neighborhood under the Brooklyn Bridge, a lifelong inspiration. (Dupré, *Bridges*, 1997, p. 88) [appositive]

There are a few genuine adepts present who throw themselves rapturously into the music, eyes shut, arms upraised, waiting, no doubt, for the onset of glossolalia. (Ehrenreich, *Nickel and Dimed*, 2001, p. 67)

Each of the cited books was written for, or is suitable for, middle school or secondary students. Present participial and other adjectival words and phrases are especially likely to occur in any genre that has a narrative sense: stories and novels; biography and autobiography; the recreation of historical events; environmental and nature writing; and other informational prose that describes a process.

In my own writing classrooms, however, I came to focus on the use of such constructions in poetry and in personal narrative or vignettes, as a prelude to teaching the expository writing, the persuasive writing, that formed the core of my freshman writing classes – and that actually fulfilled the title of the course! I found, like Francis Christensen, that dealing first with creative writing enabled students to grasp the importance of concrete detail, to become more precise in using words and more proficient in employing grammatical resources. They developed a voice as writers and began to develop confidence that they could, in fact, write.

Activity: Using Grammar to Explore Writing Options

Obtain a copy of one of Harry Noden's (2007, 2009) "image grammar" activity books for secondary and middle-grade students, and consider whether you yourself would respond positively to doing his kinds of grammar-in-writing activities. Try some out with students, if at all possible. How can you scaffold students' learning so they will use, more and more frequently and more naturally, the grammatical options Noden teaches in his books (and I do in my professional books for teachers)?

What Does "The Research" Say about Teaching Grammar to Improve Writing?

Around this time – the mid-1980s, when I began focusing first on creative writing before expository writing – I encountered George Hillocks' review of experimental research on the teaching of grammar in isolation to improve writing. In his 1986 analysis, Hillocks found that of several methods teachers employed to help students write more effectively, the only method that had a negative effect was teaching grammar as a separate subject! Reading his work (1986, and later, Hillocks & Smith, 1991), I felt confirmed in what I had discovered as a teacher: that teaching grammar separately, in the hope that it would transfer into improved writing, did not work for many students – not even with respect to teaching grammatical conventions. I had used such books as Teresa Glazier's *The Least You Should Know about English: Writing Skills* (1979 and later), assigning and reviewing exercises on basic conventions that I hoped would enhance students' ability to edit their writing, but typically the exercises had little or no effect. So I was not surprised when I read the Hillocks' conclusion from his examination of the research.

Coming to essentially the same conclusion as Hillocks about the non-value of teaching grammar in isolation, a review team based at the University of York, UK, determined that there was little evidence that teaching grammar to improve the quality or "correctness" of students' writing had a positive effect on students' writing when the grammar was taught as a separate subject, in isolation from writing. "The clear implication, based on the available high quality research evidence, is that the evidence base to justify the teaching of grammar in English to 5 to 16 year-olds is very small" (Andrews et al., 2004, p. 4; Andrews, this volume). "Having established that much, we can now go on to research what is effective, and to ask clearer and more pertinent questions about what works in the development of young people's literacy" (Andrews et al., 2004, p. 5; see also in this volume).

Despite the impoverished intellectual premises of such statistical meta-analyses (MacLure, 2005) and other issues with research studies and summaries that I (2008) and others (Mulroy, 2003) have cited, the fact is that the conclusions are congruent with many writing teachers' experiences. They, too, have found that unless they guide writers in applying the grammar they have taught, few students remember and fewer still apply it. Like me, they have found that scaffolding the use of grammar during the writing process produces the most long-lasting results, for both writers and their writing.

Infusing Grammar into the Writing Process

Of course, English teachers have not always taught writing as a process. When I was a young teacher, we typically taught a writing concept – an organizational pattern, the thesis statement, a grammatical concept, whatever – then assigned a paper, marked it up with comments and corrections, graded and returned it. One assignment, one draft, no opportunity to get help improving this particular piece of writing. Move on to the next concept, the next assignment, the next grade. My peers and I taught as we were taught. Fortunately, our students were rescued by our reading – some of us anyway – the work of writers and educators like Donald Murray (*A Writer Teaches Writing*, 1985), Donald Graves (*Writing: Teachers and Children at Work*, 1983), and his students Lucy Calkins (*Lessons from a Child*, 1983; *The Art of Teaching Writing*, 1983/1984) and Nancie Atwell (*In the Middle: Writing, Reading, and Learning with Adolescents*, 1987), all for elementary or secondary teachers. Tom Romano's *Clearing the Way: Working with Teenage Writers* (1987) and Linda Rief's *Seeking Diversity: Language Arts with Adolescents* (1991) joined the others as outstanding resources. By the mid-1970s, I was teaching future teachers how to teach writing; nevertheless, these books, mostly from the 1980s, taught me as much or more than my students about how to scaffold writing instruction and learning in general. Classics all, the books, some in second editions, remain as fresh to new readers today as they were to us back then.

What was so startling about these teachers' advice, so startling and so absolutely right, was the notion that just as we adults go through a process of writing that includes envisioning, generating ideas, drafting, revising, and editing, so too we should guide our students in that process. We should scaffold the writing process for them, treating them as apprentice writers. Of course, teaching the use of various grammatical constructions and editing concepts falls naturally into this process. And so I began – to some extent even before then – to scaffold the conscious use of grammar for my students who were growing into their own as writers, to empower them with linguistic resources they often didn't know they had.

In *Grammar to Enrich and Enhance Writing* (2008), I've included a model of the writing process, derived from the Michigan model of writing developed in the 1990s but elaborated with my suggestions on where or when, in teaching the writing process, we might include the teaching of grammatical resources, including standard conventions for writing. The model is reproduced here as Figure 11.1.

The loops in the original model are meant to suggest that the writing process is recursive rather than linear: we draft, but stop to brainstorm ideas or even to edit; we write a snippet that doesn't fit here, but might go somewhere else later; we backtrack to revise and edit (as I'm doing right now) before moving forward to draft more of the piece. Of course the actual process of writing is still more chaotic than that and, in fact, I suspect that chaos theory might offer the best explanation of this predictably unpredictable process (2008, p. 70).

Still, visual models that suggest the phases many writers go through can help teachers think about where to intervene in the writing process, including the process of using grammar more effectively and, when appropriate, more conventionally.

But how can grammar actually help writers and not just the writing? I've given a hint of that before, indicating that my students who played with the resources of language in poetry and short narratives began to realize they *could* write, an important stimulus to their attempting expository/persuasive writing in our freshman writing course. Let me give you another example, this time from a tutoring situation outside the classroom.

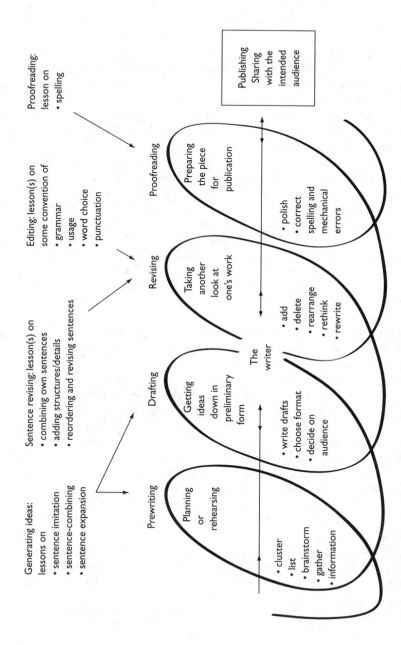

Generating ideas:
lessons on
• sentence imitation
• sentence-combining
• sentence expansion

Sentence revising: lesson(s) on
• combining own sentences
• adding structures/details
• reordering and revising sentences

Editing: lesson(s) on
some convention of
• grammar
• usage
• word choice
• punctuation

Proofreading:
lesson on
• spelling

Prewriting

Planning
or
rehearsing

• cluster
• list
• brainstorm
• gather
• information

Drafting

Getting
ideas
down in
preliminary
form

• write drafts
• choose format
• decide on
  audience

The
writer

Revising

Taking
another
look at
one's work

• add
• delete
• rearrange
• rethink
• rewrite

Proofreading

Preparing
the piece
for publication

• polish
• correct
  spelling and
  mechanical
  errors

Publishing
Sharing
with the
intended
audience

Figure 11.1 The Basic Recursive Model of the Writing Process.

Note:
The loops and the text within was prepared for the Michigan Proficiency Examination Framework for Writing by the Michigan Council of Teachers of English in 1993.

Playing with Grammar, Becoming a Writer

In the summer of 2004, I had the privilege of working on writing with a friend's son, Max Baird, who was then between his sophomore and junior years in high school. Because of Max's low self-esteem as a writer, I began by guiding Max in writing an "I am" poem that reflected his personality and character metaphorically. Usually I would have shared written examples first, but since the tutoring sessions were casual and laidback, I helped Max focus on the concept by giving two examples orally: "I am a Bilbo's pizza" and "I am a whitewater raft". I deliberately left out modifying phrases, curious whether Max would add modifiers before or after the nouns in his initial metaphors. Mostly he didn't. But in one sentence he did: *I am an aged scared* [scarred] *blue whale.*

During the first round of revisions, I showed Max how the sentence would sound if the first two adjectives were put after the noun: *I am a blue whale, aged and scared.* I also pointed out that there would be a comma after the noun – *whale* – and before the adjectives. (I did not pre-teach the concept of noun, but simply used the term incidentally as I explained.) Liking the idea of modifiers after the noun, Max then went through his "I am" statements and added modifiers to many of the other things to which he had equated himself. Interestingly, in the whale analogy he left *aged and scared* before the noun, omitted *blue*, and added new post-noun modifiers: *I am the aged and scared whale, limitless in knowledge, ancient and gigantic, loving and peaceful, graceful and magnificent.* I hadn't yet dealt with the correct spelling of *scarred*; I was focusing on content and style.

When Max shared his next draft, I showed him how to add a present participial word or phrase that would show what the thing in the "I am" statement was doing. Again using the technical term only in passing, I presented a number of examples of how words ending in *-ing* can add details after a noun as well as before. Together, we noticed that Max already had one *-ing* word (the phrase describing the whale as *loving and peaceful*). While *loving* in this context might be seen as a state of mind more than an action, it did illustrate grammatically the concept of an *-ing* word describing a noun. Max then added *-ing* modifiers to several of his nouns. Max's early drafts are shown in Figure 11.2.

I also talked about organization and the idea of leading up to those items that are most important, so they are the final images in the reader's mind. In the next draft, Max made the line about the whale the last image before the concluding "I am who I am" lines. At this point, I explained the difference in meaning between *scared* and *scarred*, and Max corrected his spelling.

With so many modifiers now following the metaphorical nouns, I also saw an opportunity to teach a useful editing concept, putting a colon after the basic "I am" statements. I explained that the colon is like a trumpet, announcing that something is coming – in this case, descriptive phrases modifying the previous noun.

Max liked the idea of using the colon this way. Ultimately, the original sentence *I am an aged scared blue whale* became:

I am the aged and scarred blue whale: limitless in knowledge, old beyond years and larger than life, loving and peaceful, graceful and magnificent,

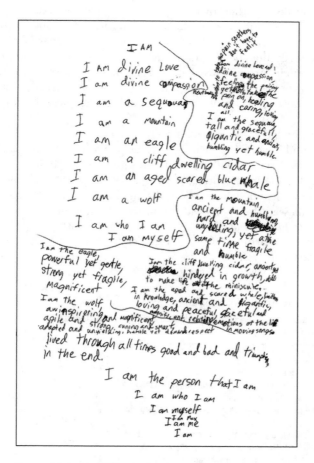

Figure 11.2 Max's Early Drafts.

relating emotions of the life in wondrous songs, living through all times both good, bad, and in between and triumphing in the end.

Would the sentence be better with a little more editing? Yes. Might the sentence be better without *all* those *-ing* phrases? Possibly. On the other hand, it illustrates what often happens when writers are learning a new skill: they tend to overuse it or apply it inappropriately or make a new kind of error in applying it (for example, adding a non-restrictive modifying construction after a noun but not including the comma needed before the modifier).

In any case, I felt it was time to stop editing. Writers can learn only a limited number of things at one time before their capacity to remember them is exceeded. More important, we teachers need to learn to keep our hands off students' writing, lest their piece become our piece. When we take over the ownership of a piece by imposing our own revisions and edits, the only lesson writers are likely to learn is that their own work is never good enough, so why try. At some point, idiosyncratic for each individual, we need to stop helping students revise and edit; learning is our goal, not a perfect paper. (When a perfect paper is necessarily the goal, we may offer to wield today's version of the proverbial blue pencil formerly used by professional editors.) Students need to consider the new things they have learned (or almost learned), bask in the glow of what they've accomplished, and publish the piece in some meaningful way.

I felt that Max and his poem were at that point. Together we reviewed the concepts I had taught and Max had applied. Then came publication. (Figure 11.3 is Max's final draft.) Max first shared it with everyone around who would look at it or listen to him read it. He then included it with his application for a much-sought-after international school, where it played a significant role in his being accepted. Finally, he allowed the poem and the process leading up to it to be included in *Grammar to Enrich and Enhance Writing* (Weaver with Bush, 2008) so teachers can see how a piece of writing can be guided from a sparse beginning to a rich and well-edited final draft.

Here's what I taught:

- the concept of putting modifiers after a noun;
- the placement of a comma between the noun and the modifiers;

I am

I am divine love and compassion: feeling the pain and wanting to take the pain so others don't have to feel it, yet learning to not take the pain on; healing and caring, loving all.

I am sequoia: tall and gorgeous, gigantic and ancient, humbling yet humble.

I am the mountain: old beyond comprehension and making one bow, hard and unyielding, yet fragile and bowing to others.

I am the eagle: powerful yet gentle, strong yet fragile—lordly.

I am the wolf: awe inspiring and magnificient, agile and strong, cunning and smart, perfected and unyielding, respectful to all yet demanding respect in return.

I am the cliff dwelling cedar: ancient yet hindered in growth, able to make life out of the miniscule yet flourishing beyond all expectations when given the right nutrient-rich environment.

I am the aged and scarred blue whale: limitless in knowledge, old beyond years and larger than life, loving and peaceful, graceful and magnificient, relating emotins of the life in wondrous songs, living through all times both good, bad, and in between and triumphing in the end.

I am the person that I am
I am who I am
I am myself
I am Max
I am me
I am

Figure 11.3 Max's Final Draft.

- the use of *-ing* words and phrases as modifiers;
- the rhetorical technique of leading up to one's strongest points or images by putting them at or near the end;
- the use of a colon to introduce a list of modifying phrases.

Did Max learn all these lessons then and there, once and for all? Of course not. That's why I emphasize that writers may need to be led through a set of steps again and again. In Max's case, we do know that he became more self-confident as a writer and, with some excellent classroom teaching, became a much stronger and joyful writer. In the fall of 2006, Max started his freshman year at Arizona State, and his strong writing helped him win a substantial scholarship!

A few concepts taught well and a few pieces done well can be much more important for a student writer's growth than many concepts and lessons taught superficially and many pieces of writing assigned without much guidance. Some students will make miles of progress with just one extended lesson; others won't. These others – many, sometimes even most, of a class – can be brought along over time, as we teachers share and discuss beautifully written literature or non-fiction prose, then scaffold the teaching of a few grammatical options and skills deeply on the way to students' producing a few final pieces done well.

Activity: Planning Lessons with the Aim of Scaffolding Learning

How could you modify what I did with Max in working with an entire class? Think about this, and maybe go so far as to create one or more lesson plans. You may wish to consider my discussion of how Jeff Henderson and I scaffolded a multi-phase lesson for his sixth graders, and what I learned about the additional scaffolding (and/or simplification!) that was needed. See Weaver with Bush (2008), *Grammar to Enrich and Enhance Writing*.

Scaffolding the Teaching of Grammar during the Writing Process

Objecting that I had the luxury of teaching Max one-on-one, you may be inclined to dismiss such teaching as impossible in the classroom. Though you'd be right that the success rate is not 100% – sometimes not nearly that at first – gradual teaching and reteaching (scaffolding) over time can make more and more of a difference. Increasing success requires skilled teaching: reflecting on what has worked, what hasn't, and why; extending or modifying our teaching accordingly; lots and lots of patience; and ideally, the collaboration of teachers that students will encounter before and after us. But even without such collaboration, dedicated teachers can scaffold grammar instruction during the writing process, ultimately helping more and more students strengthen their writing and bolster their overall competence and confidence as writers.

For mnemonic purposes, we might imagine this as a CARE process for writers, as teachers scaffold them through stages of understanding and apply key grammatical concepts:

- Concept development (concepts like participial phrase, appositive, colon use or subject–verb agreement);
- Applying concept and getting feedback (whether in a short or long piece);
- Revision;
- Editing.

Students can best be nurtured through this CARE process with their writing when they know the ultimate goal will be publication – the sharing of their work that ideally goes beyond the classroom to parents, others in the school, and perhaps the general public (as in a letter to the editor, or creative writing published in the local newspaper). Of course, from a teaching point of view, each of these phases may include multiple steps.

Here are some suggested steps leading up to more systematic teaching of revision. From my "framework for teaching grammar throughout the writing process" (2008, pp. 62–63), these possible steps can be modified according to the needs of the students:

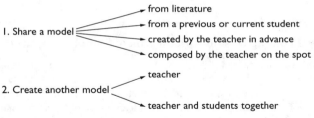

1. Share a model
   - from literature
   - from a previous or current student
   - created by the teacher in advance
   - composed by the teacher on the spot

2. Create another model
   - teacher
   - teacher and students together

3. Have students compose (or do a related preparatory activity) in small groups or pairs and share their work. Clarify as needed.

4. Have students compose a sentence or sentences individually and share their work. Check the work if desired and possible.

5. Ask students to apply the concept (that is, to use the grammatical element or writing skill) in their own writing, whether previous writing in their portfolios or writing in progress.

6. Examine the student's work to determine what scaffolding is needed in the revision process, or processes.

More difficult than these steps, of course, is teaching revision. That important step is often omitted in a time crunch, but I've found that there's an additional problem: many of us as teachers have looked at a piece of writing and seen that the sentences are similar in length and structure, sparse in detail, lacking in voice, yet had no idea how to begin helping the student revise this particular piece – even with substantial grammatical knowledge of our own. We may say, with considerable justification: Okay, I'm just going to scaffold differently next time, at least for this student or these students.

But what strategies do we have for helping students revise to make their writing more interesting more flowing, more compelling? For me, sentence-combining and sentence-expanding have been the best. Let's start with a couple of sentences from "The Big Guy", written by a sixth-grader (Noden, 1999, quoted in Olson, 1992, p. 54): "The lonely man stood in a ring holding tight to the ropes. His head was bald. His chest was hairy and sweaty." We could show the student a way to combine the second and third sentences: "His head was bald, <u>his chest hairy and sweaty</u>." This results in an absolute construction, but I wouldn't mention that to a novice writer like this middle-schooler. In my 2008 book, I've demonstrated how one could work with the entire student piece, combining some other sentences that aren't necessarily consecutive. How much I'd do would depend partly upon whether I was working individually with the student during a quick mini-conference, or whether I was trying to demonstrate to a whole class of generally more capable writers how they could look at their own and classmates' papers for sentences that might be more effectively combined.

I've included some additional steps in my albeit idealized framework for teaching grammar in writing (2008, pp. 62–63), including reteaching and revision prior to scaffolding the application of one or two editing concepts for the piece of writing in progress. Here, however, I want to continue to the other revision process I've suggested – expanding sentences.

The following examples come from seventh-grader Julie Nickelson. Her persuasive paper makes a case for wearing school uniforms. Here are two of her sentences, each with possible expansions underlined as an illustration:

> By having uniforms, we would not be distracted by the "showy" clothes that many students currently wear to school, despite the rules we have <u>against low-slung jeans, revealing necklines, tight sweaters, and the like</u>.
>
> If we had uniforms, it would help us keep focus in class, boring as it sometimes might be, for we wouldn't have to worry about fashion – what earrings Joanie is wearing today, whether Barbie's neckline offers a view of her bra, or whether Lionel's jeans are not only low-slung but so loose they're in danger of falling off.

While I never had the opportunity to work with Julie or her classmates, I often see papers like hers graded "excellent" – as mine were so very long ago – with no help offered in making the paper more interesting and convincing, more detailed and more persuasive, through the adding of detail and consequently voice. Many of Julie's sentences ended with a noun or noun phrase that invited the addition of details, so it was fun for me to imagine how I could lead her and her classmates in the adding of such details (2008, pp. 127–129).

Does scaffolding grammar instruction during the writing process really transfer to subsequent pieces of writing? I do not have enough evidence to make a claim; this could be one of the kinds of further research recommended by Richard Andrews, Debra Myhill, and others in this book. I do, though, have my own experience teaching teachers-to-be, during which I found that a sizeable majority of my students could apply the grammatical options taught, even without further scaffolding in the revision phase. And I have one particular testimonial that I can't resist sharing, from Rebecca Schipper, a teacher in the Hudsonville, Michigan system, who taught her ninth-graders "out of order adjectives" and where to place them: at the beginning of their sentences, with a comma between the adjectival and the noun; immediately after the noun; or at the end of the entire independent clause. Months later, finding that students were spontaneously using these adjectivals and other constructions she'd taught, Rebecca wrote in her professional journal:

> Well, it is February now, and the kids are using the "out of order" adjectives, appositives, and parallel constructions on their own! I am amazed that something has actually stuck with them.... Consider me sold on the idea of intertwining grammar with writing!

Knowledge about Language in the Writing Classroom

After seeing unexpectedly sophisticated use of grammar in writings from the classroom of Judy Davis, a fifth-grade teacher at Manhattan New School, I asked Judy what she had done to encourage such effective use of participial phrases. Had she taught these to the students? "No," Judy explained; she had only engaged them in reading and discussing literary pieces and the effective language employed. Without using any terminology, or any direct intervention in the writing process, Judy had scaffolded her students' use of grammar in writing – participial phrases, parallelism, and such – merely through appreciative conversation about published writing, especially poetry (see Weaver with Bush, 2008, for examples).

This encounter with Judy and her students' writing set me to thinking. In my course "Grammar in Teaching Writing", I began to experiment. At the end of the first night of class, I would put on the overhead a transparency of the following sentence from Francis Christensen (1967, pp. 12–13), with his indentations for major modifiers describing something that came before:

The swells moved rhythmically toward us,
 irregularly faceted,
 sparkling,
 growing taller and more powerful until the shining crest bursts,
   a transparent sheet of pale green water spilling over the top,
    breaking into blue-white foam as it cascades down the
  front the
   wave,
   piling up in a frothy mound that the diminishing wave
  pushes
   up against the pilings,
    with a swishsmash,
   the foam drifting back,
    like a lace fan opened over the shimmering water
 as the spent wave returns whispering to the sea.

We'd quickly discuss the fact that this is all one sentence grammatically, a cumulative sentence that begins with the main subject–verb unit and then continues with modifying phrases, modifiers of something within those modifiers, and so forth – like this sentence and much of contemporary prose.

Then – shock! – I would tell the students I wanted them to write a sentence like this, a cumulative, right-branching sentence that added detail to detail to detail. We'd compose some possible starter sentences, and then I'd ask the students to begin, not worrying for now about correctness, but simply seeing how such a sentence might unfold for them if they pushed aside their inhibitions and just wrote. I did make the concession of leaving Christensen's example on the overhead but asked students not, really, to imitate the model but just glance at it for inspiration. That typically worked.

What amazed most of the students was that they could actually produce such a sentence in the short time we had left, usually 10 minutes or less. I would collect these, take them home, and select several to show on the overhead the next class. Here is one such example out of many my students and I have enjoyed:

> The car exploded on the top floor of the parking structure, loudly and boldly, the fire began growing taller and more powerful until the flames catapulted, a giant fiery ball flooding over onto the cars beside it, melting the paint and breaking the windows as it quickly chars the whole frame, throwing dust and ash particles into the air, smoke rising in a huge cloud of smoke, the smell permeating every being within 100 feet.

After reading aloud this example (which actually has a second independent clause that could be made into an absolute), I asked the student, "Were you aware that you used parallelism? A series of participial phrases? Two absolutes?" Of course, the answer, no matter the specific paper or the exact questions, was always "No". Well, once in a while a teacher who was teaching grammar to her students knew the label for the participials, but not all of the grammar teachers did!

I used examples like these to illustrate that we all have language resources that go beyond our conscious ability to label or sometimes even to explain them (see van Gelderen in this book). However, it was also a handy way to introduce the fact that we were going to experiment consciously with such constructions as participial phrases, adjectives and adjectivals "out of order" (Noden, 1999), appositives, and absolutes. I always found examples of each in these sentences that my students generated so rapidly, though the participial phrase was always the most common, the absolute the least.

Obviously I have not found the naming of grammatical parts to be more than minimally necessary in scaffolding for students the processes of drafting and revision. Sure, I do use grammatical terminology when teaching a concept, just as I use "chair" and "table" to refer to those pieces of furniture that have, usually but not always, different appearances and different functions. When I introduce participial phrases, for example, I use the term, sometimes even with first-graders, but I teach the concept more by example than by definition, and vary my definition/explanation according to the level of the students. Quickly I shift to calling these "-*ing* phrases" some or all of the time, even with graduate students, simply because that's a lot easier to say and doesn't require students, some of them at least, stopping to think, "Now what's a present participial phrase?", while entirely missing what I'm trying to say about them.

In other words, students need to grasp the concept I'm talking about, and it's handy to have a label that will generate instant recognition on their part, a label that can help rather than impede communication. And of course, in writing classes, my students and I do attend to using specific and interesting nouns, verbs, adjectives, and adverbs. Teaching – that is, scaffolding – the effective use of adjectival phrases and adverbial clauses is especially important for developing more effective sentences. But for enriching writing by making sentences more interesting, more varied, more emphatic, more reflective of content, I find no need for students to be able to analyze and name the "parts of speech" or the parts of sentences. I briefly teach basic concepts and terms like "noun", "verb", "adjective", "adverb" – and increasingly over the school grades and years, the broader modifying functions of adjectival and adverbial, terms that cover both the single words and larger constructions that work as single-word modifiers do.

Activity: Reflection on the Value of Explicit Grammar Knowledge

When you were in middle and secondary school, or even in college, how useful was the naming of parts for your writing? How did you actually *use* those names? Perhaps to focus on using concrete nouns and colorful verbs? Did you need the names, or only the examples? Did, or would have, knowledge of subjects and verbs help in making verbs "agree" with their subjects? What about understanding independent versus dependent clauses? Did, or would have, that help you in using connecting words and punctuation conventionally? Explore these and related ideas you may think of.

So yes, experience in working with teachers and students, and the conviction – like John Erskine's and Francis Christensen's – that modifiers are vital in clarifying and expanding the basic subject and verb, have led me to focus on producing sentences instead of analyzing them, and to use a minimum of grammatical terminology as I scaffold students' use of grammar during the writing process. My teaching experience even led me to begin the grammar section of *The Grammar Plan Book* (2007) with adverbials and adjectivals, before discussing the sentence (though there is a brief recapitulation of basic terms at the beginning of the book, including parts of speech, subject and verb, and phrases and clauses).

Some editing principles can be taught, too, through conversation and example better than by terminology, especially when so many students outright reject the idea of "learning grammar". For example, many teachers find it easiest and most productive to weed out constructions like "Jimmy and me went fishing" by explaining: "You wouldn't say 'Me went fishing', would you? How would you say it?" When the student says, "I went fishing," the teacher responds something like, "Well, don't say 'Jimmy and me' either; say 'Jimmy and I went fishing'."

Though some editing concepts can be taught without terminology, I have concluded over the years that students need certain other grammatical concepts to edit consciously rather than just intuitively, based solely on their reading, which is usually not sufficient for grasping all aspects of the conventions of written mainstream English that are considered most important. For punctuating deliberately, students need over time to grasp concepts such as: subject, verb, and subject–verb agreement; independent clause and how such clauses are joined and/or separated; dependent clauses, non-restrictive modifiers, and how commas are used with them (in contrast with restrictive modifiers). These, incidentally, are the grammatical concepts students most need to understand in order to do well on the multiple-choice "English test" part of the ACT test (see my informal analysis, Weaver, 2007) and probably the SAT as well – tests which do not ask for the analysis or naming of parts, but do assess editing and revision skills for which the aforementioned knowledge helps tremendously. The Scholastic Aptitude Test, or SAT, is designed to identify high school students who are exceptionally well qualified for college. The ACT assesses a broader range of secondary students, is more widely used as part of college admissions decisions, and is now part of some state assessments of secondary students – including my own state of Michigan.

Other editing concepts can be taught through a wealth of patterned examples and contrasted non-examples, with a surprising minimum of terminology. Generally speaking, most of us learn better through extensive patterned examples, attempted application in meaningful contexts, and feedback, than we do through rules. Admittedly, though, some students like definitions, which seem to give them a sense of security. For writers, though, it's usually the scaffolding that counts.

Activity: Discussion – How *Much* Explicit Grammar Terminology Is Necessary?

When teachers use a lot of grammatical terminology with students, do students respond with understanding? Or, in your experience, is it true that a minimum of terminology and a maximum of examples and patterns and scaffolding help the most? As always, discuss with others if at all possible.

What Works

My own experience of what does and doesn't work is echoed in the teacher research of Finlay McQuade (1980) and DiStefano and Killion (1984), both quantitative experimental studies that the York researchers (Andrews et al., 2004) seemingly overlooked. Both are experimental teacher-researcher studies. While not able to exercise the controls that would make his research admirable by the narrow criteria of some experimentalists, McQuade investigated several factors regarding the effects of his popular "Editing Skills" elective class. His students' essays at the end of the editing skills class contained almost as many errors as their pre-test essays did. Most important, the post-test essays were much more poorly written, "awkwardly and I believe self-consciously construed to honor correctness above all other virtues, including sense" (p. 29). In fact, all the factors McQuade investigated turned out not to support the teaching of grammar skills in isolation as a way of improving even the taking of tests on editing skills, much less students' ability to edit their own writing. In sharp contrast, DiStefano and Killion (1984), in a substantive experimental study with contrasting Grade 4, 5, and 6 classrooms, found that the Grade 5 and 6 students in writing-process classrooms showed greater ability to create diverse and effective sentence structures and Grade 4, 5, and 6 students in such classrooms all showed greater ability to edit for conventions than students who were taught the skills in isolation.

Notice, please, what I have taken as the major criterion for success: writing that, at a minimum, is more conventionally edited than before editing-skills instruction, regardless of whether that instruction was offered in isolation or in the context of the writing process.

Activity: Teaching Editing Skills

Jeff Anderson has written two excellent books – and developed helpful videos – on teaching editing: *Mechanically Inclined* (2005) and *Everyday Editing* (2007), published by Stenhouse. If you can, obtain at least one of these and consider how, in your present or future classroom, you might draw upon Jeff's experience as a classroom teacher to teach editing and (with the 2007 book) the craft of writing – to think about how punctuation, grammar, and style can best be used to hone and communicate meaning.

In another major aspect of my teaching and publishing career, the reading process and the teaching of reading, I learned to ask an important question. When someone would say this or that "works" in reading instruction, I began to ask: "Works to accomplish *what*, exactly?" "What isn't/wasn't accomplished but could have been accomplished, or accomplished better, with different instruction?" "What, if any, are the unintended negative consequences that might have been avoided if reading were taught differently?" I came to this questioning stance when I discovered that claims for "what works" often meant simply "what works to raise test scores". It did not necessarily mean that students could, or would, read anything independently and voluntarily, much less comprehend and enjoy stories, longer fiction, or non-fiction beyond the test preparation materials.

So it is with the teaching of grammar. There has been a lot of misunderstanding about "what works" among linguists, English teachers, and those with a foot in both camps, like me, who almost became a linguist but instead became more and more a teacher of writing. Understandably, linguists aware of at least the title of my book *Teaching Grammar in Context* (1996) complained that we can't really teach grammar adequately in the context of writing. They were right, of course, if the primary aim is to teach grammar rather than writing. When we talk about "what works", we need to be clearer about the issue of "works to accomplish what?" And we need to be clearer about what is lost as well as what's gained with our approach.

I ask myself the question, "What works best – most effectively *and most efficiently* – in helping students use the resources of language and grammar more effectively in their writing?" And, of course, I keep reflecting upon my teaching, experimenting with new ideas and approaches, asking that question again and again. Across the decades, I have also increasingly asked myself, "What methods work best not only to improve students' writing, but to enhance their self-confidence as writers, as learners – and maybe even, once in a while, their confidence in themselves as human beings?"

Frankly, I suspect that a conscious knowledge of grammar, even just a bit of grammar, has little value beyond school except perhaps in speaking according to mainstream conventions of "correctness" when desired and, of course, in editing effectively, though certainly some professions may require a little more knowledge of grammar than others. I once made a deposition in a legal case involving the grammar of a sentence in an insurance policy, for instance, so I can see that those who write such documents need to have learned their grammar and punctuation well! Still, with the limited time an English teacher has to make a difference in her students' lives beyond school, I vote for teaching selected aspects of grammar to enrich writing through detail, voice and style, and related or other aspects of grammar to enhance writing through the skillful use of language conventions – whether mainstream conventions or those, say, of a dialect like African American English, when used for particular effect. I do not support the teaching of grammatical analysis as a school subject.

Moreover, we need to teach students sociolinguistic concepts, demonstrating how language varies according to time, place, purpose, and audience, in addition to factors such as home language or dialect, socioeconomic status and social opportunities, peer pressure, and education. We can share such knowledge and develop such understanding and appreciation in part through literature, such as McKissack's *Flossie and the Fox* (1986), a folktale; and, for older students, Zora Neal Hurston's *Their Eyes Were Watching God* (1937/2006) and Toni Morrison's *Love* (2003). Wheeler and Swords (2004, 2005, 2006) and Wheeler, in my 2008 book, demonstrate how such literature can be used as a starting point for scaffolding students in code-switching to mainstream English. In that same book, Roche and Gonzales demonstrate how to embed grammar and editing into the writing process for students whose native language is other than English. Beyond that, offering all our students opportunities to explore sociolinguistic information, scaffolding their opportunities to develop understanding of others' different but patterned use of language and how everyone's language use varies, can help generate greater acceptance of those whose native language, dialect, and culture is different from the mainstream.

For such personal, professional, social, and humane purposes, I see the naming of parts as playing only a minor role in the English classroom, while "knowledge of language" is far broader than the textbook study of traditional or linguistic grammars. Who knows: when we make the conscious employment of grammar and the investigation into language use more relevant to students' lives – as writers and as human beings – they may, now and then, find a little japonica, a little beauty, in what we are scaffolding for their learning. Japonica may grow not just outside the window but in our own classrooms.

References

Anderson, J. (2005). *Mechanically inclined: Building grammar, usage, and style into writer's workshop*. Portland, ME: Stenhouse.

Anderson, J. (2007). *Everyday editing: Inviting students to develop skill and craft in writer's workshop*. Portland, ME: Stenhouse.

Andrews, R., Beverton, S., Locke, T., Low, G., Robinson, A., Torgerson, C., & Zhu, D. (2004). The effect of grammar teaching (syntax) in English on 5 to 16 year olds' accuracy and quality in written composition. In *Research Evidence in Education Library*. London: EPPI-Centre, Social Research Unit, Institute of Education.

Atwell, N. (1987). *In the middle: Writing, reading, and learning with adolescents*. Portsmouth, NH: Heinemann. Second edition titled *In the middle: New understandings about writing, reading, and learning* (1998).

Bruner, J. (1986). *Actual minds, possible worlds*. Cambridge, MA: Harvard University Press.

Calkins, L. (1983). *Lessons from a child: On the teaching and learning of writing*. Portsmouth, NH: Heinemann.

Calkins, L. (1983/1994). *The art of teaching writing*. Portsmouth, NH: Heinemann.

Chomsky, N. (1957). *Syntactic structures*. The Hague: Mouton.

Christensen, F. (1967). *Notes toward a new rhetoric: Six essays for teachers*. New York: Harper & Row. Reprinted in Christensen, F., & Christensen, B. (Eds.). (1978). *Notes toward a new rhetoric: Nine essays for teachers* (2nd ed.). New York: Harper & Row.

DiStefano, P., & Killion, J. (1984). Assessing writing skills through a process approach. *English Education, 16*, 203–207.

Dupré, J. (1997). *Bridges: A history of the world's most famous and important spans*. New York: Black Dog & Leventhal.

Ehrenreich, B. (2001). *Nickel and dimed*. New York: Henry Holt.

Erskine, J. (1946). A note on the writer's craft. In W. Knickerbocker (Ed.), *Twentieth-century English* (pp. 251–259). New York: The Philosophical Library. (A 1970 edition, edited by W. Knickerbocker, was published by Ayer, Manchester, NH.)

Francis, W. (1958). *The structure of American English*. New York: Ronald Press.

Freedman, R. (1991). *The Wright brothers: How they invented the airplane*. New York: Holiday House.

Gillette, J. (1997). *Dinosaur ghosts: The mystery of coelophysis* (D. Henderson, Illus.). New York: Penguin.

Glazier, T. (1979). *The least you should know about English: Writing skills*. Fort Worth: Harcourt Brace College Pubs.

Graves, D. (1983/2003). *Writing: Teachers & children at work*. Portsmouth, NH: Heinemann.

Hillocks, G., Jr. (1986). *Research on written composition: New directions for teaching*. Urbana, IL: ERIC Clearinghouse on Reading and Composition Skills and the National Conference on Research in English. Distributed by the National Council of Teachers of English.

Hillocks, G., Jr., & Smith, M. (1991). Grammar and usage. In J. Flood, J. Jensen, D. Lapp, & J. Squire (Eds.), *Handbook of research on teaching the English language arts* (pp. 591–603). New York: Macmillan.

Hurston, Z. (1937/2006). *Their eyes were watching God.* New York: HarperCollins.

McKissack P. (1986). *Flossie and the fox* (R. Isadora, Illus.). New York: Scholastic.

MacLure, M. (2005). "Clearly bordering on stupidity": Where's the quality in systemic review? *Journal of Educational Policy, 20*(4), 393–416.

McQuade, F. (1980). Examining a grammar course: The rationale and the result. *English Journal, 69,* 26–30.

Malmstrom, J., & Weaver, C. (1973). *Transgrammar: English structure, style, and dialects.* Glenview, IL: Scott, Foresman.

Mellon, J. (1969). *Transformational sentence-combining* (Research Report No. 10). Urbana, IL: National Council of Teachers of English.

Morrison, T. (2003). *Love.* New York: Knopf.

Mulroy, D. (2003). *The war against grammar.* Portsmouth, NH: Boynton/Cook – Heinemann.

Murray, D. (1968/1985). *A writer teaches writing.* Boston: Houghton Mifflin.

Ninio, A., & Bruner, J. (1978). The achievement and antecedents of labeling. *Journal of Child Language, 5,* 1–15.

Noden, H. (1999). *Image grammar: Using grammatical structures to teach writing.* Portsmouth, NH: Boynton/Cook.

Noden, H. (2007). *Image grammar activitiy book.* Logan, IA: Perfection Learning.

Noden, H. (2009). *Introduction to Image Grammar Activity Book* (Grades 6–12). Logan, IA: Perfection Learning.

O'Hare, F. (1973). *Sentence combining: Improving student writing without formal grammar instruction* (Research Report No. 15). Urbana, IL: National Council of Teachers of English.

Olson, J. (1992). *Envisioning writing: Toward an integration of drawing and writing.* Portsmouth, NH: Heinemann.

Reed, H. (1942, August 8). Naming of parts. *New Statesman and Nation, 24*(598), 92.

Rief, L. (1991). *Seeking diversity: Language arts with adolescents.* Portsmouth, NH: Heinemann.

Romano, T. (1987). *Clearing the way: Working with teenage writers.* Portsmouth, NH: Heinemann.

Thomas, O. (1965). *Transformational grammar and the teacher of English.* New York: Holt, Rinehart. [Second edition with E. Kintgen, 1975.]

Weaver, C. (1996). *Teaching grammar in context.* Portsmouth, NH: Heinemann.

Weaver, C. (2007). *The grammar plan book.* Portsmouth, NH: Heinemann.

Weaver, C., with Bush, J. (2008). *Grammar to enrich and enhance writing.* Portsmouth, NH: Heinemann.

Wheeler, R. (2005). Code-switch to teach Standard English. *English Journal, 94*(5), 108–112.

Wheeler, R., & Swords, R. (2004). Code-switching: Tools of language and culture transform the dialectally diverse classroom. *Language Arts, 81,* 470–480.

Wheeler, R., & Swords, R. (2006). *Code-switching: Teaching Standard English in urban classrooms.* Urbana, IL: National Council of Teachers of English.

Chapter 12

Primary School Children Learning Grammar

Rethinking the Possibilities

Ruth French

Introduction: Finding the Primary School Children in the Research

Primary school children are noticeably absent from much of the research up to the 1990s on the effectiveness of teaching grammar. Absent, in that a majority of the oft-cited and largest studies were conducted with older subjects: high school or tertiary students. Absent, in that even in the subset of studies in which primary children are present in the data, they are rendered almost invisible, represented often only by test scores of experimental instruments and essays.

In this chapter I hope both to address some of the theory which I think is responsible for the comparatively limited representation of young children in the research, and to offer some redress by summarizing some research which focuses on primary school children and which includes their own views and voices.

The research upon which I will focus consists of several case studies in primary school classrooms where the children learned aspects of systemic functional grammar (Halliday & Matthiessen, 2004; 1st edition Halliday, 1985). The functional grammar in these classes was contextualized within a wider "Knowledge about Language" framework,[1] although the breadth of the metalinguistic interest and knowledge of the children cannot be fully represented in this chapter. Importantly, functional grammar was also contextualized as a strongly integrated dimension of the classes' English/literacy programs. The summary of this research will address both the accessibility of functional grammar and its utility across several areas within the English curriculum.

It's Too Abstract for Them: The Influence of Piaget

There exists a good deal of skepticism about the possibility of gainfully teaching any grammar to primary school children. This is based at least in part on the fact that grammar involves understanding abstract concepts, and there is concern from an educational psychology perspective as to whether these can be mastered by primary school-aged children.

---

1. For some background on "Knowledge about Language", see Carter, R. (Ed.). (1990). *Knowledge about language and the curriculum: The LINC Reader*. London: Hodder.

The development of abstract thought has long been considered to begin roughly at the age of 11 or 12 years. Following the work of Jean Piaget (for example, Inhelder & Piaget, 1958), teachers in training have for decades learned that children's thinking develops through a number of stages as they grow, changing gradually from the egocentric understandings of infants and preschoolers, toward concrete operational thinking typical of children aged about 7–8 to 11–12 years, and finally in the adolescent years to formal operations and abstract thought. The means by which this development occurs – whether it is essentially biological, that is, to do with physiological maturation of the brain, or whether there is a significant role for "socialization" in the development of thought – is one of the great questions of education, and one for which Piaget offered different emphases in different writings (Cole & Wertsch, 1996). In fact, despite some impressions to the contrary, Piaget was essentially in agreement with the Russian researcher L.S. Vygotsky (1962, 1978), with whom he is often compared and contrasted, that social interaction does have a role in children's intellectual development.

But the Piagetian legacy received by school teachers is not always so carefully qualified. Undergraduate textbooks in educational psychology typically use Piaget's stage theory as their benchmark explanation of child development, restating that stages and ages essentially progress together.[2] Developmental stages are presented as being biologically determined, even if environment has a minor role in keeping them moving along. In teaching there has been considerable acceptance, if often of a tacit or implied nature, of this simplified version of Piagetian theory. It has been widely held, therefore, that primary school children are essentially incapable of abstract thought; that their brains just haven't matured sufficiently in physical terms to go beyond the actual and tangible. The logical conclusion is that the ideal primary curriculum should incorporate as much concrete, hands-on activity as possible, since this will match the way young children's minds work and will therefore be "developmentally appropriate". Children will grasp more abstract ideas when their brains are ready – in adolescence.

For grammar teaching, the Piagetian legacy has been to recommend that grammar not be taught in primary school, since grammar is an abstraction – a language for talking about language – and therefore doomed to disappoint when taught to an intellectually immature audience. Reflecting on when it might be most profitable to begin learning grammar, Elley, Barham, Lamb and Wyllie (1976), commented:

> Certainly, teachers have succeeded in instructing primary school children in the exercise of sentence analysis, but, in the light of the research of Piaget and other developmental psychologists about the limited ability of pre-adolescent children to manipulate abstract concepts, it seems most unlikely that such training would be readily applied by children in their own writing. (p. 18)

---

2. For example Berk (2003) and Woolfolk (2004): two textbooks commonly used in Australian universities. In both these textbooks Piaget's stage theory is the dominant point of reference against which others' critiques or amendments are positioned.

So, is the whole enterprise of developing primary children's grammatical knowledge really just a waste of time?

Challenging the Assumptions: Possibilities from Vygotsky

There are a number of challenges which can be made to the Piagetian legacy, including questioning its view of children's abilities, and problematizing the pedagogy which it engenders.

First, there is considerable evidence that children can perform some cognitive tasks at earlier ages than Piaget suggested. This evidence covers a broad range of concepts across Piaget's areas of experimentation with children, such as "object permanence" (Baillargeon & DeVos, 1991) and spatial reasoning (Blaut, 1991, 1997). It is likely that Piaget underestimated children's abilities to some extent. Within this body of empirical research into Piaget's "stage theory", the point is also made that the fairly discrete stages described by Piaget may be more productively considered a continuum, with learning as a process of gradually thinking in a more integrated way *between* and more abstractly *about* concepts. Regarding the teaching of grammar to young school children, it seems premature to conclude from Piaget that the exercise is pointless to begin with.

Second, there is a problem with pedagogy. If Piaget's "epistemic subject" is an individual whose cognitive abilities will mature with age, then the teacher is essentially a facilitator of that development. The teacher's role involves "providing children with opportunities to create and coordinate the many relationships *of which they are currently capable*" (McInerney & McInerney, 2006, p. 49; emphasis added). That is, teaching accompanies natural intellectual development. An emphasis on child-centered, "developmentally appropriate" pedagogy represented for many educators in the 1960s a refreshing shift from the very traditional, transmission or "teacher-centered" model of education, which had been characteristic of much schooling up to that time. In the primary school context, where children were deemed to be working in Piaget's stage of "concrete operations", the teacher's role ideally was to offer many opportunities for hands-on exploration and discovery.

In recent decades, a qualitatively different approach to pedagogy has been suggested as a result of emerging interest in what have been called "social constructivist" theories of development, based on the pioneering endeavors of L.S. Vygotsky (1962, 1978) and widely known through the later work of Jerome Bruner (for example, Bruner, 1986). According to Vygotsky, culture and society have an enormous role in bringing about learning, and are not merely the setting in which learning will naturally occur. In particular, it is in interactions with enabling caregivers that children move from what they already know, to shared understandings with others, and finally to new internalized thinking: the social construction of knowledge. From this theoretical viewpoint, teaching leads learning. Teachers and caregivers interact collaboratively with children to support and extend their thinking as children learn to do new things and solve new problems. This pedagogical approach is vividly captured in Bruner's metaphor of scaffolding (Wood, Bruner & Ross, 1976).

In addition, for Vygotsky, learning is not only mediated by adults who support and lead children's development of thought, but also by tools, which may be physical tools but can also be symbolic items and systems, including language itself. In what is a major contribution to educational theory, and a distinctive feature of his approach as against Piaget's (Cole & Wertsch, 1996), Vygotsky emphasized the role of cultural artifacts or tools which permit thinking to be mediated symbolically as a means toward thought becoming fully internalized: semiotic mediation. Social constructivism argues that the question is not simply whether children can learn something or not given their age or stage of development, but rather what interactions and tools might make it possible and easier for them to learn. Here exists the potential to look afresh at grammar teaching in the primary school. Moreover, since learning is mediated by tools, the kind of thought made possible by the learning process is shaped by the kind of tools available. In teaching about grammar, the grammatical description itself may be considered a cognitive tool – a form of semiotic mediation – since it offers a way of talking about language. Grammar permits us to take language from the immediate (the story, the conversation) to the mediate (a *description* of the story or conversation). It is here that we now turn to a discussion of systemic functional grammar, the tool of choice for the research summarized in this chapter.

Activity: Reflecting on the Role of Semiotic Mediation in Learning

A famous example of how tools mediate learning is the "Forbidden colors game" (Vygotksy, 1978, chapter 3; Luria, 1992). Read one of these accounts (the latter was freely available on the Internet at the time of writing) and reflect on the methods used in this research to assist children to achieve success with an initially difficult task. In what ways does this confirm or challenge your own views about how children learn?

Activity: Designing Lessons Using "Tools" for Thinking

Consider some new, possibly abstract learning you are planning to introduce to your students, such as "metaphor in poetry". What "tools" could you provide to help your students learn? Think about both physical artifacts (e.g. materials, displays) and also the language you could use to "scaffold" the students' thinking (the texts you could use, and also your own "teacher talk" and questioning).

Why Functional Grammar?

Traditional school grammar has had a long and disputed career in education. Its usefulness for educational purposes has been questioned by studies for over a century. Conversely, and in contradiction to the ostensible wisdom of the research, traditional grammar's value has also been reasserted by academics and educators who argue its teaching should be more integrated with the English curriculum and more enjoyable than was the case historically (for example, in the United States, the work of the NCTE special interest group, the Assembly for the Teaching of English Grammar). In the search for a good grammar to teach children, transformational grammar has also been considered (Elley et al., 1976).

It is not possible in the space available here to detail the reasons why traditional school or transformational grammars may not be ideally suited for improving students' literacy, although they have their limitations (for a synopsis of these see Collerson, 1997, chapter 4). Instead we will turn to an alternative choice: systemic functional grammar, developed by M.A.K. Halliday (Halliday & Matthiessen, 2004; Halliday, 1994), hereafter often referred to as "functional grammar" or SFG. In the case studies which figure in this chapter, the researchers explored whether SFG might prove useful to primary school children. The reasons for this choice are outlined below, and while some contrasts between SFG and other grammars may appear as we progress, the focus will be mainly on the reasons for choosing to teach functional grammar.

Characteristics of Systemic Functional Grammar

There are a number of features of SFG which suggest its potential use in education. First, systemic functional grammar is a descriptive grammar, as are most grammars these days – or at least those used in linguistics. SFG does not pass judgment on dialect variations as "ungrammatical", and in this sense appeals to teachers who worry that teaching grammar involves denigrating their students' non-Standard-English home dialects. Second, SFG takes the clause as its basic unit of analysis and is therefore able to be applied to language in use, both spoken and written (rather than the basic unit of the sentence, which is a feature of written language only).

Most significantly, however, functional grammar is oriented to how meaning is made. It is designed as a way into exploring how choices in wordings create different kinds of meanings and together build up different texts to achieve diverse social purposes. It follows therefore that SFG is able to relate grammatical knowledge with knowledge of whole texts and their structure. This is one of the most powerful arguments for its potential as a resource for children's learning: that it is designed to relate the "sentence (or clause) level" to the "whole-text" level, or, in more profound terms, to relate grammatics[3] with the achievement of social purposes. In fact, for Halliday, the "way in" to understanding grammar is from the semantics down, rather than from the word-forms up. Functional grammar sits within systemic linguistics as one of the levels of analysis at which texts may be explored, but "above" the grammar lie descriptions of

3. "Grammatics" follows Halliday (Halliday, 2002, pp. 384–386) in discriminating between "learning grammar" in the sense of learning language (such as when toddlers begin to use verbs in their speech), which we achieve without conscious effort, and "learning *about* grammar" in terms of conscious metalinguistic knowledge (such as learning what we mean by "verb"). The parallel can be made: grammatics is to grammar as linguistics is to language.

whole texts: "genres" (in the linguistic understanding of the term) or "text-types". In linguistic terms, a genre is a social process: a sequence of stages through which a text moves to achieve a social goal. These stages are identifiable by their typical lexico-grammatical[4] patterns and, according to SFG, genres are in fact realized by choices at the level of the grammar. That is, the relationship between grammatical features and generic stages is not merely coincidental. The lexico-grammatical patterns *create* the stages. This linking of grammar with rhetoric, of parts with wholes, highlights where much grammar teaching in the past seems to have failed to make a connection for students. It was reported, for example, that while grammar students might improve at being able to correct sentences with errors, their writing of essays did not show any commensurate improvement.[5] With systemic functional grammar, the grammar–meaning connection is part of its design. Thus, for example, it is possible to teach children about the structure of an information report at the genre level and also to look at how features of the language at the lexico-grammatical level build the generic stages of the report.

This point about the nature and design of SFG is important from a theoretical perspective. From a Vygotskian point of view, the nature of a cognitive tool will shape the thinking or intellectual work that the tool makes possible, thus:

> beginning the study of grammatics through a functional description is likely to lead to a different kind of consciousness about the nature and use of grammatics from that produced by description of, for example, "parts of speech" or a formal description. (Williams, 2005, p. 288)

A Brief Summary of Some Systemic Functional Grammar

Before going on to discuss some of the research into children learning functional grammar, I would like to summarize briefly some distinctive features of grammatical analysis using SFG. Systemic functional linguistics may be widely *known of*, but not necessarily well known.[6] So it would be unfair to progress by assuming the reader's familiarity with Hallidayan grammar. This summary is therefore offered for the novice in SFG, with apologies for its cursoriness due both to space constraints and also the desire to talk most about the work with children.

Halliday describes three metafunctions of the lexico-grammar, that is, ways in which the jobs that language does are simultaneously encoded in text. These

---

4. In SFG, the more accurate term for the grammatical level of analysis is the "lexico-grammatical" level, which refers to vocabulary (lexis) and grammatical structure together. This is often shortened to "grammatical" in order to be more concise, and I have often followed this convention in this chapter.

5. For example, Elley et al., 1976.

6. For example, in their recent review, "The Effect of Grammar Teaching (Syntax)" (2004), Andrews and colleagues acknowledge SFG but do so quite briefly. This is not surprising since "syntax" was one of the gate-keeping search terms used to screen studies for inclusion. Halliday's approach, by his own analysis, is better described as "synesis", focusing on meaning (Halliday, 1994, p. xiv).

metafunctions are: the experiential,[7] interpersonal and textual. In the research with children to be described below, the experiential and textual metafunctions were the main focus.

- The *experiential metafunction* refers to the way we use language to represent the world – to tell what happened, the event (Process[8]), to whom or what (Participants), and when and where (Circumstances). Processes are usually realized by the word class of verb, although the terms "Process" and "verb" are not equivalent. One of Halliday's important contributions is to distinguish between different types of Processes and therefore different Participants in those Processes. For example: material or "action" Processes are performed by an <u>Actor</u> and may be done to a *Goal* (for example: "<u>The cat</u> slices *the pumpkin*") or done across a *Range* ("<u>Mrs. Piggott</u> did *the ironing*"); verbal or "saying" Processes are enacted by a <u>Sayer</u> and they may be directed toward a *Receiver* (for example: "<u>The cat</u> whispered *to the Squirrel*"); relational Processes of the attributive kind have a <u>Carrier</u> and an *Attribute* which the Carrier is assigned ("<u>The soup</u> wasn't *tasty*").
- The *interpersonal metafunction* refers to how we use language to enact social relationships and includes, in part, Mood (the Subject and Finite together, which signal the mood to be imperative or interrogative or declarative) and modality (such as the use of attitudinal lexis like "possibly" or "unfortunately").
- The *textual metafunction* refers to how language hangs together to make a meaningful message, and Halliday describes Theme and Rheme as the main resources employed in the textual metafunction. Theme is described as "the element which serves as the point of departure of the message" (Halliday & Matthiessen, 2004, p. 64). In English this is realized by first position in the clause. The Rheme is the rest of the clause, where the Theme is developed. Note that Theme is a description developed by Halliday from the work of the Prague school of linguists, and Theme has no "equivalent" in traditional grammar.

Figure 12.1 is an example of a simple functional grammatical analysis of one clause, showing the experiential and textual metafunctions only since these were the focus of the work with the children. The clause itself is drawn from a Year 6 child's work, and indicates the playfulness which was a key feature of the children's grammar work in the case studies which follow. I have included with the experiential analysis an additional row to show the more delicate description of *types* of Process and Participant.

7. More accurately, the *experiential* is one component of the *ideational* metafunction, which also includes *logical* relations expressed in language. The logical dimension refers to how word groups and clauses are put together, including, for example, the structure of the nominal group and the functions of "subordinating" clauses.
8. The use of capitalization is a convention from linguistics, which helps to discriminate between the use of a word to refer to linguistic functions and the use of the same word in a non-technical context.

Table 12.1 Simple Functional Grammatical Analysis of One Clause

This morning	a cockroach	ate	the rest of my sentence.
E X P E R I E N T I A L		M E T A F U N C T I O N	
Circumstance	Participant	Process	Participant
Circumstance of location in time	Actor	Material Process	Goal
T E X T U A L M E T A F U N C T I O N			
Theme	Rheme		

There are sometimes questions about whether Theme and Actor are not just the "subject" from traditional school grammar. While Theme, Subject and Actor may coincide in material clauses, the example in Figure 12.1 shows that it is not the case that they will necessarily be so. Note that the Theme is *not* the same as the Subject in this example (the Subject is "a cockroach"). Note also that, while in this clause the grammatical Subject is also the Actor, the clause could be rewritten as "This morning the rest of my sentence was eaten by a cockroach", in which case the Goal ("the rest of my sentence") becomes the grammatical Subject.

The value of SFG is most effectively demonstrated when looking at patterns across many clauses which make up a text rather than at individual clauses in isolation. This patterning of language across whole texts was a feature of the grammatics taught in the studies to be summarized in this chapter. Also, it is not necessary to have a complete description of all three metafunctions before beginning to use the grammar in literacy tasks; the metafunctions of SFG can offer productive insights without all three metafunctions being examined at once. For example, a focus on the experiential metafunction in a short story might show how a character is consistently the Actor of material Processes but not perhaps the Goal, and therefore demonstrate how characterization is built up in the text. Or a focus on the textual metafunction in an essay could show how the Themes construct a sense of where the argument is going and lead the reader to see its logic.

From this overview it should by now be clear that functional grammar is not a grammar preoccupied with fixing "errors" in writing and speech (although there is room to describe whether the Subject and Finite agree in the way demanded by Standard English if you want to), but rather it conceives grammar as a meaning-making resource. The notion of choice is foregrounded: not "is this (technically) right?" but rather "does this effectively do what I want/need it to do?" The grammar also sits within a theory of language which is focused on the social (unlike transformational grammars, which look inward to the hypothesized workings of the mind). For Halliday, the point of language is meaning: making sense of the world and interacting with others effectively. It is no accident therefore that systemic linguistics has been taken up by educators.

Some Recent Evidence

Background

The research I intend to draw upon in this chapter is from work with a number of schools in Sydney, Australia, and goes back to 1994. My initial connection with this research was as the classroom teacher of a case-study class, and I have since gone on to conduct my own research, some of which appears here for the first time. The research recounted here is all from case studies in primary classrooms in inner Sydney schools, and to the best of my knowledge it remains a substantial part of what is a comparatively small body of academically documented research explicitly dealing with primary school children using functional grammar.

The project "Children's Development of Knowledge about Language" was initiated and coordinated by Geoff Williams, then at the University of Sydney, and begun in 1994. Research assistance, including classroom observations and support for teachers, was provided by Joan Rothery. Over the course of the project, a total of five groups of children were the subject of case studies: four mainstream school classes of up to 30 children (two Year 6 classes and two Year 1 classes) and one smaller study of a group of 11–12-year-old volunteers who returned to their old primary school to attend a "Grammar Club" during their first year of high school. The "KAL project" sought to investigate the accessibility and effectiveness of aspects of functional grammar for primary school children. I have also included in this chapter some references to another similar project for which I was the researcher, and which involved case studies conducted in two Year 2 classes in yet another inner Sydney school.

In each of the case studies, the classroom teacher worked collaboratively with researchers so that the grammar studied in class was planned jointly, with the researchers often providing assistance with materials preparation and advice, and usually the classroom teacher leading the lessons with the children. The aspects of grammar to be taught were not cemented in advance, but rather the program was developed dynamically over time and with consideration to the pace at which the children were comfortable to learn. In planning for teaching grammatics, a strong emphasis was given to the kinds of texts the children were reading and writing in class. That is, the grammar study was integrated with the rest of the English curriculum. A wide range of mainly qualitative data was collected, with a strong emphasis on recording classroom talk – something missing in the historical grammar-teaching research.

Accessibility

One of the consistent findings of these case studies has been the accessibility to young children of aspects of systemic functional grammar. Accessibility alone may not make the study of a grammar worthwhile, but it is a necessary precursor to making any use of the grammar.

There is clear evidence in the case studies that school children from Year 1 to Year 6 were readily able to recognize and use the following grammatical descriptions:

- *Processes*, including discriminating between different Process types. Year 1 and 2 children learned about material or "action" Processes, verbal or "saying" Processes and mental or "thinking and feeling" Processes. In the Year 6 classes, relational and existential Processes were also introduced and found to be accessible to some students despite their having been given comparatively little attention in class.
- Some *Participant* roles: Children from Year 1 to Year 6 could readily identify the "Sayer" of a verbal Process and "What was said" (quoted direct speech). They could also identify the "doer" (Actor) and the Goal or the "done to" participant in material Processes.
- *Circumstances* were able to be identified by children from Year 1-age up. These are the "Where, when and how" words and phrases, or, as the term so eloquently describes them, the *circumstances* in which the Process takes place.
- *Theme and Rheme*. Theme was defined as the writer's or speaker's point of departure – and likened to the "launching pad" or "take-off runway" of the clause. Year 2 children located Themes as the first part of the sentence and, in shared whole-class and group work, identified Themes in procedures, recounts and narratives. In the Year 6 classes, the children learned that the Theme is actually a feature of the clause (these older children had been taught how to delineate clauses very early in the project and so were taught a more accurate description of Theme). Children learned that the Rheme was "the rest" and some classes discussed the function of the Rheme, such as its role in some texts of introducing new information, which may subsequently be taken up in the Theme of the next clause or sentence.
- *Conjunctions* (not an exclusively SFG term, of course).

The Year 6 children learned to identify *clauses* and many could correctly locate clause boundaries in stretches of text when working with simple and compound sentences (Williams, 2005).

One case-study group – the Grammar Club – also learned the *structure of the nominal group* and *participant roles associated with relational processes* (Williams, 2005; Williams & French, 1995). At least one member of the club could recognize, a few months after learning them, the Participant roles found with identifying-type, relational Processes – quite a difficult area of the grammar (Williams, 1998, pp. 39–40).

In addition to identifying individual grammatical elements, the children were also able to work across different metafunctions, such as looking at what experiential elements (Process, Participant or Circumstance) were positioned as Theme in different texts. Here, however, the discussion about accessibility leads into talking about ways in which the children *used* grammatics, so more detail about this aspect of the work will be developed in the next section.

Utility

In the SFG case-study classes, grammatics was found to be useful to students across a number of dimensions of their school literacy programs. Their grammatical knowledge enabled primary school children to develop:

1.   conscious control of their writing;
2.   critical understandings in their reading;
3.   improved expression in reading aloud;
4.   improved punctuation of direct speech.

I intend to focus in the following summary on the evidence for the first two of these claims, those being the claims which permit the potential of SFG to be most clearly demonstrated. The two latter claims are perhaps more straightforward and so I will more briefly address the evidence for them before concluding the chapter.

Conscious Control of Writing

A tool for making meaning, for choosing language in order to write and speak effectively and better understand what you read – this is how the SFG-based studies discussed in this chapter positioned grammatical knowledge for the children. This approach contrasts with the way grammar has historically been positioned in the curriculum. In most of the studies[9] of grammar teaching, grammar was taught in the hope it would improve students' skills in written composition, particularly by reducing the numbers of grammatical and "usage" errors they made: the focus was on grammar for accuracy. In the SFG research here described, the emphasis was on grammar for meaning. Therefore in addressing the conscious control of writing, the concern was not mainly with fixing or avoiding errors but with creating meaningful text which achieves its purpose.

In beginning to make use of grammatical knowledge, several case-study classes learned about the language of procedural texts, such as recipes, science experiment methods and other "how to" texts. Procedures are a genre which school children are often asked to write, and which can seem deceptively simple, but which (as anyone who has installed their own new TV knows) can be hard to write well. In the following work, primary school children learned functional grammar as a way to bring under their conscious control the linguistic resources needed to write procedures. That they did not already have a grasp of these resources is illustrated in the following example. The example is typical of what children in a Year 2 class wrote when they were asked to "make a poster telling Year 1 children how to write a procedure":

How to write a procedure
First write down the materials. Then write down the equipment. Last you write down the steps. Each step starts with a capital letter and for each step you need to do a different thing. by Christopher

9. To be fair, in the Elley et al. study, which used the Oregon Curriculum to teach transformational grammar (TG), the TG study was "justified on humanistic rather than pragmatic grounds" (Elley et al., 1976, p. 18). That is, TG was not taught with any expectation that it ought to improve writing.

Several children, such as Chen, also added something like: "You write the method in the right order." Clearly the children already had some metalinguistic knowledge about procedures, but this did not extend to the level of the grammatics.

In procedures, it is typical, although not obligatory, to use an imperative material Process in Theme position (Themes shown in italics):

> *Beat* the egg whites until soft peaks form.
> *Insert* one end of the string into the hole in one can.

This kind of pattern is effective in procedures, because their purpose is to tell us how to *do* something, and so the word/s which say what to *do* are usually foregrounded. However, the Theme may be varied – again for functional purposes. In the following examples, a Circumstance is the Theme, and for good reason:

> *Gently* fold the beaten egg whites into the rest of the mixture.
> *With an adult's help*, hammer the nail through the end of one tin can.

Thus, a resource from the textual metafunction of SFG – the Theme – can be realized by different resources from the experiential metafunction (in these examples, Process or Circumstance). This was a useful idea for children who learned about procedures in the case-study classes.

For example, in Williams' KAL project in 1994, a Year 6 class used SFG to improve their writing of a recipe.[10] The recipe was for a simple cheese sauce to serve on pasta as a hearty snack, and the children first cooked it by following their teacher's demonstration. They then worked with their teacher to redraft an amusing text called "Mr. Confused's Recipe for Cheese Sauce", making changes such as:

> From: The flour is then added.
> Stir until the butter and flour are bubbling gently.
> To: Add the flour and stir until bubbling.

The children were introduced to Theme as part of this joint redrafting process, and particular emphasis was given to the idea of choice. That is, that the writer can choose what to put in Theme position, and that in procedures this is typically but not obligatorily a material Process, because the social purpose of a procedure is to tell what to *do*. In the case of the "confused" recipe, the class's aim was to redraft it to make it clearer and to help ensure that the final result was tasty. One key step was the adding of milk to the roux, and for this step the children suggested to the teacher that the word "gradually" should be the Theme as a way to foreground the importance of *how* the milk was added, which of course has a lot to do with whether the sauce is lumpy or nicely smooth.

10. For further evidence of another group of 11-year-olds learning about grammatics through work on procedures, and a discussion of the relevance of Vygotskian notions of voluntary attention and semiotic mediation, see Williams (2006 [2004]).

From these beginnings with using functional grammar to develop conscious control of writing procedures, this Year 6 class went on to look at how the patterns of Theme in other texts are different from those in procedures. A particular focus was on recounts, and in this work the children learned through joint redrafting experiences how to make choices about what to put in Theme position in order to improve on their first draft recounts. They used this knowledge when independently redrafting their own written work. In the following excerpt from an interview[11] with Joan Rothery, one of the children discusses how she used her grammatical knowledge to consciously control her redrafting:

ANIELKA: Now I know about how to write it, like what's the beginning part of a clause and the different types of Themes that you can have and Participants.
...
JOAN: So, um, it would be interesting to look back at your very first recount wouldn't it, the one you wrote about [words unclear]?
ANIELKA: Yes, I think that one was a bit repetitive in, like, Theme.

When their work samples were analyzed, the written compositions of these Year 6 students demonstrated improvement in their control of Theme. They also wrote longer and more involved recounts than a parallel "non-grammar" Year 6 class, even though they knew they would be expected to redraft their work, so there was no evidence that the redrafting process was disliked (Williams, 1995).

It is not only at the older end of primary schooling that SFG can be useful to children as they learn to control their writing. Earlier, I introduced some Year 2 children's ideas about "how to write a procedure". Working in a similar way to the Year 6 children just mentioned, these Year 2 children also read and used procedures in class, such as one for making a polystyrene-cup telephone and another that they used to make chocolate milkshakes. They reread these texts and with their teacher examined the language of procedures. They later worked on other kinds of texts and compared and contrasted patterns in the language across different genres. By the end of the school year, the children's understanding of Theme had developed considerably. In the following exchange, the teacher is scribing for the children a summary of what they have learnt.

TEACHER: [addressing Beatrice] All right, what's your sentence about Themes in recounts?
BEATRICE: This year we have learnt a lot about Theme, and where it comes up.
...
We've learnt that, um, the verbs are not, the Theme is not usually verbs in recounts, because the recount doesn't usually tell you something to do, it just says what has happened.

---

11. Transcription conventions: ... indicates section of transcript ellipsed.

Beatrice was able to express a relationship between Theme and the function of a whole text – she associates "telling you something to do" (procedural texts) with verbs as Themes. This idea of the functionality of Theme had been introduced to the children from the earliest opportunity, as had the notion of choice. For example, the children noticed that this step had the word "carefully" as Theme: "Carefully make a small hole in the bottom of a cup using the pointy end of the pencil." Drawing on their concrete experience of having performed the procedure already, the children were able to do the more abstract task of reflecting on this choice of language (the selection of a Circumstance rather than Process for Theme):

TEACHER: Why do they want you to be careful? Marc?
MARC: Because you might stab yourself.
...
HEIDI: 'Cause you could've, you could've make a big hole and when you stick the toothpick in, um, the hole could be too big and it could just, um, come out.

This beginning consciousness about how language is patterned in procedures was used by the children to redraft the steps for a craft activity they had enjoyed and wanted to be able to do again at home. One group rewrote this step:

> From: The petals are made when you pull apart the layers of paper from each other.
> To: Make the petals by pulling apart the paper layers.

Not all the Year 2 children were able to apply their newly learned grammatical knowledge to writing straight away like this, but here is evidence for the beginnings of conscious control of writing. The kind of knowledge that these Year 2 children have about language is not yet at the level of the Year 6 children discussed above, but it is headed in the same direction: toward knowing how to make decisions when writing (and especially when redrafting written work) in order to help that writing do its job better. That is, using grammatics to write more effectively.

Activity: Exploring Grammatical Patterns in a Procedure

Locate a procedural text you could use with your students (e.g. a recipe, the method for a science experiment). Identify the "action Processes" – you could circle them in green. Then take a highlighter of a different color and highlight the Themes in the text. What patterns can you see? Are there any steps which don't begin with a Process? Why might the writer have chosen to place something else in Theme position in that clause?

How could you design a lesson sequence in order to help your students develop a meaningful understanding of the functionality of Theme in procedures, incorporating the idea of grammar as "choice" rather than just "rules"?

Critical Understandings in Reading

Functional grammar has proven useful to many researchers interested in critical discourse analysis. The grammar offers a shared and precise language for critics to use when analyzing text, and its orientation to social context (language both acts upon and is shaped by context) has been useful for those interested in illuminating the often implicit representations of power, inequality and exclusion to be found in texts.

Primary school children, too, can use aspects of functional grammar as critical tools for reading and discussing texts, even without knowing a lot of the grammar. Two examples of such work will be summarized here. In the first example, Year 6 children explored characterization and narrative structure in a picture book using Actor and Goal;[12] in the second example, Year 2 children used Saying Processes as a way into the structuring of another narrative picture book.

Working with the picture-book *Piggybook* by Anthony Browne (Browne, 1986), a class of Year 6 children explored the roles of Participants in material Processes. They learned about Actor and Goal, and were able to identify these grammatical elements throughout the story and to track how different characters were accorded different status by the nature of their representation in the experiential metafunction. For example, the taken-for-granted Mrs. Piggott was an Actor (doer) and her material Processes were often directed upon domestic Goals (done-to's) (see Figure 12.2).

In contrast, Mr. Piggott and his two sons, Simon and Patrick, tended to be Actors without Goals, that is, they were represented in the grammar as doing, but not doing *to* or acting upon (see Figure 12.3).

When Mrs. Piggott goes away, leaving a note saying, "You are pigs", the boys and Dad have to look after themselves. The house becomes a pigsty as they try to engage in the kind of roles usually performed so ably by Mum. When she comes back, things change for the better (see Figure 12.4).

The children created a display for the classroom wall where these and the other material clauses from *Piggybook* were shown using different colors and shapes to symbolize the different grammatical elements. Children worked in pairs to do a clause or two each, thus sharing the effort of analysis and creating a final display which represented the work of all the class members. The patterning

Table 12.2 Mrs. Piggott as Actor

Actor	Material process	Goal	Circumstance
Mrs. Piggott	washed	all the breakfast things	
	made	all the beds	
	vacuumed	all the carpets	
[and then] she	went		to work

12. This example is treated much more fully in Williams (2000) and Martin (2000) in the same volume.

Table 12.3 The Piggott Males as Actors

Actor	Material process	Goal	Circumstance
Mr. Piggott	lived		in a nice house
He	went off		to his very important job
They [the boys]	went off		to their very important school

Table 12.4 The Piggotts as Collaborative Actors

Actor	Material process	Goal
Mrs. Piggott	stayed	
Mr. Piggott	washed	the dishes
Patrick and Simon	made	the beds
Mr. Piggott	did	the ironing[1]
She [Mum]	mended	the car

Note

1. "The ironing" is technically the Range in this clause; it is really an extension of the Process. This fairly fine distinction was not made with the Year 6 children, who were content identifying "the ironing" as Goal. This is one example of how grammatics were introduced to the children at a careful pace and with attempts to avoid overwhelming them with detail. In other instances, the children pressed the teacher to learn more about some aspects of the grammar which had only been briefly mentioned in class, such as existential Processes.

of language was made clearly apparent to the children through this display, where colors and shapes vividly brought out the grammatical features of the text. This display, and others like it which the children developed throughout the project, were in Vygotskian terms mediating the children's learning of grammatics – making the abstract more visible and more manageable.

The children reflected on the shift in the patterning of the Participant roles in the material Processes in the story, and particularly on how this related to the structure of the narrative. They talked about this with their teacher and together they jointly wrote this summary of what they had noticed:

What We Learnt about the Grammatical Patterns in Piggybook

Beginning

All the Goals Mrs Piggott did were to do with housework.

Only Mrs Piggott had Goals. This shows she is the only one doing something to something else.

Mr Piggott and the boys only did things for themselves; they did not do work in the home. This is shown by the fact that they didn't have any Goals. They were the only characters that talked. They told Mrs P to hurry up.

Resolution

At the end, everyone did an action to something – to benefit the whole family, not just themselves. Everyone had Goals at the end. Now the Goals for Mrs Piggott included more than housework.

The Goals had a big role in structuring the narrative. The pattern of Actors and Goals changes at the end. This makes the Resolution.

This is an example of children using SFG productively to develop a critical sense of how grammatical patterning contributes to meaning in a narrative. In the *Piggybook* work, Year 6 children used grammatics to understand the language used to build characterization and to shape narrative.

A second example of the utility of SFG for children learning to read critically is drawn from my own work with a Year 2 class (for a more detailed treatment of this work, see French, 2009). This class read and loved the story *Pumpkin Soup* by Helen Cooper. They had learned about saying "verbs",[13] and they went on to work through the book listing all the verbal Processes. These were then displayed in the order they occurred in the text. The children were next asked to see if they could find any patterns in the verbal Processes, and while they commented freely on features to do with mathematics (counting the words, noticing repetition) and spelling (initial and final letters), none of the children commented on anything to do with literary meaning. Next the children worked with me to identify the narrative stages of *Pumpkin Soup*, using the structure Orientation ^ Complication ^ Resolution that they had already learned in class with their teacher. Labels showing the structure were placed above the "saying verbs" (see Figure 12.5):

The children were again asked if they could see a pattern, and while many still attended to how the words were spelled or tried counting them to see a pattern, some began to see a co-patterning of the lexico-grammar with the narrative structure:

HILARY: Well … it's kind of like, because they've like yelled, squeaked, wailed and stormed, and um murmured and scoffed in the Complication, it's kind of like, because it's in the Complication they're kind of like yelling words and like, screaming and shouting and like crying.

---

13. The use of the term "verb" instead of "Process" was imposed upon the researcher in this case study by the relevant state authority: the NSW Department of Education and Training.

Table 12.5 Narrative Stages of *Pumpkin Soup*

Orientation	Complication						Resolution		Re-Complication
murmured said	squeaked snapped	wailed stormed scoffed	muttered	sniffed wept	wailed squeaked	whispered yelped	shrieked	didn't say	said

And Karin was certain that the saying verbs were not varied for ornamental reasons:

RESEARCHER: Do you think that Helen Cooper, when she wrote the book, just put words like "wailed" and "stormed" and "muttered" and "sniffed" and whatever in the Complication just to make it more interesting?
...
KARIN: Not just interesting. To make it sound more like what happened in the story. How like "stormed", "wept", "sniffed" and "wailed" and "squeaked" – they're all sort of Complication-y sort of words.

These kinds of insights are neither trivial nor obvious. To these young children, the idea of finding patterns in the lexico-grammar was new and at first difficult. Yet their insights about how aspects of grammar contribute to the shaping of a whole text are qualitatively similar to those made by the Year 6 children reading *Piggybook*, if somewhat less well-formed. With support, these Year 2 children were using grammatics to make insights into the "constructedness" of story. They were using and applying simple abstract concepts in becoming critical readers. This is a far cry from the kind of grammar teaching which stops at the point of making a chart for "better words than *said*", and a different kind of comprehension experience from activities which ask young children to draw a character or retell the plot. These children are beginning to see story from a different perspective: as a crafted object, made of language which can be investigated and described, not merely as a fortuitous collection of characters and events.

Activity: Exploring Grammatical Patterns in a Narrative

Select a short, simple narrative text such as a children's picture book or a fairy tale. It may be easier to begin with a simple, single-complication narrative. Have a look at the Processes and especially the different *types* of Processes (for example: material or "action", mental, verbal) and where they appear in the story. How do these contribute to the shaping of the story and its characters?

In what ways could you help your students to see patterns in the wording of the narrative and how these relate to shaping the whole text?

Improved Oral Reading Expression

Another way in which some children have used grammatical knowledge has been in their conscious attention to verbal Processes when reading aloud. After learning about saying (verbal) Processes, the children in the 1995 Year 1 case-study class became much more attuned to how they used their reading voices, according to the observations of their teacher (Williams, 2005). While the children had not been taught about these Process types with oral reading in mind, they nevertheless were using what they had learned to attend carefully to verbal

Processes in order to read aloud with the appropriate volume and pitch: shouting, asking, whispering, crying and so on. Evidence for this includes video footage of the children playing a "Saying Processes Game", in which they selected randomly from cards showing a "Sayer" and "Saying Process", and then made up what that Sayer would have said, which they then performed with suitable expression. There is also evidence in the video material of the children's enjoyment in playing with the notion of appropriate expression, such as inventing amusingly silly counter-examples: "Miss Patricia whispered, 'Help! Fire!'"

Improved Punctuation of Direct Speech

Improved confidence in the punctuation of direct speech by young children was also observed in several classes which studied verbal Processes. In the Year 1 class just mentioned, the teacher was impressed with the facility of the children in punctuating direct speech, especially given the newness of this knowledge to them, being in only their second year of school. Evidence of this confidence in knowing where the "talking marks" go can be seen in the video footage where children make up their own sentence, writing it with marker pen on a strip of cardboard (for display later – the importance of shared knowledge and supportive classroom displays was again found in this research class) and then discuss to camera how they have punctuated it:

ANGELICA: [Reading] "Surprise Santa. I've got a surprise for you," Angelica said and shouted.
    And and I forgot the full stop at the end. [Reaches for a marker and corrects the punctuation, glancing with a smile to the research assistant.]
TEACHER: Mmm hmm.
ANGELICA: And, um, I'm going to put the ... the saying process ... in. [Picks up a highlighter.]
TEACHER: So which is that?
ANGELICA: "Said and shouted". [Circles the two processes accurately.]
ANGELICA: And –
TEACHER: And what?
ANGELICA: And I've got talking marks. Two here and two there. [Gestures accurately.]
TEACHER: And what are the talking marks around?
ANGELICA: Sorry?
TEACHER: What is, what's in between the talking marks? Can you read it to me?
ANGELICA: What I said. "Surprise Santa. I've got a surprise for you." That's what I said.
ANGELICA: And I need black to underline. [Underlines the projected speech accurately, then reaches for another highlighter.] I'm the Sayer so I have to get the orange and then I'm gonna draw a rectangle 'cause I'm the Sayer. [Draws the rectangle to accurately identify the Sayer.] ... [Looks towards the camera, smiling.] That's all I have to do.
TEACHER: OK, thank you.

My own research with a Year 2 class also found that after learning about verbal Processes and Sayers, children were much more accurate in their punctuation of direct speech. In a test of their knowledge in which they were simply asked to punctuate a passage, with no explicit mention of speech-marks in the instructions, the direct speech was punctuated much better in the post-test than the pre-test, with the mean result almost doubling.

There is evidence from a range of data sources that learning about the grammar associated with verbal Processes can improve children's expressive reading and punctuation of direct speech.

Children's Attitudes to Learning Grammar

A fair criticism of grammar teaching has been that students find the work dull and do not enjoy it (see, for example, Elley et al., 1976). What then were the findings in these SFG case studies about children's attitudes to learning grammatics?

There was ample evidence of children's enjoyment in learning functional grammar, such as the laughter and delight of Year 1 children playing the Saying Processes Game, captured on video. In my own research with Year 2 students, the children were consistently engaged and happy in the grammar lessons. Children were regularly asked to say how they felt about the work, such as by coloring in a symbol of a happy, sad or indifferent face on the bottom of a worksheet, or writing or drawing how they felt in their learning journals. Mostly the children indicated that they felt happy about their grammar work – as indeed they felt about most aspects of the school curriculum. Their learning journals included comments like:

> I feel [sic] happy because it is interesting. (Kate)
> ☺ Because learning about theme is fun. (Oliver)

When a student indicated any feeling other than "happy" it was usually because the new work had been a bit too challenging:

> *How did you feel about this work?*☹
> *Why?* One was a bit tri[c]ky. (Elizabeth)

This was important information for the teacher to know in deciding how to pace the grammar work.

Another important indication of the children's enjoyment was in their continued pleasure in the books that had been objects of grammatical study, such as *Piggybook* (Browne, 1986) and *Pumpkin Soup* (Cooper, 1999), which the children were happy to reread even after spending lots of time "studying" these texts.

Play is also evident in the children's grammar work across these case studies. A couple of examples have already appeared in the evidence surveyed above, such as the Year 1 child's amusing suggestion in the Saying Processes Game. The drawing in Figure 12.6 was one 7-year-old child's response when asked to "draw an action process":

belching

wah

Figure 12.1 A 7-Year-Old's Representation of an Action Process.

Figure 12.6 is indicative of the subversive sense of humor which is typical of young children and which was permitted to have a place in the grammar lessons I have summarized here. It is a far cry from the humorless grammar exercises which many people associate with learning grammar.

Conclusion

Primary school children can learn and use grammatics and even enjoy doing so, given the opportunity to do so in meaningful and pedagogically thoughtful ways. In considering how such outcomes may be achieved, this chapter has canvassed some exploratory case-study research in which positive classroom results were achieved in the learning of grammatics across several dimensions of the English curriculum. The studies were informed by theoretical insights from Vygotksy (particularly the valuing of collaborative activity in leading learning, and the importance of selecting "tools" or forms of semiotic mediation which encourage thought to develop along productive paths) and from systemic functional linguistics (particularly the choice of systemic functional grammar as a meaning-oriented and whole-text-friendly grammar for thinking about language patterns).

This research should encourage us to rethink both what we think children are capable of, and also what kind of role grammatics can have in the curriculum. The progress and insights of the children in these case studies indicate that abstract understandings can be opened up and explored with young learners. Indeed, it may be the case that a primary school curriculum which emphasizes the "concrete", since it is "developmentally appropriate", in fact engenders the kind of thinking it claims to merely echo. If children are given appropriate intellectual tools and support, more abstract thinking is made possible.

Metalinguistic knowledge, of which grammatics is a subset, allows us to reflect on our own and others' choices in language at arm's length. It permits a perspective released from "concrete" activity on individual texts, from isolated errors needing correction, from item knowledge about parts of speech which goes no further than the end of the exercise. Metalinguistic knowledge is to language as standing on a patch of ground is to seeing the world for the first time from the air. Or an even better analogy: to being able to visualize the world as a globe – an abstraction which we do not hesitate to put in any and every primary school classroom, despite the fact that fewer than 500 humans have ever actually seen it in concrete form from space.

Acknowledgments

The author wishes to thank Professor Len Unsworth for his careful reading of and helpful comments on an earlier draft of the chapter. Grateful acknowledgment is also due to Professor Geoff Williams for his assistance in making available for inclusion in this chapter transcriptions of classroom talk from his data bank for the "Children's Development of Knowledge about Language" project.

References

Andrews, R., Torgerson, C., Beverton, S., Locke, T., Low, G., Robinson, A., & Zhu, D. (2004). *The effect of grammar teaching (syntax) in English on 5 to 16 year olds' accuracy and quality in written composition.* London: EPPI-Centre, Social Science Research Unit, Institute of Education.

Baillargeon, R., & DeVos, J. (1991). Object permanence in young infants: Further evidence. *Child Development, 62*(6), 1227–1246.

Berk, L. (2003). *Child development* (6th ed.). Boston: Allyn & Bacon.

Blaut, J. (1991). Natural mapping. *Transactions of the Institute of British Geographers, New Series, 16*(1), 55–74.

Blaut, J. (1997). The mapping abilities of young children: Children can. *Annals of the Association of American Geographers, 87*(1), 152–158.

Browne, A. (1986). *Piggybook.* London: Julia MacRae Books.

Bruner, J. (1986). *Actual minds, possible worlds.* Cambridge, MA: Harvard University Press.

Carter, R. (Ed.). (1990) *Knowledge about language and the curriculum: The LINCReader.* London: Hodder.

Cole, M., & Wertsch, J. V. (1996). Beyond the individual: Social antimony in discussions of Piaget and Vygotsky. *Human Development, 39*(5), 250–256.

Collerson, J. (1997). *Grammar in teaching.* Newtown, NSW: Primary English Teaching Association.

Cooper, H. (1999). *Pumpkin soup.* London: Picture Corgi.

Elley, W., Barham, I., Lamb, H., & Wyllie, M. (1976). The role of grammar in a secondary school English curriculum. *Research in the Teaching of English, 10*(1), 5–21.

French, R. (2009). *Pumpkin Soup* and grammatics: A critical literacy case study with Year 2. In T. Hays & R. Hussain (Eds.), *Bridging the gap between ideas and doing research* (Proceedings of the 3rd annual postgraduate research conference, The Faculty of the Professions, University of New England, Armidale NSW) (pp. 69–84). Armidale, NSW: University of New England.

Halliday, M. (1985). *An introduction to functional grammar* (1st ed.). London: Edward Arnold.

Halliday, M. (1994). *An introduction to functional grammar* (2nd ed.). London: Edward Arnold.

Halliday, M. (2002). On grammar and grammatics. In J. Webster (Ed.), *On grammar: Volume 1. Collected works of M.A.K. Halliday* (pp. 384–417). London and New York: Continuum.

Halliday, M., & Matthiessen, C. (2004). *An introduction to functional grammar* (3rd ed.). London: Arnold.

Inhelder, B., & Piaget, J. (1958). *The growth of logical thinking from childhood to adolescence: An essay on the construction of formal operational structures.* New York: Basic Books.

Luria, A. (1992). The child and his behavior (E. Rossiter, Trans.). In A. Luria & L. Vygotsky (Eds.), *Ape, primitive man, and child: Essays in the history of behavior* (pp. 87–164). Hemel Hempstead: Harvester Wheatsheaf.

Martin, J. (2000). Close reading: functional linguistics as a tool for critical discourse analysis. In L. Unsworth (Ed.), *Researching language in schools and communities: Functional linguistic perspectives* (pp. 275–302). London: Cassell.

McInerney, D., & McInerney, V. (2006). *Educational psychology: Constructing learning* (4th ed.). Sydney: Prentice Hall.

Vygotsky, L. (1962). *Thought and language.* Cambridge, MA: MIT Press.

Vygotsky, L. (1978). *Mind in society: The development of higher psychological processes.* Cambridge, MA: Harvard University Press.

Williams, G. (1995). *Learning systemic functional grammar in primary schools.* Paper presented at the Australian English in a pluralist Australia. Proceedings of Style Council 95.

Williams, G. (1998). Children entering literate worlds: Perspectives from the study of textual practices. In F. Christie & R. Misson (Eds.), *Literacy and schooling* (pp. 18–46). London: Routledge.

Williams, G. (2000). Children's literature, children and uses of language description. In L. Unsworth (Ed.), *Researching language in schools and communities: Functional linguistic perspectives* (pp. 111–129). London: Cassell.

Williams, G. (2005). Grammatics in schools. In R. Hasan, C. Matthiessen, & J. Webster (Eds.), *Continuing discourse on language: A functional perspective* (Vol. 1, pp. 281–310). London: Equinox.

Williams, G. (2006 [2004]). Ontogenesis and grammatics: Functions of metalanguage in pedagogical discourse. In G. Williams & A. Lukin (Eds.), *The development of language: Functional perspectives on species and individuals* (pp. 241–267). London and New York: Continuum.

Williams, G., & French, R. (1995). *The Haberfield Grammar Club.* Paper presented at the Australian Systemic Functional Linguistics Association Conference, University of Melbourne, Melbourne, Australia.

Wood, D., Bruner, J., & Ross, G. (1976). The role of tutoring in problem solving. *Journal of Child Psychology and Psychiatry and Allied Disciplines, 17,* 89–100.

Woolfolk, A. (2004). *Educational psychology* (9th ed.). Boston: Pearson/Allyn & Bacon.

Part IV

Beyond Print

A Metalanguage for Multimodal Texts

Chapter 13

A Grammar for Meaning-Making

Gunther Kress

Frames and Issues: The "English and Literacy" Classroom

Two questions touch on the notion of "a grammar" in an English and literacy classroom in a fundamental way. One is: What is it that someone – whether teacher or student learner – in an English and literacy classroom needs to know? The other is: What are the social characteristics of those who are in the classroom, and above all, who are the students/learners? The first question is concerned with what the "content" of that grammar might be. The second, more profound in its implications, asks whether traditional notions of grammar can continue to be used when the social environment is such that conventions around representation no longer "hold"; when student learners assume to themselves notions of agency which undercut the power relations and forms of authority on which notions of grammar have traditionally been based.

As far as the first question is concerned, teachers, I assume, have to have a clear sense of what student learners will need as a resource, as practical means for shaping their social, cultural lives, when they leave this classroom, move on into the next classroom maybe or act in their life outside school; and certainly, when they move into their life beyond the school. I take it that the students will need to have a thoroughly firm "hold" on those resources, coupled with the means for navigating a complex social and semiotic world. I conflate these perspectives into one, namely "What does a person need in their adult social life in order to take a full part in that life, with a clear awareness of the effects of their actions?" Neither English nor "Literacy" alone can supply that, though jointly they should provide the *semiotic* resources for taking a full part in the world of meanings of their social groups, finding their way around the meanings of their society and, most importantly, making *their* meanings in their world.

As far as the second question goes, what is at issue is the very notion of "grammar" itself: traditionally seen as an authoritative compendium of entities and practices, a compelling source of rules to be followed, supported by social power – as in evaluations by others with variously serious consequences. Now, in an era of differently distributed power, of agency readily assumed by younger generations – even if that agency is not necessarily acknowledged by others – in the furtherance of *their* interests, in the era of "user-generated content" and access to the means of potentially global dissemination of that content, the questions are: "What actually is 'a grammar'?" and "On whose authority could it be founded?" and "What *are* the principles for meaning-making?"

In other words, I am concerned here with that which is to be present(ed) and engaged with, "the content and shape" of the resources for making meaning and above all with the shape of the social environment in which – differently in different places and yet similar in essential respects – the English and literacy classroom is located. I assume that for that to be seriously explored, a prerequisite is a plausible conception of communication/meaning-making/learning and, with that, a conception of students/meaning-makers/learners as agentive in their interests.

Activity: Exploration and Enquiry

Explore with others or individually your current understanding of the term "grammar": what kinds of features and aspects are included in that understanding? This understanding can be either in terms of what someone *knows* or through exploring what kinds of *knowledge* can be assumed to underlie a particular text or composition. As a follow-up activity, find a web-based text, and investigate whether or not, how and in what modes all or any of the features and aspects you identified as being part of grammar are evident in this text.

A Communicational Framing

What theoretical frame is needed for that ambitious undertaking? For me, the social has to be prior for any such theory to be plausible: it is the generative source of meaning. Clearly, the contemporary world is one in which meanings are made in many modes, each with specific affordances; and with digital media, many of which provide access and means for dissemination to most people. All texts, banal as much as culturally salient, draw on a multiplicity of modes, well beyond the use of *speech* and *writing*, as do texts, semiotic phenomena and objects which are accorded high "esthetic" value socially and culturally. The (formerly central) media of print are still in use, much as the now-dominant digital media of screens: though "generation" – as the social construction of age – and social domains, such as profession, play a crucial part in differences of practices, dispositions and habits of use. "English" everywhere – whatever the subject may have been and is now in different parts of the Anglophone world – has its place in socially and culturally highly diverse environments. "Literacy" shares with all modes the task of realizing the meanings of any message.

In that context, the English and literacy classroom is a complex social, cultural, semiotic site, more so – and different – than at any time before. Anglophone societies, responding to specific local needs, demands and histories, responding also to distinct ideological and political demands and economic requirements, expect that the "English and literacy" classroom should look in many directions simultaneously and fulfill a diverse range of needs (Kress, 1994). My suggestions in this chapter do not address such specific tasks, though I hope that they may be amenable to "translation" into the specific locations and into the terms of the local conditions encountered by readers.

Meaning-making rests on communication, so that sketching an apt theory of communication is the necessary first step in developing a theoretical frame. To get away from deeply entrenched notions around communication (including those deriving from research in classrooms), I use as my example an equally complex yet entirely different site of meaning-making (and learning), that of the operating theater. I take it to be a representative and in its forms typical instance of an environment of communication; other examples of such sites abound. Taking it as the instance, what model of communication would we come up with?

Figure 13.1 shows an operating theater; an operation is in its early stage. A scrub nurse is in the foreground. Behind her, to the right, is the "lead" surgeon; opposite him is a qualified medical doctor training to become a surgeon. Behind them, separated by a screen, is the anesthetist; far back on the right stands an operating theater technician. Representatives of four distinct professions, each with specific traditions and ways of talking and of doing are present. Their tasks are closely interrelated and integrated. Unlike the English and literacy classroom, this is first and foremost a *clinical* environment – an instance of (communication in) professional practice: a patient is here to be made better. It is, however, also a *pedagogic* site, an environment of (teaching and) learning: a trainee surgeon is

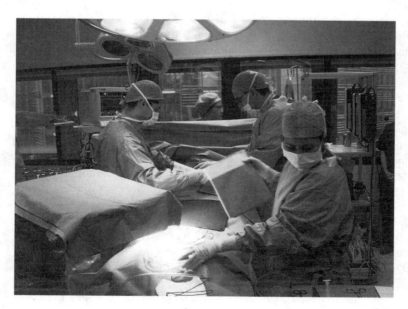

Figure 13.1 The Operating Theater (Photograph by Roger Kneebone. Used with permission).

here to become fully trained. It may be important to ask whether and in what ways the condition of a site, as a multiple social environment, is always the case, even with classrooms.

Frequently, the "same" actions become different signs in the respective "other" frame – either that of trainee or assistant. The multiple structure of an environment of communication, demanding multiple attention from all participants, is likely to be the norm rather than the exception in most situations of communication. Features of gender, class, generation, "culture", professional difference and regionality are all present here, and in different ways likely to be present in all sites. It means that communication across differences of many kinds is entirely usual and essential.

In the example, communication is multimodal: by *speech* at times, a spoken comment as instruction or request; by *gaze*; by *actions* – passing an instrument, reaching out for an instrument; by *touch*. At all times communication is a response to a "prompt": a *gaze* might produce a *spoken* comment; that leads to an *action*; *looking* at the screen by both surgeons produces a guiding *touch* by one or the other's hand; an outstretched hand is met by an instrument being passed. Communication has happened when a participant's attention has focused on some aspect of the communication; when she or he has taken that to be a message and has framed aspects of that as a *prompt* for her or himself. The *prompt* is *interpreted* by one of the participants, becoming for them a new inward *sign*; it, in turn, leads potentially to further communicational action. The semiotic sequence of attention → framing → interpretation is ceaseless; it involves all the participants, at all times, though differently in each case.

If we frame this environment *communicationally*, meaning-making is in the center; if we frame it *pedagogically*, teaching and learning become the focus. Questions differ depending on the framing: "What meanings are made?" "By whom?"; or, with a shift in viewpoint, "How does teaching happen?" and, in the same frame though with another perspective, "How does learning take place?", "What is being learned?" From the learner's perspective, any event may at any one moment need to be attended to: in my example the senior surgeon might give a spoken instruction; the scrub nurse might make a slight movement – or an explicit gesture – which the assistant/learner ought to attend to; the anesthetist might glance at him to draw his attention to something.

At any one time, any aspect of the complex dynamic communicational ensemble might be significant for the learner, so that he has to be constantly attentive to cues as potential *prompts*. It is his interest as *trainee* surgeon that turns any one of these – or none – into a *prompt* for him. It is his decision. Once turned into a *prompt*, his interest frames it and he selects features from that now specifically framed *prompt* as the basis for his response.

It is neither difficult nor implausible to substitute "student" for "trainee-surgeon" here. Even now, it is not usual to treat students as responsible for selecting from the teacher's message overall that which they might treat as a *prompt* and to interpret it as such; it is highly unusual to attribute significant agency to students – as becomes quickly apparent in forms of assessment.

Activity: Exploration and Enquiry

Select a page from a website such as YouTube or Facebook, and ask several people – maybe of different generations or professions – to make a note of what they take to be the meaning of the page; that is, what *prompt* they have constructed for themselves from that page/text. As a follow-up exercise, try to determine what principles of selection from this page seem to have been at work in each case; what kinds of transformations or transductions – changes in mode – occurred in order to produce that *prompt*. You may wish to ask your participants in what way they would respond to the original page. Focus on categories such as *mode, genre, transformation, transduction*, as well as the "categories" produced in response to the initial exercise.

Versions of a very different model of communication were active in 20th-century conceptions of communication; and to some extent they still hover around and haunt mainstream conceptions of communication and teaching alike, even though constantly modified. The dominant conception of communication in the latter part of the last century was based on Shannon and Weaver's (1947; see Shannon & Weaver, 1998) schema of *Sender* → *Message* → *Receiver* (with very many modifications and variations – feedback loops, and so on), based on electrical engineering. Here the sender (who "encodes" a message in a *code* shared by sender and receiver) is the active cause of communication. This version received its most telling critique in Roland Barthes' 1968 article "The Death of the Author" (Barthes, 1977); that insisted on the dominant role of the reader in communication. The Shannon and Weaver model implicitly rested on the stability and (potentially perfect) recoverability of the message; it was the receiver's responsibility to ensure – leaving aside "malfunctions" in the process – that the (meaning of the) message decoded was the same as the (meaning of the) message encoded. The power of the sender was not in question. In Barthes' conception, the authority for the meaning lay with the reader; the authority of the author was diminished.

Again it is not difficult to recognize affinities of this model with conceptions of teaching (and "learning"), and parallels in the notions of code and grammar. Very different models of social organization and relations of power are entailed in each of these. Ruling conceptions of communication (and learning) – which still dominate institutional sites of learning as much as they dominate popular common sense of both communication and learning – are aligned implicitly, still, with the Shannon and Weaver model; which is not to say that other models have not been advocated and used in theories of communication as in those of learning.

In the "operating theater model" of communication, three concerns are in focus. One is social interaction and interchange around meaning, oriented to the processes of constant *making* and *re-making* of meaning through the *making of signs* – simple or complex – in *representation*. *Sign-makers* and their agency as social actors are in the foreground and with them the social environments in which they make signs. Signs are made twice: once by the *initiator* of the message as the *ground* for the participants' engagement; and once by the *interpreter* who turns part of that ground into a *prompt*. The second concern is with *resources* for making meaning – a focus on *modes* and their *affordances*. The third deals with *conditions* and *means for disseminating* meaning – the *media* and their facilities. A theory of communication needs to deal with the semiotic work done in all three; and with all the meanings which result. Questions such as "Who does what kind of semiotic work and for whom?" are entailed by this model.

In principle it is neither difficult nor implausible to think of classrooms in this frame. Where the difficulty arises lies in two issues: communication depends on *interpretation*, so that the power of the *interpreter* (the student/meaning-maker/learner) is at the core; and, in this model, communication can only be understood if it is seen as an always complex interaction embedded in social environments which are contradictory, contested, fragmentary: whether between groups or between individuals, coming together from social "locations" which are always distinct in some respects. The point is: are we prepared to see classrooms in this way? That is, as an environment no longer dominated by power hierarchically organized (and exercised?); with knowledge no longer seen as flowing from that authority; as coherent; knowledge as held, disseminated and "acquired" unproblematically by student learners; in a social environment regarded as integrated, homogeneous, coherent?

In this model, the social divergences/differences between those who interact provide the generative dynamic of communication. Such differences in the classroom may be of *generation* always intertwined with other social factors: gender as well as cultural differences of many kinds. In the process of interaction, social and semiotic differences are reshaped/transformed in temporary social and semiotic accommodations. As a model of a learning environment, it accords a different position to learners and teachers to any traditional model. Here, meanings are *made* (rather than *acquired*) in transformations (and transductions – the shift from one mode to another) as the *making of signs*. The *making* of signs (rather than their *use*) is the *making* of meaning (rather than its *communication*). The *making of signs* and the making of *meaning* is *learning* – not now seen as the inert *acquisition* of *concepts*. These constant transformations and transductions constitute semiotic work and are the semiotically and socially productive force of communication. What is socially problematic in the space and site at issue – the classroom in this case – is projected into a public "space", producing temporary recordings of the social and the semiotic state of affairs as "knowledge". In transforming what is at issue in communication, it is shaped differently: meaning is made.

The defining criterion of communication is *interpretation*: only if there has been interpretation has there been communication. Interpretation is central and so, therefore, is the *interpreter*. An interpretation is always a mix of aspects of the ground framed as prompt by the interpreter, with resources brought by the interpreter, shaped, jointly, into a new semiotic entity. An interpretation is the result of a series of transformations and transductions, in which aspects of the prompt and aspects of the resources brought by the interpreter come together in a newly made, newly transformed entity. Interpretation is the defining criterion of communication: *only if there has been interpretation, has there been communication.*

Such a model does not conform to the conception of (a) grammar traditionally held.

Resources for Making Meaning

No environment of communication, of meaning-making and of learning is like any other, and so it is with the comparison of the operating theater and a classroom, ignoring significant cultural/social/national differences between classrooms. Students bring resources from outside the school into the process at issue in a classroom, while nurses and surgeons do not; the identities of students shaped outside the classroom have large effects in the classrooms, in ways that are not the case for nurses and surgeons. Students bring what are taken-for-granted notions into the classroom and these have to be accommodated there. The conditions and relations of power in both sites are different and may remain so more or less despite social changes, or become more pronounced. At the same time, if we wish to understand the principles of meaning-making, the one theory will need to serve both, even if with slight adaptations at the level of the specific environment. The question of what resources are present and may be drawn on and the relations of power which shape interactions in each site are equally relevant in each site. Rules and regularities differ, as does the degree to which they may be shaped on each occasion, but regularities there are in each case.

The texts and other semiotic phenomena which occur in that abstraction – "the 'English and Literacy' classroom" – and which certainly occur in the world beyond that classroom – are multimodal. On a screen they might consist – in the genre of video-game for instance – of *speech*; of *images*, still and/or moving; of *soundtrack* and *music*; of *gestures, actions, writing*. In the classroom they consist of *speech*; of *images* – still or moving; of *writing*; of *gesture*; of *actions* and *movement* other than gestures; of *sounds* as in soundtracks; of *3D objects*, and so on. Together these form ensembles which, in order to be seen as a text, have to exhibit a degree of coherence and which, in any case, is given coherence by the viewer/reader who engages with it (Kress, 2003; Kress & van Leeuwen, 2001).

Here arises the first issue in a grammar of meaning-making, in a grammar of multimodal texts: what categories, entities, processes and relations, what *terms* exist to name these in a "multimodal ensemble"? The terms we have and the terms, therefore, that we tend to use, were produced for grammars of "language", whether of speech or of writing. These terms do not fit the characteristics and requirements of other modes for categories, entities, processes. Put simply, images do not have *words*, do not have *verbs* or *sentences*, they have no *paragraphs*. There is no *tense* in images, though there are indications in some way relating to notions of temporality or some related notion. The same is true of music, of soundtrack, of gesture, and so on.

Here is an example. Consider *cohesion*, the formal means of producing connection and integration and *coherence*, that quality which gives the beholder/viewer/reader the sense of a semiotic entity which has a unity of meaning, as a projection of a "world" in which things belong together and belong "where they are". In order to establish *cohesion* and *coherence* between two entities, we need to be able to link "like" with "like", to show that *this* belongs with *that*, that *this entity here* is a reformulation of *that other entity there*. But if images do not have words, or phrases, or sentences, how do we establish cohesive links between an image and a "chunk" of writing? How can coherence be achieved?

However, while images do not "have" *words*, they do have "depictions"; or, as a different example, while they do not have indicators of *tense*, they do have features which refer to semiotically related notions such as ontological proximity or distance, for instance – of "realism"; of factuality or not; of "pastness" – as "that which is no longer so". Or, to take yet another example, "emphasis": *bolding* may indicate emphasis in print while *loudness* can indicate emphasis in *speech*; *intensity* of color-saturation or the use of colors at the high end of the energy spectrum may indicate emphasis in image. In other words, *high energy* is a material feature which can be used as a general semiotic feature of intensity with specific realizations in different modes: depending both on the materiality of the mode (sound, light) and the social uses of that material over time.

The theory to be used, in other words, has to be able to deal with all modes equally well; it needs to be able to work at a level which is abstract enough to provide categories and features of a general kind, which can then be instantiated in ways specific to the materiality of modes. For me that theory is "social semiotics": *semiotics* as that academic enterprise which is concerned with meaning in all forms; *social* in order to emphasize that meaning arises in "the social" and is socially made in social environments by agents with social histories, with the socially made resources of specific cultures. Social semiotics names the practices, agents and categories of meaning-making, while *multimodality* names the domain of meaning – the socially shaped resources of modes which provide the material, so to speak, for making meanings.

Activity: Exploring Features of Cohesion

Take a website which you feel is constructed for a specific group – generationally, in terms of profession or interest. Identify aspects you regard as providing *cohesion* (the *material* forms – words, syntax, color, font, etc.) and describe in words that seem fitting to you whether the characteristics of coherence (the sense that there is a *unity* of meaning, of things belonging neatly where they are) are strong or weak, tight or fragmented. As a follow up, investigate the relation between the social characteristics of the target group and the material features of the text by redesigning forms of cohesion which you regard as best for a quite different group – in terms of age/generation, interest or profession, gender.

Activity: Exploring the Theoretical Significance of Your Work So Far

Make a list of the words or phrases that you have used in your working through the three exercises so far. Consider how well each of these terms seems to do what you wanted it to do and to name; ask what better terms there might be; try to see whether the terms you have used are usable to describe *all* of the features and aspects of the sites, pages and texts that you have been considering.

Whether one uses the term "grammar" here or not is, for me, not the most significant issue; it is a point to be debated. In as much as the etymology of the word "grammar" points to "inscription", the making of a mark, it may be worth preserving the term. Insofar as the term has had a long association with notions of authority, of social power supporting and maintaining "rules" as enforced regularity of practice, it poses a problem for a theory that attempts to stress the *agency* of the meaning-makers, which stresses sign-*making* over sign *use*, for instance.

In the environment of multimodal communication, *writing* is one among a number of modes; one means of making meaning among many. Linguistics has no theoretical resources for dealing with modes such as *color, layout, image*; yet in a multimodal landscape, writing needs to be described within the one theoretical frame together with all other modes. If we are interested in the materiality – the "stuff" – of writing with its cultural regularities and potentials and are interested also in understanding multimodal textual ensembles, the theoretical consequence is the move I am proposing, from a linguistic theory to a social semiotic one. That moves attention from the *linguistic* interest in *form, formal relations* and *processes* to the *social-semiotic* interest in *meaning* and meaning-*making*. It is necessary then to point out that the linguistic phenomenon of "writing" is not identical with the social-semiotic phenomenon of the *mode* of *writing*. Semiotically, mode focuses on all potentials of a mode for making meaning in making signs, the mode of writing being no exception. That permits the continuing use of categories produced in linguistic theories (though now seen semiotically) – such as *sentence, word, subject, tense, genres* – embedded now in a focus on all other potentials for making meaning, such as *font* and *size, spacing* and *bolding, length* and features such as the means of *framing, sites of display*.

Treating writing as mode focuses attention on *affordances*: a *semiotic*, not a *linguistic* issue. It brings attention to matters such as the means of production, handwriting for instance, compared to other means; on esthetics; on the affordances of (different) script systems and on their explicit and implicit meaning effects. The category of affordances directs attention to *meaning*, to *esthetics* and to *affect*, to *ontological* and *epistemological* effects of representation; in other words, to the full spectrum of meanings.

The contemporary semiotic landscape is characterized both by multimodal representation and by the ubiquitous presence of the "screens" of digital media. The twofold and linked revolution from the medium of the book and (its centuries-long association with) the mode of writing to the now pre-eminent medium of the screen and the mode of image; from the technology of writing to the mode of image (as well as others), has had and continues to have far-reaching effects on writing (see Kress, 2003). As in all matters where meaning is the issue, the two shifts need to be understood in the environment of the deep changes in the social and economic domain, where the (19th-century nation-) state has given way in many places in the West to the (neo-liberal) market as the dominant force in shaping social practices and values. This third, larger, revolution has weakened, frayed, broken and often simply swept away the formerly firm social forms and practices, the framings of power solidified into "conventions", which had provided the frames for meaning, the naturalized semiotic frames.

At this point it is necessary to say that a grammar for meaning-making will have some – but only some – similarities with the kinds – and notions – of grammar we have been used to: notions of regularity within flux, rather than of rules authoritatively given and enforced; notions of the agency of the sign-*maker* rather than the idea of the sign-*user*; of *use* shaping the resources of the grammar rather than the categories of the grammar strictly constraining kinds of uses; of categories with application in specific domains rather than categories seen as autonomous from the social. At the same time, this is not a revolution which has swept all that formerly existed before it. In many social domains, in many professions, among older generations, older conceptions and uses of grammar remain; among many younger generations and in many social domains, there remains an understanding of these older conceptions and the practices, together with the contemporary. These lead a side-by-side existence, even if with clear social differentiation and evaluation. In the English and literacy classroom that fact needs to be constantly stressed, and uses and practices reflected on and tested.

A "grammar" for meaning-making of the kind envisaged – in a multimodally configured domain; with the media now culturally dominant; and above all with the social givens characterizing most so-called "Western", "post-industrial" or "developed" societies – needs to be a *grammar of communication* in the fullest sense, rather than a grammar of writing or even a grammar of "language" alone.

Provisionality: Rhetoric and Principles of Design

In Anglophone and Western European societies, *stability* – even though that had only ever been relative – has given way to *instability*; *homogeneity* has given way to often radical *diversity*; *permanence* has given way to *provisionality*, a condition in which crucial characteristics of the environments of communication can vary from one moment to the next. Attempts to answer the questions "why?" and "why now?" have to look at the many factors, distinct yet everywhere connected, which still are sweeping the world. The short-hand term "globalization" gathers up some of these: conditions which make it usual for the characteristics of one place to be present and active in any other, economically, culturally, technologically. In the contestation of (features of) local practices, forms and traditions with those from outside, both are transformed, in ways dependent on dispositions of power in the local site. At the same time, and as an effect of neo-liberal markets, *choice* has come to be a dominant determinant in the shaping of identity. In place of the nation state and its conception of citizenship and of a nationally conceived economy with its specific positions in a labor force, identity is now shaped through the action of choice in consumption in the market. The results in any one environment are social, cultural and semiotic instability and provisionality.

While a notion of a "grammar", as rule-governed semiotic practice, could be maintained in that former social environment of relative stability, the loss of that stability has led to the corrosion, fraying, dissolution, destruction, abandonment, of older social relations, forms, structures, "givens". That has generated far-reaching social changes in all domains of meaning: in "semiotic *production*" – in the shift from the technologies of print – with expertise restricted to few – to digital means – with expertise available to (nearly) all with competences and access to contemporary technologies; in the *dissemination* of messages – markedly in the shift from the print media – with authority and control over dissemination and productive participation lodged with few – to the (digitally shaped) media of the screen – with productive participation in production and dissemination accessible to vast numbers, as much as in the move from the ("traditional") mass-media to the new sites of "multiplicities of dissemination"; and in *representation* – in the shift from the dominance of the mode of *writing* to an insistent use of many modes, with a consequent "displacement" of *writing* to the margin in some instances of representation and communication.

Above all, agency as authorship has become widely dispersed as a taken-for-granted cultural "good" for a vast number of people, rather than the rare socially ascribed position it had been. Grooved and *dependable* conventions no longer exist, not in social interactions nor in communication and not in learning.

These conditions demand a *rhetorical* approach to communication, to meaning-making and to learning. That is, in each instance of interaction it is essential to assess the social environment and the social relations which obtain; to adjust forms of communication accordingly, along with dispositions, attention to and engagement in meaning-making and with learning. The competence of clear and detailed analysis of social environments of communication is now becoming a required commonplace.

Rhetorical analysis provides a description of the social environment in which communication takes place; communicators as *designers* employ sets of *principles* to produce the "shapes" of possible arrangements for implementation in *production* with the use of socially shaped and culturally available resources (Kress, 1994, 2003; Kress & van Leeuwen, 2001). *Design* accords recognition to the shaping *semiotic work* of individuals in their social lives and builds that recognition into theories of communication and of learning. *Design* embodies a theory of communication as meaning-*making*, based on an assumption for equitable participation in the shaping of the social and semiotic world. By contrast with *competence* – shaped by past requirements and practices and oriented to present expectations – *design* focuses on the *realization* of an individual's present *interest* oriented to *future* effects in their world.

Design is prospective, forward-looking, in a multimodally conceived world of meaning characterized by provisionality and marked by diverse, contesting social forces. With the availability of many *modes* and differing *compositional* possibilities, with different *genres* and *discourses* available to *sign-makers/designers* for the realization of rhetorical purposes, the focal issue is to use resources *aptly* in designs for the implementation of rhetorical purposes. The availability of multiple resources offers the possibility for precision in representation: the needs of specific audiences can be met as can the requirements of "what is to be communicated"; both rely on a clear sense of which resources will best serve which purposes. At this point the question of principles of design become crucial: What audience is to be addressed? What are its needs, communicationally and affectively? What is to be communicated and what resources are best to realize what is to be communicated for this specific audience? And of course: What resources are available? Equally importantly, What media are available to be used and what media are best to be used here? These questions demand specific answers, about modes to be used, about specific features of the modes – what font types for writing, what color-schemes and levels of color-saturation for images – or about potentials of media.

Without a prior rhetorical analysis of the social environment, it is not clear what form representation should take: what *modes* are *apt*, for *this* audience, for *this* purpose; what *genre* aptly captures and projects the social relations at issue – or how, as rhetor/designer I might wish to display these social relations.

In a (neo-liberal) market-dominated society, *choice* is the ruling category: identity is constructed through choices made. The sum total of choices made by me defines me as my *style*. Of course, *choice* remains subject to power; hence, in my conception, *style* is *the politics of choice*. *Style* is subject to evaluation, a further domain where power is active, and so *esthetics* becomes *the politics of style*.

Activity: Engaging in Rhetorical Design

You are about to make a specific text/site. Establish what you regard as the crucial social characteristics of the audience for whom you are about to make this text. Identify the material and design features – modes, fonts, colors and color palette, genres, size, compositional forms, etc. – you think will best allow you to achieve what you want to communicate with your semiotic product.

"Arrangements": Contemporary and Traditional Principles of Composition

The making of text for an "other" – as individual or group – has to be attentive to *esthetics* and *style* in the sense just described. Given the condition of provisionality, rhetorical assessment and aptness of design are crucial. Relevant questions become: "What color-scheme will capture and reflect how this person sees herself or himself?" "What genre of image, what forms of font, what syntactic forms in what genre of writing, will achieve the *affect* I want to produce?" No aspect of the overall design can be left unattended; what is not designed is just as likely to be interpreted as that which has been designed – though without control by me, the rhetor/designer.

The three images (Figures 13.2–13.4) of screens from one website called "The Poetry Archive"[1] may exemplify some of the issues so far discussed. The questions of rhetoric and *design* are absolutely evident – as they are with most websites. The pages/screens for teachers differ entirely from those for students or those of the children's archive; or of the page/screen called "About us". "Profession", "interest", "generation" (as the social construction of age) play their part in rhetorical analysis, in the design developed from that, and in the resulting style and the esthetics. *Writing* is present on every one of these screens, though very differently on each.

On the page "About us" (Figure 13.2), writing is there in its "traditional" form. One strong contrast between Figure 13.2 and Figures 13.3 and 13.4 concerns what I will call a difference in *arrangement*: that is, of *linearity/sequence* strongly present in Figure 13.2 and *modularity* present in Figure 13.3 and strongly so in Figure 13.4. *Arrangement* here encompasses both what *entities* are involved as well as their manner of arrangement – in the original sense of syntax. In Figure 13.2 the entities are the traditional ones of the linguistic mode of

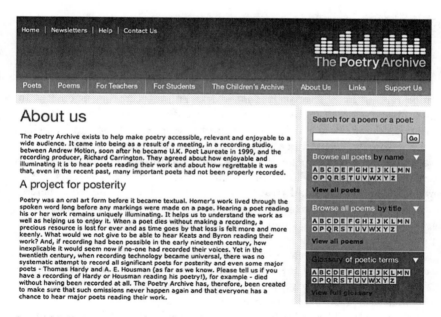

Figure 13.2 About Us (Screenshots from The Poetry Archive website at www.poetryarchive.org. Used with permission).

1. See www.poetryarchive.org/poetryarchive.

Figure 13.3 For Teachers (Screenshots from The Poetry Archive website at www.poetryarchive.org. Used with permission).

writing; and not much needs be said about them and the arrangement there, other than to say that with this screen we are still largely in the domain of traditional written representation, with some new features. By and large though, traditional forms dominate.

In Figure 13.3, the page "For Teachers", writing is also prominent; though in its appearance – both as small *modular blocks*, and as occurring together with *images*, also as *modules*, there is already a marked difference. This differs considerably from the previous example. In terms of principles of composition, *modularity* of elements is very much evident here. The entities here are mixed, as it were, between the traditional entities of writing and the contemporary modular forms. It is not clear here whether one might analyze the written elements as *paragraphs* and thereby see and treat them as traditional, or as *modules*, thereby treating them and *writing* here as already affected by new forms of arrangement. The point to me seems that one can go either way, for that is what the contemporary situation is.

Rhetorically there seems to be an assumption made here about how a teacher – rather than a member of the general public interested in poetry (as in Figure 13.2) – might approach such a page: as a busy person, who might be helped by having materials presented in bite-size form.

On the page "Children's Poetry Archive" (Figure 13.4), *writing* appears in yet another form, now largely or entirely integrated into a design dominated by irregularly shaped, rounded modules, or modules presented framed in drawn picture frames. It is a screen organized predominantly by image and by color as

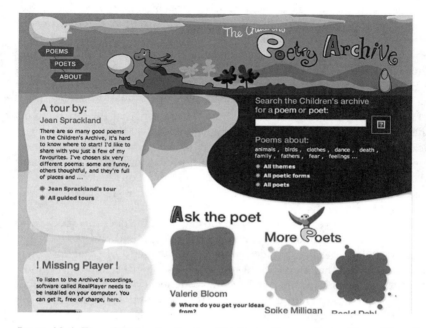

Figure 13.4 The Children's Poetry Archive (Screenshots from The Poetry Archive website at www.poetryarchive.org. Used with permission).
Note:
For copyright reasons, poets' photographs have been edited from this screenshot.

color-scheme (with animated figures on the actual site). Here, in the communicational function of this screen, *writing* is definitely not central.

This screen – for an audience of 7- to 10-year-olds – seems to be meant, in its communicational forms, in its *design*, its *style* and in its *esthetics*, to capture the attention, to meet the expectations, to be a mirror to its audience's conceptions of itself. The color-scheme here is as much and as strongly a part of the overall meaning as are the modules and their content: the desaturated (low-intensity) colors in the lower energy part of the color spectrum seem to suggest an appeal to the "sensitive", "thoughtful" child.

In Figure 13.2, the ordering/placement of the written materials presents no real difficulty. We might ask why the written part of the page appears on the left rather than on the right; but it is not a question which presents itself with any strength: the lower left of the screen seems "right" for this element. In terms of the categories of the visual grammar of Kress and van Leeuwen (2006), it is assigned to the *given/real* quadrant; which is where it ought to be according to other design principles apparent here (linearity, writing, and so on). The ordering of modules (and written parts of the overall text) on the screen of Figure 13.3 is slightly more ambivalent: is this a screen we are meant to read in a top-down direction? If so, why do we encounter the modules consisting of image and writing first, and the module/paragraphs of writing lower down? Figure 13.3 has an ordering, on the lower half of the screen, of three columns, where Figure 13.2 had two columns: their organization differs in this respect too. In other words, there are more themes/topics in the screen of Figure 13.3 than in Figure 13.2, and there is less extended written text; and the question poses itself yet again, whether a different kind of social subject is imagined and projected in this.

In Figure 13.4 the columnar arrangement is not present; on the face of it this screen is less ordered and more open to an ordering by the interest of the visitor/reader/viewer. This would correspond to the social change of the last three or four decades, which has tended to move from authoritative structures, with hierarchical relations of power into which the social subject, whether as worker or as citizen or the semiotic subject, as reader, was expected to fit – to the forms of social organization which at one level at least expect the individual, as subject or now as consumer, to be responsible for organizing the social and semiotic world according to their interests.

From this perspective, it is revealing to look again at the question of *cohesion* (the formal means of producing connection and integration) and of *coherence* (that quality which gives the beholder/viewer/reader the sense of engaging with a semiotic entity which has a unity of meaning, which is a projection of a "world" in which things belong together and belong "where they are"). If the text has traditionally been a means of providing at least a temporary coherence, in projecting a world which seems unified, it is worth asking what forms of coherence are exemplified in the three examples here; or to ask, who is assigned the task, the semiotic work of producing coherence? Figure 13.2 is, in my view, the screen which most nearly approximates coherence of the traditional kind: the devices of traditional grammar are used to achieve this, as well as the means of conventional/traditional forms of text. Lexis, syntax, textual organization (phoricity, for instance), all are used to achieve this – and so is color. This screen presents itself to us an integrated, coherent text, and projects an integrated and coherent world. In Figure 13.4, the single most significant device is color – not arrangement on the page, nor lexis, nor syntax.

Coherence – as much as forms of cohesion – have a social meaning. The reader of a coherent written text is asked to imagine her/himself as being part of a coherent social world; that is not the case for the beholder of a semiotic entity which lacks coherence. She or he faces an incoherent, semiotic entity and is faced with the task of imposing coherence on it. As social positions, Figures 13.2 and 13.4 could not be further apart.

As far as *writing* – though not only writing but all other semiotic resources and arrangements – is concerned, the site as a whole captures and represents a cross-section: from the entirely "traditional" – that is, forms that would have been regarded as unremarkable at any point over the last 60 or 70 years (minor changes apart), as in Figure 13.2; to forms which are beginning to be unremarkable now – writing in a multimodal environment, as in Figure 13.3; to forms which would not be "acceptable" to most of the overall audience (not even maybe an audience of children above the age of 10) as in Figure 13.4; and which may or may not herald the future of writing – or of *composition* more generally – in many domains of public life.

What is *design*, what does design do? Among the many different ways to think about design, I regard design as the semiotic implementation of the social accounts provided by the rhetor. In older, "traditional" approaches, with settled and stable social givens and the grammatical forms and assumptions that went with that, the tasks for *rhetoric* and *design* were profoundly different from now: present, yes, but significant only in marginal ways. When social and therefore semiotic conditions are stable, rhetoric largely has the task of reconfirming that which is expected, and design that of implementing conventional forms.

The young people addressed in Figure 13.4 are the audience which is also the audience of the school. This out-of-school site – and others quite like it in their style and esthetics – shape the settled communicational practices and identities of this group. In school, in classrooms other than English and literacy, these young people come across texts arranged on the same modular principles: in science, in geography, and increasingly, where English uses textbooks, in English also (Kress & Bezemer, 2009). The problems the school faces, with its conception of the identity and habitus of its audience, are not difficult to see. This also gives more than a slight hint of the future place of *writing*.

In these screens, *writing* is used as one of several modes, in relation to the assumed styles and esthetics of its addressees, one resource among others. While for established professionals ("About us"; "For Teachers") *writing* remains "traditional", for the young it is anything but. From the perspective of *provisionality*, it is clear *that* writing is shaped professionally and *how*, both culturally and in terms of generation. But we also know that there is no stability here even in the medium term. The *pace* of communicational/semiotic change differs in different domains, slower in some, faster in others; but there is considerable change in all domains. Comparing this site with that of the BBC shows both very much the same trends and different assumptions about the stage at which either organization assumes its audience to be – or what social features most characterize it.

Navigational Principles and the Issue of Grammar Now

Three factors now dominate: the rhetor/designer, resources and principles of design. In a former world of communication, grammar and associated textual conventions suggested what was to be done in *this* situation, *here*, *now*. The social environment was known – or at least confidently assumed to be known. The question of which mode to use did not arise – with only a slight overstatement, language was assumed to be what there was. Now, the question, first and foremost, is one of resources and choices: of a reliable account of the social environment; a clear sense of who the audience is; what its criterial characteristics are; of my social relations with that audience. From that follow questions about resources available and resources to use: modal and other semiotic resources such as genre, discourse, media. Simultaneously too, there is the question: what resources shall I use for the representation of *this* content, these meanings? Resources and principles are now the focus and choice is the ruling criterion. That is not to say that choice had not always been there: meaning has always been the effect of choice in context, as Halliday (1978) has pointed out, even in social conditions of great constraint. In the era of the neo-liberal market, the ideology of choice is dominant and seen as the ruling principle in social action and practice as much as in its effect in the individual's shaping of her or his identity.

"Le style, c'est l'homme meme", Gustave Flaubert said, showing that the insight and the process is not new. At the time of Flaubert's statement, "l'homme meme", and, as we might now say, "la femme meme" too, were tightly integrated into other identity-forming processes and structures: of citizen, of worker, of parent, of child, of teacher and student, as of many other social positions. To some extent these structures and processes exist still, though now differently embedded in the ideologies of the neo-liberal market – with the state as its servant. The traditional coexists with the contemporary, though now in contemporary scales and metrics of evaluation and with marked generational, professional and other differences.

Choice, of course, is set in fields of power, so that the formation of identity in choice is the effect of power as much as the effect of individual interest and need. *Style* is the effect of choices made, so that *style* can be seen as the effect of the politics of choice. *Styles* in their turn are subject to (e)valuation in the wider social field, also shaped by power, so that *esthetics* can be seen as the effect of the politics of style. In this approach, both style and esthetics apply to all semiotic entities, to the results of all semiotic work of *design* and *production*, with no distinction made at the first level between a "high" and a "low" esthetics: all social-semiotic action is subject to evaluation and to the category of esthetics therefore. This becomes both a central principle in design – what esthetic characterizes the individual, this group? – and a central heuristic principle: what social site or place does this esthetic point to, what principles of choice and what dispositions to style and meaning?

In relation to the Children's Poetry webpage, we could track back – always as a process of hypothesis – to the choices made and the meanings assumed in the choices made: the rounded irregular shapes of the modules, the genres of illustration, the color-scheme, the choice of modes and the foregrounding of modes, and so on. The conception of a grammar of meaning-*making* here is entirely different to the conception of a grammar resting on the process of the *realization* of meaning. The meaning-maker – in full awareness of the social environment; of the requirements of the audience in relation to that which is to be communicated; of the affordances of the semiotic resources – *designs* the semiotic entity, whether as text or other semiotic object.

As navigational aids go, all that is missing are two parts of one overarching frame: at one end the consideration of ethics as the politics of evaluation and of value – the evaluation of the effects of my semiotic actions on those who are its likely recipients and interpreters; and at the other end, of rhetoric as the politics of communication. That keeps the approach firmly framed.

The English classroom had been, in many places and in many periods, a space for the consideration of value, both as ethics and as esthetics, as induction into sensibility, into what was "good" or "best". Traditional grammar had, to a large extent, overlaid and displaced those concerns with a naturalization of social power in assumptions about what was "correct" in language.

So what of a grammar of meaning-*making* in the English and literacy class-room? No doubt that there will again be periods of stability, periods when long periods of stable power have produced new conventions with resources which will by then have become the contemporary commonplace, unremarkable, usual, not seen as complex but seen as what is. But this is not that moment. There cannot, at the moment, be a grammar of the hitherto traditional kind. In its stead the English classroom will need to be the place where conditions and resources for communication are the issue – set in a frame of understanding of difference, diversity, power and ethics – and where solidly founded understandings of these issues can provide its members with the means for interpreting the texts of others as well as making meanings in their interest, apt for the conditions in which they find themselves. Whether we call that a grammar, a new grammar, or whether we treat that as an understanding of agency, resources and principles of design is a lesser issue.

PS: Naming, Principles and Categories

The Poetry Archive website presents the characteristic features of the contemporary landscape of communication – not fully, not in great detail, but in broad outline. There are screens which seem "conventional" enough and there are screens which would cause some upset to some traditionalists in education, politics, the media and no doubt some parents as well. You cannot learn writing of the "traditional" manner from the children's webpage; and there might be a worry that the teachers themselves are addressed in a manner nowhere near conventional enough. But that is the issue: the contemporary period is one in which a vast variety of forms of representation are available and are used. Some of these point to, and suggest, former ways of doing things; some are thoroughly located in the present; and some point to a future that no one can fully predict – other than to say with certainty that it will not be in any way like the past. The complex and confusing present is not an anarchic mess, a fact indicated in this website: the young are addressed with one "esthetic" and the poetry reading public – by and large an educated, sensible, maybe somewhat traditional lot, oriented to the spoken word in poetry and to writing when they buy a volume of poetry – in quite another. Generation, social domain, profession, all have their role in that. It is not an anarchic situation, though it is highly complex.

In this post-script so far, I have used the terms *contemporary*, "*conventional*" and "*traditional*", the last two in inverted commas to indicate some distance, some hesitation. I would not now want to have to define "traditional", for instance: after all, which period would I reference? "Conventional" presents similar problems. Nor have I used "new" or "digital"; and put neither an "e-" nor an "m-" in front of any noun: all of these nouns, morphemes, particles, adjectives bring their problems (Kress & Pachler, 2007). Yet members of any generation do have a sense about something that it is more of the present and less of the past, what belongs to the era of digitally framed and facilitated communication and, more than that, what comes out of the present – unframed seemingly, compared to the strong social (and semiotic) framings of a not-so-

distant past. This makes me interested in a crucial enterprise: the renaming of
the practices of our present, rather than the continuation of the misleading use
of terms from the past.

The task, as I suggested, is to begin elucidating principles of design, of composition and of arrangement, as well as the resources available for use in these, as a
crucial issue. I am exploring the difference between *principles of design* and *principles of composition*. *Design*, for me, provides an overarching conception in
which my interest interacts with the resources available for me to shape overarching meaningful conceptions; these express my *interest*, my wish to shape
some aspect of the world, some entity, object, text. Principles of composition
then are the means of "implementing", "realizing" these conceptions through the
use of culturally available shapes, frames and semiotic resources of all kinds.

Contemporary principles of design and of composition differ markedly from
those of a not-so-distant past, enough to attract strong comment and dismissive
evaluation: "cutting and pasting", "downloading", "plagiarism" even, are the
terms used to signal rejection, unease and incomprehension of these principles.
So what are some of these – both principles of design and principles of composition, beyond those mentioned in the body of the chapter?

Were I to contemplate building a new house, what might I regard as *principles
of design* to discuss with an architect? I might say that I want the house to be
light and airy; to be energy-neutral in use; to be built from renewable resources;
to have clear open spaces; to fit with the building style of the region and of my
immediate vicinity; to make it easy for the people in the house to withdraw to
"their" space yet to have communal spaces that suggest congenial interaction;
and to have these "interpreted" in a contemporary form. These seem to me to be
principles of *design*. They express my interest, my "dreams", my conceptions of
how I would want to shape the space in which to conduct my life. These are principles which are both an expression of "me" and principles which are wholly
socially formed and culturally given.

In many instances these principles would be indistinguishable from *compositional principles*: what size rooms there should be; what specific arrangement of
rooms – where the "master" bedroom might be in relation to the kitchen or the
shower and toilet, or the terrace.

Some similar thinking needs to be done in relation to representation and
communication. In my representation do I want it to be "traditional" and "conventional" or very much "up with" contemporary forms? Do I want it to be
formal or informal, to suggest relations of solidarity or power? Am I attempting
to locate myself in a professional domain? Do I want to distance myself generationally from certain groups or seek affinity? Do I wish to seek institutional affinity or not? Which media of dissemination, which site of appearance for my
message, will best indicate the meaning I wish to make about myself, the world
and my place in that world in relation to others? What esthetic am I aiming for
as a desirable mirror for my audience? And also, what semiotic work do I wish to
attribute to my audience? Am I suggesting that they treat my design as authoritative without possibility of change or amendment for the "readers" or do I leave
to them the task of designing the page, the screen, the *meaning*?

Quite different *principles of composition* can achieve these *principles of design* – some or all. Do I want a temporal/sequential or a spatial/modular composition? Is the composition to be governed by linearity or modularity? What choices of mode and what modal ensembles/orchestrations will best realize my design? What means of achieving cohesion – in the linearly displayed "text", whether with image foregrounded or with other modes dominant? What role do I give to layout – how integrated should the text or the semiotic entity be or appear? What reading path, if any, shall be indicated? Should it be displayed or enacted/performed? How do I wish to produce salience? Through *intensity* – in whatever mode it might be, or through *placement* of an element, or through *size*?

References

Barthes, R. (1977). The death of the author. In *Image–music–text* (S. Heath, Ed. & Trans.) (pp. 142–148). London: Fontana.

Halliday, M. (1978). *Language as social semiotic*. London: Edward Arnold.

Kress, G. (1994). *Writing the future: English and the making of a culture of creativity*. Sheffield: National Association of Teachers of English.

Kress, G. (2003). *Literacy in the new media age*. London: RoutledgeFalmer.

Kress, G., & Bezemer, J. (2009). Writing in a multimodal world of representation. In R. Beard, D. Myhill, J. Riley, & M. Nystrand (Eds.), *The Sage handbook of writing development* (pp. 167–181). London: Sage.

Kress, G., & Pachler, N. (2007). Thinking about the "m" in m-learning. In N. Pachler (Ed.), *Mobile learning: Towards a research agenda* (pp. 7–32). (WLE Centre Occasional Papers in Work-based Learning 1). London: WLE Centre.

Kress, G., & van Leeuwen, T. (2001). *Multimodal discourse: The modes and media of contemporary communication*. London: RoutledgeFalmer.

Kress, G., & van Leeuwen, T. (2006). *Reading images: The grammar of visual design* (2nd ed.). London: RoutledgeFalmer.

Shannon, C., & Weaver, W. (1998). *The mathematical theory of communication*. Chicago: University of Illinois.

Chapter 14

Schemas for Meaning-Making and Multimodal Texts

Anne Cloonan, Mary Kalantzis and Bill Cope

Introduction

It has become commonplace to observe that communication in the 21st century is no longer limited to print-based forms of literacy. The digital world's reduction of the elementary modular unit for the production of textual meaning from the character of the printing press to the zeros and ones that underlie computer code has resulted in the ability to make, store and distribute sound, language and still and moving images through the same media because they can all be reduced to a common platform. Far from the analog world, the proliferation of new communications technologies has shifted the capacity for combining representational modes from technical specialists to households, classrooms, cafes and libraries. Meaning is made in ways that are increasingly multimodal – in which linguistic modes of meaning interface with visual, audio, gestural and spatial patterns of meaning (New London Group, 1996, 2000).

Observations on the unprecedented transformations in communication due to the pace of change have also become commonplace. To take one measure, the scale of Internet access has reached a point where one-sixth of the world's population has access to the Internet with one-half of the world's population due to be online by 2012. These figures belie divisions among regions, countries and age-groups. However, speed and scale of growth in Internet access in regions with the lowest current access rates, such as Africa, Asia, Latin America and the Middle East, are clearly apparent (Internet World Stats, 2006).

A profound shift is also occurring in the balance of agency as workers, citizens and learners are increasingly required to be users, players, creators and discerning consumers rather than the audiences, delegates or quiescent consumers of an earlier modernity. Students increasingly spend time in their out-of-school lives using multimodal forms of communication and social networking tools in online worlds, transforming their expectations of and orientations toward texts, literacies and pedagogies.

Against this backdrop, state and national curriculum guidelines increasingly embed the need for teachers to attend to digital forms of literacy enabled by contemporary media technologies, and to teach an extended repertoire of new and traditional literacies. But while teachers are encouraged to incorporate multimodal texts and literacies into the classroom, professional learning and other resources are confined to knowledge about technology and its practical uses rather than knowledge of the *meaning-making* capacities of various modes.

Various contributions have been made to the development of theoretical accounts of aspects of multimodality (Kress & van Leeuwen, 1996; New London Group, 2000; Unsworth, 2001). These accounts of multimodal meaning, while widely acknowledged, were not generated out of classroom practice. The core concepts and language in these accounts for the most part remain highly theoretical, and have not been widely explicated for teachers and students. The development of an accessible and generative multimodal metalanguage, a means by which students and teachers can articulate the functions of components of multimodal designs, has been identified as an urgent agenda item in developing students' multiliteracies capacities (New London Group, 1996, 2000; Unsworth, 2001).

This chapter explores a case study of expanded literacy pedagogies in which multimodal meaning-making is incorporated. In this case, the stimulus for renewed literacy teaching was a professional learning research project (Cloonan, 2005, 2008a, 2008b) involving early-years literacy teachers (students aged 5–10). This chapter will outline the context of the professional learning research, including two key schemas drawn from multiliteracies theory with which participating teachers engaged – a *multimodal schema* and a pedagogical *knowledge-processes schema*. Following this, it will detail the classroom literacy pedagogical context in which multimodal texts were encountered and created by students. Teacher attention to different modes of meaning (linguistic, visual, gestural, audio and spatial) as a result of engagement with multiliteracies schemas will be analyzed. A *dimensions-of-meaning* schema will support this analysis. Further possibilities for teacher generation of a multimodal metalanguage using the dimensions-of-meaning schema will be explored.

Activity: Map Your Own Use of Multimodal Texts and Multimodal Metalanguage

Think about the multimodal texts you use and those you've seen used in classrooms. Include digital and non-digital examples. What metalanguage do you use to talk about multimodal texts? What metalanguage have you heard other teachers use? List the sorts of terms used in describing, using or producing such texts.

The Context of the Research

The teacher referred to in this chapter was a participant in a project which supported professional learning and the classroom application of multimodal pedagogies. Teachers were engaged as co-researchers of their own classroom practice and scholarship (Cochran-Smith & Lytle, 1993; Darling-Hammond 1997; Elmore, 2002). They engaged with theoretical schemas through participatory action research (Carr & Kemmis, 1986; Kemmis & McTaggart, 2005). The schemas were drawn from multiliteracies theory and included a *multimodal schema* (New London Group, 1996, 2000) and a *pedagogical knowledge-processes schema* (Kalantzis & Cope, 2004, 2005).

The multimodal schema frames literacy meaning-making resources as linguistic, visual, audio, gestural and spatial. Multimodality is the interplay of the different modes. The multimodal schema is underpinned by the notion of "design" to describe linguistic, visual, audio, gestural, spatial and multimodal codes and conventions or grammars. The word "design" has a fortuitous double meaning, simultaneously describing intrinsic structure or morphology, and the act of construction. Design in the sense of construction is something you do in the process of representing meanings, to oneself in sense-making processes such as reading, listening or viewing, or to the world in communicative processes such as writing, speaking or making pictures.

As designers, students draw on "available designs", existing design elements, be they linguistic, visual, audio, gestural, spatial or multimodal designs in meaning-making. Students are involved in "designing" by harnessing available designs to make meaning for their own purposes. Students produce "redesigned", or transformations of, meaning, which then become available designs for other meaning-makers to draw upon.

The pedagogical knowledge-processes schema presented four (or eight finely differentiated) pedagogical orientations,[1] as follows:

1. student experiencing, be that experiencing the known or the new;
2. student conceptualizing, be that conceptualizing by naming or by theorizing;
3. student analyzing, be that analyzing functionally or critically; and
4. student applying, be that applying appropriately or creatively.

Teachers researched their own classroom practices and reflected on these in interview. They documented and published context-specific pedagogical applications of multimodal teaching as "Learning Elements" (Kalantzis & Cope, 2005). A "Learning Element" is a teacher-developed pedagogical sequence written on a "Learning Element template" which can be published online. It has a Teacher Resource section which is designed to be accessed by other teachers and a Student Resource section for learners to use. The "Learning Element template" contains a series of prompts for teacher consideration when developing pedagogical sequences. Informing the prompts are the four pedagogical knowledge processes. Teacher authors engaging with the template are prompted to develop a "Learning Element description" (a short overview of the sequence of lessons being developed), a "Learning Focus"; "Knowledge Objectives"; "Knowledge Processes"; and "Knowledge Outcomes".

---

1. The four "knowledge processes" relate to the orientations in the four-part multiliteracies pedagogy of situated practice, overt instruction, critical framing and transformed practice (New London Group, 1996, 2000).

The pedagogical context of the teaching of multimodality addressed in this chapter consists of 14 lessons developed by a case-study teacher, Robyn (a pseudonym). Robyn taught a class of school entrants in an inner-suburban, multicultural school in Melbourne. She documented the 14 lessons in a "Learning Element", entitled "Body Talk: Making and Interpreting Meaning".

In response to the prompt for a short description of the sequence of learning planned, Robyn wrote:

> This Learning Element guides learning about expression and feelings enabling students to classify and articulate a range of feelings. Children are involved in posing for digital photos and exploring meaning through hands, stance, and eyes. Through the use of literature, illustration, movement and sound, students analyze layers of meaning, deconstructing and reconstructing multimodal texts.

Robyn also wrote a "Learning Focus" for the "Learning Element" which reads: "All children make and interpret meaning as part of their everyday lives. They have been successfully interpreting facial expressions, tone and gesture in a variety of settings." In interview, Robyn elaborated on purposes for planning and developing the particular set of knowledge objectives, knowledge processes and knowledge outcomes described in the "Learning Element". Robyn describes consideration of the meaning-making experiences of students on entry to school as well as consideration of students' lifeworld experiences:

> When Preps[2] come to school they come from a variety of different entry points and they've all got to learn a new language at school and a new way to make meaning. The thing they know most about is themselves; so we worked on themselves and their own facial expressions and we played lots of games using facial expressions and getting to know the language of feelings and things like that.

These rationales suggest that Robyn's multimodal literacy pedagogies were inclusive of gestural and visual meaning-making modes in the literacy program – a literacy focus broader than print. Robyn's aims seek to engage students with the interplay of modes of meaning – rather than only the technology – of digital culture. They seek to engage students with the meaning-making potential of gesture, visual and audio modes, modes traditionally studied in the arts curriculum, in interplay with the linguistic mode. Robyn's documentation then shows 14 lessons to which she has ascribed visual "tags" of the eight finely differentiated pedagogical "Knowledge Processes".

Data relating to Robyn's movement toward classroom enactments influenced by the "multimodal schema" and "pedagogical knowledge-processes schema" is given in Table 14.1 and will form the basis for discussion in this section. Lesson

2. "Preps" are students in their preparatory year of schooling in Victorian schools; the first year of formal education.

Table 14.1 Robyn's Data Categories for Discussion of Breakthrough Multiliteracies Practices

No.	Lesson Title	Multimodal Emphasis	Pedagogical Knowledge Process	Pedagogical Knowledge Objective/s
1	Verbalizing expressions and feelings	Gestural *Peer and personal gestures, mirrored reflections*	experiencing the known	Discuss the meaning that gesture, expression and sound make in books, magazines and videos.
2	Classification, articulation of feelings	Gestural in visual *Expressions in magazine images; bingo cards*	experiencing the known	As above
3	Posing for digital photos	Gestural in visual *Expressions and gestures in digital photos*	experiencing the new	As above
4	Exploring how hands, stance, eyes and actions add meaning	Gestural in visual *Expressions, gestures and stances in peer and personal digital photos* *Isolated body parts in peer and personal digital photos*	conceptualizing naming	Meaning is represented in multimodal form. To explore how modes can affect the construction and interpretation of meaning. To recognize that literacy encompasses various modes.
5	Exploring literature	Visual including gestural and linguistic *Picture story book characters*	conceptualizing theorizing	As above
6	Exploring illustration	Visual including gestural and linguistic *Picture-book and "story map"*	analyzing functionally	To talk about print, gesture, sound, and expression as part of meaning – how do they help meaning?

7	Exploring movement	Gestural in visual *Animation*	analyzing functionally	As above
8	Exploring sound	Audio *Speech, music, sound effects in interplay with visual animation*	analyzing functionally	As above
9	Making links	Linguistic *Response to audio (speech, music, sound effects), and visual (animation)*	analyzing functionally	As above
10	Posing for a Body Talk video	Gestural *Expressions, gestures and stances in filming process*	analyzing functionally	As above
11	Analysing gesture (no audio)	Gestural in visual *Process of viewing film*	analyzing functionally	As above
12	Making meaning explicit	Linguistic and visual *Reflection on gestural representation*	analyzing functionally	As above
13	Music analysis	Audio *Musical resources*	analyzing functionally	As above
14	Linking music and mood in video	Audio in visual *Musical resources in interplay with visuals on video*	applying appropriately	To articulate (using metalanguage) their own interpretations. To use gestural and audio literacies to add extra meaning to illustrated texts.

number in sequence; lesson title; multimodal emphasis; deployment of pedagogical knowledge processes; and deployment of pedagogical knowledge objectives are reproduced, highlighting the language of teacher planning. The following discussion shall focus on the lessons referred to in Table 14.1.

Multimodal Pedagogies: Theory-Influenced Teacher Choices

Robyn's initial classroom practices focused on "interpreting" movements and facial expressions through mirror games incorporating peer discussion of possible interpretations of reflected gestural representations. Focus then shifted from student-mirrored reflections to represented images of people in magazines, involving students in a search for pictures of people adopting various stances and facial expressions. Students sought, sorted and labelled images according to the feelings expressed – for example, happy people, sad people, thoughtful people and angry people.

Analysis and discussion of the results showed that the range of expressions represented in the magazines was quite limited, so a commercial game, "Expression Bingo", was used to further build language around a broader range of possible meanings of facial expressions. In the "Learning Element" Robyn entitled the first two enactments "Verbalizing expressions and feelings" and "Classification and articulation of feelings", the titles reflecting the heavy emphasis on the development of student language for describing meaning made through gesture. Robyn "tagged" these two enactments with the pedagogical knowledge process "experiencing the known", which in the tradition of immersion pedagogy, or the multiliteracies pedagogical orientation of "situated practice", involves recruiting learners' knowledge from their lifeworlds (Husserl, 1970).

Robyn then worked in rehearsal with groups of students exploring various expressions (and stances) before students made their own selections of expressions for photographic documentation. The third lesson was entitled "Posing for digital photos" and tagged as "experiencing the new", since many of the students were unfamiliar with digital photography. Experiencing the new involves immersing students in new information and experiences but, in the Vygotskian sense of scaffolded instruction, where the new learning is in the zone of proximal development (Vygotsky, 1978). The three initial lessons in the sequence drew on the progressivist-influenced pedagogies of connecting with students' lifeworld experiences. This was achieved via a focus on students' own gestural representations and an incorporation of images of other children – peers, in magazines and on cards.

Concepts of gestural meaning-making are traditionally found in drama, dance and physical education curricula. However, the influence of the *multimodal schema* was evidenced by Robyn's focus on actual gestures and visual representations of gestures during literacy teaching.

Lesson 4, which Robyn entitled "Exploring how hands, stance, eyes and actions add meaning", showed a shift in pedagogy with her tagging of "conceptualizing by naming". The focus of traditional overt instruction, conceptualizing by naming involves defining and applying concepts, while conceptualizing by theorizing involves the connection of concepts in discipline knowledge through generalizing schemas or models.

Interpretations of possible feelings shown through expressions were sought and photos were also categorized according to the feelings expressed, for example, happy people; sad people; thoughtful people; angry people. Individual body parts were cut out from the photographic representations and students prompted to analyze the sections and determine possible gestural meanings to justify their points of view, concluding that gestural meaning can be conveyed in particular through eyes, mouth and hands. A poster with the sentence stem "We show our feelings with our..." and the words "mouth", "eyes" and "hands" completing three sentences were accompanied by cut-out sections of the students' photos. Students also drew representations of a "feeling" highlighting representations of "eyes", "body" and "mouth".

As described in the focus statement, Robyn expanded the focus to include children's literature, enabling links with gestural meanings portrayed by characters' expressions and implied actions. In this way Robyn led students into the "conceptualizing by theorizing" knowledge processes, exploring meaning-making concepts in different modes: linguistic, visual and gestural (and later audio) modes, making explicit the transferability of concepts. Lessons 5 and 6, "Exploring literature" and "Exploring illustration" involved readings and discussion of meanings in stories, the words of the stories; the way the print was presented (print size, type); and how the print and pictures made students feel. Students cumulatively documented their reactions to a range of books in a grid under the three headings: "Print"; "Picture"; "How it makes me feel".

In lesson 7, "Exploring movement", Robyn introduced an animated version of *Rosie's Walk*, without audio, ensuring focus on gestures in animated form. Robyn narrated the story, so students had access to the linguistic textual resources, but not audio tracks. "They saw the pictures [from the book] moving and they got that concept of what was happening; the fox really following and Rosie not watching, but they didn't have any idea of what sounds would be accompanying it." Robyn replayed the animated version of the story in lesson 8, "Exploring sound", this time with the accompanying audio (music, sound effects and the verbalized text read in a male American, mid-West accent):

> They were really cued in to what sound effects [were in the animated text]. I noticed that when they heard the sound effect they'd anticipated, or it was something different, they turned to each other and they'd look ... they were really listening for that sort of thing ... and watching them move to the music.

Lesson 9, "Making links", involved students in considering the meaning that each mode contributed to the narrative. Robyn's focus on gestural, visual and linguistic meanings reflects the continued influence of the *multimodal schema*, achieved through focusing attention on individual modes of meaning. Robyn expressed surprise at the students' ability to use language to describe their learning artifacts:

I'm seeing how adaptable the children are at using the language to suit the purpose and changing already. When we were doing the drawing of *Rosie's Walk*, one little child came up to me showing me his picture and pointed to a part of his picture saying "the fox has got a sad mouth because he's feeling unhappy" and just making those connections and using the language that I was using, and we're already going from quite general language about our feelings and the modes to quite specific language.

Robyn's focus showed receptivity to the children's responses which resulted in further focus on isolated modes of meaning from the *multimodal schema*, as described in this interview:

> When we were reading *Rosie's Walk* ... children started to say what sound effects, just spontaneously, that might happen, and I thought it would be interesting for them to watch the video [of *Rosie's Walk*] without the sound and see what sort of connections they made.

Utilization of a cross-platform text (picture-story book and animation) enabled teaching of a range of modes of meaning from the *multimodal schema*, initially linguistic (through reading the print) and visual (through directing attention to the story in the pictures). When asked to reflect on deployment of multiliteracies theory at this point, Robyn commented:

> [Prior to this] I kept saying, "What I'm doing is just natural ... I'm a fraud because I am not doing anything new". Then I actually got the brainwave of bringing in the audio. And then I felt "yes I have taken my learning and their learning another step".

Drawing on traditions of critical pedagogy, Robyn "tagged" the explorations of individual and combined linguistic, visual (illustration), gestural (animated movement), and audio (music, narration and sound effects) modes of meaning, *analyzing functionally*. Analyzing functionally investigates cause and effect; it involves considering the use of any knowledge, action, object or represented meaning. In contrast, *analyzing critically* interrogates human purposes and positions, querying the perspectives, interests and consequences of any piece of knowledge, action, object or representation.

The emphasis on analytical knowledge processes, specifically analyzing functionally, continued with lessons 10–13: "Posing for a Body Talk video", wherein students identified, rehearsed and acted and filmed feelings; "Analyzing gesture (no audio)", during which students viewed and analyzed each other's films and discussed possible interpretations; "Making meaning explicit", involving students reflecting on the experience of acting for camera and watching the footage in terms of "what I used", "how I felt when I did it", and "how I felt when I watched myself"; and "Music analysis", where students considered the mood created by various types of recorded music.

Despite the applied objectives, "for the students to be able to articulate [using metalanguage] their own interpretations of meaning" and "to be able to use gestural and audio literacies to add extra meaning to chosen illustrated texts", Robyn did not "tag" any lessons as *applying creatively* and only one, lesson 14, as *applying appropriately*. "Applying appropriately" involves learner application of knowledge in a typical situation, in the tradition of applied or competence-based learning. While this may involve a typical or accepted application, it is never merely replicated but always transformative to some degree. "Applying creatively" involves learners in the innovative application or use of learning in a different situation, involving original and hybrid possibilities. Engagement with the pedagogical knowledge processes as a heuristic highlighted a possible lack of explicit scaffolding and documenting of attempts to apply new knowledge.

However, while Robyn's documentation shows that students had little opportunity to explicitly apply their learning, Robyn engaged and tracked students in applying their learning in an ongoing way throughout their daily encounters at school, as she describes:

> [e]ven though we've only been doing this unit for a very short time, I'm seeing how adaptable the children are at using the language to suit the purpose and changing already ... making those connections and using the language that I was using.

Robyn's documentation addresses areas of meaning-making prompted by the *multimodal schema*, as can be seen in the "Multimodal emphasis" column of Table 14.1. This is corroborated by Robyn's description of the meaning-making resources foregrounded in the lessons documented on the "Learning Element",

> I focused usually just on the visual literacies, but using the video I was able to think about audio literacy and how much emphasis that adds to meaning and trying to get the children to see that, and that was a really good starting point to move on when we look at our videos of ourselves doing actions, to talk about what sort of sound effects or what sort of music will match that mood and that feeling. So where I want to go is looking at audio literacies and more on gestural literacies. Then much further down the track we'll probably be looking at the spatial too, as we're learning. So once I would only have focused on maybe the visual side and the alphabetical side, but now there's that whole range that I'm aware of.

The influence of the *multimodal schema* can be seen in the data-set relating to Robyn's classroom enactments in this teaching sequence, focusing on gestural, visual, linguistic and audio meaning-making resources. Robyn's focus on meaning-making modes in the 14 literacy lessons documented on the "Learning Element" and corroborated by teacher interview and staged filming data are represented in Table 14.2 below.

Table 14.2 Robyn's Teaching Focus – Mode

Robyn: Teaching Focus: Mode (numerals indicate number of lessons)	Lesson No.	Total No. of Lessons	%
Linguistic including:		2	14
• Linguistic response to audio and visual (1)	9		
• Linguistic reflection on gestural (1)	12		
Visual including:		2	14
• Visual including gestural and linguistic (2)	5, 6		
Gestural including:		7	50
• Gestural (2)	1, 10		
• Gestural in visual focus (5)	2, 3, 4, 7, 11		
Audio including:		3	22
• Audio (1)	13		
• Audio in interplay with visual (2)	8, 14		
Spatial		0	

Two of the 14 lessons focused on print linguistic meaning resources: one a response to audio and visual in an animation; the other a reflection on gestural representation in film.Two of the 14 lessons focused on visual meaning-making. Both of these lessons addressed different meanings of pictures and print in a range of children's literature and a picture-book study involving illustration and print meaning.

Seven of the 14 lessons focused on gestural meaning-making, two of which addressed actual student gestures or gestural presentation (Martinec, 1999) including exploration of students' peer and personal expressions and gestures; mirrored reflections and expressions; and gestures and stances in the process of being filmed. Five of the gesture-focused lessons addressed gestural meaning-making embedded in visual resources, or gestural representation (Martinec, 1999), expressions in images from magazines and on game cards; expressions, gestures and stances in photographs of children, including cut-outs of isolated facial features and body parts; and gestural representation of characters in animation; and viewing a film of students for gestural meaning.

Three of the 14 lessons focused on audio meaning resources: one lesson focused on a range of musical resources. A second audio-focused lesson explored the interplay of audio with visual meaning including speech, music and sound effects in interplay with visual animation, and a third focused on musical resources in interplay with visuals when constructing a video. As Robyn explains:

> When I first thought about multiliteracies it was still probably within the context of an English block of teaching. I think the most powerful thing that I found is how it is in all learning and how we've really got to be aware of that and make those links, taking it from just looking at it in one area, one subject area [English], across all subject areas ... I didn't think I'd go that far in my learning, and teaching too.

Prior to engagement with the multimodal and pedagogical knowledge-processes schemas in the professional learning research project, Robyn focused English teaching and learning, and literacy teaching and learning, on learning language. Teaching engaged with a range of the modes from the multimodal schema challenged modes which constitute literacy meaning-making and placement of literacy and English into a daily block of time dedicated to literacy. Multimodal literacies were evident across all subject areas.

Activity: Consider Robyn's Teaching of Multimodal Literacies

Reflect on Robyn's sequence of lessons designed to develop multimodal literacies. Identify the modes and the pedagogies she has emphasized in her teaching. Compare this with a sequence of lessons you have taught or are currently teaching. Which modes and pedagogies do you emphasize? Which do you not emphasize? Reflect on your knowledge of metalanguage in the various modes? What conclusions can you draw?

Emerging Teacher-Generated Multimodal Metalanguage

Describing and comparing how meaning is constructed within isolated and combined modes of linguistic, visual, gestural, audio and spatial designs of meaning requires language which is accessible to young students and able to be generated by teachers and students in various teaching contexts.

Work from the multiliteracies project recommends that each of the above modes can productively be considered in terms of *dimensions of meaning* (Cope & Kalantzis, 2000). The dimensions-of-meaning schema draws on systemic functional linguistics (Halliday, 1994; Martin, Matthiessen & Painter, 1997) and critical literacy traditions (Fairclough, 2000; Gee, 1996) and offers a series of open-ended questions to broaden understanding of how elements of meaning are structured and how cultural and ideological knowledge of meaning can be deepened. The five dimensions of meaning to which the questions would be directed are:

- *Representational meaning*, which relates to who and what the design represents; and what's happening in the design.
- *Social meaning*, which considers the way meaning connects the producer and the recipient.
- *Organizational meaning*, which involves the composition of the meaning.
- *Contextual meaning*, which relates to the context of the meaning and how context and meaning interrelate.
- *Ideological meaning*, which involves the possible motivations of the creator and consequent positioning of receiver.

The multimodal schema and the dimensions-of-meaning schema were incorporated into a matrix (see Table 14.3) in order to analyze Robyn's generation and deployment of a multimodal metalanguage as evidenced through teacher prompts and teacher-specified goals (Cloonan, 2008a).

Each of these dimensions and examples from Robyn's documentation of her teaching practice will now be discussed.

Representational meaning is explored through questions such as, *What do the meanings refer to?* This directs attention to the "participants" represented and the "being and acting" the meanings represent. This dimension prompts a consideration of who and what the text represents; and what's happening in the design. Examples of Robyn's emerging metalanguage relating to the representational

Table 14.3 Modes and Dimensions of Meaning Matrix

	Linguistic	Visual Still/Moving	Audio	Gestural	Spatial
Representational					
Organizational					
Social					
Contextual					
Ideological					

dimension of meaning addressed the gestural, visual, linguistic and audio modes of meaning, including:

- Emotions and "states" are conveyed through gestures and facial expressions.
- Various body parts can indicate meaning: hand gesture, stance, mouth, eyes.
- Words describe feelings and expressions.
- Pictures can tell a story the same as or different from the words.
- Sound conveys meaning: noises can include sound effects and music.

Social meaning is explored through questions such as, *How do the meanings connect the persons they involve?* relating to the roles of participants in the communication of meaning; the commitment the producer has to the message; interactivity; and relations between participants and processes. This dimension prompts consideration of the way the meaning connects and relates to the producer and the recipient. Examples of Robyn's emerging metalanguage relating to the social dimension of meaning addressed the visual and audio modes of meaning, including:

- Words can make us feel different ways.
- Color can affect how we feel about a text.
- Music can affect the mood of a text and how we respond.
- Sound effects add emphasis to match mood.
- Feelings can be in response to sound on a video.

Organizational meaning is explored through questions such as, *How do the meanings hang together?* relating to mode of communication; medium; delivery; cohesion; and composition. This dimension prompts consideration of the composition or shape of the meaning and the way it communicates meaning. Examples of Robyn's emerging metalanguage relating to the organizational dimension of meaning addressed the gestural, visual, linguistic and audio modes of meaning, and included:

- The words go from left to right across many pages.
- Reading the text involves making meaning from the words, the illustrations, the layout and the music.
- The meanings from the visuals and the words can be different, that is, the words can say one thing and the pictures can say another.
- Whole body movements and expressions show feelings.

Contextual meaning is explored through questions such as, *How do the meanings fit into the larger world of meaning?* prompting consideration of the context of the meaning and how context and meaning interrelate. Examples of Robyn's emerging lexicon relating to the contextual dimension of meaning addressed the gestural/visual modes of meaning, including:

- Feelings can be expressed in different ways.
- Expressions can be "read" in different ways.
- Particular presentation styles assist in meeting different audience needs.

Ideological meaning is explored through questions such as, *Whose interests are the meanings skewed to serve?* drawing attention to the possible motivations of the creator and consequent positioning of receiver. Secondary questions relate to indications of interests; attributions of truth value and affinity; space for readership; deception by omission if not commission; and types of transformation. Examples of Robyn's emerging metalanguage relating to the contextual dimension of meaning addressed the gestural/visual and audio modes of meaning, and included:

- Gestures in images can show real or "pretend" feelings.
- Expressions in visuals texts can be selected for different purposes.
- Sounds can be used to design a particular mood.

Analysis of the *dimensions of meaning* (representational, social, organizational, contextual and ideological) addressed when teaching various modes of meaning (linguistic, visual, gestural, spatial, audio, multimodal) offers insight into teachers' choices and emphases. In Robyn's case, the *representational* dimension of meaning was most heavily emphasized across the linguistic and visual (incorporating representations of the gestural) modes of meanings. The *social* dimension of meaning was emphasized when teaching about the audio, and the *organizational* dimension was most heavily addressed in the linguistic mode. The *contextual* dimensions of meaning addressed were in the gestural/visual modes and the *ideological* dimensions of meaning addressed were in the gestural/visual and audio modes of meaning.

In relation to a teacher-generated multimodal metalanguage, Robyn (and the other teachers involved in the project) deployed rich, student-friendly examples of different dimensions of modes in classroom discussions with students. The dot points in this discussion, which were examples of planning language gleaned from Robyn's "Learning Element", indicate examples of these. However, also evident was that teachers' attempts lacked specialization of terms and a systematic framework as they grappled with emerging understandings of modes as meaning-making resources.

Further Explorations with Multimodal Metalanguage

Robyn's work – particularly lessons 6–9 in which she engaged students with linguistic, visual, gestural and audio modes present in classic picture-book and animated versions of *Rosie's Walk* – was the stimulus for further exploration of the *multimodal/dimensions-of-meaning* matrix. Drawing on Robyn's technique of isolating the modes of meaning for independent study, a series of critical questions or prompts around the cross-platform text, *Rosie's Walk*, have been generated. Possible multimodal metalanguage has also been generated, in response to the prompts.

Table 14.4 shows the linguistic resources from the text of *Rosie's Walk* (Hutchins, 1968) as well as prompts which draw attention to each of the dimensions of meaning. These are accompanied by "possible metalanguage" related to the linguistic mode.

Table 14.4 Engaging with Linguistic Resources

The linguistic resources (32 words in total) describe the uneventful journey of a hen as she walks around a farmyard.

Critical Questions	Possible Linguistic Metalanguage
Representational: What's happening in the words of this text? What do the words tell us about?	*Representational:* Recount of a journey. Character: Rosie: a hen. Actions: walking. Circumstances: various farmyard places, mill, pond, etc. (book: written words, animation spoken words)
Social: How did you feel when you heard the words of the story? What in the words made you react like that?	*Social:* One sentence narrative recount, detached third person, past tense, economical use of words
Organizational: How do the words hang together? How does it start?	*Organizational:* Sentence begins with a noun phrase with character and species in theme position, verb phrase the process she undertook, followed by three word prepositional phrases.
Contextual: What are the words like? Do you know of other words put together like these?	*Contextual:* sentence beginning acts as an orientation, each phase "poetic" in its succinct description; uneventful; no plot complications
Ideological: What was the writer trying to make you think about Rosie? (The fox?)	*Ideological:* hen positioned as purposeful, safe, and oblivious. Linguistic (written words in book and narrated in animation) fail to mention stalking fox's harmful attempts omitting plot complications and resolutions

Table 14.5 briefly describes the role of visual resources from the same text as well as prompts which draw attention to each of the dimensions of meaning. These are accompanied by "possible metalanguage" related to the visual mode, including still and moving images.

Table 14.6 briefly describes the audio from the same text, as well as prompts which draw attention to each of the dimensions of meaning. These are accompanied by "possible metalanguage" related to the audio mode.

While the dimensions-of-meaning schema was deployed as an analytical tool in the professional learning research project on which this chapter draws (Cloonan, 2008a), Tables 14.4–14.6 show the schema's potential as a pedagogical tool when used in conjunction with the multimodal schema. Consideration of dimensions of multimodal meaning may deepen knowledge of systems and structures, and broaden cross-cultural knowledge of modes. Questions about dimensions of meaning could generate multimodal metalanguage which could increasingly form the basis of a functional grammar. Such considerations would not include rules of correct usage that teachers might have students learn. Rather, they are concepts teachers and students can use to assess the reasons why particular design choices are made in particular cultural and situational contexts.

In this project, it was found that teachers' attempts to develop multimodal metalanguage lacked specialization of terms and a systematic framework. However, teachers offered rich examples of student-friendly language which addressed dimensions of meaning across linguistic, visual, audio and gestural modes.

Activity: Teaching the Dimensions of Multimodal Literacies

Again reflect on the sequence of lessons you have taught. Using Table 14.3, identify the dimensions of multimodal meaning you emphasized in this sequence. Notice the dimensions you addressed and those you didn't. Using Table 14.3 as a guide, suggest lesson foci which would address all dimensions of meaning.

Conclusion

Increasingly removed from the word-centered era of print literacy, contemporary communication is characterized by multimodality in which written text is increasingly interconnected with visual, audio and other modes of meaning. This shift requires new literacy educational responses. Students need to learn to "read" and create the new multimodal designs and to find ways to cross discourse borders.

This chapter has described changes in early-years literacy pedagogies in response to the complex changes brought about by digital technology. The pedagogical shifts were a result of teacher engagement with theory within the context of a professional learning research project. Within this reflective context, the *multimodal schema* influenced teacher choice of the modes of meaning addressed as part of literacy teaching. The *pedagogical-processes schema* influenced teacher

Table 14.5 Engaging with Visual Resources

The visual resources not only illustrate the events described in the linguistic resources; they depict an additional character (a fox) surreptitiously preying on the hen, although all attempts to harm her are unsuccessful and amusing.

Critical Questions	Possible Visual Metalanguage
Representational: What's happening in the (moving) images? What are the (moving) pictures about? **Social:** How do the (moving) images make you feel? What in the (moving) images made you react like that? **Organizational:** How did what you saw hang together? **Contextual:** What are the images like? Do you know of other images put together like these? **Ideological:** What are the illustrator and animator trying to make you think about characters? Why do you think they wanted you to think this?	**Representational:** Two main characters, a hen walking and a fox stalking, and elements such as coop, buildings and lake denote circumstances as a farm. **Book:** still images: **Animation:** edited stills images; animated images and images involving lens and camera movement such as pans, zooms and dollys show a hen's journey around a farmyard oblivious to a fox's harmful attempts **Social:** The shot angles are predominantly at eye level, although fox is positioned higher on the page as it prepares to jump, lower following failed attempts. The shots are mainly offers, rather than demands with character gaze directed within the text **Organizational:** Rosie's steadfast left to right march around the farm forms the main reading path for these images. Her profiled body, particularly her feet and crest provide strong left to right vectors, supported by the vectors of the fox's eyes **Contextual:** pen and ink drawings with heavy use of line, dots and patterns are reminiscent of colonial cross-stitch **Ideological:** humanizes characters positioning hen as oblivious, naive (or perhaps clever) and fox as bad (although hapless) rather than an animal hunting for food. Safety and humor obvious despite predatory themes

Table 14.6 Engaging with audio resources

Rosie's Walk (narrated by male voice with an American mid-West accent; musical accompaniment and percussive sound effects)

Critical Questions	Possible Audio Metalanguage
Representational: What's happening in the sounds? What sounds did you hear? Who and what do the sounds tell us about?	**Representational:** Audio journey of repetitious cycles with narrated words, music, sound effects. Narrator (mid West American accent); Music (banjo, violin, string bass); sound effects (percussion)
Social: How did characters feel? What in the audio makes you think that? How did you feel when you heard that section? that instrument? that sound effect?	**Social:** Major key. Invites optimism. Quadruple (4/4) beat denotes a *march*. Invites an evenly rhythmic foot-tapping or hand-clapping response. Cycles build to climax/resolution
Organizational: How did what you heard hang together? What did you hear first? Then what?	**Organizational:** Informal tuning up of violin; Narrator introduces title; Laughter; Violin solo introduction; Verse: banjo carries melody; string bass accompaniment; Chorus: violin carries melody with string bass. Repetitive structure of verse and chorus
Contextual: What was the music like? Do you know of other sounds put together like these? What do these sounds mean for the story?	**Contextual:** Laughter foreshadows comedy. Mid-West American accent and use of string instruments (violin and banjo) and marching beat (string bass) denotes hillbilly or country and western style
Ideological: What did you think the audio designer was trying to make you think about Rosie?	**Ideological:** Constant, prominent bass line and banjo melody depict Rosie (hen) as steadfast, focused and safe in undertaking walk around the farmyard. Sound effects accompanying fox's failures emphasize humor and safety.

choice as to how students engaged with various textual designs, through knowledge processes of experiencing, conceptualizing, analyzing and applying. Broad curriculum goals and teacher choices of mode and pedagogy formed the context for the development of a multimodal metalanguage. Applications of the schemas were context-specific, allowing teachers to design learning attuned to the learning needs of their students.

The schemas presented are instruments of inclusion and enablement – inclusion in the sense of starting with and respecting the experiences, languages and discourses of students, and enablement in the sense of providing learning experiences through which students will be able to access the most powerful contemporary forms of self-expression and communication.

Teacher generation of a multimodal metalanguage or grammar occurs within the context of literacy pedagogy and broad curriculum goals. The variation in pedagogical contexts affects the teaching and learning direction of multimodal metalanguage, as teachers design sequences of learning experiences to meet specific situational needs and objectives. The diversity presented by the learners in any particular cohort will indicate entry points and learning needs for designs of literacy pedagogy.

The development of an accessible, pedagogically context-friendly, multimodal metalanguage remains an urgent research agenda. It is apparent that teachers have not yet moved to technical ways of describing the multimodal, such as those grammars described by Kress and van Leeuwen (1996), Martinec (1999), Unsworth (2006) and van Leeuwen (1999). This is perhaps not surprising given the relative newness and the emergent nature of theoretical schemas which offer specificity of articulation, particularly in relation to the visual (Kress & van Leeuwen, 1996); and the paucity of advice available, particularly in relation to the gestural (Martinec, 1999), audio (van Leeuwen, 1999) and spatial (van Leeuwen, 2006) modes. Questions remain as to what levels of technical language to describe the multimodal is appropriate for students at various stages of schooling.

The *pedagogical knowledge-processes* and *multimodal schemas* enable teachers to create classroom literacy experiences which engage students with an expanded range of text-types. Used in conjunction with these, the *dimensions-of-meaning schema* offers rich potential for enabling descriptions of the features and functions of multimodal texts within the classrooms context. Research partnerships, with teachers engaging with theoretical schemas and researching and reflecting on their own practice, offer exciting possibilities in developing pedagogically context-friendly, multimodal metalanguage.

References

Carr, W., & Kemmis, S. (1986). *Becoming critical: Education, knowledge and action research* (3rd ed.). London: Falmer Press.

Cloonan, A. (2005). Professional learning and enacting theory (or trying to be a lifelong/lifewide teacher-learner while hanging on to your sanity). In M. Kalantzis & B. Cope (Eds.), *Learning by design*. Melbourne: Victorian Schools Innovation Commission in association with Common Ground Publishing.

Cloonan, A. (2008a). *The professional learning of teachers: A case study of multiliteracies teaching in the early years of schooling.* Unpublished PhD thesis, RMIT University, Melbourne.

Cloonan, A. (2008b). Multimodality pedagogies: A multiliteracies approach. *The International Journal of Learning, 15*(9), 159–168.

Cochran-Smith, M., & Lytle, S. (1993). *Inside/outside: Teacher research and knowledge.* New York and London: Teachers College Press.

Cope, B., & Kalantzis, M. (2000). Designs for social futures. In B. Cope & M. Kalantzis (Eds.), *Multiliteracies: Literacy learning and the design of social futures* (pp. 203–234). London: Routledge.

Darling-Hammond, L. (1997). *Doing what matters most: Investing in quality teaching.* New York: The National Commission on Teaching and America's Future.

Elmore, R. (2002). *Bridging the gap between standards and achievement: Report on the imperative for professional development in education.* Washington, DC: Albert Shanker Institute.

Fairclough, N. (2000). Multiliteracies and language. In B. Cope & M. Kalantzis (Eds.), *Multiliteracies literacy learning and the design of social futures.* South Yarra: Macmillan.

Gee, J. (1996). *Social linguistics and literacies: Ideology in discourses* (2nd ed.). London: Taylor & Francis.

Halliday, M. (1994). *An introduction to functional grammar* (2nd ed.). London: Edward Arnold.

Husserl, E. (1970). *The crisis of European sciences and transcendental phenomenology.* Evanston: Northwestern University Press.

Hutchins, P. (1968). *Rosie's walk.* New York. Aladdin.

Internet World Stats. (2006). *Internet usage statistics – The big picture: World internet users and population stats.* Retrieved July 26, 2007, from www.internetworldstats.com/stats.htm.

Kalantzis, M., & Cope, B. (2004). *Designs for learning.* Retrieved August 12, 2007, from www.wwwords.co.uk/pdf/viewpdf.asp?j=elea&vol=1&issue=1&year=2004&article=3_Kalantzis_Cope_ELEA_1_1_web&id=139.132.1.1.

Kalantzis, M., & Cope, B. (2005). Learning in theory. In M. Kalantzis & B. Cope (Eds.), *Learning by design* (pp. 9–155). Melbourne: Victorian Schools Innovation Commission in association with Common Ground Publishing.

Kemmis, S., & McTaggart, R. (2005). Participatory action research. In N. Denzin & Y. Lincoln (Eds.), *The Sage handbook of qualitative research* (3rd ed., pp. 559–603). London: Sage.

Kress, G., & van Leeuwen, T. (1996). *Reading images: The grammar of visual design.* New York: Routledge.

Martin, J., Matthiessen, M., & Painter, C. (1997). *Working with functional grammar.* London and New York: Hodder Headland Group.

Martinec, R. (1999). Cohesion in action. *Semiotica, 1/2,* 161–180.

New London Group. (1996). A pedagogy of multiliteracies: Designing social futures. *Harvard Educational Review, 66,* 60–92.

New London Group. (2000). A pedagogy of multiliteracies: Designing social futures. In B. Cope & M. Kalantzis (Eds.), *Multiliteracies: Literacy learning and the design of social futures* (pp. 182–202). Melbourne: Macmillan.

Unsworth, L. (2001). *Teaching multiliteracies across the curriculum: Changing contexts of text and image in classroom practice.* Philadelphia: Open University Press.

Unsworth, L. (2006). *E-literature for children: Enhancing digital literacy learning.* London: Routledge.

van Leeuwen, T. (1999). *Speech, music, sound.* London: Macmillan.

van Leeuwen, T. (2006). *The discursive construction of social space.* Paper presented at the "Multimodal texts and multiliteracies: Semiotic theory and practical pedagogy" national conference of the Australian Systemic Functional Linguistics Association, University of New England, New South Wales.

Vygotsky, L. (1978). *Mind in society: The development of higher psychological processes.* Cambridge, MA: Harvard University Press.

Chapter 15

Resourcing Multimodal Literacy Pedagogy

Toward a Description of the Meaning-Making Resources of Language–Image Interaction

Len Unsworth

Introduction

It is now widely accepted that literacy and literacy pedagogy can no longer be confined to the realm of language alone, and that reconceptualizing literacy and literacy education needs to include the role of images (as well as other modes of meaning-making). In Australia, State English syllabi generally require students to learn about the role of images in their comprehension, and to a lesser extent, their composition of various kinds of texts. However, while either traditional or some form of functional grammar (influenced by the systemic functional linguistics (SFL) of Michael Halliday and his colleagues (Halliday & Matthiessen, 2004; Martin, 1992) is required to be taught, no such comparable metalanguage for describing the meaning-making resources of images and image–text interaction is included or recommended as a resource for developing multimodal literacy.

Faced with the requirement to address the multimodality of texts, the prescription of verbal grammar and the absence in syllabi of comparably theorized resources for describing the meaning-making resources of images, some teacher educators and teachers have made use of the "grammar of visual design" developed by Kress and van Leeuwen (2001/2006), extrapolating from SFL accounts of language. The commonality of the systemic functional theoretical approach to language and image as social semiotic systems facilitates an articulation of visual and verbal grammar as descriptive and analytical resources in developing students' comprehension and composition of multimodal texts. However, beyond accounting for the independent, albeit sometimes strategically aligned, contributions of language and image to the meaning of composite texts, is the challenge of systematically describing resources for the construction of meaning at the intersection of language and image.

This chapter will outline recent work addressing this challenge. In the next section I will outline the key tenets of systemic functional semiotic theory that facilitate its use in describing meaning-making resources within and across a variety of modes of meaning including language and images. The subsequent section, and main body of the chapter, will outline ongoing research dealing with the development of descriptions of meaning-making resources of image–language interaction. Finally, I will suggest – on the basis of research reporting the pedagogic efficacy of the metalanguage of SFL, some work on the pedagogic use of the grammar of visual design and the discussion in previous sections of the emerging research on descriptions of image–language interaction – that teachers, teacher-educators and researchers consider further the pedagogic potential of existing and emerging metalanguage drawing on systemic functional semiotic approaches to multimodal texts.

Key Tenets of Systemic Functional Social Semiotic Theory

The strength of SFL in contributing to frameworks for the development of intersemiotic theory emanates from its conceptualization of language as one of many different interrelated semiotic systems, and hence the assumption that the forms of all semiotic systems are related to the meaning-making functions they serve within social contexts. SFL proposes that these meaning-making functions can be grouped into three main categories, or metafunctions. These are the three types of meaning-making that are inherent in all instances of communication, regardless of whether the communication is via language, image, music, sculpture or some other semiotic mode. The three kinds of meaning-making or metafunctions are related to three corresponding situational variables that operate in all communicative contexts.

Any communicative context can be described in terms of these three main variables that are important in influencing the semiotic choices that are made. The first of these, *field*, is concerned with the social activity, its content or topic; the second, *tenor*, is the nature of the relationships among the people involved in the communication; and the third, *mode*, is the medium and channel of communication. In relation to language, *mode* is concerned with the role of language in the situation – whether spoken or written, accompanying or constitutive of the activity, and the ways in which relative information value is conveyed. These situational variables are related to three overarching areas of meaning, or metafunctions: "ideational", "interpersonal" and "textual". For example, if I say, "My daughter is coming home this weekend", ideationally this involves an event, a participant and the circumstances of time and place associated with it. Interpersonally it constructs me as a giver of information and the reader/listener as a receiver (as well as perhaps suggesting I have at least some acquaintance with the listener). Textually, it locates "my daughter" as the "Theme" or orientation or point of departure for the interaction, simultaneously suggesting that "my daughter" is given information that we both know about ("Given") and the new information is that she is coming home "this weekend" ("New"). If I say, "Is my daughter coming home this weekend?" the ideational meanings remain the same – the event, the participant, the circumstances have not changed. But the interpersonal meanings have certainly changed. Now I am demanding information, not giving it (and there may be some suggestion of estrangement between the listener and me). Similarly, if I say, "This weekend my daughter is coming home", the ideational meanings are still the same, but this time the textual meanings have changed. Now the orientation (Theme) is the weekend and this is the given or shared information. What is new or unknown concerns what my daughter is doing. So the different structures reflect different kinds of meaning, which in turn reflect different aspects of the context. The metalanguage of systemic functional grammar derives from this linking of language structure, meaning and context.

It is this metafunctional aspect of SFL and its link to the situational variables of social contexts that has provided a common theoretical basis for the development of similar "grammatical" descriptions of the meaning-making resources of other semiotic modes. For example, Kress and van Leeuwen (2001/2006) proposed that images, like language, also always simultaneously realize three different kinds of meanings. Images construct not only representations of *material reality* but also the interpersonal interaction of *social reality* (such as relations between viewers and what is viewed). In addition images cohere into textual compositions in different ways and so realize *semiotic reality*. More technically, the "grammar of visual design" formulated by Kress and van Leeuwen (2001/2006) adopted from SFL the metafunctional organization of meaning-making resources:

- *Representational/ideational* structures verbally and visually construct the nature of events, the objects and participants involved, and the circumstances in which they occur.
- *Interactive/interpersonal* verbal and visual resources construct the nature of relationships among speakers/listeners, writers/readers, and viewers and what is viewed.
- *Compositional/textual* meanings are concerned with the distribution of the information value or relative emphasis among elements of the text and image.

Activity: Exploring the Three Dimensions of Meaning

Select a one-page magazine advertisement to examine and discuss with two friends. The first person discusses only representational/ideational meanings (in the language and the images), the second person only the interpersonal meanings, and the third person only the compositional/textual meanings. Consider, as a group, the significance of teaching students to attend to all three dimensions of meaning in the images and language of the text.

Activity: Inquiry

A number of publications (Callow, 1999; de Silva Joyce & Gaudin, 2007; Unsworth, 2001) deal with the teaching of Kress and van Leeuwen's (2001/2006) "grammar of visual design". How might such approaches to explicating the meaning-making resources of images be used to enhance the interpretive comprehension of students with whom you are primarily concerned?

Toward a Metalanguage of Image–Language Interaction

Describing Resources for the Intermodal Construction of Ideational Meaning

What is being investigated here is the space of integration between language and image in order to provide a theoretical description of the dynamics of interaction between them in meaning-making (Lim, 2004). In terms of ideational meaning, this interaction may be characterized as ideational *concurrence* (Gill, 2002), *complementarity* or *connection*.

Ideational Concurrence

Ideational concurrence was described by Gill (2002) as referring to ideational equivalence between image and text. This was operationalized as the image and text having an equivalent participant–process–phenomenon configuration. For example, the first image in Anthony Browne's well-known picture-book, *Gorilla* (Browne, 1983), can be transcoded as: "Hannah is reading a book about gorillas while sitting on the floor." This concurs with the verbal text: "She read books about gorillas." Roth and his colleagues (2005) quote a caption from a Brazilian school science textbook accompanying a sequence of three images of a European partridge in winter, late winter and spring: "The European partridge, during winter, shows white plumage, blending with the snow. At the end of winter, it starts to change its plumage, and acquires a coloration that blends with the dry vegetation where it lives" (p. 88). This image–language relation is regarded as exposition, since the triptych of images portrays the change in plumage with the seasonal change. Concurrence may entail some form of redundancy across modes, but this is not a simple intermodal duplication of meaning.

In examples from children's literature like the one from *Gorilla* (Browne, 1983), the image–text relation is one of instantiation. The language conveys the habitual nature of the activity while the image indicates one instance, adding to the meaning of the language version that, at least on some occasions, this reading was done while sitting on the floor in the house. The degree of redundancy is variable depending on the context of the process or activity common to the language and image. For example, image three in *Gorilla* depicts the father walking along the street with a briefcase. This concurs with, and provides an instantiation of, the text: "He went to work every day." The image clearly suggests additional meanings such as what kind of work he did and, to some extent, how he got to work.

A further means by which ideational concurrence is achieved intermodally is perhaps the most immediately arresting to the reader/viewer. This is the phenomenon of "homospatiality", discussed by Lim (2004), and refers to texts where two different semiotic modes co-occur in one spatially bonded homogeneous entity. One example shows the linguistic representation, "snaaap", which visually appears with the "sna" segment forming one arm of an inverted "v" shape and the "aap" segment forming the other arm, so that it appears that the word itself has "snapped", as indicated in Figure 15.1.

Figure 15.1 Homospatiality.

Ideational concurrence then, is consistent with Lemke's (2002) notion of the multiplicative nature of the meaning-making capacity of multimodal texts being the logical product of the capacities of the constituent semiotic systems. In other words the visual–verbal interface is synergistic, producing a total effect that is greater than the sum of the contributions of each modality (Royce, 1998). At this point we could summarize our partial framework for understanding the construction of ideational meaning at the intersection of language and image as a set of semantic options for intermodal relations as indicated in Figure 15.2.

Ideational Complementarity

Ideational complementarity refers to the situation where what is represented in images and what is represented in language may be different but complementary and joint contributors to an overall meaning. One type of ideational complementarity is *augmentation* – where each of the modes provides meanings additional to and consistent with those provided in the other mode. Martinec and Salway (2005) refer to this as "extension", but provide only examples that indicate the text adding to the meaning of the images. In a study comparing school science explanations in books, on CD-ROMs and on the World Wide Web, Unsworth (2004) included data where the image extended the meanings of the text. For example, an explanation of the water cycle on the Classroom of the Future website (www.cotf.edu) included evaporation from the soil and the movement of clouds in its diagram but did not mention these in the main text.

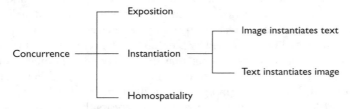

Figure 15.2 Ideational Occurrence.

The augmentation of the text by images is fundamental to the construction of interpretive possibilities in literary picture-books for children. This can be seen where significant segments of the narrative are conveyed by several pages that consist of images alone. In *Where the Wild Things Are* (Sendak, 1962), for example, the conduct of the "wild rumpus" is conveyed by images alone in three consecutive double-page spreads. But also, where images and text are co-present, significant elements of the action of the story frequently occur within the images only. For example, on page nine of Anthony Browne's *Gorilla* (Browne, 1983), the text foreshadows subsequent events: "In the night something amazing happened." Then the images on this page are exclusively responsible for conveying just what the amazing event was. It is these images only that depict Hannah's toy gorilla growing into a real gorilla (Gill, 2002). Juxtaposed images and text in picture-books have also been shown to jointly construct activity sequences.

Gill, extending her work on ideational concurrence in picture-books, described the nature of this joint image–text construction of meaning as "distribution". Distribution, however, seems to be appropriately discussed within ideational complementarity. According to Gill (2002), there are two types of distribution. Intra-process distribution refers to the portrayal by images and text of different aspects of a shared process. For example, the image(s) might depict the end result of a process described in the verbal text. This occurs in *Gorilla* when the text indicates that Hannah and the gorilla crept downstairs and Hannah put on her coat and the gorilla put on her father's hat and coat. The image shows them standing in the doorway so dressed. Inter-process distribution occurs when images fill a gap in the ideational flow of meaning in the verbal text. For example, later in the story of *Gorilla*, the text indicates that it is time to go home and then indicates that they danced on the lawn, which is clearly in front of Hannah's home. But the text makes no reference to their actually going home. This is conveyed by the image of the gorilla walking along the street with Hannah on his shoulders.

Another form of ideational complementarity is *ideational divergence*, where the ideational content of text and image are opposed. Ideational divergence does not seem to have figured in the research dealing with inter-semiotic concurrence and complementarity, and it is not mentioned in the system for image–text relations proposed by Martinec and Salway (2005). Nevertheless, it is clearly important in children's literary picture-books. For example, in the "Shirley" books by John Burningham (1977, 1978), the text and images of Shirley's parents convey a narrative of a typical beach visit or of a child taking a bath, while the images of Shirley depict her as participating in exciting adventures such as her encounter with pirates. Similarly, McCloud (1994) has drawn attention to the role of ideational divergence in the narrative art of comic books. In his category of image–text relations, he uses the term "parallel combinations" to denote instances where "words and pictures seem to follow very different courses – without intersecting" (p. 154).

A simple framework summarizing these types of image–text ideational complementarity is shown in Figure 15.3.

Slightly refined versions of the descriptions of image–text relations summarized in Figures 15.2 and 15.3 were used in an Australian Research Council-funded study

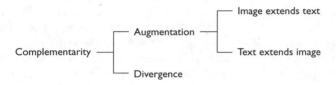

Figure 15.3 Ideational Complementarity.

I conducted from 2006 to 2008 using the New South Wales Basic Skills Test (BST).[1] This study focused on explicating the different types of image–language relations that primary school students needed to negotiate in responding to reading-comprehension test questions, and indicating the relative difficulty level of these different types of intermodal meanings. The results are reported in more detail elsewhere (Unsworth & Chan, 2008), but, in summary, from the data analysis there appeared to be an ordering of the types of image–text relation according to item difficulty. To determine the significance of this finding, the data were subjected to a one-way analysis of variance (ANOVA), which confirmed a difference in the mean item difficulty for each of the image–text relation types – in decreasing order of difficulty: "augmentation", "exposition" then "equivalence" (the latter term being described as "instantiation" in this chapter). Clearly many students find the increased strategic work required in negotiating image–text relations of augmentation very challenging. Current work suggests that this is also the case with online reading of multimodal texts (Chan, 2009; Unsworth, 2009). It is therefore very important for teachers to be able to distinguish the different types of image–text relations and to deploy explicit descriptions of these in teaching integrative reading of image and language in developing students' comprehension strategies.

Connection

There are two types of *connection* between images and text. The first is *projection* and most commonly involves the quoting or reporting of speech or thoughts. The second type involves the *conjunctive relations* of time, place and cause.

Projection in the Martinec and Salway (2005) system refers to either a "locution", which is the quoting or reporting of wording, or an idea, which is the quoting or reporting of thought. They cite the speech or thought bubbles in cartoons as the typical realizations. But a further realization of projection in language–image interaction occurs where a verb in the text "projects" or quotes what a character says or is thinking and the verbal or mental quotation is realized by images rather than language. It also refers to the juxtaposition of quoted

1. An Australian Research Council (ARC) Linkage Grant led by Len Unsworth from the University of New England in conjunction with the Educational Measurement and Schools Assessment Directorate of the New South Wales (NSW) Department of Education and Training (DET), 2006–2008, entitled *New Dimensions of Group Literacy Tests for Schools: Multimodal Reading Comprehension in Conventional and Computer-Based Formats.*

speech and a participant in the image represented as the obvious source of the quote. The latter form of projection commonly occurs in magazine advertisements where the participant looks directly at the viewer from a social or close-up position, thereby making contact that "demands" a pseudo-interpersonal interaction. The juxtaposed quote then is very strongly assumed to be attributed to this represented participant. One example of such an advertisement is provided by Cheong (2004). It shows a "demand" image of a smiling young woman at a medium close-up position holding a poster with the logo of the "M1" company that offers an attractive, weekly, "off-peak" discount for energy consumption. The quote spans the width of the advertisement and is located just above the head of the woman: "I get the feeling that M1 wants me to enjoy value – and enjoy life. Everything they offer is brighter, nicer and more fun!"

Image projection from a verb in the text occurs in the picture-book *Hyram and B* (Caswell & Ottley, 2003). In this story Hyram and B are two toy teddy bears who have lived on the shelf in a second-hand shop longer than any other toys. They have shared memories of their traumatic days of being discarded and their understandings of loneliness. Eventually, a young war orphan named Catherine takes B home, turning the world of the two bears upside down. But later, Catherine returns to the shop and collects Hyram. Two, consecutive, double-page spreads deal with Hyram's recounting his earlier life to B. In the first of the double-page spreads, B says: "Hyram sleeps a lot. He told me about it once." The verb "told" projects what is realized both verbally and visually in the next double-page spread as Hyram recounts his experience; and this past experience is also recalled visually in the illustrations. On a later double-page spread, the verb "remember" on the right-hand page projects B's memories represented only by the images on the left-hand side of that double page and also on the subsequent double-page spread.

Conjunction refers to the *connection* of images and text in terms of causal, temporal or spatial relations. The third-last double-page spread in *Hyram and B* constructs causality at the intersection of image and text. The left-hand third of this double-page spread shows the following text (in column format) with a rear-view image of Catherine holding B in her arms with "action" lines suggesting that she is trembling or that she is rocking B.

> Catherine loves me.
> Catherine understands the secret language of bears.
> She understands what it means to be lonely. (Caswell & Ottley, 2003, no page numbers)

The remaining two-thirds of the left page and the entire right-hand page show an explosive warfare scene with fire and a helicopter in the background, artillery and a damaged tank in the foreground as well as a rear-view image of a red-headed girl in an almost parallel pose to the separate image of Catherine on the far left page onto which this warfare image is partially superimposed. This parallelism suggests why "Catherine understands the secret language of bears" and why she "understands what it means to be lonely".

Temporal relations between images and text can also be seen in picture-books where juxtaposed images and text jointly construct activity sequences. One example of this is in Allan Baillie's book, *Drac and the Gremlin* (Baillie, 1991) where the young girl, Drac, is pursued by the "Terrible Tongued Dragon" (the family's large and very friendly dog). The text reads:

> She turns to fight.
> But the Dragon is too big, too fierce.
> The terrible tongue is poised to destroy her. (Baillie, 1991)

The sequence of images on the page facing this text includes images that "fill in" the event sequence between the second and the last line of this text segment. Through the combination of images and text we construct the event sequence of play between the girl and her pet dog.

The framework describing meaning made at the intersection of image and language through *connection* can be summarized in Figure 15.4.

An overall framework describing ideational meaning-making at the intersection of image and language can be summarized as indicated in Figure 15.5.

Activity: Exploring Ideational Meaning-Making

In a number of countries, literary picture-books are an important part of the English curriculum for primary and secondary school students. Select your favorite picture-book for work with either younger or older students and locate and discuss examples of ideational meaning-making at the intersection of image and language as described above.

Activity: Enquiring into Literary Picture-Books

David Lewis (2001) has detailed the use of Kress and van Leeuwen's "grammar of visual design" as a resource for the interpretation of contemporary literary picture-books. An example of its application to the work of the popular picture-book author, David Wiesner, also deals with online references to his work (Unsworth & Ortigas, 2008). What is to be gained from "a grammar of visual design" in understanding images in picture-books compared with other approaches to images (for example, Anstey & Bull, 2000; Arizpe & Styles, 2003; Keifer, 1995)?

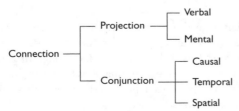

Figure 15.4 Connection.

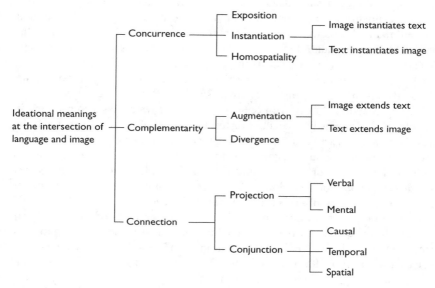

Figure 15.5 Ideational Meanings at the Intersection of Language and Image.

Image–Text Relations in the Construction of Interpersonal Meaning

Interactive and Evaluative Meaning

Interpersonal meaning in SFL includes interactive and evaluative meaning. Interactive meaning refers to the roles of interactants in giving information (making statements) or providing goods and services (making offers) or demanding information (asking questions) or ordering goods and services (giving commands). The grammar of visual design proposed by Kress and van Leeuwen (2001/2006) indicates that visually only two interactive roles can be portrayed: a "demand" image has the gaze of one or more represented participants directed to the viewer and hence "demands" some kind of response in terms of the viewer entering into some kind of pseudo-interactive relation with the represented participant; an "offer" does not have the gaze of any represented participant directed to the viewer and hence provides a portrayal for the viewer's contemplation.

Evaluative meaning in SFL has traditionally been confined to commentary on the truth of what is represented linguistically. This is realized by polarity (yes or no) and by the system of modality, which realizes possibilities between positive and negative polarity, such as degrees of certainty and probability (perhaps/of course; possibly/probably/certainly), and degrees of usuality and frequency (sometimes/usually/always). In the grammar of visual design, evaluation also focuses on the truth or credibility of images, also referred to as modality (Kress & van Leeuwen, 2001/2006). Modality value, however, is related to "coding orientation". Within a naturalistic coding orientation, high modality is a reflection of the fidelity of the representation with the natural world, such as that achieved in a high-quality color photograph. Within a scientific coding orientation, fidelity may be calibrated more in relation to the representation of conceptual clarity rather than naturalistic reality.

Martin has extended SFL perspectives on evaluation by proposing an "appraisal network" including three main systems – *attitude, engagement* and *graduation* (Martin, 2000; Martin & Rose, 2003). This work has also been made available in a form easily accessible to teachers and students (Droga & Humphrey, 2002). Here I will deal with the category of attitude only. Within attitude there are a number of subcategories: Affect refers to the expression of feelings, which can be positive or negative, and may be descriptions of emotional states (for example, happy) or behaviors that indicate an emotional state (for example, crying). Subcategories of Affect are "happiness", "security" and "satisfaction". Appreciation relates to evaluations of objects, events or states of affairs and can also relate to the characteristics of people but not their behavior. Appreciation is further subdivided into "reaction", "composition" and "valuation". Reaction involves the emotional impact of the phenomenon (for example, thrilling, boring, enchanting, depressing). Composition refers to the form of an object (for example, coherent, balanced, haphazard) and valuation refers to the significance of the phenomenon (for example, groundbreaking, inconsequential). Judgment can refer to assessments of someone's capacities (brilliant, slow), their dependability (tireless, courageous, rash) or their relative normality (regular, weird). Judgment can also refer to someone's truthfulness (frank, manipulative) and ethics (just, cruel, corrupt). Recent research has noted how image–text relations co-construct interaction but the main impact from an interpersonal perspective seems to be the construction of evaluative stance.

Portraying Interpersonal Interaction through Image–Text Relations

The Economist magazine advertisement analyzed by Royce (1998) shows a monochrome photograph with a medium to close-up, eye-level view of a young woman whose gaze is directed at the viewer, and whose frontal plane is parallel with that of the viewer. These visual features realize a pseudo-interpersonal relation of direct involvement at a personal level with a demand for a response. Positioned immediately above this image is the following question in the largest font on the page: "Does your environmental policy meet your granddaughter's expectations?" Royce notes how this question, with its second-person address and similar features in the subsequent text, effects a joint image–text initiation of interaction, which he refers to as "Reinforcement of Address". Similar examples are provided in work by Cheong (2004).

Communicating Evaluative Stance through Image–Text Relations

As far as interpersonal meaning is concerned, verbiage–image relations, according to Martin (2002), are more concerned with evaluative stance than interaction.

He argues that a key function of images is to co-articulate attitude (including Affect, Judgment and Appreciation). In doing so, images operate in a similar way to imagery, provoking an evaluative reaction in readers, and the images are typically positioned to do this so that they preview the value positions to be constructed in the subsequent verbiage. For example, in Nelson Mandela's *The Illustrated Long Walk to Freedom* (Mandela, 1996), in the section dealing with the 1976 Soweto uprising, the well-known photo of the body of 13-year-old Hector Pieterson being carried from the fray is positioned as a full-page image on page 147, preceded by its caption in the right-hand margin of the previous page. The main text dealing with the Soweto uprising then appears overleaf. The photo previews and amplifies the reaction induced by Mandela's verbal imagery. In SFL terms, Martin suggests that the photo functions as an evaluative interpersonal Theme, naturalizing the stance from which the remaining verbiage can be read. Additional examples are provided by Martin's (2002) analyses of other sections of this text and further examples from his analyses of the Australian government report (1997) *Bringing Them Home* on the generations of Aboriginal children taken from their families and placed in alternative care.

Activity: Using Images to Manipulate Response

Work with a friend to select a newspaper article about a contemporary politician and search the Internet for multiple images of this politician. One of you should then replace any images in the original newspaper article with at least two images designed to influence the reader to be sympathetic to the politician, and the other person replaces any original images with at least two designed to influence the reader to be hostile to the politician. Discuss the joint role of the selected images and original text in influencing reader response to the politician.

Activity: Enquiring into the Use of Images in Student Composition

Image–text relations are most often discussed in relation to reading. However, the role of images in students' writing development in a contemporary multimodal world cannot be disregarded. Work by David Baxter and Andrew Simpson (2008) and Mary Macken-Horarik and Maria Adoniou (2008) gives some insight into the impact of images on student writing development. Consider how you might incorporate the role of images and image–text relations in designing writing tasks for your students.

Textual/Compositional Meanings in Image–Text Relations

The descriptions of compositional meanings in images by Kress and van Leeuwen (2001/2006) have been extensively applied by them to image–text relations. Studies of school science books have shown how layout resources of Given/New, Ideal/Real, and Framing are deployed (Veel, 1998). Typically these studies show that what is likely to be familiar to students, whether in the form of language or image, is placed in the Given position on the left and that which deals either visually or verbally with unfamiliar, technical information is placed in the New position on the right. While these Given/New structures are consistent with the usual left-to-right progression in reading, the Ideal/Real structures in school curriculum texts do not necessarily map strategically onto our practice in working from top to bottom of the text. Students might be advised to examine the specific, concrete information of the Real positioned at the bottom of the layout before addressing the more abstract, conceptual and generalized information of the Ideal positioned at the top. Often the salience of concrete images in the Real will influence students to adopt such a reading path (Unsworth, 2001).

It has been noted, in Martin's (2002) work discussed above, that the descriptions of the compositional meanings in multimodal texts need to be extended to take account of the role of images as Interpersonal Theme. Further extensions are suggested in the work by Jewitt (2002) dealing with the compositional resources for constructing character in the Novel as CD-ROM version of Steinbeck's *Of Mice and Men* (Steinbeck Series, 1996).

From her *Of Mice and Men* study of the Novel as CD-ROM, Jewitt (2002) has suggested that the spatial relationship between image and verbiage on each of the screens is itself a meaning-making resource. She argued that writing serves as a visual element, a block of "space" that makes textual meaning beyond its content. Jewitt indicated that on the CD screens, the blocks of writing were positioned in different places: the left or right side, along the bottom or top length of the screen, or in the top or bottom corner. The size and position of the block and its location combined to reveal or conceal different parts of the image layered "beneath it". In this way, a block of writing emphasizes different aspects of the image on screen. According to Jewitt, the image at times cuts across the lexis and grammar of the written text to create a visual mood and rhythm, which she illustrated with one image of George and Lennie that runs across four screens of changing text:

> In the first screen, the block of writing sits above George's head as he talks to Lennie about what he could do if he left him. In the second screen Lennie is visually obliterated by George's angry talk of leaving, visually foregrounding George. In the third screen, as George's anger subsides, the block of writing is placed on the screen so that both George and Lennie are visible. (2002, p. 184)

Jewitt suggested that the visual arrangement of image and writing on screen indicates the intensity of emotion being experienced by the character of George in such a way as to suggest the alignment of the viewer with George's point of view, and also to emphasize the relative agency/passivity of the characters of George and Lennie in the novel. Whether negotiating the meaning of newspaper stories, or literary narratives (in book or electronic media), layout features such as framing are crucial elements in the interpretation of the meanings at stake and in establishing the evaluative stance of the writer in relation to those meanings (Macken-Horarik, 2003b; Unsworth, 2006a).

Although the ideational, interpersonal and compositional perspectives on the meaning-making resources of image–language interaction have been discussed separately here, it must be remembered that in reality these meanings are always made simultaneously in all texts, and critical understanding of the interpretive possibilities of texts needs to be based on an integrative view of all three perspectives.

Activity: Exploring the Relationship between Arrangement and Meaning

Collect a range of contemporary consumer artifacts such as DVD case covers, wrappings from food containers, book covers, clothing labels, t-shirt slogans and so on, and consider the relative positions of the images and the language and the significance of this positioning in interpreting the meanings of these artifacts. What would be the impact of rearranging the image/text layout arrangements?

Activity: Enquiring into the Role of Images in News Reporting

Helen Caple (2008) has shown that in many news stories today images have assumed the most prominent role and they are central to the overall organization of the story. Select the same event reported in at least two different newspapers and discuss the images used in each story and their role in the overall organization of the stories.

Conclusion: the Pedagogic Potential of a Systemic Functional Perspective on Metalanguage and Multimodality

There is significant support for the view that redefining literacy in the electronic age entails the development of a metalanguage that will facilitate metatextual awareness of image–text relations (Kamil, Intrator & Kim, 2000; Kress, 2003; Macken-Horarik, 2004; Richards, 2001; Russell, 2000). Metalanguage entails systematic, technical knowledge of the ways in which the resources of language and images are deployed in meaning-making. English syllabi currently require a significant commitment by teachers and students to understanding and using metalanguage. Such an investment in teaching and learning can be productive if the metalanguage functions as a tool to enhance the development of critical social literacies.

For this to happen, the metalanguage must be based on systematic accounts of the meaning-making potential of contemporary multimodal texts and also be capable of expansion/modification in response to the expansion of meaning-making potential with the ongoing emergence of new forms of communication. This chapter suggests that systemic functional semiotic theory has much to offer in this respect. However, the work on grammars for exploring the co-articulation of image and verbiage is in its infancy (Kress, 2001; Macken-Horarik, 2003a). While little classroom research has been done on the pedagogic use of such emerging grammars, there is some evidence that young children can productively use aspects of Kress and van Leeuwen's visual grammar in work with picture-books and with multimedia CD-ROMs (Callow & Zammit, 2002; Howley, 1996). There is also evidence for the efficacy of the metalanguage of SFL in literacy development and learning in primary/elementary and secondary/high school contexts (Quinn, 2004; Schleppegrell, 2004; Schleppegrell, Achugar & Oteíza, 2004; Torr & Harman, 1997; Williams, 1999, 2000). What is suggested here is that the theoretical bases of the social semiotic research arising from SFL are providing a generative and inclusive framework for the transdisciplinary development of a metalanguage of multiliteracies.

While the research on an evolving metalanguage of multimodality is in the very early stages and emerging descriptions remain quite tentative, at least one firm, practical implication for English teachers lies in the robustness, broad application and practical usefulness of the metafunctional principle deriving from SFL. That is the principle that all texts, visual and verbal, separately and in combination, always simultaneously entail ideational, interpersonal and textual/compositional meanings. This principle is frequently reflected in the rationale of the English syllabi of different school systems, such as the current Years 1–10 English curriculum for Queensland Schools (Queensland Studies Authority, 2005, p. 1).

The metafunctional principle is widely accepted as central to our understanding of contemporary and emerging forms of multimodal texts and provides a sound and accessible basis for English teachers to further examine the pedagogic potential of metalanguage. Detailed accounts of the ways in which SFL and the grammar of visual design can be used together in the English classroom are now well documented (Callow, 1999; Christie, 2005; Christie & Unsworth, 2005; Cope & Kalantzis, 2000; Goodman & Graddol, 1996; Jewitt, 2005; Jewitt & Kress, 2003; Kress, 2003; Unsworth, 2001, 2006b; Unsworth, Thomas, Simpson & Asha, 2005). It is hoped that this chapter, by stimulating critically constructive responses to, and envisioning beyond, what is presented here, will encourage further collaborative work among teachers, teacher educators and researchers in exploring the nature and role of a metalanguage that will facilitate development of the multiliteracies pedagogies appropriate to the multimedia world of our children in the 21st century.

References

Anstey, M., & Bull, G. (2000). *Reading the visual: Written and illustrated children's literature*. Sydney: Harcourt.

Arizpe, E., & Styles, M. (2003). *Children reading pictures: Interpreting visual texts*. London and New York: Routledge/Falmer.

Baillie, A. (1991). *Drac and the gremlin*. Ringwood, Victoria: Penguin/Puffin.

Baxter, D., & Simpson, A. (2008). Secondary school English, literacy examinations and attitude: Utilizing appraisal to interpret values in image/text relations. In L. Unsworth (Ed.), *New literacies and the English curriculum: Multimodal Perspectives* (pp. 309–327). London: Continuum.

Browne, A. (1983). *Gorilla*. London: Julia MacRae.

Burningham, J. (1977). *Come away from the water, Shirley*. London: Cape.
Burningham, J. (1978). *Time to get out of the bath, Shirley*. London: Cape.
Callow, J. (Ed.). (1999). *Image matters: Visual texts in the classroom*. Sydney: Primary English Teaching Association.
Callow, J., & Zammit, K. (2002). Visual literacy: From picture books to electronic texts. In M. Monteith (Ed.), *Teaching primary literacy with ICT* (pp. 188–201). Buckingham: Open University Press.
Caple, H. (2008). Intermodal relations in image nuclear news stories. In L. Unsworth (Ed.), *Multimodal semiotics: Functional analyzes in contexts of education* (pp. 123–138). London/New York: Continuum.
Caswell, B., & Ottley, M. (2003). *Hyram and B*. Sydney: Hodder Headline.
Chan, E. (2009). Image-language interaction in online reading environments: Challenges for students' reading comprehension. Paper presented at the 44th RELC International Seminar "The Impact of Technology on Language Learning and Teaching: What, How and Why". Singapore, April 20–22, 2009.
Cheong, Y. (2004). The construal of ideational meaning in print advertisements. In K. O'Halloran (Ed.), *Multimodal discourse analysis: Systemic functional perspectives* (pp. 163–195). London and New York: Continuum.
Christie, F. (2005). *Language education in the primary years*. Sydney: University of New South Wales Press.
Christie, F., & Unsworth, L. (2005). Developing dimensions of an educational linguistics. In J. Webster, C. Matthiessen & R. Hasan (Eds.), *Continuing discourse on language: A functional perspective* (Vol. 1, pp. 217–250). London: Equinox.
Commission (Human Rights and Equal Opportunity). (1997). *Bringing them home: National inquiry into the separation of Aboriginal and Torres Strait Islander children from their families*. Sydney: Human Rights and Equal Opportunities Commission.
Cope, B., & Kalantzis, M. (Eds.). (2000). *Multiliteracies: Literacy learning and the design of social futures*. Melbourne: Macmillan.
de Silva Joyce, H., & Gaudin, J. (2007). *Interpreting the visual: A resource book for teachers*. Sydney: Phoenix.
Droga, L., & Humphrey, S. (2002). *Getting started with functional grammar*. Marrickville, Australia: Target Texts.
Gill, T. (2002). *Visual and verbal playmates: An exploration of visual and verbal modalities in children's picture books*. Unpublished BA (Hons) dissertation, University of Sydney.
Goodman, S., & Graddol, D. (1996). *Redesigning English: New texts, new identities*. London: Routledge.
Halliday, M., & Matthiessen, C. (2004). *An introduction to functional grammar* (3rd ed.). London: Arnold.
Howley, P. (1996). *Visual literacy: Semiotic theory, primary school syllabus documents and classroom practice*. Unpublished Bachelor of Education Honors thesis, University of Sydney, Sydney.
Jewitt, C. (2002). The move from page to screen: The multimodal reshaping of school English. *Visual Communication, 1*(2), 171–196.
Jewitt, C. (2005). *Technology, literacy, learning*. London: Routledge.
Jewitt, C., & Kress, G. (Eds.). (2003). *Multimodal literacy*. New York: Peter Lang.
Kamil, M., Intrator, S., & Kim, H. (2000). The effects of other technologies on literacy and learning. In M. Kamil, P. Mosenthal, P. Pearson & R. Barr (Eds.), *Handbook of reading research* (Vol. 3, pp. 771–788). Mahwah, NJ: Lawrence Erlbaum.
Keifer, B. (1995). *The potential of picturebooks: From visual literacy to aesthetic understanding*. Englewood Cliffs, NJ: Merrill/Prentice Hall.

Kress, G. (2001). Sociolinguistics and social semiotics. In P. Cobley (Ed.), *Semiotics and linguistics* (pp. 66–82). London: Routledge.

Kress, G. (2003). *Literacy in the new media age*. London: Routledge.

Kress, G., & van Leeuwen, T. (2001/2006). *Reading images: A grammar of visual design* (2nd ed.). London: Routledge.

Lemke, J. (2002). Travels in hypermodality. *Visual Communication, 1*(3), 299–325.

Lewis, D. (2001). *Reading contemporary picturebooks*. London: Routledge Falmer.

Lim, V. (2004). Developing an integrative multi-semiotic model. In K. O'Halloran (Ed.), *Multimodal discourse analysis: Systemic functional perspectives* (pp. 220–246). London and New York: Continuum.

Macken-Horarik, M. (2003a). A telling symbiosis in the discourse of hatred: Multimodal news texts about the "children overboard" affair. *Australian Review of Applied Linguistics, 26*(2), 1–16.

Macken-Horarik, M. (2003b). Working the borders in racist discourse: The challenge of the "children overboard affair" in news media texts. *Social Semiotics, 13*(3), 283–303.

Macken-Horarik, M. (2004). Interacting with the multimodal text: Reflections on image and verbiage in *artexpress*. *Visual Communication, 3*(1), 5–26.

Macken-Horarik, M., & Adoniou, M. (2008). Genre and register in multiliteracies. In B. Spolsky & F. Hult (Eds.), *The handbook of educational linguistics* (pp. 367–382). Malden, MA: Blackwell Publishing.

Mandela, N. (1996). *The illustrated long walk to freedom: The autobiography of Nelson Mandela*. London: Little, Brown and Company.

Martin, J. (1992). *English text: System and structure*. Amsterdam: Benjamins.

Martin, J. (2000). Beyond exchange: Appraisal systems in English. In S. Hunston & G. Thompson (Eds.), *Evaluation in text: Authorial stance and the construction of discourse* (pp. 142–175). Oxford: Oxford University Press.

Martin, J. (2002). Fair trade: Negotiating meaning in multimodal texts. In P. Coppock (Ed.), *The semiotics of writing: Transdisciplinary perspectives on the technology of writing* (pp. 311–338). Begijnhof, Belgium: Brepols & Indiana University Press.

Martin, J., & Rose, D. (2003). *Working with discourse: Meaning beyond the clause* (1st ed.) (Vol. 1). London/New York: Continuum.

Martinec, R., & Salway, A. (2005). A system for image-text relations in new (and old) media. *Visual Communication, 4*(3), 337–371.

McCloud, S. (1994). *Understanding comics: The invisible art*. New York: HarperCollins.

Queensland Studies Authority. (2005). *Years 1–10 English syllabus*. Retrieved September 7, 2005, from www.qsa.qld.edu.au/yrs1to10/kla/english/syllabus.html.

Quinn, M. (2004). Talking with Jess: Looking at how metalanguage assisted explanation writing in the middle years. *Australian Journal of Language and Literacy, 27*(3), 245–261.

Richards, C. (2001). Hypermedia, internet communication, and the challenge of redefining literacy in the electronic age. *Language Learning and Technology, 4*(2), 59–77.

Roth, W., Pozzer-Ardhenghi, L., & Han, J. (2005). *Critical graphicacy: Understanding visual representation practices in school science*. Dordrecht: Springer.

Royce, T. (1998). Synergy on the page: Exploring intersemiotic complementarity in page-based multimodal text. *Japan Association Systemic Functional Linguistics Occasional Papers, 1*(1), 25–50.

Russell, G. (2000). Print-based and visual discourses in schools: Implications for pedagogy. *Discourse: Studies in the Cultural Politics of Education, 21*(2), 205–217.

Schleppegrell, M. (2004). *The language of schooling: A functional linguistic perspective*. Mahwah, NJ: Lawrence Erlbaum.

Schleppegrell, M., Achugar, M., & Oteíza, T. (2004). The grammar of history: Enhancing content-based instruction through a functional focus on language. *TESOL Quarterly, 38*(1), 67–93.

Sendak, M. (1962). *Where the wild things are.* London: The Bodley Head.

Steinbeck Series. (1996). *Of mice and men.* New York: Penguin.

Torr, J., & Harman, J. (1997). Literacy and the language of science in year one classrooms: Implications for children's learning. *Australian Journal of Language and Literacy, 20*(3), 222–237.

Unsworth, L. (2001). *Teaching multiliteracies across the curriculum: Changing contexts of text and image in classroom practice.* Buckingham: Open University Press.

Unsworth, L. (2004). Comparing school science explanations in books and computer-based formats: The role of images, image/text relations and hyperlinks. *International Journal of Instructional Media, 31*(3), 283–301.

Unsworth, L. (2006a). *Describing meaning-making at the intersection of language and image: Towards a metalanguage for multi-modal literacy pedagogy.* Paper presented at the Future Directions in Literacy, University of Sydney.

Unsworth, L. (2006b). *E-literature for children: Enhancing digital literacy learning.* London and New York: Routledge/Falmer.

Unsworth, L., Thomas, A., Simpson, A., & Asha, J. (2005). *Children's literature and computer-based teaching.* London: McGraw-Hill/Open University Press.

Unsworth, L., & Chan, E. (2008). Assessing integrative reading of images and text in group reading comprehension tests. *Curriculum Perspectives, 28*(3), 71–76.

Unsworth, L. (2009). *Bridging new literacies and national assessment programs in literacy.* Paper presented to the National Conference of the Australian Literacy Educators' Association, Hobart, July 9–12, 2009.

Unsworth, L. & Ortigas, I. (2008) Exploring the narrative art of David Wiesner: Using a grammar of visual design and learning experiences on the World Wide Web. *L1: Educational Studies in Language & Literature, 8*(3), pp. 1–21.

Veel, R. (1998). The greening of school science: Ecogenesis in secondary classrooms. In J. Martin & R. Veel (Eds.), *Reading science: Functional and critical perspectives on the discourses of science* (pp. 114–151). London: Routledge.

Williams, G. (1999). Children becoming readers: Reading and literacy. In P. Hunt (Ed.), *Understanding children's literature* (pp. 151–162). London: Routledge.

Williams, G. (2000). Children's literature, children and uses of language description. In L. Unsworth (Ed.), *Researching language in schools and communities: A functional linguistic perspective* (pp. 111–129). London: Cassell.

Chapter 16

Rules of Grammar, Rules of Play

Computer Games, Literacy and Literature

Andrew Burn

Computer games and English still seem like uncomfortable bedfellows. Thrown together, they evoke old (but still smouldering) anxieties about cultural value, which those who teach English, those who train English teachers and those who research literacy perennially encounter and negotiate. It's a sharper version of the persistent clash of the values of literary studies and the values of studying popular culture. In many Anglophone contexts, these differing traditions are realised as the awkwardly related domains of English and literacy education on the one hand, and media education on the other.

So one version of this debate is, in what kind of curricular world would we teach literature and computer games in the same breath, as it were? How would we negotiate the different tastes, values, structures, reading practices, conceptual understandings, situated experiences which they seem to involve?

Behind this apparent fault-line or fracture – between the content of the literature curriculum and the media curriculum – lies another ancient fault-line: between literature and language. My argument here will be, of course, that we need to repudiate this fracture (again), with its old stories of literature versus linguistics graduates, language versus literature exams, the colliding ideologies of appreciation on the one hand and analysis on the other. But I will argue here that, while the old debates are given fresh life by the instance of computer games, they are also offered new solutions, new slices at the Gordian knot, new exits from the labyrinth. On the one hand, games extend the experience of popular narrative for children. My ideal example here is currently Harry Potter – how do we need to reconceive literacy to understand how children experience the *mythos* of Harry Potter across book, film and computer game, in the context of what Henry Jenkins calls "convergence culture" (Jenkins, 2006)? On the other hand, however, games are based on design principles, even grammatical structures, which are directly comparable to those which operate in other systems of signification, including language.

I hope to show in this chapter how we might think about all of this; as well as how we might approach it with students in the classroom. While this kind of work can, of course, be carried out at different levels of complexity with any age-group, the examples I will use here are mostly drawn from the lower end of the secondary phase – Year 8 in the United Kingdom (age 12–13). The examples come mostly from a funded research project in which we developed a game-authoring software tool for children to use in school.[1]

Activity: Playing a Game

Find a game, and play it as you read.

Many teachers do not play computer games: only 16% of teachers sampled in a current project included games in their frequent media use. The rest of this chapter will make much more sense in conjunction with an exploration of a game. You might consider *Harry Potter* (any of the games in the franchise) or *Tomb-Raider IV*. These both have the advantage of relating to a well-known franchise, and so are easily "mined" for material on representation, literacy across different media (literature, film, game), and so on. Alternatively, if you are an experienced gamer, choose any game you feel motivated to play.

Game-Grammar and Social Semiotics

In thinking about what kind of "grammar" games might use, I have found social-semiotic theories of visual design useful. Kress and van Leeuwen (1996) adopt three overarching functions of visual media which I will follow in this chapter.[2] They call these *representational, interactive* and *textual*; though I will change the last category to *compositional*, which I find more transparent.

So here, we can think about *representation*: how games represent aspects of the world, or construct fictional worlds, in ways that will seem familiar in many ways to the core business of English and of media education. We can look at how elements of narrative such as characters, events and locations are constructed, what kinds of meanings they convey, and why they are important to those who made the text or those who read, watch and play it. In the case of a trans-media text like *Harry Potter*, we can also consider how these aspects of narrative change across book, film and game.[3]

We can look at how games allow forms of *interaction* between participants: how the game addresses the player; how the designer addresses the player through the game; how the player engages with this address, and returns with particular responses, demands, actions.

And finally we can look at how games are organised and *composed*: what design principles lie behind them; how they cohere, both as narratives and as games.

---

1. *Making Games*, funded under the PACCIT-Link programme (People at the Centre of Communication and Information Technology), by the Economic and Social Research Council and the Department for Trade and Industry. The development of the software was carried out by Immersive Education Ltd. The partner schools in the project were Parkside Community College, Cambridge and Charles Edward Brooke Community School, Lambeth, London.
2. Derived from Halliday's three linguistic metafunctions: ideational, interpersonal, textual (1985).
3. All the film adaptations of the *Harry Potter* novels have been adapted as computer games across a range of platforms, by the UK company Knowonder, commissioned and published by Electronic Arts. For a full discussion of literacies across book, film and game, see Burn (2004).

These categories can help us (and, at a different level, our students) to explore in what ways games carry out functions that are similar to those of other narrative media. However, as scholars in the new field of game studies often point out, and as anyone who has played a computer game knows, games are also different from older media. Most obviously, they are playable. Students of games have, then, had to reconsider fundamental notions of *game* and *play*, and have proposed various versions of each, and of the relationship and distinctions between them.

An often-cited model is that of the French play theorist Roger Caillois, who distinguished between two forms of play: *ludus* and *paidea* (1958/1979). The former is strictly rule-governed; the latter is more open and chaotic. A couple of examples might help. If we think about young children playing "I'm the King of the Castle", we can see that there are vague kinds of rules. There must be a castle (a mound, a box, a table) to be conquered, and to make a physical distinction between high and low, the territory of winner and loser. There's a rule that specifies a "win–lose" state. But other than that, there are no complex rules. The richness of this game will come from more open-ended playful activities – the language children will use to assert status, compete, make jokes; the gestures that signify victory, the objects or clothing, real or imaginary, that might signify kingship. So we can say that here, the emphasis is on *paidea* rather than *ludus*: open play rather than structured game.

By contrast, nought-and-crosses is very clearly a game. It has many rules: two players, turn-taking, straight lines, three-in-a-row, a three-by-three grid, noughts versus crosses, and so on. The play here is clearly closer to Caillois's *ludus* than his *paidea*.[4]

I'm not suggesting that 12-year-old students necessarily learn about Caillois's concepts – though of course older secondary students could learn this with rather less difficulty than they might encounter in learning about subordinate clauses, laws of motion or the formula for quadratic equations. But more simply, and maybe more importantly, 12-year-olds, if asked to identify the features of games, will produce long lists which can be further scrutinised, classified, conceptualised, interrogated: which items are really criterial for this to count as a game; which are dispensable; which are more or less important; do some apply to play and others to games, and so on. Such lists in classrooms where I have worked have included rules, competition (and cooperation), winning and losing, points and scoring systems. We will look at these in more detail below.

After this general consideration of the nature of games and play, I will take each of Kress and van Leeuwen's overarching categories in turn, and explore how they can be applied to game-texts.

Representation

There are many reasonably straightforward questions we can encourage students to ask about how games represent the world. How are women represented? Urban life? Technology? Conflict? History? The family?

---

4. I am grateful here to Eric Zimmerman, co-author of *Rules of Play* (2004), for an entertaining demonstration of the value of noughts and crosses (tic-tac-toe in the United States) as an exemplar of game rules at a conference in London.

However, I will concentrate here on how games might represent the world in narrative form, by constructing sequences which in language would be called transitive. The French narratologist Gerard Genette proposes that the verb is the central category in narrative, since narratives revolve around action (1980). In simple terms – certainly accessible to 12-year-olds – they are at least partly about who does what to whom. In the terminology of systemic functional linguistics, on which Kress and van Leeuwen partly base their grammar of visual design, this becomes a transitive sequence of Actor, Action, Goal.

Now, English teachers may want students to learn these kinds of structure in language grammar, though they may use other terms (Subject, Verb, Object). They may well look at how time is managed in language, through tense, for example. They may look at how particular kinds of narrative action are represented by particular kinds of lexical choice (how the soldiers in Wilfred Owen's "Dulce et Decorum Est", for instance, march, stumble, choke, drown). They might look at how point-of-view is represented through the system of *person*: how, for instance, the "friend" back in England who perpetrates the "old lie" of "Dulce et Decorum Est" is addressed in the second person by the poet/soldier/narrator:

> If you too could walk behind the wagon that we flung him in...
> You would not tell to children ardent for some desperate glory
> The old lie: Dulce et Decorum Est pro patria mori.

What, then, is the equivalent of the verb in game-narratives? In some ways, it might look quite similar to our experience of narrative action in older media. In the game of *Harry Potter and the Chamber of Secrets*, the player (as Harry) *flies* around Hogwarts, *plays* Quidditch, *intrudes* into the Slytherin common-room disguised as one of Malfoy's friends, *enters* the Chamber of Secrets, *fights* and *kills* the Basilisk. These "verbs", or narrative actions, are, however, generalised representations of how the player experiences Harry through play. At the game equivalent of sentence level, something rather different is happening. Harry the avatar[5] (the player's representative in the game) is a programmed entity only able to perform six actions – to move forwards, backwards, left or right; to cast spells; or to jump. These actions are related to keyboard strokes in the PC version of the game: arrow keys, left mouse button and space-bar respectively. We can call these actions *playable actions*.

The values of literary composition, which emphasise rich variety and inventiveness, originality of expression and a naturalistic modality in representing human behaviour, may seem to collide violently with such restrictive, mechanised constructions of narrative action. However, three points need to be made.

First, these actions are *amplified* by the visual and auditory semiotic. If I press the forward arrow key to move the avatar to the edge of a dark precipice, perhaps triggering in the process a deep chord in a minor key, I will experience this

---

5. The avatar is the player's representative in the game, usually the player-controlled protagonist. The word is derived from Sanskrit, originally signifying the descent of a god to Earth in human form.

action as something like "teetering dangerously". This is a frequent experience in the first game of the *Harry Potter* franchise.

Second, these actions are elements of play as well as elements of narrative. As such, they can be seen as part of a *restricted language* (Halliday, 1989). So, just as the limited moves of a knight, pawn or bishop in chess contribute to complex and rich forms of play, so the restricted moves the player in a computer game is able to manipulate can produce skilful play and a rich narrative experience, as any committed player of the *Tomb Raider* series will tell you in relation to Lara Croft's actions of running, climbing, jumping, shimmying and shooting.

Third, the playable actions are complemented by two other kinds of action outside the control of the player. One can be called *existential action*: small programmed actions which show that the character is alive, by keeping them dynamic or investing them with human-like properties – restlessness, boredom, impatience. These include animations which produce small movements of the body or turns of the head, or occasional speech a character is programmed to utter if they have been inactive for a determined period of time. The other is *nonplayable actions* which take place outside the play sequences, in scenes known as "cut-scenes" to gamers, which are effectively short films designed to provide backstory, narrative fills or instruction to the player. These scenes, since they are simply animated films, do not depend on the restricted language of the playable actions, and are thus unrestricted, and can show any action the designer wishes.

These kinds of complementary actions enrich the semiotic repertoire the text offers the player. We may only have six movements available to us as players – but narratively we experience many more.

Nevertheless, the game apologist may still fail to satisfy the committed student or teacher of literature. After all, all these movements, however varied, are effectively programmed to be produced by a machine. What passes for a character is really a bundle of media data (visual design, animation, wireframe) animated by algorithmic instructions. How can this compare with the richness of literary character, with its psychology, its development through the narrative, its roundedness, its mimetic or referential repleteness in relation to the people of the real world? By comparison with the characters of literature, computer game characters must seem reductive, crude, unconvincing, devoid of aesthetic merit or representational adequacy. Admittedly, I'm making up these arguments, or attributing them to an invented caricature of the literature-loving English teacher. Yet I have encountered arguments like these when presenting games to English teachers or teachers in training.

What might the counter-arguments be? There are several, it seems to me.

The first is made by Marie-Laure Ryan, in an article for the inaugural issue of the game-studies journal *Game Studies* (Ryan, 2001). She points out that some kinds of narrative make good games, while others don't. Those that do are ones with what E.M. Forster called "flat" characters, as opposed to "round". Ryan argues, then, that games work better with characters like Alice, Sherlock Holmes, Harry Potter and the heroes of fairytale rather than Emma Bovary, Oedipus or Hamlet. The point here is not Forster's point, that flat characters mean inferior narratives; rather that they mean different ones, with different merits, functions, effects. This seems to me a good argument, though perhaps it needs qualifying. A teacher in training who followed a Master's module I taught last year successfully made a computer game with his Year 7 class (11–12-year-olds) based on Hamlet. Key missions were: to discover if the Ghost was Hamlet's father or an infernal demon; to rescue Ophelia from suicide; to discover the identity of Hamlet's father's murderer; to choose between killing Claudius or letting him live. So the play was interpreted here as a series of games, albeit somber ones.

Ryan's argument is similar to one made by Janet Murray (1998), who points out that computer game characters resemble the heroes of oral narrative. Walter Ong calls these "heavy heroes" (2002), and argues that they are characterised by a few simple traits, and by an agonistic mode of action (they solve problems through external physical action rather than through internal psychological processes). Again, the point is not that heavy heroes belong to inferior narratives; just to ones whose functions, cultural provenance and modes of representation are different from those of the European novel or the Renaissance drama (although both also boast respectable lists of heavy heroes too).

I mention these two genres deliberately, because they dominate the literary canon to which the sensibility of English teachers is still often directed, and around which syllabuses and curricula in the Anglophone world are most commonly constructed. In relation to narrative and narrative characters in particular, this seems to me to produce what is really an ideology of representation. This is rooted in claims for certain "realisms": a representation of psychology, and a representation of the physical world confined by the rules of naturalism. This ideology made life difficult for genres which did not conform, fantasy and folktale in particular. These narrative forms become, especially in the 19th and 20th century, driven elsewhere, into children's literature and popular fiction – what becomes known dismissively as "genre" fiction.

What is in danger of being under-represented in the curriculum here are not only the contemporary popular forms of the comic-strip, blockbuster movie and computer game, but also their antecedents in oral narrative: the Norse sagas, the Homeric epics, *Beowulf*, the Robin Hood ballads, the Child ballads, and so on.

It may seem that I've drifted rather from the question of "grammar" into much broader concerns with genre, literary values, narrative types, cultural histories. The drift is, however, strategic. The humble, functional units of grammatical structure are of no interest to children or English teachers except insofar as they might be culturally weighted building blocks of larger textual and discursive entities. There is a direct line from the formulaic actions of Harry Potter and Lara Croft to the larger narrative characteristics of their respective computer games. The formulae here are those which determine transitivity, and the part the player takes in this transitivity; and also those which govern what a character is – the bundle of media objects (visual designs, animation cycles, units of recorded speech) held together by algorithms that configure and articulate what we see and experience as movement, dialogue, magic powers, combat, discovery, and so on. If this kind of mechanized characterization seems anathema to us as English teachers reared on the representational ideologies of modern literature, we need to pause and reflect. My argument is that these formulaic grammars, necessarily computable, necessarily configured to respond to the skill, improvisation and quick wits of the players, are not so dissimilar from the Homeric epithet or Old English kenning, or the formulaic representation of action which repeats the details of warrior-death in the Iliad, or of the wielding of a quarter-staff in the Robin Hood ballads.

Activity: Analysing Characters

Choose a player-character in the game you are playing, or a game you have played, and analyse its properties, focusing especially on the actions it can perform. Which actions are delegated to the player? Which are not? How does it feel to perform those actions? Also consider other features of the character: the visual design, any backstory the game provides, and the narrative function of the character. Compare it to similar characters in film and literature. What differences and similarities can you find? How are these differences and similarities judged or valued by English teachers, and by students?

A valuable extension of this activity would be to conduct it with a class. It is relatively easy to play a PC game projected on a whiteboard with a whole class, with one student playing and the others observing, note-taking, commentating. If this proves difficult, an alternative would be to ask students to bring in screenshot images of player-characters from games they have played, and to use these as a basis for discussion. The aim here is to explore, for yourself as a teacher, but also with students, what the common features are of a narrative protagonist, across different media; but also what particular features games provide. The wider aim is to extend students' understanding of narrative and fiction, by extending the range of narrative forms and media beyond the literary, while also taking games seriously as a cultural form.

Interaction

Interaction is the word Kress and van Leeuwen use to indicate how meaning is jointly constructed by texts (and their authors) and readers or spectators. It derives from Halliday's (1985) *interpersonal* metafunction, but implies a relation to texts (and more recently screens) as well as other people – a mediated relationship, in other words. Other people use different words. Jay Lemke uses *orientation*, which suggests the way the text is turned to face the audience, as well as the audience's stance towards the text (Lemke, 2002).

This function of grammar can include many things. Among the most important features in relation to narrative texts seem to me to be:

- how audiences are positioned in relation to the text in general (Kress and van Leeuwen look, for instance, at the use of horizontal and vertical angle in visual texts, which is a commonplace approach also for media teachers);
- how audiences are located in relation to specific characters, especially the protagonist: what Genette calls *focalisation*;

- the systems of *mood* and *modality*: is a narrative text offering information, asking a question or making a demand? How is it making claims for what is credible, authentic, definite or vague, real or fantastic? And how do audiences judge and engage with these claims?

The first of these three has traditionally been thought of, by both English and media teachers, in terms of the idea of *address*, perhaps. The second invokes older ideas of *identification*. The third has usually been conceived of through the notion of *realism*. Such notions were – and still are – victims of the lang–lit fracture. They were and are deployed as ways to think about narrative texts, whether literary or media; but they were disconnected from the study of language structures which operated in another part of the English curriculum, separated out like egg yolk by academic qualifications, curriculum prescriptions and examination syllabuses. What social semiotics offers to do, perhaps, is to remix the omelette.

How, though, do these systems work in computer games? I will consider this question under three sub-headings: how, in games, the functions of representation and interaction become newly articulated; how the literary and filmic notion of focalisation can also help explain how the player relates to the protagonist; and how systems of modality might operate in game texts.

Representation Becomes Interaction

The first point to make is that games make possible an unprecedented relation between the representational function and the interpersonal function. In conventional narratives, the transitive sequence of Actor–Action–Goal is provided by the text: the interactional function of the audience is to observe and interpret. In games, what we mean by interactivity (in its common sense) is that either of the end-terms in this sequence becomes occupied by the player, who performs the middle term. We literally become the Actor or Goal; we literally perform the action. We leap with Lara; cast spells with Harry's wand; manipulate Gandalf's staff; strike with the huge sword of Cloud Strife, the elfin warrior hero of *Final Fantasy VII*; slash and block as Iorek the armoured bear with the Wii-mote and nunchuk of the Nintendo Wii in the game adaptation of *The Golden Compass*. Or, on the receiving end of the transitive sequence, we take hit points from Draco Malfoy; lose life force to the Balrog in *Lord of the Rings*; die of spider venom in the forests of the popular online role-playing game, *World of Warcraft*. To say "Gandalf strikes" or "Harry casts" now means something different, partly because the player (in respect of these defined actions) has become the Actor, partly because the material substance through which the action is constituted has changed.

It is clearly different from the collection of letters which signifies the action in print. It has more in common with the animated motion that forms the signifier material in moving image texts. But it also includes the programmed properties of the action, triggering quantified consequences such as depletion of life points, increase of score, release of reward objects. And finally, it includes the physical action of the player with the interface – the stabbing of keys on the PC keyboard; the urgent use of buttons and joysticks on Playstation consoles; the mimetic waving of the Wii-mote and nunchuk. Are these "grammatical"? They seem to work in ways analogous to the qualifiers of verbs in language, adding degrees of urgency, or confidence, or skill. More profoundly, they raise phenomenological questions about the embodiedness of player engagement with the game-text.

Focalisation

Focalisation is realised through the grammar of language in many ways, as Genette (1980) explored in Proust. It was the term Genette proposed to cover, as he said, "who sees" – how our perceptions of the narrative are determined by our location in relation to particular characters, and especially the protagonist. Film theorists have gone on to consider how focalisation works through the grammar of the moving image through conventions such as shot distance, voiceover narrative, camera position, frequency of representation of the focalised character. These and other elements of film grammar locate us closer to one character than another; determine whose eyes we "see" through; give us privileged access to that character's thoughts, beliefs and motives; establish, or at least invite, our sympathy; make possible our empathy.

How does this work in games? Perhaps the most obvious thing is that it is in some ways a more fixed relation. The player-character, or avatar, is unambiguously the representative of the player in the game, like the incarnation of a divinity which the Sanskrit origin of *avatar* signified. We are close to the protagonist because, at least to the degree that we perform the playable actions, we *are* the character. This degree of focalisation surpasses anything that was possible in older narrative forms, with the possible exception of theatre, in which, as Hamlet succinctly observed, an actor can "drown the stage with tears/And cleave the general ear with horrid speech" in his lament for Hecuba. Indeed, as some game theorists have observed, playing a narrative game does resemble playing a character in a play, or perhaps the invasion of the stage by the audience (Laurel, 1991; Murray, 1998).

However, as with other kinds of focalisation, distance can be established as well as proximity. We may operate some of the character's actions, but, as observed above, not all of them. We play as amnesiacs in a perpetual dramatic present tense – any representation of actions before the moment of the game narrative have to be supplied to us, in cut scenes, as flashbacks, in the same way that they would be in literature or film. We are also distanced by our perceptual connection with the character. Game players have a clear conception of first- and third-person play: first-person play means looking through a character's eyes, seeing only their gunhand in the case of first-person shooters; third-person play often means, in 3D adventure games, being permanently positioned behind and just above the character. Both positions are, perhaps, closer to variations on a first-person narrative in literature or film: there is nothing, in the player–avatar relationship, that is close to a third-person literary narrative. So we are always attached to our avatars by invisible umbilical cords – but by the same token at one remove from them, especially in the third-person view, where we observe them from a vantage-point.

Students are able to conceptualise these relations, and to do so involves not a little intellectual challenge. Their talk in one of our research interviews about how they relate to, in this case, Harry Potter in the second game adaptation, shows how they are able to articulate their engagement with this aspect of game-grammar. It also shows that the structures of the game-text offer only possible meanings – the game-text can only offer us a system of meaning-potential (Halliday, 1989). Some children in these research interviews did not feel as if they "were" Harry; merely that they were controlling him from above:

ANNIE: You're in the third person, you're watching Harry move around, so you're not looking at it from the first person, so you're not really being Harry Potter, you're just watching him and controlling what he's doing.

By contrast, one girl who was a committed Harry Potter fan felt quite different:

GEMMA: You're controlling it, really, and it's actually like you're there, and you're the one that's doing it, you're Harry Potter.

Her much more intense experience of the text's focalising devices derived from her dedication to the whole Potter phenomenon: the drawings of Harry on her bedroom wall; the board game she had made of the third novel; the improvised dramas she played out with two friends in the school playground. Her enthusiastic immersion in the figure of the avatar extended, naturally, to a willing acceptance of the claims for credibility and authenticity made by the whole game-text – the aspect of game-grammar indicated by the idea of modality, the subject of the next sub-section.

Modality

Social semiotics provides a way to think about how the text's claim to credibility is negotiated through the judgements of its audience, who may choose to accept or reject such claims. These systems of modality are various, and construct believability in different ways. They may build a credibility rooted in naturalistic representation, or, conversely, in a fantasy modality; they may assert the reality of a documentary take on the world or a comic-strip take; they may root their credibility in fidelity to the conventions of a particular genre, appealing to its fans to distinguish between the real thing and pale imitations.

In the case of games, it can be said that at least two systems of modality are working in parallel at any given time. One relates (at least in narrative-styled games) to the narrative system; the other to the ludic system. The narrative modality is similar to its counterpart in other narrative media, with the exception that the player's attachment to the avatar weights the modality in certain ways. The designers of the game will certainly hope that the player–avatar relation raises modality, a hope evident in exhortations on the box-cover of the second Harry Potter game adaptation to "Be Harry Potter and unlock the mystery at the heart of the Chamber of Secrets!"

How do players judge narrative modality? Examples identified in research include players who develop fan work online, in which they embellish the story of the game, writing "spoilers" which provide satisfying endings or fanfiction which fills in the complex backstories of characters and other narrative events. At the finer "grammatical" level, they may make judgements about the credibility of the graphic design and 3D experience, analogous to ways in which readers of literature might respond to passages of descriptive prose. This reviewer of *Harry Potter and the Chamber of Secrets*, for instance, gives a critical account of the visual style of the game, corresponding to what Kress and van Leeuwen call "naturalistic modality": "The graphics improved in the second game – they aren't perfect and are a bit angular and 2-dimensional in places (like the trees and I once got caught in a corner and couldn't get out without rebooting my system)" (Tak, 2003). Meanwhile, for another reviewer, the game is found to be effective in its provision of a convincing emotional experience through its use of music, in a modality judgement that corresponds to what Kress and van Leeuwen call a "sensory modality": "The sound is fabulous. I love the Harry Potter music, it portrays mystery, innocence, and curiosity. Precisely what the game needs" (Bill, 2003).

By contrast, the ludic modality is built through the game system, and the experiences it offers: meeting challenges that are achievable but sufficiently difficult; collecting objects, scoring points, fighting enemies, progressing towards a win-state but in constant danger of triggering a lose-state, managing quantified resources to meet the challenges. It is clear that players can switch between narrative (or representational) modalities and ludic modalities without any sense of contradiction. So, in the online role-playing game *World of Warcraft*, as in any game of this genre, players toggle between screens which represent their avatar in colourfully realised scenes of fantasy adventure and screens which represent resources such as clothing, weapons, magic spells, health points, currency, membership of groups and other social and political affiliations, and so on, as simple icons, numbers, written descriptions, charts, inventory boxes. This kind of modality can be said to correspond to what Kress and van Leeuwen call a "technological modality" – the kind of claim to veracity made in visual media by charts, maps, technical diagrams.

Not only can players switch between this technological modality and the naturalist modalities of the game – they can also make different modality judgements. So the reviewer quoted above, who was so impressed by the music of the *Harry Potter* game, made a quite different judgement about the ludic modality:

> The gameplay in this game is rather basic. Everything leads one way, and the player has no real freedom, to roam the castle and explore all the other things they want. E.g., talking to characters going on hidden quests, sneaking out, etc. The game could be vastly improved by the adding some RPG characteristics. (diablo2)

For example, harry could have an inventory, a quest log, and character attributes such as dexterity, strength, charisma, and mana. Harry should also level up, or in a vaguer term improve as time passes, not only in skill but in vitality. (Bill, 2003)

The representation of low modality here includes judgements of three ludic aspects of the game: the ludic topography, the ludic function of non-player characters, and the generic attributes of Role-Playing Game (RPG) avatars, which typically develop through the game by the player's management of the kind of resources referred to by this reviewer (for a detailed account of RPG generic structures, see Carr, Buckingham, Burn & Schott, 2006, chapter 2).

The focus of this chapter so far has been on how players *experience* games, and on how teachers and students might think critically about them, conceptualise them. The next section will address the compositional function of game-grammar by considering how children might *create* their own games, based on our research with schools and game-authoring software.

Activity: Analysing Gameplay

Try analysing the gameplay of the game you are playing in terms of the categories used in this section: interaction, focalisation, modality. What exactly does interaction mean here? Exactly how are you becoming the narrative's protagonist (or not)? How are you positioned in relation to the player-character? How does this relate to the system of person (first-person; third-person); and how does this system work differently in the game you're playing from the way you are familiar with in literature? What about the game seems more or less credible or convincing to you? How can this be seen in terms of the notions of modality offered in this section? How is this different from more traditional debates about realism in literary texts?

Again, this activity can be extended to work with your class. One way to do this would be to ask the class to write reviews of games they have played. Encourage them to include a section on "gameplay", and to develop this as thoughtfully as possible, to address at an appropriate level the kinds of issue covered in this section.

Composition

The grammars of game-composition are hybrid and multimodal. They range from the grammar of coding in the design of the game's skeleton, the game engine, to the grammars of visual design in the 3D modelling of environments and characters, and moving image design in the animation of characters and objects. They extend to the grammar of speech, whether represented as spoken or written language; and music composition, an important design specialism in the games industry, with its own dedicated fan following in the case of some game franchises.

In my field, media education, we have concentrated on a few key principles of game design when working with students in schools. I will mention only two here, because they seem fundamental to me; and also because they have interesting implications for the (related) teaching of grammar and narrative in the literacy/literature curriculum.

The first concept is *rule*. This is well-known as a basic building block of game design (for example, Juul, 2003; Salen & Zimmerman, 2004). I have considered the notion of rule above in relation to simple games like noughts and crosses, as well as complex games like chess.

When we developed an authoring tool for children to use to design their own games, we built into it a unit we called the "rule editor" (see Figure 16.1). This allows users to determine the conditions under which an event occurs: in this example, *if key/is clicked/Sci-fi Door opens*.

This kind of rule-building is at the core of game-grammar. The narrative of games is entirely conditional. Nothing can happen, at least nothing in the ludic sense, without some choice being made by the player: to turn left or right; to enter a room or not; to pick up a gun or a magic potion; to be a mage or a Night-Elf; to shop or to fight. At the level of this kind of rule, conditionality is evident in the narrative effect (the door will only open if the key is clicked), in the programming (the key and the door must both be connected to the code that specifies the *if/then* or *when/then* sequence); and in the language grammar, which is always an if-clause.

This can teach us – and students, if we choose to make it explicit – something about game-design, something about the language of computer programming, something about language grammar and something about the grammar of narrative. In fact, in the research project in which this software was developed, we chose to focus with the students on the cultural aspects of rules, asking them to think of examples of rules and why rules are necessary or important or enjoyable.

Students understood that many games they were familiar with used rules – but had often not applied this idea to computer games. One boy's list made it clear that he was able to conceive of rules across different kinds of game: tennis, pool, pontoon, cricket, and the Second World War-themed computer game *Call of Duty*. He was also able to consider the cultural significance of rules, and how they can provide pleasure: "The reason games have to have rules is if there wasn't rules in a game you wouldn't have any challenges or boundaries, limits too, and that would spoil the fun and cause you not to have anything to complete."

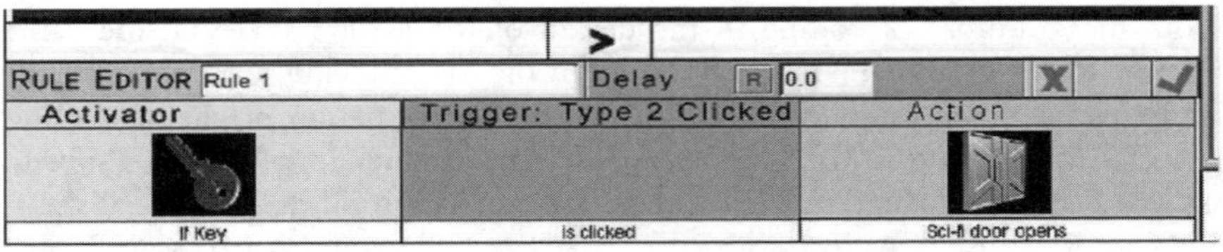

Figure 16.1 Rule Editor from the Missionmaker Game-Authoring Software.

The other element of ludic "grammar" we focused on explicitly was *econo-mies*: quantified resources. In fact, everything in a computer game is quantified in some way, but our interest here was in those resources available for the player to manage: health points, hunger, time, the weight of objects, quantity of ammu-nition, vulnerability levels of player and non-player characters – all resources which, in the software we used in this project, can be determined by the young game-designers.

When we asked them to think about economies, they were able both to define them and to give examples:

> ECONOMIES are the objects that get used through the game. They can be collected or deducted. They are the base of the game, they help give the player some challenges. An example of some economies are: the time left on the game. How much oxygen you have left.

This definition gives a good sense of the writer's conception of the positive and negative trajectories of economies, and of their numerical nature ("deducted").

Unlike the notions of transitivity, person or modality referred to earlier, the concepts of rule and economy have no direct counterpart in language grammar, and may seem alien to those most comfortable with the meaning systems of lan-guage, or even the broader semiotic systems of "older" media such as film. However, there are profound connections. As we have seen, rules relate to the conditionality of games, part of their structures of mood; and in turn, this pro-duces a quite different kind of narrative, one based on options and choices at every turn. So, rather than leave students with the idea that ludic grammar was something divorced from narrative grammar, we asked them for examples of stories they knew which contained rules and economies. An example given by a boy of a "rule" in narrative was that Frodo's sword, Sting, in *The Lord of the Rings*, glows blue when orcs are near; while a girl suggested *Hansel and Gretel* for an example of a narrative economy: the breadcrumbs the children drop to find their way out of the forest.

Naturally, an important aspect of the composition of the children's games was their coherence, both in narrative and ludic terms. We found examples of games with strong ludic coherence and weak narrative coherence – where objects were strongly connected by rules to make a satisfying game, but had no narrative sig-nificance. An example was an object in an Egyptian-themed game which effect-ively triggered an event, programmed by the student to do so, but was incoherent in the game's representational system: a safety-pin. Conversely, we found games with strong narrative coherence but weak ludic coherence, such as a Victorian-themed game with a clear plot about the murder of a lady and the revenge taken by her ghost; but a fragmented sequence of ludic challenges with no overall structure or development.

In relation to multimodal texts in general, Jay Lemke emphasises the impor-tance of *textual cohesion* as a feature of their organisation or composition (Lemke, 2002), and this was clearly the case in these students' games. There were simple links between cause and effect in objects juxtaposed in the game space: a player's key would open a safe, for instance. These kinds of coherence resembled conjunctive cohesion in language. In more ambitious designs, objects quite far removed from each other would refer back and forwards across the time and space of the game, resembling more closely referential ties in language. The strength or weakness of these cohesive ties were part of what made the games robust and successful, or rambling and unsatisfying.

An example can be seen in Figure 16.2. This is part of a level of a game made by two Year 8 girls (aged 12–13). It is a screen from the design software, rather than from the game as a player would encounter it. In it, the player finds a gun, but then has to seek elsewhere for the ammunition, which the girls have partially hidden in a lake – it can be seen towards the bottom right-hand corner of the image of the gameworld. There is, then, a referential link between ammo and gun; though, unlike such a link in a conventional narrative, the establishment of the link here has to be made by the player, so rather than a fixed semantic pair, it can be seen as a provisional semantic triad – two objects articulated through a player action (pick up the ammo).

The cohesion between gun and ammo is then tied to another player action – firing the gun – which is in turn tied to the goal of this action, a stormtrooper who can be vaguely seen behind the translucent column. The column is a "trigger volume", which the girls have programmed to trigger the stormtrooper to "seek and destroy the player" if the player should enter the space defined by this shape. This object would, of course, be invisible to the player when they play the game.

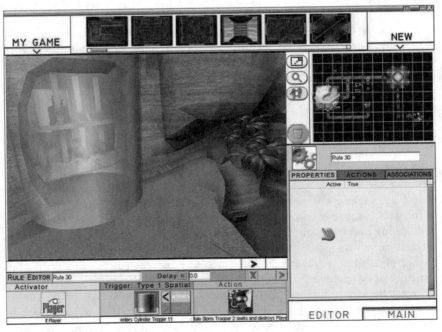

Figure 16.2 The Design Screen of a Game Made by Two Year 8 Girls.

The tight cohesion of this sequence, in which objects, actions and participants are articulated within processes of narrative causality, is evidence of a well-designed game. At the same time, it can be seen as evidence of two kinds of motivation on the part of these young designers. One is an educational motivation – a desire to follow the processes which have been modelled by the teacher (and to some extent "taught" by the software). The other is a broader interest in the pleasures of First-Person Shooter games – the awareness of a need for narrative suspense, for a difficult but achievable objective, for a clear demarcation of conditions of winning and losing. These cultural properties are achieved in part by the closely woven cohesion of the sequence, which results in the player searching for the ammo, trying to avoid the stormtrooper, just visible through the gate, and trying to avoid falling into the lake (which would end the game).

Activity: Making Games

Plan and deliver a game-design activity for your class. The ambitious version of this might involve using game-design software, such as the Missionmaker software described in this section; or other commercial alternatives, such as the low-cost package The 3-D Game-Maker (http://t3dgm.thegamecreators.com). While there are many technical issues to consider here, such as those covered in this section, the general aim is to encourage students to design a game which has a coherent and satisfying narrative as well as a coherent and satisfying game-structure, the two being closely integrated. The possibilities for exploring narrative structure, introducing students to the idea of ludic structure and to key concepts such as rule and economy are plentiful.

The less ambitious version of this activity would be to develop proto-design activities, which might include: planning a multi-level game as a chart (a little like a board-game), with missions, narrative information, obstacles, different character types, rewards, alternative routes, economies, rules and a specified win–lose state at the end; designing characters; drawing screenshots; making promotional material; making a walkthrough (a player's set of instructions for how to play a game); writing reviews for game magazines. These activities allow for the exploration of the cultural context of game production and play: who makes games, who plays them, what institutions are involved, how players respond.

Conclusion: Game-Grammar and Game-Literacy,

I have tried to show, then, how a social-semiotic model of "grammar" could be applied to computer games, and how it could make sense of the relationship between their narrative and ludic functions.

However, such an analytical framework is pointless as a formal exercise, and a social-semiotic approach would always privilege the cultural and social functions of the text in question here and the ways the player engages with it. To do this, I would argue that we need to locate any such textual approach within the sort of structure which in Cultural Studies is often referred to as the "circuit of culture" (for example, du Gay, Hall, Janes & Negus, 1996). This model imagines a cyclical relation between textual production and audience engagement, in which the regime of production and its economic and political context feeds into the regime of consumption and interpretation, with its various functions (the acquisition of cultural capital; the building of identity; the growth of literacy; the experience of pleasure; the exercise of cultural taste and affiliation to particular communities of taste and interpretation). This movement from production to consumption, from text to reader, involves other processes, such as regulation – how various interventions might come between, in this case, a game and its player, such as age-classification by national regulatory bodies (games are regulated partly by the BBFC[6] in the United Kingdom, partly by PEGI,[7] the European self-regulatory system devised by the industry); or constraints imposed (or not) by parents; or the common prohibition of gaming in school computer labs.

Finally, the processes of play, interpretation, distinction and consumption feed into the appropriation by players of resources provided by the game-texts, in the production of their own texts. These might be fan texts such as fanfiction, walkthroughs, spoilers, fan art (cf. Jenkins, 1992; Burn & Schott, 2004); or they might be new games such as the ones made by the children in our project, which use cultural resources such as genre, narrative types, play conventions and the visual and programming resources of the software. In any of these cases, the grammar of the game-text corresponds to the grammars of play, fanwork and player design: the same narrative structures, representational structures, interactional functions and compositional processes are at work.

The assumption of the circuit of culture is that these new texts feed back in some way into the industry and the next cycle of production. There are plenty of examples of how this might happen in game culture: player experts who become sponsored by the industry; "modders" who modify the original game texts in ways which the industry recognises and capitalises on; fan communities whose desires are picked up by the company and may influence subsequent designs. However, the articulation between audience production and the industry is necessarily fragmentary, highly selective and based in, as well as reproductive of, a starkly unequal power relation. This is not to bemoan the grip of global corporatism (though this can have stifling and domineering effects, not least on smaller "independent" elements of the industry itself), or to overplay the passivity of player-audiences. It is, however, to warn against over-enthusiastic celebration of the power of players, consumers and – in the case of education – the agency of children. Such agency certainly exists, often in dramatic and spectacular ways, and it is the job of teachers to nurture it; but it does not abolish or neutralise the power of media institutions.

It may seem again that my argument has drifted away from the question of grammar and literacy. However, my concern here is that the formal properties of games as texts must not be dislocated from the cultural cycle in which their social

6. British Board of Film Classification.
7. Pan-European Game Information.

meanings are offered, constructed, challenged and remade. As with any "grammar" or "literacy", to conceive of it, or to explore it with students in school, without proper attention to its social and cultural functions is pointless, and invites all the old accusations of reductiveness, mechanistic formalism, decontextualised exercises, and so on. Game "grammar" can connect with the semiotic systems of language, film and other media conventionally bundled within English curricula at three levels: the micro-systems of syntagmatic structure; the macro-systems of broader discursive patterns, in particular those of narrative and argument; and the contextual structures of cultural function and use. All three are necessary if teachers are to gain any useful sense of how students' experience of games, beyond and within the classroom, can enrich and extend their understanding of the making of meaning and its purpose.

References

Bill. (2003). Review (number 6) of *Harry Potter and the Chamber of Secrets*. Retrieved 18 August 2007, from www.videogamereview.com/sf-1/befid-54214/pid-20519335/nrr-20/Harry-Potter-and-the-Chamber-of-Secrets-for-Windows/review/productreviewscrx.aspx?dnatrs=genre_mining_action-9440_ea_electronic_arts.

Burn, A. (2004). Potter-literacy – from book to game and back again: Literature, film, game and cross-media literacy. *Papers: Explorations into Children's Literature, 14*(2), 5–17 [reprinted in *Contemporary Literary Criticism, 217,* April 2006].

Burn, A., & Schott, G. (2004). Heavy hero or digital dummy: Multimodal player–avatar relations in *Final Fantasy 7. Visual Communication, 3*(2), 213–233.

Caillois, R. (1958/1979). *Man, play and games.* New York: Schocken Books.

Carr, D., Buckingham, D., Burn, A., & Schott, G. (2006). *Computer games: Text, narrative, play.* Cambridge: Polity Press.

du Gay, P., Hall, S., Janes, L., & Negus, K. (1996). *Doing cultural studies: The story of the Sony Walkman.* London: Sage.

Genette, G. (1980). *Narrative discourse.* Oxford: Blackwell.

Halliday, M. (1985). *An introduction to functional grammar.* London: Edward Arnold.

Halliday, M. (1989). *Spoken and written language* (2nd ed.). Oxford: Oxford University Press.

Jenkins, H. (1992). *Textual poachers: Television fans and participatory culture.* London: Routledge.

Jenkins, H. (2006). *Convergence culture.* New York: NYU Press.

Juul, J. (2003). The game, the player, the world: Looking for a heart of gameness. In M. Copier & J. Raessens (Eds.), *Level up,* Digital Games Research conference proceedings, University of Utrecht, 4–6 November 2003.

Kress, G., & van Leeuwen, T. (1996). *Reading images: The grammar of visual design.* London: Routledge.

Laurel, B. (1991). *Computers as theater.* Menlo Park, CA: Addison Wesley.

Lemke, J. (2002). Travels in hypermodality. *Visual Communication, 1*(3), 299–325.

Murray, J. (1998). *Hamlet on the Holodeck.* Cambridge, MA: MIT Press.

Ong, W. (2002). *Orality and literacy: The technologizing of the word.* London: Routledge.

Ryan, M. (2001). Beyond myth and metaphor: The case of narrative in digital media. *Game Studies, 1*(1). Retrieved 10 August 2009, from www.gamestudies.org/0101/ryan.

Salen, K., & Zimmerman, E. (2004). *Rules of play: Game design fundamentals.* Cambridge, MA: MIT Press.

Tak. (2003). Review (number 3) of *Harry Potter and the Chamber of Secrets*. Retrieved 18 August 2007 from www.videogamereview.com/sf-1/befid-54214/pid-20519335/nrr-20/ Harry-Potter-and-the-Chamber-of-Secrets-for-Windows/review/productreviewscrx. aspx?dnatrs=genre_mining_action-9440_ea_electronic_arts.

Games

Call of duty. (2003). Infinity Ward/Activision.
Final fantasy VII. (1997). Square Soft.
Harry Potter and the chamber of secrets. (2002). Knowwonder/Electronic Arts.
Lord of the rings: The return of the king. (2003). Hypnos/Electronic Arts.
The golden compass. (2007). Shiny Entertainment/Sega of America.
Tomb-raider 4: The last revelation. (1999). Core/Eidos.
World of warcraft. (2004). Blizzard.

Contributors

Richard Andrews is Professor of English at the Institute of Education, University of London. His recent publications include *Argumentation in Higher Education* and *Re-Framing Literacy* (both Routledge). He is also co-editor of the *Routledge Handbook on English, Literacy and Language Teaching*, and of a recent edition of *As You Like It* for the Cambridge Schools Shakespeare. His research interests include e-learning research methodologies, writing development and writing from a multimodal perspective.

Andrew Burn is Professor of Media Education at the London Knowledge Lab, in the Institute of Education, University of London. He has researched and published work on many aspects of the media, including young people's production of computer games, digital video in schools and media literacy. His most recent book is *Making New Media: Creative Production and Digital Literacies* (2009). He spent many years in secondary schools as a teacher of English, Media and Drama.

Frances Christie is Emeritus Professor of Language and Literacy, University of Melbourne and Honorary Professor of Education and of Linguistics at the University of Sydney. Recent books are *Language Education in the Primary Years* (2005) and (with B. Derewianka) *School Discourse: Learning to Write across the Years of Schooling* (2008). She is co-editing two new volumes: (with A. Simpson) *Literacy and Social Responsibility: Multiple Perspectives* and (with K. Maton) *Disciplinarity: Functional Linguistic and Sociological Perspectives*.

Urszula Clark is Reader in English at Aston University, Birmingham, within the School of Languages and Social Sciences. She is Deputy Director of the Aston Centre for Interdisciplinary Research into Language and Diversity (InterLanD). Her research and teaching interests include issues relating to pedagogic theories of discourse, language, region and identity, and stylistics. Publications include: *War Words: Language, History and the Disciplining of English* (2001) and *Studying Language: English in Action* (2007).

Anne Cloonan currently lectures in undergraduate and postgraduate Language and Literacy Studies and conducts research in the School of Education at Deakin University, Australia. Her most significant contribution to the field of language and literacy education has been her research into teachers' learning of multimodal forms of literacy and their implementation of multiliteracies theoretical schemas in classrooms. This focus built on her earlier work as a senior project officer with the Department of Education, Victoria.

Bill Cope is Research Professor in the Department of Educational Policy Studies, University of Illinois. He is also Director of Common Ground Publishing, a company which develops mixed-medium print and Internet publishing software now located in the Research Park at the University of Illinois. He is a former First Assistant Secretary in the Department of the Prime Minister and Cabinet and Director of the Office of Multicultural Affairs in the Australian Federal Government. His most recent books are edited collections: *The Future of the Book in the Digital Age* (2006) and *The Future of the Academic Journal* (2009).

Ruth French, B.Ed. (Hons), is an experienced primary school teacher with a long-standing interest in language and literacy in education. She is a PhD candidate at the University of New England, Armidale, Australia. Her current research is focused on young school children's learning of aspects of functional grammar.

Craig Hancock has been working as a writing teacher with Educational Opportunity Program students at the University at Albany since 1986. His book, *A Meaning-Centered Grammar* (2005), looks at traditional grammar from a functional perspective. He continues to lobby publicly for the reintegration of language study into the English curriculum.

Hilary Janks is Professor in the School of Education at the University of the Witwatersrand, Johannesburg. She is the editor and an author of the *Critical Language Awareness* series of workbooks and the author of *Literacy and Power* (2009). Her teaching and research are in the areas of language education in multilingual classrooms, language policy and critical literacy. Her work is committed to a search for equity and social justice in contexts of poverty.

Professor Mary Kalantzis is currently Dean of the College of Education at the University of Illinois, Urbana-Champaign. Before then, she was Dean of the Faculty of Education, Language and Community Services at RMIT University in Melbourne, Australia, and President of the Australian Council of Deans of Education. With Bill Cope, she is co-author or editor of: *The Powers of Literacy* (1993); *Productive Diversity* (1997); *A Place in the Sun: Re-Creating the Australian Way of Life* (2000); *Multiliteracies: Literacy Learning and the Design of Social Futures* (2000); *New Learning: Elements of a Science of Education* (2008), and *Ubiquitous Learning* (2009).

Martha Kolln retired as Associate Professor of English from Penn State University, where she taught grammar, composition and rhetoric for 25 years. She is the author of *Understanding English Grammar* (with Robert Funk), now in its eighth edition, and *Rhetorical Grammar: Grammatical Choices, Rhetorical Effects*, sixth edition (with Loretta Gray). She lives in State College, Pennsylvania, with her husband of 59 years.

Gunther Kress is Professor of Semiotics and Education at the Institute of Education, University of London. His interests are in understanding principles of representation, meaning-making and communication in contemporary social environments, building on a social-semiotic theory of multimodal representation and communication. Pertinent publications include: *Linguistic Processes in Sociocultural Practices* (1984/1989); *Social Semiotics* (1988, with Hodge); *Reading Images: The Grammar of Graphic Design* (1996/2006, with van Leeuwen); *Multimodal Discourse: The Modes and Media of Contemporary Communication* (2002, with van Leeuwen); *Literacy in the New Media Age* (2003); and most recently *Multimodality: A Social Semiotic Approach to Contemporary Communication* (2009).

Terry Locke is Chairperson of the Arts and Language Education Department at the School of Education, University of Waikato. His recent books include *Critical Discourse Analysis* (2004) and *Resisting Qualifications Reforms in New Zealand: The English Study Design as Constructive Dissent* (2007). His research interests include constructions of English as a subject, all aspects of subject English pedagogy, the relationship of ICT to literacy, and issues of classroom pedagogical discourse. He is coordinating editor of the journal *English Teaching: Practice and Critique*.

Debra Myhill is Professor of Education at the University of Exeter, and is Head of the Graduate School of Education. Her research interests focus principally on aspects of language and literacy teaching, particularly writing and grammar, and talk in the classroom. She is the author of *Better Writers*; *Talking, Listening, Learning: Effective Talk in the Primary Classroom*, and co-editor of the *Sage Handbook of Writing Development*.

Graeme Trousdale is Senior Lecturer in English Language at the University of Edinburgh. His main research interests concern grammatical variation and change in English, particularly the relationship between formal and functional change. He is also interested in the teaching of language and linguistics in pre-university education in the United Kingdom, and is currently the chair of the Committee for Linguistics in Education, which is sponsored by the Linguistics Association of Great Britain and the British Association for Applied Linguistics.

Len Unsworth is Professor of English and Literacies Education and Head of the School of Education at the University of New England, Armidale, Australia. Recent publications include *Researching Language in Schools and Communities* (2000); *Teaching Multiliteracies across the Curriculum* (2001) (with Angela Thomas, Alyson Simpson and Jenny Asha); *Teaching Children's Literature with Information and Communication Technologies* (2005); *E-Literature for Children and Classroom Literacy Learning* (2006); *New Literacies and the English Curriculum* (2008); and *Multimodal Semiotics* (2008).

Amos van Gelderen is Senior Researcher at the SCO-Kohnstamm Institute of the University of Amsterdam. His dissertation (1992) concerned linguistic and phonetic analysis of oral performances. He studied language learning and language education in primary and secondary education, both for mother-tongue and foreign languages. Recent research topics include: effects of training self-regulation and lexical fluency on foreign-language writing, componential analysis of reading and writing proficiency in Dutch as a first language and English as a foreign language, and the function of learning explicit grammatical rules for writing in comparison with implicit learning of rules.

Constance Weaver is currently Heckert Professor of Reading and Writing at Miami University, Oxford, Ohio. Her long-standing interest in teaching a limited amount of grammar for and along with writing is exemplified by the landmark *Grammar for Teachers* (1979 and still in print), followed by *Teaching Grammar in Context* (1986), the edited *Lessons to Share* (1998), and two recent books, *The Grammar Planbook* (2007) and, with Jonathan Bush, another theoretically grounded book with more emphasis on practice, *Grammar to Enrich and Enhance Writing* (2008).

Index

Entries in *italics* indicate figures

affordance 241
arrangement 245–6
assessment 80
attitude 286–7
audio meaning-making 265
augmentation 280
avatar 302–3

Bakhtin, M. 179
Bernstein, B. 11, 39–42, 45, 51, 171–5
Bruner, J. 208

Cameron, D. 99–103
choice (ideology of) 249–50
Chomsky, N. 24, 26–7, 44, 60, 186
cognitive grammar 35
coherence 240, 248, 307
cohesion 240, 248, 307–9
communication 235–9
composition 29–30, 252–3
computer games 15, 294–311
conjunction 283–4
connection 282–4, *284*
context of culture 180
context of situation 180
contextual meaning 267
critical discourse analysis 156–68, 220–4
critical literacy 63–5, 67, 174–5, 266
critical theory 29
cultural reproduction 41

Dartmouth Conference 58–9
design 243–9, 252–3, 256
dialect 45, 81
dimensions-of-meaning schema 255, 266–8, 270
discourse 156, 176
distribution 281

economies 307
English as subject 41
English Review Group 47
error correction 30, 34, 111, 130–1, 213
esthetics 244–50
evaluative meaning 285–7

Fairclough, L. 156, 172
field 277
Flaubert, G. 250
focalisation 302–3
formal grammar 22–3, 25, 31, 38, 44, 91, 94, 99, 102–3; definition of 92n3, 112
formalist linguistic theory 57, 60
four resources model 153–4, 175–6
Framework for Teaching English (England) 48
"functional" English 50
functional grammar 56, 59–61, 64–5, 103

game 296
generative (transformational) grammar 7, 24, 26, 28, 35, 104, 186, 210
genre 56, 61–2, 67, 179–80, 211, 299; types of 3, 63; Australian genre school (SFL genre theory) 3, 7–8, 12–13, 56–65, 124
gesture 260–3
grammar (definition of) 4, 92n1, 233–4, 241
"grammar in context" 135–8
Grammar Wars 1–2, 34, 42–50, 55–9
grammatics 12, 210n3, 210–11, 214–28
Graves, D. 63

Halliday, M.A.K. 8, 12, 14, 353, 44, 55–7, 59–63, 65, 67, 174, 180, 210–11, 213, 250, 276, 303
Hasan, R. 62–4, 180